Economic Incentives and Environmental Policies

EUROPEAN SCIENCE FOUNDATION

This series arises from the work of the ESF Scientific Programme on Environment, Science and Society: an economic and institutional analysis (ESS).

The Scientific Steering Committee of the ESS Programme is composed as follows:

Economic Incentives and Environmental Policies

Principles and Practice

Edited by

HANS OPSCHOOR

and

KERRY TURNER

Kluwer Academic Publishers

Dordrecht / Boston / London

Library of Congress Cataloging-in-Publication Data

Economic incentives and environmental policies : principles and
    practice / edited by J.B. Opschoor and R.K. Turner.
        p.   cm.
      ISBN 0-7923-2601-6 (HB : acid free paper)
      1. Environmental policy--Economic aspects. 2. Environmental
    protection--Economic aspects.   I. Opschoor, Johannes B. (Johannes
    Baptist), 1944-   . II. Turner, R. Kerry.
    HC79.E5E272   1994
    333.7--dc20   93-41913

ISBN 0-7923-2601-6

Published by Kluwer Academic Publishers,
P.O. Box 17, 3300 AA Dordrecht, The Netherlands.

Kluwer Academic Publishers incorporates
the publishing programmes of
D. Reidel, Martinus Nijhoff, Dr W. Junk and MTP Press.

Sold and distributed in the U.S.A. and Canada
by Kluwer Academic Publishers,
101 Philip Drive, Norwell, MA 02061, U.S.A.

In all other countries, sold and distributed
by Kluwer Academic Publishers Group,
P.O. Box 322, 3300 AH Dordrecht, The Netherlands.

Printed on acid-free paper

02-0396-150 ts
First published 1994
Reprinted 1996

Printed in the Netherlands

The *European Science Foundation* is an association of its 55 member research councils, academies, and institutions devoted to basic scientific research in 20 countries. The ESF assists its Member Organisations in two main ways: by bringing scientists together in its Scientific Programmes, Networks and European Research Conferences, to work on topics of common concern; and through the joint study of issues of strategic importance in European science policy.

The scientific work sponsored by ESF includes basic research in the natural and technical sciences, the medical and biosciences, the humanities and social sciences.

The ESF maintains close relations with other scientific institutions within and outside Europe. By its activities, ESF adds value by cooperation and coordination across national frontiers and endeavours, offers expert scientific advice on strategic issues, and provides the European forum for fundamental science.

This volume arises from the work of the ESF Scientific Programme on Environment, Science and Society: an economic and institutional analysis (ESS). This programme stimulated a number of successful collaborating networks between economists, policy analysts, lawyers and natural scientists across Europe.

Further information on ESF activities can be obtained from:

European Science Foundation
1, quai Lezay-Marnésia
F-67080 Strasbourg Cedex
France

Tel. (+33) 88 76 71 00
Fax (+33) 88 37 05 32

Contents

1. Environmental Economics and Environmental Policy Instruments: Introduction and Overview

KERRY TURNER[1] and HANS OPSCHOOR[2]
[1] *University of East Anglia, Norwich, U.K.*
[2] *Free University, Amersterdam, The Netherlands*

1. Merging Environment and Economics in Decision-Making

Historical Background

Once the decision to promote environmental quality and sustainable resource use was made, policy-makers began looking for tools or instruments with which to achieve their objectives. This process has gone on, albeit in piecemeal fashion, since at least the late 60s. In the new phase of environmental policy that came about as a result of the report of the World Commission for Environment and Development, *Our Common Future* (WCED, 1987), an increased emphasis has been put on the application of so-called economic instruments. They represent potentially effective as well as efficient incentives to economic agents to modify their behavioural patterns in environmentally friendlier directions. In fact, the title of this section is a direct quote from the WCED report, and it may be appropriate to demarcate the position of this book within environmental economics and even within the wider setting of environmentalism by sketching the contours of WCED's analysis.

The Brundtland commission was the first official commission to adopt the notion of sustainable development as a prerequisite for continued societal existence. It was mainly responsible for putting this notion on the international agenda. Due to the way the notion was interpreted in the report, an enhanced role for environmental economics in actual policy has become a distinct possibility. Chapter 2 of that report outlines the main strategic imperatives for achieving sustainability. Critical objectives for environmental and economic policies compatible with sustainability are (WCED, 1987, p. 49):

- reviving economic growth,
- changing the quality of growth,
- meeting essential basic needs,
- ensuring a sustainable level of population,

Hans Opschoor and Kerry Turner (eds), Economic Incentives and Environmental Policies, 1–38.

 - conserving and enhancing the resource base,
 - reorienting technology and managing risk, and last but not least,
 - merging environment and economics in decision-making.

The latter strategic imperative is subsequently described by the Brundtland Commission as the common theme throughout all other elements of this strategy (ibid., p. 62). It is meant to induce a change in attitudes, objectives and institutional arrangements at all levels.

According to the Commission the need for this merger emanates from the existence of and pervasive nature of environmental externalities, institutional myopia, sectoral self-interest, etc. Substainability requires changes in the legal and institutional frameworks that will enforce the common interest (i.e., global environmental interdependency) as well as decentralised management of resources (ibid., p. 63). Moreover, it requires that environmental objectives be built into more general financial and economic policies such as taxation, trade incentives, etc. (ibid., p. 64). It is in this context that WCED appears to refer to the argument that environmental costs ought to be incorporated in prices. The Commission's arguments are then more fully elaborated in its chapter or industrial development. In its discussion on the use of energy and materials, WCED advocates full (including environmental and resource) costing as a pricing policy (ibid., p. 217). Finally, when discussing strategies for sustainable industrial development, the use of economic instruments is directly advocated (ibid., p. 220 ff).

After the WCED report was published, the 1992 United Nations Conference on Environment and Development (UNCED) was announced. And, from the very outset, economic issues were important in the preparation for that conference, In Washington DC a conference was held to assess the possible contribution to the UNCED-process as early as January 1990 (US EPA, 1990). It discussed issues such as resource pricing, economic instruments, etc. Subsequently, prior to the Bergen ECE-conference in preparation for UNCED (May 1990) the scientific community in the ECE region held a conference on Sustainable Development, Science and Policy (Bergen, 8–12 May 1990) in which one of the five participating groups at the conference discussed the 'economics of sustainable development'. It also formulated recommendations on how to elaborate in economic terms the notion of sustainability, the feasibility of sustainable economic growth, resource valuation problems complicated by uncertainties and time preference, the measurement of economic growth, and instruments for securing sustainability (Anon., 1990). These were fed, via the subsequent Governmental conference, as well as through the global science conference ASCEND (Vienna, November 1991), into the preparations for UNCED.

At the ASCEND conference, economic issues were discussed as part of the institutional side of global environmental issues, and a number of barriers to sustainability as well as ways of dealing with these barriers were identified. Amongst the latter were economic instruments and resource pricing to implement notions such as 'the polluter and user should pay' (Lang, Opschoor and Perrings, 1992). Finally, at UNCED itself a number of economically significant positions were accepted.

To begin with, the fundamental importance of patterns of production and consumption in the industrialised market economies was recognised as a major contributor to environmental degradation.

Secondly, the right of developing countries to continue to develop was underlined. The two together point to the need to redistribute the access of the planet's limited 'environmental space', and the need to use that space efficiently and sustainably. At various places in the main outputs of the conference itself there is recognition of the polluter (and user) pays principle, the need to internalise environmental costs, the precautionary approach to environmental change, and the use of economic instruments ('Declaration of Rio' and 'Agenda 21').

The growing severity and pervasiveness of pollution in the industrialised economies had led the OECD (Organisation for Economic Cooperation and Development) to elaborate, and in 1972 to adopt, the Polluter-Pays-Principle (PPP) as a background economic principle for environmental policy. The basic tenet of PPP is that the price of goods or service should fully reflect the total cost of production and consumption. Its aim is to integrate use of the environment (including its waste assimilation capacity) into the economic sphere through the use of price signals and the use of economic instruments such as pollution charges and permits (although the use of regulation to internalise externalities is also consistent with PPP) (OECD, 1992).

Effective international use of the PPP requires a coordinated approach because environmental regulations can become a source of trade distortion if some countries subsidise private investment in pollution control while others do not. To encourage uniform application of the PPP, the OECD Council stipulated that the PPP should constitute a fundamental principle of pollution control in Member Countries in 1972 (implemented in 1974). Internationally, the PPP has become a principle of non-subsidisation of polluters. Nevertheless, some Member Country governments argued in favour of accelerated national programmes for pollution reduction measures. This led to the acceptance of certain exceptions to the strict PPP. Financial aid could be given to a polluting sector if that sector was already suffering from significant economic difficulties. But the aid could only be given for a fixed amount of time in a clearly defined programme and international trade distortion must be avoided.

In 1989 the OECD adopted a Recommendation on the Application of the PPP to Accidental Pollution. This links the economic principle and the legal principle relating to damage compensation. Currently, OECD is investigating the question of how the PPP could be extended to address global pollution issues such as climate change.

At the European level, the focus of much environmental legislation has shifted towards the European Commission in Brussels, through the medium of environmental directives. According to Article 189 of the EEC Treaty of Rome, a directive shall be binding, as to the result achieved upon each Member State, but shall leave to the national authorities the choice of form and methods. Piecemeal moves to protect the environment up until the single European Act of 1987 were consolidated under the Act and environmental protection was given an explicit place in the Treaty via Articles 130R, 130S and 130T. The establishment of the internal market as from 1 January 1993 will require the harmonisation of different national laws and environmental measures will also need attention in this context. The goal of uniform minimum environmental standards has the advantage of preventing 'pollution havens', and allowing the establishment of a safety margin approach in the areas of human health and ecosystem damage where scientific data is deficient and uncertainty is high. Variable minimum standards, on the other hand, seem to be more realistic given the existing differences among EC regions in terms of industrial and population concentrations. It can also be argued that regions that produce strong transboundary pollution should be made to maintain higher standards, A European Environmental Agency would presumably have to negotiate such standards.

The PPP was endorsed by the EC in a 1975 Recommendation which attached application conditions similar to those of the OECD and was included in the Single European Act. While the PPP itself will continue to evolve it has now been buttressed, to a greater or lesser extent, by four basic principles, all of which will play a part in guiding environmental policy in the future. The full of list of the principles is as follows:

(i)   the PPP to force those creating the pollution to pay the costs of meeting socially acceptable environmental quality standards;

(ii)   the prevention or precaution principle, which explicitly recognises the existence of uncertainty (environmental and social) and seeks to avoid irreversible damages via the imposition of a safety margin into policy; it also seeks to prevent waste generation at source, as well as retaining some end-of-pipe measures;

(iii) the economic efficiency/cost effectiveness principle, applying both to the setting of standards and the design of the policy instruments for attaining them;

(iv)   the subsidiarity principle, to assign environmental decisions and enforcement to the lowest level of government capable of handling it without significant residual externalities;

(v)   the legal efficiency principle, to preclude the passage of regulations that cannot be realistically enforced.

The European Community in its Fifth Environmental Action Plan is proposing to broaden the range of instruments of environmental policy, including an economic approach of 'getting the prices right' (Commission of the EC, 1992, Par. 7.4). Targets and actions proposed include the development of indicators of renewable resources, modification of key economic indicators to better reflect environmental effects, application of the polluter pays principle, and the introduction of a transparent system of pollution charges, deposit/refund systems etc.

Overall, there can be little doubt that as society demands increasingly stringent pollution controls, costs and regulatory intrusiveness are set to escalate significantly. For economists therefore the balance of argument will fall even more heavily in favour of the exploitation of the market's mechanisms for revealing information, as compared with the excess costs and bureaucracy associated with a strategy based solely on regulatory controls. Governments will be forced to search out cost minimizing procedures to reduce the projected cost burden of future environmental policy. Economic incentives carry with them the promise of just such cost-effectiveness benefits (Helm and Pearce, 1991).

The policy relevance of the so-called economic instruments for environmental policy will be obvious by now. What about the academic interest?

Traditionally, actual environmental policy has been buttressed by enabling instruments of the 'command-and-control'-type: *direct regulation* through e.g., permits, zoning, standards. On the other hand, economic theory from very early on has perceived environmental degradation in terms of negative externalities (see notably Pigou, 1920, p. 184). Pigou advocated the internalisation of these and other externalities through a centrally imposed system of bounties and taxes (Pigou, 1920, pp. 192–195). This is the Pigovian tax (Baumol and Oates, 1975, p. 30) Alternatives to this system of charges are: decentralised approaches via property rights (Dales, 1968) and/or bargaining (Coase, 1960). From 1960 onward, and especially since 1975, a vast literature on the theoretical merits and demerits of economic instruments has emerged (for a review, see Bohm and Russel, 1985); a first broad review of empirical applications was published by OECD (Opschoor and Vos, 1989). By the end of the 80s, it had become clear that much of the original debate on economic instruments had remained too remote from the realities of the economic process and of the environmental degradation this process had induced; a more pragmatic – but still cost-effective – approach was advocated by economists.

A final background factor worth mentioning, is the collapse of the centrally planned economies of Central and Eastern Europe, which reinforced an upsurge of sympathy for, and interest in, market-based approaches and market analogues to be used across a range of policy contexts. The phrase 'market-oriented environmental policy' may now itself be assuming some political value (Stavins and Whitehead, 1992). The economies in transition appear to offer good testbed conditions. At the same time, there was a concern over the rapidity and the simplicity of this swing of the pendulum from command and control approaches, to market based mechanisms, also in these emerging market economies. To several economists working in the area of environmental economics, this provided another rationale for analysing economic instruments and market based approaches to environmental problems.

The European Science Foundation's Interest in Environmental Policy Instruments

Since 1990 the European Science Foundation has run a programme called: Environment, Science and Society (ESS). The programme brings together a large number of environmental economists and other social scientists from most European countries, to collaborate in six Task Forces and three Pilot Studies on a range of issues relevant to the understanding of environment-society interactions, the problems that arise at that interface and ways to deal with these problems. Task Force II of ESS has concentrated on the academic and policy aspects of the development, the implementation and the evaluation of such instruments – especially in the industralised market economies such as those in Western Europe.

The research programme has focused upon both theoretical and empirical work on economic incentives. At the theoretical level, attention was given to the dynamics of instruments choice in various policy and economic contexts, and to the means to evaluate economic instruments in terms of their effectiveness and efficiency. At the empirical level, work was done to investigate the performance of economic instruments in reality, and to explore options for new approaches on the interfaces of technology, economy and the environment.

In carrying out this research programme, the Task Force hoped to find clues to new instruments or new combinations of instruments to tackle environmental destruction, and to make new theoretical and methodological inroads into the territory of the physical environment – a territory that economists since the days of the Physiocrats have mostly been alienated from.

The *modus operandi* of the Task Force has been to work collaboratively on a number of papers as elaborated in a first workshop (June 1990). There were three subsequent workshops in which intermediary products were scrutinised and refined, each (set of) author(s) being allocated one special discussant from within the Task Force and each product being discussed intensively by the entire Task Force. As the papers reached their final stages, the editors have of course gone through them carefully, but also each draft final paper was reviewed by an external expert drawn from the sphere of (environmental) policy making or (environmental) policy analysis (see list of authors and reviewers at the back of this volume). Reviewers were selected on the basis of extensive international and practical economic experience. In the light of the reviewers' findings the editors have invited the authors to finalise their contributions (August/September 1992). Comments on the policy relevance of the various contributions, will be incorporated in the overview presented in Section 3 of this chapter.

This volume therefore contains the final results of this work, it has three parts:

- Economic Analysis of Environmental Policy Instruments,
- Economic Instruments: Empirical Aspects,
- Product Cycles, Innovation and the Design of Economic Instruments.

Before discussing the project's results (Section 3 below), this introductory chapter will introduce the notion of economic instruments in some more detail (policy analytical as well as economic detail).

2. Economic Instruments: Concept and Theories

The Management of Environmental Impacts of Economic Activities

Economic activities generate several types of environmental pressures on the environment:

(i)   input demands (e.g., materials, energy, intermediate products);
(ii)   pollution/waste flows;
(iii) ecosystems modification, e.g., by spatial claims for roads, etc.

These pressures are normally buffered by absorptive systems and processes (e.g., waste assimilation, pollution absorption, resilience of ecosystems to disturbance, etc.) and regenerative processes in the environment. If these pressures exceed the buffering capacities, then they lead to environmental change; if that change leads to a reduced capacity of the environment to satisfy human needs, then one can speak of environmental degradation.

Environmental degrading may lead to policy responses in terms of e.g., measures aimed at reducing environmental pressure or enhancing environmental buffering capacities. Environmental policy uses a range of instruments to realise these objectives; as we shall see, such instruments may include various incentives to economic agents, to change their behaviour in an environmentally desirable way.

Environmental policy has been an explicit feature of the policy scene since, say 1970. Early environmental policy strategies focused on environmental impacts and ways to treat, eliminate or remedy these. Preventative approaches did play a role but most policy measures were restricted to stimulating end-of-pipe measures reducing emissions or discharges per unit of performance (output or consumption). As we argued above, environmental policy since the mid-1980s is moving into a new phase with associated new emphases both in terms of overall strategies and the combination of enabling policy instruments.

The focus is shifting to *prevention* rather than cure or mitigation of environmental degradation. In fact, radical preventative strategies are being discussed, aiming at far-reaching basic technological innovations at source: minimum waste technologies. Much attention is being given to the sequence of changes within environmental systems once materials have been released into these systems. Some environmental policy (i.e., in the transboundary air pollution context) is being influenced by the critical load concept. This defines how much pollution the environment can tolerate without experiencing harmful biological effects. It provides a crude measure of the different tolerance levels of ecosystems to airborne pollution stress induced by emissions of sulphur and nitrogen (Brodin and Kvylenstierna, 1992). Persistent pollutants (Red and Black List substances) will be subject to strict regulatory control or outright bans.

Public policy concerning pollution control is therefore being influenced by a range of criteria and this poses a formidable challenge in terms of the design of future control strategies. The strategy has somehow to encompass conflicting policy objectives – see Table 1. No single approach scores well on all the criteria listed in Table 1 and trade offs are inevitable.

In a very general sense one may say that environmental policy instruments are the environmental policy maker's tools in attempting to alter societal processes in such a way that they become and remain compatible with some notion of sustain-

Table 1. Comparative evaluation of different decision frameworks

Regulatory approach		Economic efficiency	Equity	Administrative simplicity	Acceptability	Risk reduction
No risk (bans) zero emissions	PP	v. low	v. high	high	v. high	v. high
Risk-based (regulations)		low	high	high	high	high
Technology-based (standards)		v. low	low	v. high	high	high
Risk-benefit analysis	CBA	high	low	low	low	low
Cost-benefit analysis (augmented by economic incentives		v. high	low	low	low	low

PP = precautionary principle; CBA = cost-benefit approach. Adapted from Lave and Malès (1989).

ability as made operational in the policy maker's environmental objectives. The substance of 'sustainable development' or related environmental policy objectives is not the subject matter of this volume (for that, see Pearce and Turner, 1990; Turner, 1992; Opschoor, 1992).

In seeking to ensure sustainable use of environmental resources and the maintenance of stricter levels of environmental quality, environmental policy can make use of (mixes of) two basic strategies (Figure 1, routes a and b):

(a) engaging in public projects and programmes aimed at preventing, compensating and eliminating environmental degradation or at providing substitutes for traditional behavioural patters, such as: collective treatment facilities, environmental sanitation and (re)construction programmes, new forests, bicycle paths and railway lines;

(b) influencing the decision making process at the micro level, i.e., that of the environmentally relevant (economic) agents such as consumers, producers, investors. The second strategy is discussed in more detail below.

Rational decision makers will base their decisions about their activities via a comparison of the various options open to them. they will compare the costs and

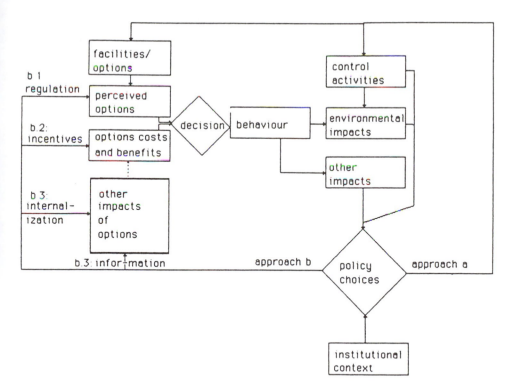

Fig. 1. Environmental policy approaches.

benefits relevant to them, that each of these options presents. Costs and benefits here are taken to be generalisations of all (dis)advantages relevant to the decision maker as somehow aggregated by his/her individual weighting system.

In such a situation, decisions can basically be influenced in three different ways (Figure 1, left hand side):

(1) alteration of the set of options open to agents;
(2) alteration of the cost and/or benefits relevant to agents;
(3) alteration of the priorities and significance agents attach to environmental change (i.e., altering the structure of agents' costs and benefits).

Route (1) involves: providing new alternatives or forbidding (or licencing) old ones. Typically, this has been the route followed by environmental policy in most industralized countries; it has been called the 'command-and-control' approach. Instruments used in this approach have included a whole range of 'direct' regulations (i.e., regulations directly influencing behaviour from an internal 'leverage point') such as: standards, bans, permits, zoning, quota, use restrictions, etc. These instruments will be referred to below as *regulatory instruments*, or RIs.

Route (2) leads to the application of economic incentives or market stimuli. the motivation relied upon here is that if environmentally more appropriate behaviour is made more rewarding in the eyes of the agent involved, then attitudes and behaviour will 'automatically' shift in favour of these socially more desirable alternatives. Options can be made more or less (financially or economically) attractive by applying charges or levies, granting subsidies, implementing tax differentiation etc. (see below for a more complete list). Such instruments will be referred to below as *economic instruments*, or EIs. In this way the environmental concerns can in a certain restricted sense be 'internalised' by altering the agent's context rather that the agent's value structure or preferences.

Route (3) would entail approaches such as: education, information extension, training, but also: social pressure, negotiation and other forms of 'moral suasion'. Here the mechanism is: a change of perceptions and priorities within the agent's decision framework, or: a full 'internalisation' within the preference structure of the agent. These instruments could be referred to as *suasive instruments*, or SIs.

In the past, all countries' environmental policies (including strongly market oriented ones such as those in the USA) entailed the use of RIs in a 'command and control'-strategy (Opschoor and Vos, 1989). Several developments since the late 60s or early 70s may explain why the subject of instrument choice has gained increasing prominence on the public agenda:

(i)   increasing and empirically based doubts as to the general *optimality* of traditional instruments especially RIs, and

(ii) changes in policy contexts leading to a search for instruments more in *accord* with the new situation.

In fact, these notions of 'optimality' and 'concordance' can be used to categorise two sets of criteria (to be) used in instrument choices.

Concordance criteria have to do with the acceptability of instruments:

(a)   consistency with policy developments such as deregulation, policy integration, international harmonization;

(b)   implications for other policy objectives e.g., in fields such as public finance, the distribution of net income, etc.

(c)   the acceptability of instruments (and their impacts) to vested economic and political interests.

Optimality criteria are concerned with whether instruments will do the desired job and at an acceptable performance level. They deal with the effectiveness and efficiency of instruments. By efficiency is meant both the static aspects (i.e., what levels of administrative costs are associated with the instruments) and the dynamic ones (e.g., to what extent will the various instruments induce technological innovation and/or diffusion). By effectiveness is meant the degree to which predetermined environmental objectives are achieved through the use of a certain instrument (note that impacts beyond environmental ones have been incorporated here in the concordance criteria).

EIs are instruments that provide *incentives* to economic actors inducing them to behave in an environmentally more appropriate or acceptable way. Their potential merits include: effectiveness, efficiency, flexibility, incentives for innovation. If properly chosen, they will ensure that enforcement efforts are minimal. In so far as they apply to sources of environmental degradation, EIs are more appropriate in a policy context that places priority on prevention.

The incentives provided may take the form of:

(i)   direct alteration of price or cost levels;

(ii)   indirect alteration via financial or fiscal means;

(iii) market creation and market support.

Direct alteration of price and cost levels occurs when, for example, charges are levied on products (product charges) or on the processes that generate these products (emissions charges, input charges, feedstock charges), or when deposit-refund systems are put in operation. Indirect alteration takes place when, for example, direct subsidies, soft loans or fiscal incentives (e.g., accelerated depreciation) are provided to induce environmentally clean technologies; enforcement incentives (such as non-compliance fees and performance bonds) can also be put in this category. Market creation is often done on the basis of changed legislation or regulation: emissions trading, quota auctioning etc as a consequence of limiting emissions or catches in a certain area, insurance schemes in response to changed liability legislation, etc. Market support occurs when public or semipublic agencies take responsibility for stabilizing prices on certain markets (e.g., for secondary materials such as recycled paper or ferrous metal).

There are several rationales for using EIs, *inter alia*:

(a) charges/subsidies may be used to correct for market price distortions due to government failure to effectively impose the internalization of environmental maintenance and replacement costs;

(b) they may be used to provide behaviourally relevant incentives to polluters and resource users in order to arrive at some allocative optimum;

(c) they may be used to provide funds for public or private investment schemes or environmental programmes;

(d) they are being advocated (increasingly) as an appropriate base for general taxation (to replace schemes based on income, profit or value added) in situations where environmental quality and natural resources have become scarcer means of production than labour or manmade capital.

If we define EIs loosely, i.e., if we include financial and fiscal instruments that may not have had the intention of modifying the behaviour of polluters and resource users, then it is possible to produce an impressive list of EIs actually in use. Opschoor and Vos (1989) presented a review of the situation in 6 countries (Italy, Sweden, USA, France, FRG, The Netherlands). These case studies yielded a total of 85 EIs, or 14 per country. Roughly 50% of these were charges, only about 30% were subsidies and the remainder were other types such as deposit-refund systems and trading schemes. Among the more successful schemes EIs are the Dutch water pollution charge, some US experiences in emissions trading, and some deposit-refund schemes in Sweden.

In a dynamic setting, environmental policy instruments aim at accelerating both technological innovation and the process of diffusion (or penetration) of new technology (Dosi et al., 1988). The impact of regulatory approaches on actual patterns of innovation and diffusion of environmentally friendlier technology is still a matter for empirical analysis (Georg and Jorgensen (1990: 6). But it is clear that even though economic conditions (e.g., cost differentials) do affect choices on technologies, two additional features also have to be considered. Firstly, in a context of uncertainty, innovation is more often than not the result of firms' market based interactions with others (clients, suppliers, etc.). These interactions produce multiple influences on the products' and processes' environmental performance 'upstream'. Secondly, diffusion-promoting activities will influence these decisions.

Innovation can then be seen as the outcome of a complex process within a 'structure of cooperation'; depending on e.g., the level and type of innovation (process or product) and the actors involved, different policy instruments may provide different stimuli resulting in different environmental impacts.

The impact of charges and other economic incentives on the rate and direction of innovation is largely unknown. Empirical evidence as far as it exists, casts some doubts on the dynamic efficiency of e.g., effluent charges (Georg and Jorgensen, 1990; see however Schuurmans, 1989). They may have sizable effects only in so far as firms with significant waste loads are affected, evasion by illegal dumping can be prevented and the charges can be tailor-made to generate incentives to innovative in the appropriate directions.

The complexity of the process of innovation precludes straightforward and simple broad-brush preventive instruments; rather, context-specific and often complex (i.e., mixes of elements of command and control, incentive and suasive approaches) will have to be developed. And analysis will have to make use of tools that can handle complex ramifications of the effect of interventions pervading the economic system and the environment through processes and interdependencies not easily captured by static welfare theoretic models or even by dynamic control-theoretical approaches. This conclusion goes against the tendency to analyse instruments in ideal-type form and in a generic fashion (e.g., 'the' efficiency and effectiveness features of product charges) as well as in a welfare economic setting.

The Economic Theory of Economic Instruments for Environmental Policy

Before looking at attempts to more realistically analyse and evaluate economic instruments, let us summarise what mainstream theory has to say about economic instruments.

A standard result of the economic theory of pollution is that a socially optimal level of economic activity does not coincide with the private optimum if there are external costs present. The issue arises therefore of how to reach the social optimum. One school of economic thought associated with Coase (1960) emphasises the importance of property rights and bargaining between polluters and sufferers. The Coasian tradition rejects intervention by the government (via taxes, subsidies or standard-setting) in favour of market bargaining underpinned by appropriate property rights in order to achieve the social optimum.

Figure 2 illustrates that when left unregulated, the polluter will try to operate at $Q\pi$, where his profits are maximised. But the social optimum is at Q^*. Thus private and social optima appear to be incompatible. However, the introduction of property rights may change this situation. If the sufferer from pollution has the property rights then it could pay the polluter to compensate the sufferer (up to the level of activity

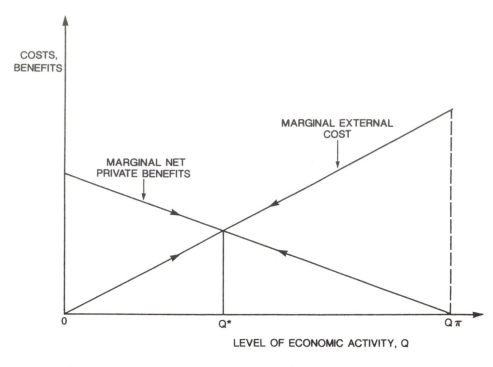

Source: adapted from Pearce & Turner (1990)

Fig. 2. The bargaining solution to the pollution problem.

Q^*). Beyond Q^* it is not feasible for such compensation to take place because the polluter's net gains become less than the sufferer's losses. Thus starting at O and giving the sufferer the property rights, there is a 'natural' tendency to move to Q^*, the social optimum.

It the property rights are vested in the polluter then the analysis in Figure 2 starts at $Q\pi$, with the sufferer given the opportunity to compensate the polluter until again the level of activity Q^* is reached. The 'Coase Theorem' therefore lays down that regardless of who holds the property rights, there is an automatic tendency to approach the social optimum via bargaining. If this analysis is correct then government regulation of externalities is redundant, the market will take care of itself (Pearce and Turner, 1990).

A number of criticisms of and complications with the Coase theorem have subsequently been explored in the literature. These include the existence of imperfect competition, high transactions costs, difficulties of polluter and sufferer identification and threat-making behaviour. Pearce and Turner (1990) have concluded that the Coase Theorem is important in forcing advocates of environmental intervention to define their terms and justify their case more carefully than they might otherwise have done. But there are many reasons why bargains do not, and cannot, occur. This much said let us now turn to the alternative school of economic thought associated with Pigou which does advocate intervention in the form of price and cost adjustments implemented via a tax/subsidy approach.

What is frequently advocated is a particular type of intervention – a tax on the polluter based on the estimated damage (external cost) done. The ideal 'Pigovian' tax, on efficiency grounds, must exactly reflect the costs of pollution at the margin. However, it is often impractical to tax the pollution precisely and therefore a number of proxy solutions are often adopted. But because charges or other market-based instruments such as permits equalise the level of marginal pollution abatement costs among firms, they provide the right incentive for the most cost-effective total investment in pollution clean-up. So compared to standards set without taxes, charges will tend to be a lower-cost method of achieving a given standard (Baumol and Oates, 1972) – see Figure 3.

In Figure 3, three polluting firms are being regulated in order to achieve an overall standard equivalent tonne, S_2, of pollution abatement. The government could, for example, either set a standard such that each firm is made to abate pollution by

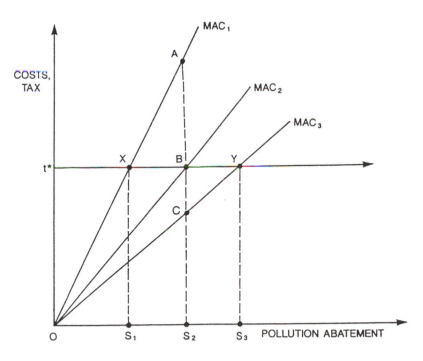

Source: Adapted from Pearce & Turner (1990)

Fig. 3. Taxes versus uniform standards setting.

an amount OS_2, or it could set a tax t^*, so that firm 1 goes to point x, firm 2 to point B and firm 3 to point Y. Total costs of abatement will be higher under the standard-setting solution than the tax solution:

Under standard-setting,

total abatement costs = TAC_{st} = OAS_2 + OBS_2 + OCS_2.

Under the tax,

TAC_{tax} = OXS_1 + OBS_2 + OYS_3.

TAC_{st} − TAC_{tax} = S_1XAS_2 − S_2CYS_3, but $S_1XAS_2 > S_2CYS_3$.

so

$TAC_{st} > TAC_{tax}$

Marketable permits offer the same advantage as the charge in the Baumol and Oates Theorem context. By giving the polluters a chance to trade their pollution emission/discharge permits, the total cost of pollution abatement is minimised compared to the more direct regulatory approach of setting standards. Figure 4 illustrates a simple two polluter situation, in which the MAC curves are the demand curves for permits. Polluter 1 buys OQ_1 permits and polluter 2 buys OQ_2 permits, if the price is P*. The higher cost polluter (2) therefore buys more permits than polluter (1). As long as polluters have different costs of abatement there is an

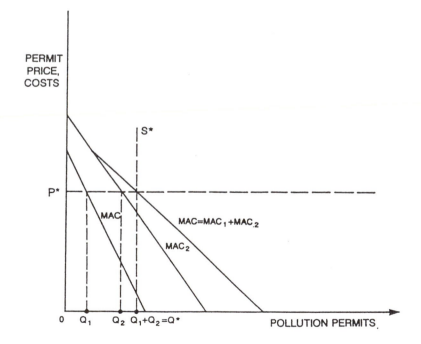

Fig. 4. Cost minimisation with marketable permits.

automatic market – low-cost polluters selling permits and high-cost polluters buying them. Trading ensures a cost-effective total abatement result.

Stavins and Whitehead (1992) have compared the advantages and disadvantages of pollution charges and permits. They observe that while permits set the level of control, charges establish the marginal costs of control. Permits allow a total pollution level to be set but cannot control pollution abatement expenditure. If the pollution context is one in which threshold effects in terms of damages (human health etc.) are known to be present, then permits may have a comparative advantage. Because charges do not control the actual level of pollution abatement they are better suited to situations in which damage impacts are fairly certain and relatively constant over a certain dosage rate range; as well as situations in which small changes in abatement costs cause significant changes in production levels.

Charges carry a dynamic incentive effect and augment the process of technological change. Permits lack this facility, since technical progress can cause control costs and permit prices to fall rather than emission levels. It may also be the case that permit systems may be the more susceptible to strategic behaviour. Such systems require competitive market conditions in both the permit and product markets.

Governments throughout Europe and North America have relied on the regulatory and not the economic instruments approach to pollution control. They have typically set standards (technology or performance-based) for classes of industry or the so-called scheduled processes across industrial categories. While this regulatory standards approach is biased against technological innovation (i.e., it provides no incentive for regulated polluters to exceed their prescribed target level of abatement) it has still proved attractive to control agencies. What it does provide is a measure of environmental quality 'certainty' (as long as there is adequate monitoring and enforcement). This certainty is particularly important when persistent and toxic substances are being released into the ambient environment.

The regulatory approach has recently been buttressed by the support given by some European governments and the European Commission to the so-called precautionary principle. A broad definition of this principle says that caution should be exercised when setting emission standards, and emphasis should be placed on the prevention of pollution via source reduction measures rather than the sole reliance on end-of-pipe treatments. Figure 5 illustrates a possible range of definitions of the precautionary principle (Ramchandani and Pearce, 1992; Pearce, Turner and O'Riordan, 1992).

At the extreme is what can be called the 'Strict' Precautionary Principle (SPP in Figure 5). The assumption behind the enforcement of such a standard would be that the future effects of current discharges/emissions are unknown, but may in the future impose significant damage cost burdens. The implication of this approach is that all potentially hazardous releases are considered an unacceptable risk to the future safety of the environment. SPP is therefore a zero release goal. In reality,

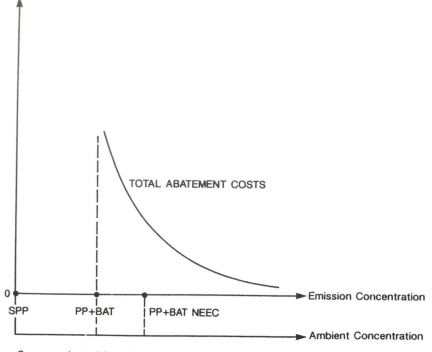

Source: adapted from Ramchandani & Pearce (1992)

Fig. 5. The precautionary principle.

however, zero emission is practically impossible due to technological limitations, or impracticable because of excessive costs. The Precautionary Principle emission standard is based on the emission/discharge quality, and receiving environmental status and quality has little or no effect on the determination of such standards.

The critical load (CL) concept which has recently been adopted as the basis for international negotiations on reducing air emissions of sulphur and nitrogen (to combat acidification and entrophication), on the other hand, does take the receiving environment explicitly into account. Critical loads are thresholds of damage which indicate the degree to which deposition will have to be reduced if emissions are to be 'environmentally acceptable' (i.e., lack of harmful biological effects). CLs undoubtedly represent cost-effectiveness improvement over the simple approach of uniform percentage emission reduction, since the effects and costs of abatement do vary across regions. However, they should still be used with some caution if inefficient environmental policy is to be avoided. In Figure 6, CL occurs at an ambient concentration level OC_{CL}, 'damage' occurs due to a breaching of the assimilative capacity of the environment, or because of the breaching of a threshold related to the accumulated stock of persistent pollutants.

But a biologically determined CL_b is not necessarily equivalent to an 'economic' CL_e. The latter is defined in terms of human welfare and the perception and valuation of environmental changes. In Figure 6 we assume for convenience that the two critical loads are the same. If we consider just two locations 1 and 2, economic damage in 1 is measured by MD_1 (marginal damage) and in location 2 by MD_2. Even if the two locations are identical in bio-physical terms they may still vary

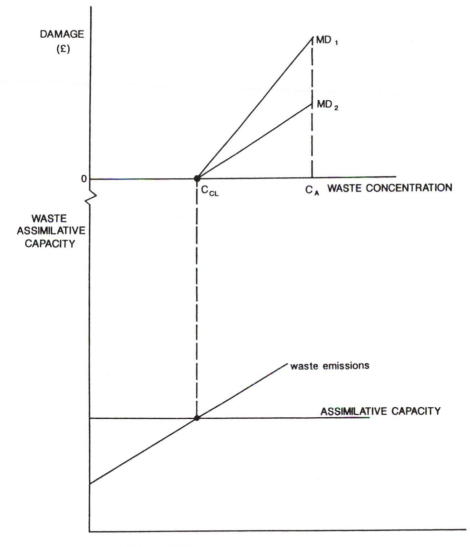

Source: Pearce (1992)

Fig. 6. The critical load approach to pollution control.

in economic damage (measured in terms of willingness-to-pay to prevent damage). Thus area 1 could be an area of high recreational demand or cultural importance relative to area 2. Using the CL approach both sites would be treated equally since they both face the same 'excess load' situation. But damage (in economic terms) will be different at the two sites. At site 1 it is $C_{CL} \cdot d_1 \cdot C_A$ and at site 2 it is $C_{CL} \cdot d_2 \cdot C_A$, and $C_{CL} \cdot d_1 \cdot C_A > C_{CL} \cdot d_2 \cdot C_A$. Hence the CL approach runs the risk of economic inefficiency (Pearce, 1992).

For this reason, target loads, which are set nationally, need to take into account not only environmental sensitivity but also, among others, technical and economic considerations. Thus the CL approach and the SPP approach may be modified by referring to technological capability. Releases of pollution can then be controlled in line with Best Available Technology (PP + BAT in Figure 5). The problem then becomes that any given time a best technology does not exist. Another layer of control can always be added, or there is a bench-scale technology under test and promises more effective pollution control (Lave and Mäles, 1989). In the USA and Germany the authorities choose the most advanced technology that is commercially available, reliable, has an 'acceptable' level of control and is available at a 'reasonable' cost. In the UK, BAT is interpreted as a technique which is deemed to be 'available' only if it is 'procurable' and also if it has been developed (or proven) at a scale which allows its implementation in the relevant industrial context with the necessary business confidence.

Given only the prevailing state of relevant technology and innovation, a PP + BAT solution may impose a more or less strict standard on emissions than a CL approach. The actual relative level of PP + BAT standard will depend on the type and availability of existing technologies, the interpretation of the BAT concept by pollution control authorities, the degree of acceptance of the PP in certain contexts and countries and the assimilative capacity of the environment.

The PP and BAT approach is given an even more practicable orientation when the costs of achieving a specified emission target level are explicitly considered. This results in the establishment of a PP + BATNEEC approach (see Figure 5). The NEEC portion of BATNEEC means that the presumption in favour of BAT can be modified by two sorts of 'economic cost' considerations i.e., whether the costs of applying BAT would be excessive in relation to the environmental protection achieved: and where the costs of applying BAT would be excessive in relation to the nature of the industry and its competitive position. There is, however, no great consistency in the way authorities have interpreted the term excessive cost. Sometimes what is referred to is a financial cost to the polluting firms (i.e., pollution abatement equipment, etc. and/or loss of market competitiveness); and at other times the wider external costs of pollution are included.

Critics of the technology-based standards approach tend to focus on its vagueness in terms of guidance on questions such as how clean should the environment be made, what are acceptable risks and what precisely are excessive costs (e.g., what do we do with threatened plant closures in areas of high unemployment?). Difficult ethical, political and economic efficiency questions are shrouded rather than illuminated by this approach, value judgements are made implicitly rather than explicitly.

Given the realities of the political economy of regulation (see, for example, Verbruggen, De Savornin Lohman and Fraschini and Cassone in this volume) future environmental policy will remain at least partially anchored to the regulatory approach. Economic incentive mechanisms may find their greatest potential future use in the context of ambient quality improvement strategies and objectives. The UK provides a good illustration of this situation. Future water pollution policy, for example, is likely to include an incentive charging instrument. But the traditional regulatory system of 'consented' discharges will be retained in order to 'guarantee' the status quo ambient quality certainty.

A gradual move into cost-recovery charging and then into incentive charging is the most likely future scenario.

3. Some Results and their Relevance for Policy and Economics

As we noted at the end of Section 1, Task Force II of ESS has concentrated on the academic and policy aspects of the development, the implementation and the evaluation of economic instruments.

At the theoretical level, we looked at the dynamics of instrument choice and the means to evaluate economic instruments by simulations which run through various types of models. Also the performance of some operational economic instruments was studied empirically, and options for new approaches on the interfaces of technology, economy and the environment were explored. This volume is therefore composed of:

- Economic Analysis of Environmental Policy Instruments
- Economic Instruments: Empirical Aspects
- Product Cycles, Innovation and the Design of Economic Instruments.

We summarise the main results for each part, and conclude with some crosssectional observations. In this summary we incorporate the observations made by the team of external reviewers who were especially asked to comment on the policy relevance of the various chapters. It goes without saying that we recognise their inputs with deeply felt gratitude. The reviewing has been organised as an anonymous process; hence the individual contributions of reviewers cannot be explicitly acknowledged. The composition of the group is given at the end of this volume.

Economic Instruments in Economic Analysis

Earlier on in this chapter we presented an overview of the fundamental economic analysis underlying market based instruments and the conceptual framework within which instruments are to be evaluated. Part 1 of this volume extends this at several levels. First, there is an evaluation of the types of instruments currently in use and the reasons for preferring them from a political economy-oriented perspective (Verbruggen and De Savornin Lohman). Then there is an analytical approach to the design of incentives schemes in a more political framework than the one traditionally employed in neoclassical economics, a principal-agent model (Conrad and Wang).

Verbruggen begins by observing that currently used sets of instruments are inadequate to achieve increasingly stringent policy targets for environmental quality. He even speaks of an 'instruments crisis'. This crisis can be overcome by finding new instruments or new combinations of instruments, by applying these (new) instruments at the appropriate links in product chains (see Opschoor and Bertrolini in Part III), and by applying them at the appropriate level (which increasingly has to transcend that of the state). He sees an important future role for economic incentives because in particular he believes that economic instruments are less vulnerable than regulations to undesirable manipulation and do not provide shelter to established industries. Why, then, is there an apparent preference for regulatory approaches? Verbruggen explains this using a stylised analysis of the dominant motives of the various actors in the game of instruments selection: government, industry, etc. His analysis is based on a 'rent seeking' approach in a principal-agent context. He finds a rationale for regulatory approaches in coalitions between government and industry, at the expense of the consumers (given that the regulatory approach is less cost effective) and the environment. He also develops the case for an international approach, based on the transboundary nature of many environmental problems and the economic systems (product chains, international markets, etc.) that give rise to them. The central message is that it is important to establish the appropriate level to address certain problems and there is no single optimal solution to this problem.

De Savornin Lohman goes further in attempting to understand the historical preference for the regulatory approach, by more or less playing devil's advocate (to mainstream economic thinking). He is skeptical about the efficiency arguments normally put forward in favour of charges; he shows that there is no reason to expect that the administrative costs of economic instruments are generally lower than those of regulatory instruments. And, by looking at the empirical data on current practice he does not observe any marked increase in the use of economic instruments, nor any convincing swing to attitudes in favour of them. To meet some of his own points, he develops an incentive mechanism that might work but has only been utilised in restricted fashion so far: a system of incentive charges with refunding to pollution abaters. Why are such obvious schemes not more extensively used? In order to understand this he develops the idea of 'policy arenas' in which all stakeholders interested in particular (environmental) policies engage in a joint process in which the choice of instruments is but one element inseparably linked with many others. He provides grounds for assuming that the arenas in which instruments for air and water quality policies are designed, might not be conducive to incentive charging systems as they are prone to lead to dislocating conflicts between the parties involved. Rather, one looks for a regulatory strategy as this option is more likely to lead to mutual accommodation. Thus, the cost effectiveness of interventions is traded off against impact predictability (both in terms of economic and environmental results). Even if he possibly overestimates support for established strategies (such as the 1972 definitions by OECD of the 'polluter pays principle') or underestimates the advantages of economic approaches as the appropriate basis for a growing inclination to harness market forces, De Savornin Lohman makes a range of relevant points very frequently absent in economists' analyses of environmental policy instruments. But, as one reviewer remarks, the analysis is perhaps too pessimistic on the future of economic instruments as the current debate on e.g., energy taxes, exemplifies.

As a side remark, Verbruggen also points out (something underlined heavily by our external review panel as well) that there may be win-win situations and dynamic gains from national and regional attempts to restructure economic activities, in terms of economic benefits (secured competitiveness, employment and growth), and of environmental impact (green and clean industrial patterns and activities). Internalising environmental costs in market prices (e.g., through economic instruments) might in the long run have major competitive advantages. As one reviewer point out, even going regionally for increasingly tight environmental standards might provide the region with a long run competitive advantage on the world market; the innovations these tighter standards may give rise to, could eventually become the general norm.

Leaving the perspective of institutional and political economic approaches with the feeling that the right combination of instruments may not yet have been developed, we turn to the neoclassical economic perspective for insights into future instrument developments. Conrad and Wang develop an iterative procedure (within a principal-agent frame) to establish improved incentives schemes, including schemes that actually contain the features of combined incentive-refund schemes as discussed by De Savornin Lohman. They assume that the policy maker may wish to minimise environmental damage plus the net value of the transfers involved in the incentive scheme, or may wish to maximise social welfare functions of that nature subject to constraints satisfying vested interests (such as established industries whose profit levels should be considered). They thus allow for trade-offs between efficiency including a polluter pays-philosophy, and the realities of the bargaining situation the environmental policy maker may find himself emboiled in. The pricing rules or incentive schemes Conrad and Wang come up with are, as they observe, 'ad hoc', and hence they plead for the development of an overall, normative approach in which alternative incentive schemes can be evaluated, or the range of possible incentive schemes can be narrowed by searching for optimal (or perhaps 'satisficing') options. In this new approach, it is indeed important to start with well-founded social welfare functions. One reviewer questioned the Pareto-relevance of a function in which transfers also appear.

As a commentary on Parts I and II of this volume, one reviewer adds some general observations on the preferences for particular instruments, especially on the positions taken in the standards-versus-charges-debate. Industry is inclined to reject charges imposed by national authorities as it fears erosion of its competitive position internationally, as a consequence of cost rises that charges may induce; industry is also inclined to assume that it has more influence on the outcomes of a standards based approach than on the process of charge setting. Our reviewer agrees with Verbruggen and de Savornin Lohman that administrators have a relative preference for standards as their environmental effectiveness is likely to be more predictable (this is the certainty concept we examined earlier in this chapter). Moreover, administrators may feel that they have less grip on polluters in the case of charges. He adds to the analysis of De Savornin Lohman the point that administrators may not be all that rational and may simply prefer standards because these are well known and long used instruments (bureaucratic inertia), especially given the fields that many environmental administrators in the early days of environmental policy originated from (e.g., public hygiene, engineering, law); this point is highlighted as well in Opschoor and Vos (1989). Environmental pressure groups, this reviewer adds, also tend to prefer a standards based approach because charges are often seen as implying the sale of a property right, i.e., the right (or 'license') to pollute.

Economic Instruments in Economic Reality

In this Part, instruments are studied as they are applied to a range of environmental compartments (air, water, soil) and economic sectors (energy, agriculture) in a variety of countries (Italy, Sweden, Germany). These national contexts provide a useful comparison between an economy which lacks any market-based pollution control instrument (Italy) and economies which have a relatively long experience of pollution charges, albeit in a limited number of applications.

Fraschini and Cassone analyse the performance of water pollution policy in Italy. They conclude that an outsider might observe the water policy development in Italy as '. . . a process governed by a reluctant regulator'. It appears that effective rent-seeking strategies as applied by producers as well as consumers can explain the prevailing preferences for regulatory instruments. Moreover, they point to a culturally relevant element: pollution is regarded as a public bad to a much smaller extent than the various rent seeking opportunities are seen as collective goods. In such cases, the agents 'capture' the regulators or principals. Thus, RIs are used in the Italian water policy much more than EIs, and if EIs are used, their incentive impact is low. Fraschini and Cassone confirm some of the points raised in part I by De Savornin Lohman. However, the authors also give some pointers to the prospects for and impediments to developing a more efficiency-oriented approach in environmental policy. In this context, they point out the significance for the further development of economic instruments, of the acceptance in principle in Italian legislation, of the concept of damage liability.

Piacentino looks at the domestic policy aspects of introducing carbon dioxide taxation measures at the international level. He analyses the economic consequences of having such incentives schemes, beyond the typical efficiency approach of standard economic analyses. It is precisely such 'concordance' considerations (see section 2) that are increasingly dominating public debates over instrument choice. Piacentino's study results in a wide and deep perspective of the elements to be taken into account in the political economy of instrument analysis, evaluation and design. He discusses distributional considerations (revenue flows from the private sector to government, different impacts for different income groups, sectorial redistributions and sectoral restructuring as a consequence of substantive carbon taxes, etc.). He concludes *inter alia* that the taxation level should not be so high as to cause unmanageable stress on budgetary redistributive activities and hence that carbon taxation may not result in an adequate level of control of emissions; moreover, there may have to be tax differentiation between sectors or groups of energy consumers, and revenue rechanneling, to prevent undesirable economic and social disruption. Furthermore, consideration of the possible macro economic considerations suggests that energy taxation should be integrated with overall budgetary and fiscal policy.

Even though much of his analysis is of the qualitative and ex ante type, Piacentino's views have been confirmed by much more quantiative, empirical and policy simulation work, done by Dutch economists looking at energy and carbon charges and their economic impacts (Central Planning Bureau CPB, 1992). From that work (based on the introduction in one step of a substantive charge raising energy prices by about 50% either in the OECD – case A – or in the Netherlands alone – case B) the following predictions can be derived: in case B (relevant in connection with Piacentino's analysis) GNP and consumption would drop by some 6–7% over the entire period 2000–2015 (compared with a baseline of no charge) and national employment would fall by 4% by the year 2000 (levelling off to a

1% fall by 2015); activity levels in major sectors such as agriculture, chemicals, metals and petrochemicals would drop by 10–20% and remain at these lower levels; meanwhile energy use could drop 35%, out of which only 5–10% is real energy conservation and the remainder is the result of relocation of productive activities outside the national jurisdiction. In case A (an OECD-wide charge) initial economic effects (on GNP, consumption etc.) are much lower, but due to charge evasive relocations of industries to outside the OECD region, effects in 2015 may become as bad as in the B-scenario, or worse: minus 3% employment and a drop of 13% in NNI; relocation effects would concentrate and intensity in (petro)chemicals and metals; energy use in the Netherlands would go down by 30%, out of which 20–25% would be due to relocation rather than energy conservation. Much of the above rests heavily on assumptions about the long term elasticity of energy demand, the response of industry (in terms of relocation) and the possibilities for mitigating measures in terms of import and export facilities to protect the domestic or regional economy against relocative tendencies (as also suggested by Piacentino). In fact, the CPB-study quoted took a rather pessimistic approach to these points: e.g., low (and given) elasticities, strong response in terms of relocation, no mitigating policies at the border. Also, the type of model used may not be the most appropriate. It was basically a macro economic model with a sectorial breakdown, but without explicit behavioural and response functions to endogenously deal with differences in relative prices, intersectoral effects etc. As editors we feel that these results support the case for more in-depth research on ways to improve the environmental effectiveness and to mitigate the economic and distributional impacts of substantial charges.

One reviewer points at the importance of macro economic effects but at the same time he remarks that a revenue neutral approach would do much to counteract them. The above data from one particular case study indicate that this may be true to a much less convincing degree than the reviewer hopes. The issue is of extreme policy relevance and requires further work.

He also points out that energy conservation has benefits in terms of other environmental and economic effects (e.g., reductions in emissions of acid forming compounds, energy savings etc.). This too is an important policy issue: there may be no-regret arguments cancelling out some of the adverse economic effects. Another reviewer goes on to say that the debate about the severe economic consequences and the low environmental effectiveness of carbon charges is besides the point given the dynamic effects of having a regional (e.g., European) approach in terms of longer term competitive innovation. Hence a regional approach (with perhaps some protection at the common border) might in the long run be an economic advantage. Again the issue is so policy relevant and the information so deficient or contradictory, that further environmental economic research work is required.

Conrad and Schroeder's study takes the ESF project several steps further in the direction of more appropriate analytical tools capable of handling such indirect economic repercussions as discussed by Piacentino. They develop a so-called 'applied general equilibrium' model based on an input-output matrix representing (in principle) all economic interlinkages, and extended with coefficients incorporating air pollution into the model. Actually, the model developed is a subset of 'temporary equilibrium' models that allow for a more realistic adjustment process between short and long term demand and supply conditions. Changes in prices can then in each period affect price-dependent input-output coefficients which may induce alterations in sectoral structure, substitution, investment patterns and patterns of capital stock formation. The model is used to simulate various economic instruments and emissions standards, in terms of impacts on, e.g., GNP, employment, consumption, production structure, etc.. AGE-models are necessary to better rank alternative policy instruments. Such models are also increasingly being used. But in order to solve real-world problems, they need to be refined and made more sophisticated. The study by Conrad and Schroeder points out directions in which to develop general equilibrium modeling for that purpose.

It seems clear that the application of economic instruments to the agricultural sector and its attendant environmental problems is a formidable challenge. The existing complexity of the interrelated market and government failures that already afflict the agricultural industries in Europe undoubtedly constrains the role that economic instruments could potentially play in any policy move to encourage a transition to what we might call sustainable farming. Thus the general application of a range of economic instruments does not represent a panacea for the unsustainable agriculture that currently exists.

Gren has used econometric tools to investigate how Swedish farmers behave in terms of pesticides use and how sensitive they are to income losses due to pest attacks; it is this risk-oriented approach that represents an extension to traditional analysis in this field. She develops a model for farmers' input choice, and derives pesticides demand functions. She then evaluates three different instruments (a charge, a regulation, and a tradeable permit) to affect pesticides consumption, in terms of cost efficiency and effects on farmers' incomes. In order to do this, she uses a non-linear programming approach for finding the minimum costs for different reductions in pesticides use. She finds that a 50% reduction of pesticides use can be achieved efficiently via a charging or a trading system; regulation through non-tradable quota would be 40% more costly in terms of the net value of yield losses. However, in terms of the distributional impact, charges are much more severe than either a direct regulation or a tradable quota. A permit market would do the job efficiently with least distributional impacts. This, of course, depends on the initial distribution of permits, as the general literature on trading indeed suggests. Gren starts with an initial distribution free of charge. Here, again, the results may be interesting in themselves, but it is the methodological step forward that is even more important.

Nutzinger takes us back to the realm of qualitative analysis: he looks at institutional problems in the implementation of economic incentives in a search for a sustainable agriculture, in the European Community, based on German experience. He looks at nitrogen taxes, pesticides taxes and water user charges. In economic reality (as opposed to the artificial world of competitive equilibrium) already existing regulations and policy interventions may create a setting in which efficiency-based considerations do not necessarily provide first-best solutions. As Nutzinger puts it: the idea of internalising externalities via a Pigovian tax does not make much sense in a world of seriously distorted commodity prices, especially if they are fixed for the sake of income stabilisation. This is particularly the case in the area of agriculture, dominated as it is by national and European policy interventions. His work is directed at finding out conditions under which such a situation is, or is not a problem for the application of particular economic instruments. Nutzinger feels that economic instruments can be helpful as second best approaches. Sometimes – as in the case of a nitrogen charge – a charge might help in alleviating disequilibria that are the consequence of distortive agricultural policies. In other cases, regulatory approaches seem appropriate (e.g., in the area of pesticides policies; see, however Gren on this issue). Nutzinger prefers this approach as he finds it difficult to relate a charge to pesticides' toxicity; Gren's charge was not related to toxicity, but to the amount of pesticides actually applied. In a Pigovian approach the latter is in itself second best. The overall conclusion is, that typically a combination of regulatory and economic instruments will prove to be a pragmatic and effective policy avenue.

Finally, the application of a specific water charge for farmers would probably lead to a more efficient use of increasingly scarce groundwater reserves. But it would not influence the deteriorating water quality problem, nor, in his view, would it do much to discourage the most intensive farming methods. This finding, if correct, is in direct contrast to that of the nitrogen tax and its impacts which provides for both pollution abatement in the short run and deintensification of farming methods and practices over the longer run.

As one reviewer mentions, a fundamental aspect of instruments choice is the spatial scale. If standards are to be met at the regional level, then economic instruments may be more effective. However, if quality standards are to be met at the farm level, then a regulatory approach could be more appropriate.

Looking at both the Gren and the Nutzinger chapters, one referee wishes a distinction to be made between short term and long term impacts of economic instruments in the agricultural sector. This is because the response elasticities will differ markedly, given that expected new technological options will become available in the short to medium term. The implication is, that in a dynamic sense it may not be efficient to modernise farming systems now. High tax rates might thus induce inefficient patterns of investment at the farm level. This may be true, but at the same time it could lead us to environmental cul-de-sacs. Much depends on the actual path of innovation, cost differentials, etc. It is correct that a full analysis of the relative merits of the various instruments would have to take these dynamic effects into account, and in fact Kemp *et al.* (in part III) will deal to some extent with this point.

The same reviewer suggests that long term elasticities may in themselves be underestimated or could be enlarged by preference-oriented instruments of the SI-type. We have come across this thought also in relation to the energy demand elasticities.

Product Cycles, Economic Instruments and Innovation

In the final part of the volume, four studies are put together that are design-oriented.

Two papers (by Opschoor and Bertolini) deal with the fact that specific final products are the end-results of chains of economic activities each leading to their own environmental impacts. Given this, the notion of 'cumulated' environmental impact makes sense. When it comes to the issue of instruments to address environmental impacts, the question becomes: at which 'leverage point' in the product chains would specific sets of economic instruments have what economic and cumulative environmental effects?

Pearce and Turner investigate the economic and environmental merits of alternative waste policy options and waste management instruments. Finally, Kemp *et al.* seek incentives to explicitly induce cleaner technologies. They explore factors affecting the decision to supply and adopt cleaner technologies. These four chapters share an awareness of the complexities of introducing instruments in the actual economic process, of the wide ranging and often intractable interrelations between economic and environmental systems, and of technological change as a necessary part of the solution to the problems at hand. They all are attempting to penetrate into the new ground thus demarcated.

Looking closely at real-world materials cycles and product cycles, provides frustrating insights into what is in fact behind the 'pure' models of the textbook in environmental economics: very complex webs of inter-related economic activities and multi-dimensional inter-compartmental environmental processes.

Opschoor explores the Chlorine chain, in order to come up with suggestions about the use of simulation modeling based on 'materials-products'-chains as a new tool in evaluative approaches to instruments analysis. Materials product chains are pragmatically truncated subsets of linked materials cycles and product chains, these links being of a (bio)chemical, technological and economic nature. Chains analysis and modeling thus links the materials approach and the economic approach.

Chain management – a relatively new policy concept in some countries – aims at manipulating chains to optimise their environmental impact or to efficiently reach predetermined environmental targets. The notion of the product chain implies that there are several leverage points at which to apply administrative pressure; it is to be decided which sets of instruments to apply at which of these leverage points. An attempt is made to generally indicate which type of instrument could be used efficiently and effectively at which of these leverage points or stages in the product cycle. This is made more realistic by looking at different instruments which could affect the PVC chain, both on the basis of process knowledge and by using an ad-hoc dynamic simulation model. The reviewer judges this extension of the materials balance approach to integrated dynamic simulation the main contribution of this chapter. The conclusion is, that the more one tries to approximate reality, abstract theories and analytical solutions for solving issues related to instruments selection rapidly become less convincing and realistic, ad hoc studies appear more attractive. Environmental economics would become richer and more relevant, if it would open itself up more to such less elegant but more useful approaches. The reviewer of this chapter adds to this the desirability of extending the approach by designing modules which track the pathways of compounds through the environment with ambient concentrations (to be confronted with quality standards or critical loads) as the end result. This would indeed enhance the policy relevance of the approach.

Bertolini studies wastepaper recycling from the perspective of the need to limit the entropy of the materials system.

In this chapter the product-chain approach is applied to the waste-paper flows. The focus taken is that of a need for policy interventions which stimulate waste reduction and materials conservation.

Several specific areas for policy interventions can be identified in this chain; these are referred to as 'pressure blocks'. They are:

- incentives to reduce the use of virgin inputs;
- stimulating recycling and recycling technology;
- instruments in the area of recovery and disposal;
- disincentives on final demand.

In each of these pressure blocks, several ways of stimulating more environmentally friendly economic behavior are, or can be used; they differ substantially in terms of effectiveness, efficiency, financial effects and their distributional impacts. Moreover, the performance of these various instruments may be affected by differences in side conditions (e.g., market structure, domestic versus international market). This is substantiated in the various sections on options for intervention in the various pressure blocks.

At each set of pressure points in the product chain, different economic incentives will affect materials demand and waste volumes differently, thus affecting the structure of the waste paper market. By using the concept of entropy, a tool is developed to compare and evaluate different waste flow systems – defined as matrices showing flows of wastes of different grades through subsectors within the waste paper market. The entropy within these systems, however, is only one criterion for comparing them, apart from differences in economic and environmental impacts and their distributions.

From an empirical analysis of data from a range of European countries, it appears that these countries differ greatly in terms of their recovery rates (i.e., their efforts in collecting waste paper domestically) and their recycling (or utilization) rates. Most countries are improving their recovery performance, and recycling rates have increased even more (except Belgian and German recycling rates). Countries with recycling rates below their recovery rates are likely to promote exports of (parts of) their waste paper flows, especially when they have strict and effective policies on waste incineration and landfilling/dumping. This could explain exports of waste paper by e.g., Germany.

It appears that in many countries, rapidly increasing recovery rates have pushed up collection costs whilst depressing prices of secondary materials.

On theoretical grounds it is argued that recovery and disposal can be regarded as substitutes rather than complements and therefore recovery activities should be financially rewarded as such, over and above the revenues drawn from the market value of recovered materials. However, recycling itself may not be a 'good' thing per se and the costs and benefits of an extension in recycling activities are analysed by Turner and Pearce in Chapter 12.

Turner and Pearce also focus on the waste stage, where various processing options may technically exist and where incentives will dictate how the waste flows will actually be distributed over these various alternatives. They employ a cost-benefit framework to analyse these, and conclude that waste minimisation or recycling maximisation are not necessarily socially worthwhile things in themselves. This, according to the reviewers, is a conclusion of great importance. Turner and Pearce develop criteria for evaluating economic instruments and on that basis compare packaging taxes, disposal charges, deposit-refund systems, and permit trading. Again (as with Opschoor's and Bertolini's paper) it appears that no case exists for general conclusions: from an efficiency point of view, the choice of the optimal (mix of) instruments depends on the materials flow to be manipulated.

The authors do however advocate a greater reliance on economic instruments (rather than direct regulation) in order to increase the efficiency of municipal waste management policy. But they also show that the alternative policy instruments need to be evaluated in terms of a range of criteria, not just economic efficiency. Thus environmental effectiveness, equity, administrative cost-effectiveness, acceptability, institutional concordance and revenue raising properties are all criteria that should be included alongside economic efficiency.

On this basis, they see great merit in a simple packaging waste tax, based on the costs of disposal and littering. It may also be possible to design and implement a simple curbside disposal charge. Deposit-refund systems seem to fare less well than taxes/charges, at least in terms of the schemes that have operated in a number of countries since the early 1970s and directed at beverage containers. Nevertheless, there may be an important role for deposit-refund type systems in the context of hazardous waste. Finally, transferable permits applied to waste management problems present an essentially open research question, as no empirical examples as yet exist.

Finally, Kemp et al. discuss incentives to induce cleaner technologies. They firstly explore the factors affecting the decision to supply and adopt cleaner technologies by analysing three case studies. Amongst the determinants of innovation that are studied by Kemp et al. are: market demand ('demand pull') 'appropriability conditions' (conditions affecting the extent to which innovations can be protected against imitation), transfer of knowledge and information. Secondly, they compare policy instruments that can be employed to induce innovation. It turns out that there is a risk on the side of the regulator in terms of stimulating the 'wrong' technological trajectory; and market signals provide very imperfect guidelines for allocating R&D-budgets: the effects of policy instruments depend on the economic context in which they are applied. The case studies suggest that stimulation of clean technology requires context-specific combinations of technology forcing standards and charges, supported by communicative instruments. Once again, leaving the neat textbook world of certainty means that immediately the attractiveness of specific policy instruments and/or analytical tools is less clear and the case for more, practically oriented, often unorthodox research becomes increasingly strong.

The cases relate to three (intermediate) products (e.g., low solvent paints and coatings) and this represent only part of the problem, as the reviewer points out: emissions related policy interventions such as air pollution standards have led (and are leading) to major technological advances such as the catalytic converter, at the same time blocking advance along other trajectories, such as the lean burn engine. Kemp et al. provide another example of this in their case of CFC-substitutes. The indirect or second order influences of instruments choice on technological development should prove a highly policy relevant field of analysis. The reviewer finally would have liked to have seen the empirical justification for the authors' statement that subsidies for investment in pollution control technology are 'less useful'. We believe that such evidence can indeed be found, so that the argument might stand.

4. Where Do We Go From Here?

That, as we can learn from Lewis Caroll, depends on where we want to go. Looking back at this project, we have indeed reached certain conclusions.

1. Environmental degradation may lead to policy responses in terms of e.g., measures aimed at reducing environmental pressure or enhancing environmental buffering capacities.
Environmental policy uses a range of instruments to realise these objectives.

2. Given a 'rational' approach, policy makers would select instruments so as to achieve their objectives in an optimal manner (that is: with reference to criteria such as effectiveness and efficiency) and with reference to the 'concordance' of instruments with current political trends or policies (e.g., compatibility with principles such as 'the polluter pays'), societal acceptability, compliance/enforement aspects, etc.

3. Economic instruments are instruments that provide *incentives* to economic agents to induce them to behave in a more environmentally appropriate or acceptable way. Their potential merits include: effectiveness, efficiency, flexibility, incentives for innovation.
There is quite a variety of economic instruments, including charges, tradable permits, subsidies, deposit-refund systems, compliance incentives, market support.
The policy relevance of so-called economic instruments for environmental policy is well established and no longer rests on theoretical or academic arguments only. The call for increasingly stringent quality standards inevitably means escalating policy-response costs and therefore enhances the appeal of cost-effective market-based instruments.

4. There has been a tendency to analyse instruments in ideal-type form and in a generic fashion (e.g., 'the' efficiency and effectiveness features of product charges). The complexities of the interactions between environmental and economic processes, as well as the dynamics of innovation preclude straightforward and simple broad-brush recommendations on instruments; rather, context-specific and often complex (i.e., mixes of elements of command and control, incentive and suasive natures) instruments will have to be developed.

5. Environmental administrators have (or used to have) a relative preference of command-and-control-instruments such as standards and permits, as (i) their environmental effectiveness is likely to be more predictable, and as (ii) they appear

to provide a better grip on polluters. This is the 'certainty' dimension we have stressed at various points in this chapter. Also, they may prefer a regulatory approach because they are familiar with the use of such instruments given the fields that many environmental administrators in the early days of environmental policy emanated from.

6. Rent-seeking by polluters explains preferences for non-economic instruments as effectively expressed by economic agents.

7. Factors affecting acceptability include income distributional effects, impacts on sectorial and overall economic activity and employment, etc. The overall economic consequences of using environmental policy instruments are very significant elements in the public debates over instrument choice. They can be substantial, especially in the short run. But the dynamic effects of having a strict regional (e.g., European) approach to environmental quality might include potential long term competitive advantages in terms of marketable new products and technologies.

8. A range of quantitative tools is applied to study the impacts of using certain types of instruments in order to assess their performance or to make ex ante evaluations and recommendations. This range includes macro-economic models, applied general equilibrium models, various econometric tools, non-linear programming, dynamic simulation models. Most of these are used in this volume. Major improvements to the quality of policy recommendations in the area of environmental policy instruments can be expected from the development of general equilibrium and dynamic simulation models.

9. (Semi-) quantitative performance criteria to evaluate environmental policy instruments as used in the various contributions in this volume, include:

- effects on environmental quality, emissions etc. ('environmental effectiveness')
- effects on sectoral levels of production or productivity (e.g., the value of yield losses)
- effects on GNP or NNI
- effects on consumption, purchasing power or welfare
- effects on (sectoral and national) employment
- effects on investment
- relocational impacts
- administrative costs and revenue flows
- effects on income distribution, sectorial income shares, etc.
- cost impacts and related impacts on profitability and competitiveness
- international trade and balance of trade impacts

Qualitative performance criteria used, include:

- acceptability
- legality
- compatibility/concordance with policy principles.

These aspects can be captured by the following categories:

- environmental effectiveness
- efficiency and cost effectiveness
- societal acceptability (equity aspects, impacts on interest groups, side effects on other element of (social) welfare functions),
- concordance with policies, principles, conventions etc.

10. Existing regulations and policy interventions may create a setting in which efficiency-based consideration of environmental policy instruments would at best indicate second-best solutions. Internalising externalities via economic instruments may not make much sense in a world of seriously distorted markets (i.e., in a complex situation involving multiple market and government failures).

11. Economic instruments are potentially relevant in policy contexts that are based on a preventative approach. Typically, economic incentives will operate best in combination with, or in support of, other instruments such as direct regulation. Hazardous pollutants are best dealt with via regulation, although deposit-refund systems could play a valuable role in the solid and chemical waste fields.

12. Environmental policy must adopt a 'materials-product' approach to environmental degradation. In such an approach policy interventions affect the economic process at different point in the product chain. The 'instruments' question then becomes: at which 'leverage points' in the product chains would specific sets of instruments have which economic and cumulative environmental effects?

13. Waste minimisation or recycling maximisation are not necessarily socially optimal policy strategies.

14. The effects of policy instruments depend on the economic context in which they are applied. A priori general rules are inferior to case-by-case analysis.

15. The impact of charges and other economic incentives on the rate and direction of innovation is a much claimed advantage of such instruments but actual outcomes are not well documented. There is a risk on the side of the regulator, however, that more interventionist policy may stimulate the 'wrong technological trajectory.

16. As one tries to better approximate reality, abstract theories and analytical approaches to solving issues related to instruments selection rapidly become less convincing and realistic. Case studies appear more attractive. Environmental economics would become richer and more relevant, if it would open itself up to these less elegant but potentially more useful approaches.

17. Because of the uncertainty over some pollution damage functions and the monetary valuation of such damage, actual incentive charging schemes, for example, to combat water pollution will not conform precisely to the 'pure tax' (based on marginal damage costs) version. In the UK, it is likely that a charge based on pollution load, river volume and river quality (as expressed in a broad classification scheme based on general usages) will be adopted. The charge level will initially be set at a low level and then gradually increased. However, more research is required on a catchment-wide basis before we can be reasonably confident about the impacts of such a charging scheme.

18. The problem posed by diffuse pollutants is not adequately addressed in the incentive charging literature and the same is true for groundwater contamination. What instruments might be applied and at what points in the economic-environment chain is an under-researched question.

19. The problem of intertemporal bias and the discount-rate debate remains unresolved.

20. The extent to which tradeable permits might be introduced across a range of pollution and resource management problems requires further investigation. International trading in greenhouse gases, permits related to waste recycling targets and the combined problem of point and diffuse water pollution mitigation are all possible applications.

But, again, where do we go from here? In our view environmental economics must be developed in such a way that it becomes more policy relevant based on proper theoretical as well as empirical foundations. There is a need for sustainability oriented, practically usable insight based on technically sound economics. New insights on how to manipulate the economic process, and tools to analyse and evaluate alternative (if they exist) ways of manipulation, are required.

On the basis of our project for the European Science foundation, we point out the following promising research avenues:

(1) Refinement of the theoretical capacity and enhancement of the empirical basis of instruments evaluation in environmental economics by a well-structured international programme of coordinated in-depth case studies.

(2) Improvement of models currently in existence and development of new models and model applications in order to better capture the intricacies of economic and environmental interrelationships and the environmental and economic impacts of alternative environmental policies, strategies and instruments.

(3) Research (empirical, qualitative and where possible quantitative) on the influence of policy failure and market distortion, on environmental policy instruments' performance, especially under conditions in which such failures pose problems for the application of particular economic instruments.

(4) The environmental and economic costs and benefits of different paths or speeds of innovation in particular sectors (e.g., agriculture, energy, transport)

(5) Research on the economic and cumulative environmental effects of applying specific sets of instruments at different 'leverage points' in a range of selected product chains and for selected materials.

(6) Broadening the scope of (dynamic) product-materials chain models by incorporating modules tracing the impact of 'emissions' on ambient environmental quality.

(7) Case studies of the indirect or second order influences of instruments choice on technological development: how and in what way do economic instruments provide incentives or pose barriers to the development of specific technological options?

(8) Research on the incidence and size of macro economic impacts of far reaching environmental policies. Empirical and prospective research on industries' responses to alternative environmental strategies and instruments, in terms of relocation. Associated with this, research into mitigating measures to protect domestic or regional economies against relocative tendencies.

(9) Research on the positive dynamic impacts (through technological innovation and sectorial restructuring) of regional, international environmental policies.

(10) Research on long term elasticities for products that have a large environmental impact, and on how to increase these elasticities.

References

Anon. (1990) Sustainable development, science and policy, Conference Report, Bergen, 8–12 May 1990, Norwegian Research Council for Sciences and the Humanities, Oslo.

Baumol, W. J. and Oates W. E. (1975) *The Theory of Environmental Policy*, Prentice-Hall, Englewood Cliffs, N.J.

Bohm, P. and Russel C. S. (1985) Alternative policy instruments, in A. V. Kneese *et al.* (eds), *Handbook of Natural Resource and Energy Economics*, Vol. 1, North-Holland, Amsterdam.

Central Planning Bureau (1992) *Long Term Economic Consequences of Energy Charges* (in Dutch), CPB Working Documents No. 43, The Hague.

Coase H. (1960) The problem of social cost, *Law and Economics*.

Commission of the EC (1992) *Towards Sustainability. A European Community Programme of Policy and Action in Relation to the Environment and Sustainable Development*, Par. 7.4, Commission of the European Communities, March 1992, Brussels.

Dales, J. H. (1968) *Pollution, Property and Prices*, Toronto Univ. Press, Toronto.

Dosi, G., Freeman C., *et al.* (1988) *Technology and Economic Theory*, Pinter Publ., London, New York.

Georg, S. and Jorgenson U. (1990) Clean technology: Innovation and environmental regulation, paper presented at the Venice Conference of the European Association of Environmental and Resource Economists, Venice, April 1990 (unpublished).

Helm, D. (1991) *Economic Policy Toward the Environment*, Blackwell, Oxford.

Lang, W., Opschoor, J. B., and Perrings, Ch. (1992) Institutional arrangements, in *An Agenda of Science for Environment and Development in the 21st Century*, ICSU, Paris.

Lave, L. B. and Males, E. H. (1989) At risk: The framework for regulating toxic substances, *Environ. Sci. Technol.* **23**(23), 386–391.

Opschoor, J. B. (1992) *Environment, Economics and Sustainable Development*, Wolters Noordhoff, Groningen, 1992.

Opschoor, J. B. and Vos, H. B. (1989) *Economic Instruments for Environmental Protection*, OECD, Paris.

Pearce, D. W. (1992) Using critical loads to determine environmental policy, Unpubl. CSERGE Note, University College London.

Pearce, D. W. and Turner, R. K. (1990) *Economics of Natural Resources and the Environment*, Harvester Wheatsheaf, Hemel Hempstead.

Pearce, D. W., Turner, R. K. and O'Riordan, T. (1992) Energy and social health: Integrating quantity and quality in energy planning, CSERGE Working Paper GEC 92-05. University College London and University of East Anglia.

Pigou, A. (1962) *The Economics of Welfare*, MacMillan, London.

Ramchandani, R. and Pearce, D. W. (1992) Alternative approaches to setting effluent quality standards, CSERGE Working Paper WM 92-04. University College London and University of East Anglia.

Schuurmans, J. (1989) *The Price of Water* (in Dutch), Gouda Qunit, Arnhem, The Netherlands.

Stavins R. N. and Whitehead, B. W. (1992) Market based incentives for environmental protection. *Environment* 34, pp 7–11 and 29–42.

Turner, R. K. (1992) Speculations on weak and strong sustainability. CSERGE Working Paper GEC 92–26, University of East Anglia and University College London.

US EPA (1990) *United States Workshop on Economics of sustainable Development: Report to the 1990 Bergen Conference*. Washington DC, Jan. 23–26, 1990, US EPA.

World Commission for Environment and Development (WCED) (1987) Our common future, Oxford University Press, Oxford.

PART I

Economic Analysis of Environmental Policy Instruments

2. Environmental Policy Failures and Environmental Policy Levels

HARMEN VERBRUGGEN
Institute for Environmental Studies, Free University, Amsterdam, The Netherlands

1. The Instrument Crisis

In many developed countries, environmental policies experience what may be called an instrument crisis. This crisis manifests itself in the general recognition that there is a wide and even growing gap between the formulation of environmental policy goals and standards on the one hand, and the implementation and realisation of these goals and standards on the other hand. There is a policy failure: the achievements of environmental policies fall seriously short in many fields. In this respect, falling short has two dimensions. Officially formulated environmental goals are not attained in the planned period of time, especially so with respect to diffuse and mobile sources of pollution (cf., RIVM, 1991, section 1.1; RIVM, 1992). Or in case of attainment, the social costs are relatively high (Nelson, 1991). The obvious reaction, that with stricter standards and a more comprehensive and improved enforcement this gap can be reduced, fails to appreciate the nature of the instrument crisis. More of the same is just not enough. The real causes of the instrument crisis are three-fold:

(1) a far from efficient and effective application of environmental policy instruments;
(2) the lack of application of environmental policy instruments at the most efficient and effective policy level;
(3) the insufficient mutual coordination, and sometimes even inconsistency, between the different policy levels, i.e., local, state, national, regional and international.

In other words, environmental policies are usually not implemented with (an) optimal (combination of) instruments at the optimal policy level. The challenge for the 1990s is to improve the implementation of environmental policies, both with respect to instrument choice and policy level. This means that one has to seek for other and new combinations of instruments that must be applied at the most efficient and effec-

Hans Opschoor and Kerry Turner (eds), Economic Incentives and Environmental Policies, 41–54.
© 1994 *Kluwer Academic Publishers. Printed in the Netherlands.*

tive links in the production-consumption-waste chain. Given the increasing economic and international environmental interdependence, a shift to supra-national policy levels seems inevitable in many cases.

This contribution first of all attempts to show that there is a general disposition among governments to seek out the wrong type of environmental policy instruments. Next, attention will be paid to the policy problems inherent to the absence of a self-evident environmental regulator at transboundary and international levels. Finally, some lessons are drawn and recommendations are formulated to improve environmental policy performance.

2. Environmental Policy as Economic Policy

It is true that environmental policy, more than any other aspect of government policy, has to cope with additional and rather specific problems which seriously complicates the formulation of policy answers to environmental problems (cf, Opschoor, 1992).

First of all, at least in the short run, environmental policy has to make a stand against powerful forces, inherent in market economies, that generate economic growth and tend to take these economies beyond what is ecologically sustainable.

Second, a specific characteristic of environmental degradation, namely the distance factor, provide ample opportunities for 'cost shifting' or 'displacement of costs' (Pearce and Turner, 1990; Opschoor, 1989). The effects of environmental degradation often manifest themselves at large distances, both in terms of space and time, from the source. Consequently, the cost of environmental degradation can be passed on without punishment to other sectors, other countries and future generations.

Third, the relationships between ecological and economic variables are characterised by uncertainty, time-lags, discontinuities and risks. This frustrates the formulation of environmental goals as well as the application of the designed instruments. For instance, quite often the nature and extent of environmental damage is difficult to assess on purely scientific grounds, let alone assign a monetary value to this damage.

Fourth, environmental problems are all pervasive, ranging from isolated cases of soil contamination to climate change. Hence, environmental issues often cannot be restricted to small groups or sectors of society. This characteristic is largely responsible for competence issues between government ministries and departments mutually, and between the different policy levels within a country.

Notwithstanding these highly complicating factors, it is argued here that the implementation problems and instrument crisis of environmental policy has more to do with the phenomenon that environmental policy is increasingly becoming an integral part of economic and industrial policy. Especially in smaller countries like the Netherlands, the traditional instruments of economic and industrial policy have lost importance (Zalm, 1990). A deliberate anti-cyclical budget policy has fallen into disuse. The same holds for interventionist wage and price policies. An exchange rate policy is also not vigorously pursued since, in the Netherlands for instance, the guilder is linked to the German mark. And for the EC countries in general, there is no or little room left for a national trade policy, a regional policy and policies to improve the economic structure. All these policy fields have come to be governed by EC directives or GATT rules. And, as will be explained in Section 5, these supra- and international regulations may seriously interfere with national environmental policy, particularly at the level of policy instruments.

If the traditional instruments of economic and industrial policy either fall into disuse or are delegated to higher, supra-national levels of decision, the national governments, not surprisingly, would look for other instruments and policy fields to attain their economic policy goals. Employment, income distribution and international competitiveness are among the most sensitive goals. In any case, the impact of other policy fields particularly on these sensitive goals has to be extensively scrutinised, as there are hardly any traditional instruments left for a correction of possible negative effects. In this way, environmental policy has also become economic and industrial policy, even trade policy.

It is not argued here that the goals of economic and environmental policy are always in conflict. There are obvious examples where the restructuring of a backward economic sector both increases the economic viability of that sector and its environmental performance. Likewise, an accelerated innovation and diffusion of environmental technology in response to stringent government regulation may very well improve competitiveness in the sector that invests in the new technology, and it may open up new market opportunities for the technology supplying sector. The argument is that environmental policy is not judged on its own merits alone. This inhibits both the effectiveness and the efficiency of environmental policy.

3. Political Economy Aspects of Environmental Policy Instruments

Generally, environmental policy instruments are subdivided in three different categories: communicative instruments, direct regulation (command-and-control) and economic instruments. All three categories of instruments aim at influencing private decision making in order to attain environmental goals. It is also important to realise that all three categories entail effects on prices, incomes and international competitiveness. But here, the similarity ends. These categories of instruments greatly differ in at least two respects (Baumol and Oates, 1988; Bohm and Russell, 1985).

First, they differ in the extent, directness and time profile of their price and income effects. The price effects of regulatory instruments are not immediately visible, but with a certain time-lag, additional investment costs in response to environmental regulation show up in prices. The same is true of the voluntary agreements between government and specific branches or sectors of the economy in order to attain environmental goals, the so-called covenants. By contrast, economic instruments change the system of relative prices most directly, and consequently, have immediate visible and clear-cut effects on prices, income distribution and a country's competitive position in international trade.

Second, the instrument categories differ in their presumed efficiency. At least in principle, economic instruments combine the properties of effectiveness in environmental terms and efficiency in economic terms (Baumol and Oates, 1988). A general advantage of these instruments is that they encourage emission reduction by those who can achieve them at the least cost. They also provide an ongoing incentive to apply the most efficient abatement strategies through more efficient and cleaner technologies. This static and dynamic efficiency property is generally not ascribed to direct regulation. Inflexibilities in the setting of standards leads to static inefficiencies, ignoring abatement cost differences between firms. Direct regulation does not induce cleaner technologies either (Kemp, et al., this volume). On the contrary, as long as standards are in force, newer and cleaner technologies are often kept from the market in favour of the existing abatement technologies with which these standards can be met. Moreover, it becomes evermore clear that direct regulation results in a relatively heavy burden on the government budget, since the administration and enforcement costs often prove to be relatively high. The present experiences even raise serious doubts whether an ever growing web of environmental regulation can after all be administered, monitored and enforced by government agencies.

It is not argued here that economic instruments can be applied to solve all problems. Each instrument can have its place, depending on the pertinent circumstances such as the nature of the environmental problem at hand, the available technologies, market conditions and the number of polluters. The social and institutional acceptance and the possibility and the cost of administration, monitoring and enforcement are also of importance in this connection. So, in the case of a few, large polluters with similar cost abatement functions, direct regulation, preferably of the progressive, technology-forcing type or voluntarily agreed long-term environmental objectives may be highly efficient. In a situation of many diffused polluters with relatively great differences in abatement costs, emission charges are preferable.

Yet, recent experiences with environmental policies in a number of OECD countries show that governments have relied mainly on regulatory instruments, usually complemented by fund-raising charges facilitating environmental programmes (Opschoor and Vos, 1989). The use of economic instruments is marginal and fragmented, notwithstanding the recently intensified discussions on the use of these instruments in various countries, the EC and international organisations. Some movement can be observed away from direct regulation. At least in the Netherlands, the government prefers voluntary agreements with those producers and/or consumers who are directly involved in the attainment of environmental goals.

In general, this revealed instrument preference is neither effective, nor efficient, especially in the longer term. Policies stay behind the facts, and there is a growing irritation about the continuous revisions and tightening of standards.

The preference for regulation and voluntary agreements can only properly be understood if the interest and motives of the parties involved in the political process are analysed. Some aspects of the environmental instruments choice are examined below, explicitly taking account of the increased 'fuzziness' of environmental goals and (short-term) economic policy objectives.

4. The Playground of Environmental Policy

Two main actors can be distinguished in the political process of environmental policy formulation: on the one hand the government and its officials, on the other hand (specific sectors of) industry, agriculture or the service sector, represented by employers' organizations and trade unions. Along the sideline are (organisations of) consumers, environmental experts and environmental pressure groups. The latter groups are usually not directly involved in the process of policy formulation. Below, these actors' motives are presented in stylized form.

Government

The main interest of politicians is to maximize public support in order to be re-elected through the ballot box. Concern about environmental issues ranks high in public opinion. We may therefore assume that governments wish to pursue an environmental policy and try to attain environmental goals. This is the well-known motive for Government action in the public-choice setting of the political process. However, the objective function of the government includes environmental standards to be maximized, under the following conditions:

– no political harmful adverse effects on income distribution and employment;
– no adverse effects on international competitiveness.

Moreover, the context of setting of these policy objectives and the conditions is one of uncertainty and hidden or open obstruction. The uncertainty refers to the divergent set of variables included, both on the ecological and the economic side. Think, for instance, of the vast amount of information required and the difficulties in quantifying environmental and health damage, the problems of finding the proper level of charges, the money value of marginal environmental damage, and the lack of insight into the marginal and average costs of producers and the cleaner technologies available.

To gather information and to obtain cooperation instead of obstruction, the government has hardly any other choice but to go for a consultation with the industry involved. Usually, this consultation results in a discussion and negotiating platform, where both parties are supported by their own experts and negotiators. This platform can acquire a more or less formal status if both parties agree upon a common secretariat.

Industry

The interest of industry lies in an uninterrupted conduct of business, and to maintain its (inter)national competitive position. In addition, industry will seek to improve its competitiveness through environmental policy. For, as we have explained, there are hardly any traditional instruments in operation to improve the structure and productivity of industry. Thus, the objective function of industry with respect to environmental policy includes:

- minimize environmental cost;
- maximize time and scope to comply with environmental standards;
- longer-term certainty about the level of environmental standards, and
- rent-seeking.

The importance attached to each of these objectives varies by sector of industry, even by firm. There are, for instance, serious initiatives in specific sectors of industry and individual firms to take the lead in the greening of industry. These voluntary initiatives are found especially in economically viable and internationally significant corporations. Cases in mind are the Business Charter of Sustainable Development of the International Chamber of Commerce (ICC, 1991) and the Global Environment Management Initiative (GEMI, 1991/92), a multisectoral organization of 200 US chief executives. Their annual report states that 'GEMI participants believe in the fundamental precept that business, by taking control of its environmental destiny, can spur change from within and create a forum for sharing solutions among industry worldwide'.

Long-term strategic considerations are at the root of these initiatives, namely the insight that environmentally unsound business practices will not be tolerated in the long run, either by politics, or by the market. Hence, the voluntary greening of industry is a well-understood, anticipating and proactive strategy to guarantee a firm's long-term continuity. There are also firms that try to create a new competitive edge with environmentally-sound products, anticipating a further greening of consumer preferences.

However positive these initiatives might be, they make clear above all that firms try to get rid of the costly and time-consuming government interventions by keeping ahead and solving their environmental problems in their own, more efficient way. A reactive attitude is simply too costly. Voluntary initiatives and agreements provide them with the necessary freedom of action and are much more attractive. This means also that these proactive industries have the same arguments in their objective function as the more passive ones, although the mutual weights of the objectives will differ. Offensive industries, for instance, might attach less weight to minimization of environmental cost in the short run and the maximization of time to comply to environmental standards. Only the genuine, idealistic ecological entrepreneur, serving a tiny segment of the market, falls outside this typology.

5. Rent-Seeking in the Framework of Environmental Policy

Due to the government's need of information and cooperation, industry is provided with ample rent-seeking opportunities. Rents are conceived as artificially contrived transfers (Tollison, 1982). Controls in general, and certainly environmental policy controls, create resource-using activities to influence those controls. This rent-seeking or directly unproductive activity take two forms.

First, there are the direct attempts to become eligible for a subsidy programme. Various justifications can be and are actually put forward (Verbruggen, 1990). For instance, in case the government wishes to observe environmental standards higher than those generally required, the industry claims financial assistance to remain internationally competitive. It is also argued that financial assistance is justified to speed up the enforcement of direct regulations, or to support producers, sectors or regions that have to cope with serious economic problems as a consequence of imposed regulations. It will be clear that these justifications fall under the heading of economic policy. In those cases where a financial assistance programme is granted to cover a proportion of abatement investments, it will also be clear that we are in fact dealing with subsidies mainly serving as a lubricator to solve negotiating problems and buy cooperation. This type of environmental subsidy is often not in line with the polluter pays principle which states that the polluter has to bear the costs of keeping environmental quality at some publicly determined level. From a theoretical point of view, subsidy programmes should only be granted to production processes and products generating external benefits, which, in environmental terms can be conceived as less detrimental or neutral to the environment.

Of particular importance in this respect can be the financial support of research, development and introduction into the market of cleaner products, technologies and processes. The above described pro-active industries, for instance, try to become eligible for this type of subsidies, quite often successfully.

The second form of rent-seeking is less direct and less visible. It boils down to the argument that, in return for providing information and cooperation, the industry is afforded specific types of market protection. To understand the forces and mechanisms that can lead to protection, the influential work of Buchanan and Tullock (1975) is called to mind. They examined the political processes that lead to the formulation of rules and regulations rather than economic instruments like penalty taxes and charges in control of pollution. The argument runs as follows.

First, the application of economic instruments amounts to a charge for an environmental resource which was previously free to industry. This can be conceived as a legislated change in property rights. In order not to antagonize the affected sector, the government prefers to dissipate the scarcity value of the environmental assets to the producing firms through regulation and the issuing of emission permits.

Second, industry prefers emission standards because they serve as a barrier to entry to new firms, and consequently result in higher profits. By contrast, an equilibrium under a emission charge can only be attained after a sufficient number of firms have left the industry, as they represent an additional cost to firms. However, their argument is based on, at least, three assumptions that violate reality. The first is that the government has full information. The second is that regulation takes the form of individually assigned production quota, whereby the government must prevent new entrants. The third is that two idealized instruments are compared: direct regulation through production quota **versus** an emission tax. In actual practice, however, not only are multiple instruments applied, there is also a great deal of variation in the performance of instruments (Hahn, 1989). Production quota for environmental reasons are seldom applied: usually environmental regulation dictates a certain input use or mandates a specific technology.

This does not mean that Buchanan and Tullock's conclusions are not valid. On the contrary, for many years the political process indeed resulted in the formulation of rules and regulations, and one of the aims of industry is still rent-seeking. Maloney and McCormick (1982) demonstrated that the usually applied technology-based regulations will lead to enhanced industry profitability. Entry limitations, or perhaps better formulated, sheltering of established firms, can be achieved in various ways.

Not infrequently, differential, i.e., more stringent, pollution-control requirements are imposed on new firms. Maloney and McCormick (1982) see this as the environmental quality analogue to grandfather clauses. At least, established firms are granted more time, more scope and, quite often, financial assistance to comply to environmental standards. In the case of product-specific regulation, established firms enjoy the advantage of prior information with respect to product specifications to be met within a certain time span. Moreover, these firms can, through negotiations, influence the product specification and the compliance period. To a high degree, the technology is then fixed as well. This means the creation of a barrier to innovation.

The inalienability of emission permits and licences also favours established firms. Thanks to the consultation procedures, established firms more easily find their way in the bureaucracy and more often succeed in getting the required permits and licences. The cumbersome licensing procedures may amount to a real barrier to entry. Although of a different nature, it may not remain unrecorded that once permits and licences are obtained, or industry-specific standards are in force, enforcement generally tends to be low due to high monitoring and enforcement costs.

Yet another way of sheltering by way of environmental policy can be obtained in case an agreement is afforded legal status and embraces the entire sector to prevent free-riding behaviour. The costs of overcoming free riders will then be placed upon the government.

The mechanisms at work in the political process can only be supported by fragmented and casual empiricism. Ample evidence, however, is provided by those involved in the process of policy formulation. And a reasonable case can be made for it if it is acknowledged that the government's interest in the negotiating process also lies in its compliance with economic policy goals.

The question arises to what extent the playground of environmental policy formulation resembles a competitive rent-seeking model, yielding a Nash equilibrium (Becker, 1983). The economic approach to political behaviour assumes competition among pressure groups for political influence to further their own interests. These interests are served by regulation, as correcting a market for a market failure induces a transfer of wealth from the consumer to the producer. The demand for regulation, and hence producer protection, is met by the political process, the regulator, who is after direct political support, i.e., votes (Peltzman, 1976). Political equilibrium depends on the efficiency of each group in producing political pressure.

The analysis of Buchanan and Tullock (1975) is also placed in this public-choice setting, completed by the argument, already referred to above, that the government's preference for regulation has also much to do with its reluctance to legislate a change in property rights. According to Maloney and McCormick (1982), there is a firm coalition between social reformers (environmentalists) and producer groups which slightly changes the competitive rent-seeking model. There is extra political support from environmentalists on the side of the producer to seek environmental regulation, because both may profit from output reductions at the expense of the welfare of consumers. Thus, both these analyses are based on the competitive rent-seeking model. The fact that Maloney and McCormick assume a firm coalition between environmentalists and producers does not detract from this model, as it only reinforces the political pressure of both groups vis-à-vis the government.

The political-economy aspects treated here can be viewed differently. First, the government does not need to be conceived solely as a maximizer of public support when embarking on an environmental policy. The government has more objectives, namely acquire information and cooperation, and the attainment of economic policy goals. This means that the government is placed in a much more complex situation, where several, often conflicting goals have to be met to maximize public support, not just serving the group producing the strongest political pressure as in the competitive rent-seeking model. It is rather the context of compromises and give and take that characterizes the playground of environmental policy. In this context, the government seeks a coalition with the producer groups, and this departs from the competitive rent-seeking model. Thus, second, the goals of the government and producers can be compatible, and this coalition supports a regulatory approach. Third, the coalition between government and industry is at the expense of consumers' wealth as well as the efficiency and effectiveness of environmental policy.

6. The Optimal Policy Level and International Regulators

The instrument crisis is also due to a weak coordination between the different policy levels and the absence of an environmental regulator at higher, supra-national policy levels. There is no international system of environmental governance. For three reasons, this seriously frustrates environmental policy implementation.

First, instruments cannot be applied at the most effective and efficient policy level. As Tinbergen (1954) explained, the optimal policy level is that level where no externalities occur any more beyond that level. Or, as the subsidiarity principle of the European Community (EC) states, the scope for Community policy is limited to those cases in which policy objectives can be better attained at the Community rather than the national level.

Second, production and consumption activities in any country often imply the use of natural resources and polluting impacts in other countries. This means that the production cycle from extraction and production of raw materials, to production of intermediates, products and finally waste, is spread over different countries. This seriously complicates an integrated management of the production cycle, a production chain or cradle-to-grave approach. The international trading system is central to this issue, because trade not only facilitates an efficient allocation of resources, it also facilitates the spread of environmental degradation. It is one of the causes behind the above-mentioned distance factor which provides the opportunities for 'displacements of costs'. Here, the production chain and the optimal policy level approach coincide. To reconcile these two approaches, two points of view are in order (Van der Meer and Verbruggen, 1992). On the one hand, from an efficiency point of view, it is preferable to tackle the source of the market failure as closely as possible. In addition, for the same reason it is preferable to minimize the number of market interventions. On the other hand, a resource-oriented approach requires that policy measures bite as early as possible in the production cycle. It will be clear that there might be trade-offs between these objectives. The first objective refers to the optimal policy level in terms of economic efficiency, whereas the second objective seems to be especially relevant for physical efficiency considerations.

Third, both national and international environmental policies, the latter in the form of multilateral agreements, interfere with increasing force with existing international regulation and agreements such as those relating to international trade, economic integrations and international investment. For instance, the international trade principles and rules of the GATT do not recognise that the world market can function imperfectly with respect to environmental goods. Not only is this insight lacking, there is also no guiding principle to deal with environmental market imperfections, such as the polluter pays principle of the OECD. This constitutes a fundamental shortcoming. The provisions that are present in the body of GATT rules to overcome this shortcoming or to limit its consequences, are very limited and highly uncertain in their possibilities and scope (Verbruggen, 1991). Due to a lack of guiding principle and legal precedents it is not clear what 'can and may'. More or less the same is true for the EC. Although a framework for EC environmental policy was established in 1987, including the subsidiarity principle, the prevention principle and the polluter pays principle, the Member States still grope in the dark over the legitimacy of environmental policy implementations at the national level. The Single European Act sets out that, with a view to an undistorted free market, harmonisation of environmental measures is still the leading objective. However, Member States are, in principle, allowed to exclude national regulations from Community harmonisation measures, provided, of course, that these national regulations do not constitute a disguised barrier to trade. The burden of proof for deviating and country-specific environmental standards lies with the Member States.

It is increasingly clear that environmental policies and trade rules are getting in each other's way. These tensions and lack of clarity are gratefully acknowledged by sectors of industry who often rightly argue that stricter national regulations are either not compatible with international rules, or just not effective in environmental terms, whereas national industry only stands to loose international competitiveness.

7. An International System of Environment Governance

In order to overcome the lack of compatibility between different policy levels and improve the efficiency and effectiveness of national and international environmental policies in general, an international system of environmental governance should be established. It is, however, neither necessary nor desirable to establish just one such international environmental regulator, for instance at the UN level. On the contrary, the preference to establish environmental regulators at an optimal policy level implies that numerous multi-lateral environmental agreements should be concluded, all addressing specific environmental problems and agreed upon by the various numbers of participating countries, depending on the scale of the environmental problem addressed and the countries involved. Thus, a convention on climate change should be reached by as many countries as possible, as is also the case with conventions on preserving biodiversity or on trade in toxic wastes. But environmental problems on a regional scale should be subject to separate regional agreements, for instance transboundary air pollution to Europe, to be concluded among Western and Eastern European countries, or pollution of the North Sea to be agreed upon among the North Sea States. A number of environmental commodity agreements could be envisaged for different renewable and non-renewable natural resources, directed towards a sustainable management of these resources. Apart from the consuming countries, such agreements would, in any case, differ in the number and composition of producing countries. Each multilateral environmental agreement can formulate its own modalities, assignments of responsibilities, transfer of financial resources and technology, instruments and monitoring and enforcement provisions, together with the establishment of institutional capacities and processes at the appropriate level.

However, recent experiences of international cooperation in this area is littered with under-resourced inefficient and ineffective agreements. Their international legal status is weak and, as indicated above, these agreements often interfere with existing international regulation and agreements. To strengthen the legal status of multilateral environment agreements, their compliance mechanism, and ensure their compatibility with existing international rules a common framework for these agreements should be developed.

This framework should include:

(1) An international charter of basic principles and guidelines on how the world community should manage its environmental resources and how to deal with local, transboundary and international environmental problems. The principles and guidelines of this charter should be sufficiently concrete and operational and should establish the status of, inter alia, the polluter pays

principle and its deviations, the precautionary principle and the responsibility and liability for environmental damage, also in a transboundary context.

(2) International legislation to structure environmental agreements;
(3) An international institution to ratify and review international environmental agreements;
(4) Amendment of the GATT, in order to establish the legitimacy of the use of trade measures in the context of environmental agreements (Verbruggen, 1991);

Such a framework has to ensure compatibility between the different policy levels, preferably in such a way that they mutually support and reinforce each other.

8. Conclusions

Implementation of environmental policy objectives fails, partly because of an instrument crisis: currently used instrument are not sufficient to achieve currently relevant policy goals.

The first manifestation of the instrument crisis is the wrong choice of instruments. Direct regulation instruments better meets the objectives of both government and industry than using economic incentive instruments, although it is at the expense of consumers' wealth and the effectiveness and efficiency of environmental policy. From the point of view of industry, voluntary agreements are even more desirable. The more so if, after an agreement has been reached, the agreement can become generally binding for the entire sector, to prevent free-riding behaviour. In this respect, economic incentive instruments and forms of liability for environmental effects are superior, because they are less vulnerable to manipulation and, in principle, do not shelter established firms and do not deny the possibilities for new entrants. A complicating problem inherent in the use of economic instruments is that they raise revenues, which in turn, can be an important incentive for rent-seeking activities. There is a strong tendency to return these revenues to the affected sector, in particular to those who suffer most. This may jeopardize the attainment of the environmental goals in view.

In addition, the instrument crisis is also due to weak coordination between the different policy levels and the absence of an environmental regulator at higher supra-national policy levels. It has been argued that a differentiated system of multilateral and international environmental agreements has to be concluded to facilitate policy formulation and implementation at the optimal policy level. A common international framework is needed to guarantee the effectiveness and efficiency of these agreements.

Acknowledgement

This contribution is a revised and extended version of my contribution 'Political economy aspects of environmental policy instruments', in F. Dietz, F. van der Ploeg and J. van der Straaten (eds) (1991) *Environmental Policy and the Economy*, North-Holland, Amsterdam, pp. 141–149. Helpful comments were gratefully received from the taskforce members, a reviewer and the editors.

References

Baumol, W. J. and Oates, W. E. (1988) *The Theory of Environmental Policy*, Cambridge University Press, Cambridge, New York.

Becker, G. S. (1983) A theory of competition among pressure groups for political influence, *Quart. J. Economics* **98**(3), 37–400.

Bohm, P. and Russel, C. S. (1985) Comparative analysis of alternative policy instruments, in A. L. Kneese and J. L. Sweeney (eds), *Handbook of Natural Resource and Energy Economics*, Elsevier, Amsterdam.

Buchanan, J. M. and Tullock, G. (1975) Polluters' profits and political response: Direct controls versus taxes, *Amer. Economic Rev.* **65**(1), 139–147.

GEMI, 1990/91 *Annual Report*, Washington, D.C.

Hahn, R. W. (1989) Economic prescriptions of environmental problems: How the patient followed the doctor's orders, *Journal of Economic Perspectives* **3**(2).

International Chamber of Commerce (ICC) (1991) *Business Charter for Sustainable Development – Principles for Environmental Management*, Paris.

Maloney, M. T. and McCormick, R. E. (1982) A positive theory of environmental quality regulation, *J. Law and Economics* **25**.

Meer, G. J. van der, and Verbruggen, H. (1992) *Sustainable Resource Management*: Survey of policy aspects, advisory council for research on nature and environment No. 61-III, Rijswijk.

Nelson, R. H. (1991) Why capitalism has not won yet. *Forbes*, November 25.

Opschoor, J. B. (1989) *No Deluge After Us* (in Dutch). Kok/Agora, Kampen.

Opschoor, J. B. (1992) this volume, Chapter 10.

Opschoor, J. B. and Vos, J. B. (1989) *Economic Instruments for Environmental Protection*, OECD, Paris.

Peltzman, S. (1976) Toward a more general theory of regulation, *J. Law and Economics* **19**.

Pearce, D. and K. Turner (1990) *Economics of Natural Resources and the Environment*, Harvester Wheatsheaf, Hemel Hempstead, UK.

RIVM (1991) *National Milieuverkenning 1990–2010*, Samson H. D. Tjeenk Willink, Alphen aan de Rijn.

RIVM (1992) *The Environment in Europe: A Global Perspective*, Bilthoven.

Tinbergen, J. (1954) The theory of the optimum regime, in J. Tinbergen *Selected Papers*, North Holland, Amsterdam, pp. 264–304.

Tollison, R. D. (1982) Rent seeking: A survey, *Kyklos,* Vol. 35, Fase 4.

Verbruggen, H. (1990) Subsidies as an instrument for environmental policy, in R. Gerritse (ed), *Producer Subsidies*, Pinter Publ., London, New York.

Verbruggen, H. (1991) Contours of a sustainable international trade system, *Internat. Spectator* **45**(11), 686–691.

Zalm, G. (1990) Mythen, paradoxen en Taboes in de economische politiek, Inaugural Lecture, Faculty of Economics and Econometrics, Free University, Amsterdam.

3. Economic Incentives in Environmental Policy: Why are They White Ravens?

LEX DE SAVORNIN LOHMAN
Institute for Environmental Studies, Free University, Amsterdam, The Netherlands

1. The Instrument Crisis

The first part of the paper reviews two empirical surveys, covering 1987 and 1991, respectively, of the use of financial instruments and economic incentives in environmental policies of OECD-countries. It turns out that the use of economic incentives is limited, however with the second survey indicating an increase in official interest in such instruments.

The second part focuses on one of the findings of the second survey, i.e., the predominance of direct regulation in policies on water and air pollution. An explanation for this is offered from the angles of environmental and cost-effectiveness, administrative costs, distributional impacts and institutional contexts.

2. Empirical Surveys of Economic Instruments

In 1989 a comprehensive survey was published of ecnomic instruments for environmental protection in OECD-countries (Opschoor and Vos, 1989). The survey, taking stock of the state of affairs in 1987, included charges, tax differentiations, deposit refunds, tradable permits, subsidies, environmental liability and non-compliance fees. It turned out that environmental charges were applied mainly for financing purposes, not to affect behaviour of economic agents. Any incentive effects were mainly coincidental to financing purposes. As 'pure' incentive instruments only tax differentiations were applied to some extent, equalizing prices of non-leaded and leaded gasoline and of cars with and without catalytic converters.

Tradable permits were only used in the United States, basically to bring some flexibility into the prevailing rigid direct regulation policies for combating air pollution. Existing deposit refunds had mainly been instituted for economic purposes.

Another finding was that economic instruments were not used autonomously, but as adjuncts to schemes of direct regulation.

Hans Opschoor and Kerry Turner (eds), Economic Incentives and Environmental Policies, 55–67.
© 1994 *Kluwer Academic Publishers. Printed in the Netherlands.*

In all OECD-countries direct regulation appeared to be the cornerstone of environmental policies.

In 1991 the survey was repeated, although data collection was not as extensive and systematic as in the 1987 survey. Data were gathered from a variety of sources, with data quality differing between countries in terms of detail and vintage. Nevertheless, judging by cross-checks, data quality for major OECD-countries and countries with mature environmental policies appeared to be satisfactory.[1]

The 1991 survey included charges, tax differentiations, deposit refunds and tradable permits, and excluded subsidies, environmental liability and non-compliance fees. Also official proposals were surveyed to get a view of future developments.

A distinction was made between *financial instruments (FI)* and *economic incentives (EI)*. Financial instruments are designed exclusively to raise revenue for specific environmental expenditures. Economic incentives have incentive effects as their primary motive, while any revenues are non-dedicated. A mixed category has also been distinguished, consisting of financial instruments that actually have incentive side-effects.[2]

The main conclusions of the 1987 survey appeared to be still valid in 1991. Direct regulation continues to make up the core of environmental policy in OECD-countries.

It is also the case that the Scandinavian countries have applied financial instruments and economic incentives fairly extensively. This may be accounted for by these countries' high environmental aspirations. Also the Scandinavian countries have experienced a 'legitimacy crisis' over direct taxation, stimulating them to go for environmental taxation as a financing alternative.[3]

Judging by the number of official proposals, in the early nineties official interest in FI and EI is increasing. Among these proposals, the share of instruments with intended incentive effects was substantial.[4] However, it is difficult to judge to what extent the proposals will actually be put into effect. Neither can it be safely concluded that there was a shift in *relative* emphasis towards economic incentives, as the 1987–1991 period demonstrated a general rise in environmental aspiration levels.

Table 1 provides the results of the 1991 survey.

In Table 1 no distinction has been made between financing charges and incentive charges. It is instructive to make this distinction for policies on air and water pollution, as in these fields there is a choice between direct regulation and incentive charges on emissions.

It turns out that in air and water pollution policies there are only three instances of 'pure' incentive charges on emissions, with financing purposes subordinate: the NO_x-charge in Sweden, and SO_2-charges in Norway and Sweden.[5] These charges are applied in addition to direct regulation.

Table 1. Financial instruments and economic incentives

Country	Charges				Tax differential	Deposit refund	TDP[a]
	Emission	User	Product	Admin.			
Denmark	2	3	7	1	2	1	–
Finland	2	3	5	5	2	1	–
Norway	3	2	7	1	2	4	–
Sweden	3	3	6	4	1	3	–
Austria	2	1	1	–	2	2	–
Germany[b]	2	2	1	1	2	2	–
Netherlands	2	2	2	2	2	2	–
USA[b]	–	3	2	–	–	1	4
Canada[b]	1	2	–	–	1	1	–
Japan	2	–	–	–	1	–	–
Switzerland[b]	1	2	–	–	1	1	–
Belgium	3	2	–	2	1	1	–
France	2	2	1	1	1	1	–
Italy	1	2	2	–	–	–	–
Spain	2	2	1	–	–	–	–
United Kingdom	2	3	–	2	1	–	–
Australia	–	2	–	–	–	–	–
New Zealand	–	1	–	–	1	–	–
Greece	–	–	–	–	1	1	–
Ireland	–	–	–	–	1	–	–
Portugal	1	1	–	–	1	1	–
Turkey	1	–	–	–	–	1	–
Yugoslavia	–	–	–	–	–	–	–

[a] TDP = Tradable permits.
[b] Federal or strongly decentralized country with instruments at non-federal level.
Bold printing (Denmark)   = good quality data
Italics (Canada)   = medium quality data
Roman printing (Turkey)   = little data available.

The instruments that do appear in practice are the following:

• User charges, levied on emissions.
  In water pollution policies user charges, with revenues earmarked for collective treatment, are common. In most cases the charge is fixed and no actual
  measurement of emissions takes place; moreover charge rates are generally
  moderate, not sufficient for any appreciable incentive effect.
  In a few cases actual emissions are measured and the charge rate is such that
  an incentive effect is to be presumed.[6] But these effects are coincidental to
  the primary purpose of financing collective treatment.

- Financing emission charges.
  Especially in air pollution policy there are earmarked charges to finance public
  expenditure on environmental problems, among others for subsidizing pollution abatement at sources.
- Emission charges as an enforcement instrument.
  In Germany and Italy water pollution charges are designed as a complement
  to direct regulation, to promote compliance to permit conditions.

In no case is there emission charging without a concomitant permit policy.

How to account for the prevalence of permit giving and collective treatment,
and the subordinate significance of incentive charges on emissions?

Case studies of specific policy fields could answer this question. But there must
be broad reasons for the general tendency noted above. In the remainder of this paper
an attempt is made to offer such a general account by comparing policies of permit
giving and emission charging from the viewpoints of environmental and cost-effectiveness, administrative cost, distributional impacts and policy-making contexts
('public policy arenas').

3. Environmental and Cost-Effectiveness

As a reference case a Baumol-Oates emission charge, designed to achieve a
prespecified ambient standard, is compared to a policy of permit giving.[7] Abatement
cost functions of sources are not known with certainty.[8] The central question is: what
type of uncertainties are involved in charging and permit giving respectively?

For the environmental regulator the charge involves an 'environmental effectiveness risk', as sources' reactions are not known for certain. The exact shape of
the aggregate abatement costs schedule is uncertain.

Theoretically the charge rate can be set in a process of 'trial and error', but
this leads to transition costs if there are irreversibilities in abatement investment
(Ugelow, 1990). Also environmental regulators cannot 'experiment' with charge
rates, as society is not the policy-makers' laboratory. In democracies administrative law as well as political expediency limit the liberty of policy-makers to change
policy parameters, especially taxes.

It is sometimes suggested that 'progressive introduction' of incentive charges,
by raising rates stepwise, would solve these difficulties. Indeed, progressive introduction *according to a fixed pre-determined schedule* does address the issue of
irreversibilities in abatement investment, by foregoing some environmental benefits
in a transition period. But such a procedure, with a fixed timetable, does not
address the problem of uncertainty about polluters' reactions, that can only be tackled
by leaving the policy-maker free to experiment with charge rates.

So the trial and error approach is beset with practical difficulties. At minimum the 'first shot' needs to be rather good.

As society made it the job of environmental regulators to attain physical environmental results, they face a strong incentive to be adverse to the environmental effectiveness risk.[9] So for the environmental regulators it is rational to discount incentive effects of charging and treat them as 'co-incidental'.

There are indeed some grounds to take a dim view of the predictability of sources' reactions to emission charges:

- Sources' lacking knowledge of (costs of) abatement technologies. Getting knowledge about alternative treatment methods, recycling opportunities or the potential for product, process or input change is a costly process in itself, with an uncertain outcome.
- Opportunity costs of capital.
  Fixed investment in emission abatement competes with sources' own investments in 'core business' activities. Risk premia, implicit in internal profitability rates and required payback periods, are substantial.
- Preference for variable costs.
  Paying an emission charge, a variable cost, is a reversible policy; investing in abatement equipment is not.
- Opportunities for shifting the charge to others.
  Sources with market power, or facing inelastic demand curves, may find it easier to shift the charge to suppliers or customers. In multi-product firms the burden can be shifted to other products with low demand elasticity.

It is difficult enough to construct a 'schedule of aggregate abatement costs', but one may even wonder to what extent such a construct has real significance for managerial decisionmaking. In an environment of pervasive technological, financial and market uncertainty sources primarily have to figure out *what* trade-offs to face, and secondarily *how* to do that.

Permit giving, the discretionary rationing of environmental resources, attains definite physical targets, but involves a cost-effectiveness error as sources' individual abatement cost schedules are not known perfectly to the policy-maker. The size of this error depends on the degree to which the environmental regulator can and does take into account any knowledge on abatement costs in the setting of permits.

If the aggregate abatement cost function is perfectly flat, any permit policy is cost-effective. More realistically, if there is a limited number of technologies, some feasible for small sources and others (due to indivisibilities) only for large, a policy of technology standards differentiated according to sources' size would already improve on the cost-effectiveness of a crude 'equal percentage emission reduction' permit policy.

This example of a 'sophisticated' physical regulation policy serves to make the point that it need not be the privilege of policy-makers intent on charging to take into account differentials in abatement costs. Any knowledge a policy-maker possesses on abatement costs can be used just as well to get some 'economic sense' in a permit policy.

The presumed efficiency advantage of charging rests on the proposition that it is easier for the policy-maker to estimate the aggregate (across all sources) schedule or marginal abatement costs, than to get to know individual sources' abatement cost schedules. This proposition is unassailable in the abstract, but as a practical point it may not count for much. It has already been established above, that even in a pure trial and error setting the first shot will have to be rather good. Now, how does the policy-maker make his first guess? Any estimate of an aggregate abatement cost schedule can only be derived 'bottom-up', from a limited class of typical individual abatement cost schedules. So in setting a charge the policy-maker will have to delve into the array of different abatement cost schedules. Why then should he not use this knowledge to pursue a differentiated permit policy? The knowledge that is required to get a charge close to environmental effectiveness is the same knowledge that makes a permit policy approximate cost-effectiveness.

Whether environmental regulators actually pursue permit policies with regard to cost effectiveness would be an interesting subject for empirical analysis.[10] It is in the interest of environmental regulators to minimize resistance from sources, and therefore they may indeed choose to press for emission reductions primarily from sources with low abatement costs. On the other hand they may also reduce sources' resistance by mitigating their policy and compromise on the environmental target to be achieved.[11]

So for the environmental regulator the choice between charging and permit giving essentially is one of 'risk preference'. Charging involves an environmental risk, while permit giving involves a cost-effectiveness risk. If environmental regulators are charged with attaining physical environmental results, they will prefer to take the cost-effectiveness risk, and may (but need not) use any knowledge they can get on abatement costs to make their permit policies more cost-effective.

4. Administrative Cost

How do administrative costs of emissions charging and permit giving compare? And what are the incentives for sources of non-compliance?

In implementing a charge or permit policy there are three successive stages: specification of the policy for individual sources, emission monitoring and enforcement.

Specifying an emission charge is straightforward, as usually the charge rate is specified exactly in formal legislation.

Specification of a permit policy is a more laborious affair, as formal legislation on permits usually limits itself to the setting of a framework, by prescribing the application of policy principles such as 'best practical means' or 'best technical means'. Setting permit conditions requires the administrator to assess specific technical and/or economic opportunities for every source.

Regarding monitoring, with a charge the exact amount of emissions must be monitored in order to correctly calculate the charges due. With permit giving the regulator only has to make sure that the source does not exceed the allowed emission rate. Therefore in principle the monitoring of a charge involves a greater administrative effort. However, if the charge is implemented by a system of self-reporting coupled with occasional checks, or by fixed administrative assessments requiring sources to apply for easements, the administrative burden may be limited. Even more relevant, if the charge is implemented as an input charge, the monitoring task is substantially alleviated. Implementing an emission charge as an input charge is appropriate, if there is a direct link between the input and the emission, i.e., if end-of-pipe abatement technologies are not feasible.

Enforcement procedures, with charges as with tax legislation generally, are usually routine and effective. If sources refuse to pay, the tax bill keeps piling up while in addition a fine is due. Also, the charge rate is an upper limit to the potential benefits to be reaped by non-compliance. In enforcing permits however, regulators have no convenient measure for the benefits of non-compliance. Sources can capture benefits by putting compliance off.[12] Non-compliance penalties are usually fixed sums, independent of the period of non-compliance.

Also with permits sources have greater scope to argue, in court or in contacts with bureaucrats and politicians, that permit conditions are 'unreasonable', while with a charge sources cannot challenge the rate.

The above observations on specification, monitoring and enforcement are anything but conclusive. Naturally, the precise balance of pluses and minuses is contingent on the specifics of concrete situations. But if anything, the administrative cost and non-compliance incentives of charging should be smaller than with permit giving. This raises the question why, in practice, environmental bureaucrats do exhibit a general preference for permit giving.

Without pretending to answer this question definitively, one can speculate a little on conceivable bureaucratic motives. A preference for permit giving may be accounted for by a logic of budget maximisation, making bureaucrats prefer more cumbersome regulation. Also the nature of bureaucrats' work connected to charging is less attractive. Administering a charge is a routine job, with low prestige, comparing unfavourably with the work of permit giving where one is visibly in the business of 'protecting the environment'.

5. Distributional Impacts

The account offered thus far focuses on motives of environmental bureaucrats who prefer permit giving to charging. But surely environmental bureaucrats are not omnipotent: polluters, politicians and the interests of consumers and taxpayers have their role to play.

So the question remains how charging and permit giving look to other interest groups in society. What are the distributional impacts of these instruments?

Charging and permit giving start from different distributional principles. Charging can be an application of the so-called 'Extended Polluter Pays Principle (PPP)' (Pezzey, 1988). It requires polluters to pay for all environmental resources used, leaving them the free option of emission abatement or resource use in return for payment of the charge.

Permit giving starts from the 'Standard PPP'. The Standard Polluter Pays Principle requires polluters to pay for the degree of emission abatement (or environmental clean-up) prescribed by public authorities, leaving residual emission free of charge.

If the original state of affairs is one of free emissions, i.e., of property rights on environmental resources belonging entirely to polluters, the 'Extended Polluter Pays Principle" involves a more radical redistribution than the 'Standard Polluter Pays Principle'. The difference is that charging involves a transfer payment for residual emissions, an element that is absent in permit giving.

Now if it is true that the political process exhibits 'distributional inertia', i.e., prefers smaller redistributions to larger ones, the political feasibility of charging is lower in principle.

Empirical confirmation for the hypothesis of distributional inertia is provided in Rolph (1983) and Welch (1983).

Also it should be noted that it is the less radical Standard PPP, not its Extended version, that has been codified as a principle for environmental policy-making by OECD. And it is the Standard PPP that is implicit in the predominant policy practice of user charges for collective treatment and financing charges for public environmental expenditure. So there is empirical evidence for the statement that the Standard PPP, not the Extended PPP, is in conformity with prevailing normative conceptions about property rights.

An alternative account for the inferior political feasibility of charging can be found in the nature of the interests damaged and favoured by charges or permit policies. Benefiting from an emission charge are the taxpayers, a large group with a dispersed interest, while the interests of (producer-)polluters damaged by the charge are usually concentrated. Because of their greater individual stakes the polluters' grouping faces a stronger incentive to expand resources for influencing the political process to their advantage. An active interest group of taxpayers is more difficult to conceive, as free rider incentives are substantial.[13]

So the concentrated interests of polluters may succeed in 'capturing'[14] the environmental regulator and getting a policy of permit giving effected.

However it should be noted that the Standard PPP embodied in a policy of permit giving is not necessarily more advantageous to polluters than the Extended PPP embodied in a charge policy. It is conceivable that the additional abatement costs of a permit policy outweigh the transfer component of the charging alternative. If this is so, the charge would be in the polluters' interest.

Moreover, if one leaves the framework of comparing abstract instruments and allows for hybrids, it appears that the environmental regulator and the polluters jointly could have the best of all worlds by the combination of an incentive charge with an integral rebate of revenues. If the rebate is provided in an allocatively neutral manner to the polluters collectively, the efficiency benefits are reaped while the transfer component is eliminated.

Why do we not see this appealing option occurring in practice? The empirical material of the first section of this paper does not show any example of an incentive charge combined with an integral rebate of revenue.

To account for this apparent anomaly two implicit assumptions of the framework of 'instrument choice', adopted thus far in this paper, should be noted.

First, it is assumed that goals and instruments are established separately. The environmental target is assumed to be given, embodying society's valuation of environmental resources. Policy instruments are conceived as intrinsically neutral means of achieving the target. The choice of instruments does not influence the choice of targets.

Second the political perception of (re-)distributional impacts is assumed to be irrelevant. Whether redistributional impacts are affected 'visibly' via public finances, such as with a charge, or 'invisibly' via producers' costs and output prices, such as with permit giving, is assumed to be immaterial.

In the following section these assumptions, that are implicit in the imagery of instrument choice, will be dropped.

6. Public Policy Arenas

Public policy is made not in the minds of policy-makers, but in concrete 'arenas' consisting of affected actors with their specific interests, resources, values and responsibilities. Different policy *issues* go with different arenas. But the same goes for *instruments*: different policy instruments imply different arenas.

It is argued below that the typical policy arena of charging, makes actors' conflicting interests and values explicit, while the arena of permit giving allows mutual accommodation. As explicit conflicts are sand in the wheels of public policy-making, the political feasibility of charging is inferior.

To make this point clear, a distinction between 'political' and 'administrative' arenas is essential.

Public policy consists of the dual process of formal legislation and concrete administrative deeds.

Formal legislation is made in the *political arena*, involving a wide array of actors: politicians, their voter constituencies, interest groups, competing fractions of the bureaucracy etc. etc. The way in which formal legislation gets its shape, is the progressive creation of political legitimacy. The necessary inputs for obtaining legitimacy are 'publicness' and 'openness': the handling of policy issues in the legislation process must be observable and, directly or indirectly, be accessible for (groups of) citizens who feel affected. Publicness and openness, while essential for the creation of legitimacy, do breed conflict by calling forward an open articulation of interests and values from a wide spectrum of actors. This hampers mutual accommodation and agreement: the more stakes are involved, and the higher their social visibility, the more difficult it is to attain agreement. It is more difficult to strike a deal in public than in private. Putting it differently: in public issues can only be settled by reference to *generalized* values, as what is publicly given to one cannot be denied to the other. In private however it is possible to favour one (group) at the expense of another.

All this is different in the administrative arena, in which formal legislation is implemented. *Administrative arenas*, usually consisting of a less wide spectre of actors, produce *administrative deeds*. The production process is one of mutual accommodation between bureaucrats and affected interests, on the basis of interpretation of formal legislation.

Compared to their political counterparts, administrative arenas are hidden and closed. Therefore the opportunities for mutual accommodation are better. Administrative decisions do not necessarily require legitimation by generalized values: in view of their lower observability administrative deeds can embody 'discretion' and be based more on the particulars of a case.

There is no uniform distribution of tasks between the political and the administrative arena. Some policy instruments are affected in political arenas, while others get their concrete shape largely in administrative arenas.

Taxes and charges are in the first category, the one of politicized instruments. The principle is that there should be 'no taxation without representation'. Details of taxes and charges, such as tax basis, rate and enforcement procedures have to be written in the law. The explicit purpose in tax legislation is to give the administrative arena minimal room for manoeuvre. The very legitimacy of taxes is their impersonal administration.[15]

So any tax or charge scheme, whether it is designated as 'environmental' or not, is strongly politicized. This is the case even if the charge scheme is accompanied, as was suggested at the end of the previous section, by a compensating rebate: details of the rebate are a political bone of contention as well.

Permit giving, on the other hand, is shaped largely in the administrative arena. With permit giving the political arena limits itself to the setting of a framework, the articulation of values and/or policy principles to be observed. The keyword is 'administrative discretion': the political process sets an environmental target to be achieved, or formulates policy principles, such as 'best technical means', 'best practical means', 'the standstill principle' etc. But the all-important details, determining the actual impacts of the policy on affected actors, are hammered out in the administrative arena.

With permit giving the political arena is freed from the painful task of coupling words with deeds, of putting principles to practice. Politicians can satisfy environmentally minded voter constituencies with *physical* targets of symbolic value. Polluters do not need to speak out openly against environmental values: they are given the opportunity to look after their interests in the administrative arena, in which they can capitalize on their superior information about abatement technologies and their costs. Compared to this the appeal of a charge policy is bleak, with the costs of environmental protection being presented publicly, while the commanding aspect, the environmental target, remains implicit.

7. Beyond Instrument Choice

Empirical surveys of economic instruments show that incentive instruments are 'white ravens' in environmental policies. The actual choice of policy instruments in air and water pollution is a case in point. How can one account for this?

Comparing emission charges and permit giving, it appears that incentives working on environmental regulators make them prefer the cost-effectiveness risk of permit giving to the environmental risk of charging. The (nature of) administrative efforts with permit giving may suit environmental bureaucrats' preferences better.

Permit giving is in accordance with the prevailing distributional standard implicit in the 'Standard Polluter Pays Principle'. Also, compared to a policy of charging, permit giving is in principle more conducive to the concentrated interests of polluters, improving its political feasibility.

However, an incentive charge coupled with a rebate of revenues, could achieve cost-effectiveness without breaching distributional constraints on the political process. To explain the fact that this apparently attractive instrument is not chosen in practice, the section on 'public policy arenas' has explored the notion that in public policy-making the primary choice is not between instruments, but between policy arenas producing instruments. It then appears that charges are determined in conflict-ridden political arenas, while permits are shaped largely in administrative arenas better suited to mutual accommodation.

Notes

[1] Detailed results are in: de Savornin Lohman, A. F.: *Financial instruments and Economic Incentives in OECD-countries*, Institute for Environmental studies, unpublished paper September 1991.
[2] The Dutch water pollution charge is an example of the mixed category. Its revenues are earmarked for financing water purification equipment, but its rate is so high that it actually has incentive effects (Bressers (1983) and Schuurman (1988)).
[3] This has been confirmed in interviews with members of the official Norwegian, Swedish and Finnish committees that have been instituted to prepare proposals for economic instruments.
[4] Of all proposals 76% officially intend incentive effects. Of existing FI and EI 55% intends, or actually demonstrate, incentive effects.
[5] The SO_2-charges are implemented as a product charge on mineral oil sulfur content, to be rebated in case of SO-emission abatement.
[6] For the Dutch water pollution charge an incentive effect has been demonstrated by Bressers (1983) and Schuurman (1988).
[7] To simplify matters, spatial dimensions of environmental damage are abstracted from.
[8] If abatement costs were perfectly certain, the rationale for charging would vanish. The policy-maker can then devise a set of permits so that cost-effectiveness is achieved.
[9] An attitude that is compounded by a general non-belief in the efficacy of economic incentives due to the professional training of environmental bureaucrats, that is preponderantly one in law or technology.
[10] Klink, Krozer and Nentjes (1991) analyze an example of a cost-conscience permit policy, i.e., Dutch policy on heavy metals water pollution.
[11] This point will be taken up in the section on public policy arenas.
[12] This point is made in White (1976).
[13] This logic can also be invoked to explain the prevalence of abatement subsidies.
[14] The capture theory of public regulation was introduced in Stigler (1971).
[15] Interestingly this is an achievement of modern democracies. In the old days monarchs distributed taxing competences at their will among local lords, who were left a free hand in extorting the money from their subjects. Essentially, this is still the way it goes with permit policies.

References

Bressers, J. (1983) Beleidseffektiviteit en waterkwaliteitsbeleid, Doctoral dissertation, Enschede 1983.
Klink, J., Krozer, Y. and Nentjes, A. (1991) *Technologische Ontwikkeling en Economische Instrumenten in het Milieubeleid*, NOTA, Den Haag 1991.
Opschoor, J. B. and Vos, J. B. (1989) *Economic Instruments for Environmental Protection*, OECD, Paris.
Pezzey, J. (1988) Market mechanisms of pollution control: 'polluter pays'. Economic and practical aspects, in R. Kerry Turner (ed), *Sustainable Environmental Management, Principles and Practice*, Belhaven Press, London.
Rolph, E. (1983) Government allocation of property rights: Who gets what? *J. Policy Analysis and Management* 3(1), 45–61.
Schuurman, J. (1988) *De Prijs van Water*, Gouda Quint, Arnhem, The Netherlands.
Stigler, G. (1971) The theory of economic regulation, *Bell Journal of Economics* 2, 3–21.

Ugelow, J. (1990) The economic incentive of pollution control charges: Exceptions to the 'rule'?, Paper presented to Workshop on Environmental Economics, Copenhagen, November 1990.

Welch, W. (1983) The political feasibility of full ownership property rights: The cases of pollution and fisheries, *Policy Sciences*, 165–180.

White, L. J. (1976) Effluent charges as a faster way of achieving pollution abatement, *Public Policy*, Winter 1976, 111–125.

4. On the Design of Incentive Mechanisms in Environmental Policy

KLAUS CONRAD and JIANMIN WANG
University of Mannheim, Germany

1. Introduction

The theory of incentives in environmental policy is concerned with the problem an environmental authority faces, when its own objectives do not coincide with those of the polluters. Negative externalities in production and consumption degrade the quality of the environment in an excessive way. The public goods property of natural resources, like air and water, is a standard example of the failure of markets and hence for the need of public regulation. It is the task of the environmental authority (the principal), to invent instruments for environmental policy in order to internalize the social cost of production and consumption caused by the polluters (the agents).

The objective of this paper is to derive from the theory of incentives and from the principal-agent theory some simple instruments which could be implemented in environmental policy. We first present the incentive theory in a framework appropriate for incentive regulation in environmental policy, i.e., the principal-agent framework. Then we design some pricing rules which may satisfy criteria for an optimal instrument from the point of view of the environmental authority.

2. A Family of Pricing Rules from a Simplified Principal-Agent Perspective

The basic principal-agent model consists of one principal and n agents. In the context of the economics of environment the principal is a public institution which acts in the public interest. The agents are n polluting firms with private information on production and abatement technologies. Based on these technologies firm i emits e_i units of a pollutant which can be observed by the principal. The cost of the observation will be neglected to simplify the discussion. The principal responds by announcing an incentive scheme. Such a scheme could be a monetary rule like

Hans Opschoor and Kerry Turner (eds), Economic Incentives and Environmental Policies, 69–85.
© 1994 *Kluwer Academic Publishers. Printed in the Netherlands.*

a pricing scheme or a quantity rule like a standard. The agents react to that scheme by an action which could be an effort in abatement activities. The principal cannot observe that effort, however he can observe the result of it in terms of a change in emissions or in output. The principal now pays a bonus or collects a malus and revises his incentive scheme for the next period. This two stage game can end up at a social optimum the principal had in mind, or it can go on forever.

We next derive a family of solutions for protecting the environment, based on the principles of incentive theory. We assume that the authority knows the social damage function $D(e)$ with respect to total emission $e = \Sigma_i e_i$, and that the firms know their abatement cost functions $C_i(e_i)$. $D(e)$ is a simplified damage function because it assumes that each polluter's emissions are equally harmful, and that current damage depends only on current emissions. Our two stage game between the authority and the firms is now the following one: At the first outset the authority announces a bonus/malus scheme $f(e_i, \lambda)$, which depends on the emission level e_i of firm i in the whole period and on an initial parameter λ, which will be revised at the end of the period in order to adjust the scheme to the observed state of the environment. For analytical simplicity we assume $f(e_i, \lambda)$ to be linear in e_i and in λ. The first stage of the game is then to announce a value for the parameter λ. In order to determine its value, the authority optimizes a utility function $u(D(e(\lambda)), f)$, whereby the emission levels e_i and total emission e are considered to be functions of λ. We assume that the authority minimizes the sum of total damage and of the bonus/malus payments:

$$\min_{\lambda} D(e(\lambda)) + \Sigma_i f(e_i(\lambda), \lambda) \tag{1}$$

The bonus/malus scheme could be subsidies for abated emissions and/or emission taxes. In the latter case f becomes negative. The objective function reflects the trade-off problem between low damage values but high subsidy payments for the government. High subsidies would require an increase in taxes distorting allocation decisions in other markets. There are, of course, other economic effects which could enter the objective function. Kwerel (1977) minimizes damage and the sum of firms' abatement costs. In such a case a combination of instruments is required for optimal regulation in order to motivate the firms to tell the truth about their abatement cost situation. Dasgupta, Hammond and Maskin (1980) also base their optimal pollution control on the fact that the authority considers abatement costs of the regulated firms but under imperfect information. By choosing (1) as our objective function, no information on firms' technology and behavior is required at the initial stage of the regulatory process. We assume, however, the cost-minimizing behavior by firms is public information used by the authority to determine λ (see the following paragraphs).

The first-order condition for optimizing problem (1) is

$$D'(e) \cdot \Sigma_i \; \frac{de_i(\lambda)}{d\lambda} + \Sigma_i \left(\frac{\partial f}{\partial e_i} \frac{de_i(\lambda)}{d\lambda} + \frac{\partial f}{\partial \lambda} \right) = 0 \qquad (2)$$

since $e = \Sigma_i e_i$. Hence, a bonus/malus scheme $f(e_i, \lambda)$ with a parameter λ satisfying (2) is an optimal scheme from the point of view of the authority in order to minimize (1).

At the first stage of our game the firm i learns about the parameter λ, announced by the authority, and chooses an action e_i (in our case the emission level e_i) which minimizes the sum of abatement costs less the bonus/malus scheme. Each firm i ($i = 1, \ldots, n$) minimizes

$$\min_{e_i} \; C_i(e_i) - f(e_i, \lambda). \qquad (3)$$

Given the theoretical complexity resulting from our environmental regulating problem we assume that output and the prices of the inputs are unaffected by the decision to abate. We will relax this assumption in section 4 by considering imperfect competition in output markets.

The first-order condition is

$$\frac{dC_i(e_i)}{de_i} - \frac{\partial f(e_i, \lambda)}{\partial e_i} - \frac{\partial f(e_i, \lambda)}{\partial \lambda} \frac{d\lambda}{de_i} = 0. \qquad (4)$$

Dividing by the differentiated inverse function of $e_i = e_i(\lambda)$ and then summing over i yields

$$\Sigma_i \frac{dC_i(e_i)}{de_i} \frac{de_i}{d\lambda} - \Sigma_i \left(\frac{\partial f}{\partial e_i} \frac{de_i}{d\lambda} + \frac{df}{d\lambda} \right) = 0. \qquad (5)$$

Ideally, if the authority wants its optimal scheme to be consistent with firms' behavior it should incorporate their behavior in determining an appropriate λ. This means that (5) can be used to integrate optimal behavioral conditions given by (2) and (5). We substitute (5) in (2) and obtain

$$D'(e(\lambda)) \; \Sigma_i \frac{de_i(\lambda)}{d\lambda} = -\Sigma_i \frac{dC_i(e_i)}{de_i} \frac{de_i(\lambda)}{d\lambda}.$$

If the authority chooses for instance a λ such that at the resulting emission levels all marginal abatement costs are equal across firms, then this λ lead to

$$D'(e(\lambda)) = -\frac{dC_i(e_i)}{de_i}, \quad \text{for all } i.$$

This is a well-known condition for cost-effectiveness of an environmental policy instrument.

If we add the sum of the objective functions (3) and of (1) we realize that we obtain an objective function in the sense of Kwerel; i.e., the minimization of damage and of abatement costs. The important difference between Kwerel's and our approach is that we do not assume that the authority attempts to achieve that firms reveal their abatement costs. The authority uses the instrument f to affect the objective function of the firms and by this the emission levels. Under cost-minimizing behavior of the firms, the bonus/malus scheme leads to optimal levels of emission minimizing damage plus firms' abatement costs, i.e., levels minimizing Kwerel's objective function of the authority. However, in our indirect regulatory approach via the bonus/malus scheme the authority does not have to deal with the asymmetry in information about abatement costs.

At the second stage of the game the authority observes all e_i, adds them up to e and calculates λ. With e_i and λ known for each firm, the bonus/malus scheme can be realized. Then the game starts all over again for the next period. From the characterization of the game one recognizes that the process starts with a specification of the rule f, called pricing instrument in environmental policy. It ends with the realization of the scheme. In the next section we will choose some simple examples for linear schemes f.

3. Some Simple Incentive Schemes

We assume that the transfer payment rule $f(e_i, \lambda)$ is a linear function in e_i, and that λ is a given constant, i.e.,

$$f(e_i, \lambda) = \lambda(e^*_i - e_i) \tag{6}$$

where e^*_i is a benchmark for e_i and constant. This means that if the emission level e^*_i is higher than the benchmark level e^*_i, the firm must pay a penalty. If e_i is lower than e^*_i, f is positive and the firm gets a bonus for its low emission level. For λ to be optimal we obtain from (2)

$$(D'(e) - \lambda) \, \Sigma_i \, \frac{de_i}{d\lambda} + (e^* - e) = 0. \tag{7}$$

The firms' cost-minimizing emission levels e_i follow from (4)

$$-\frac{dC(e_i)}{de_i} = \lambda, \quad \text{for all } i. \tag{8}$$

If the authority would have perfect information by knowing the cost-minimizing emission levels emission levels $\hat{e}_i$, it would choose $\lambda = D'(\hat{e})$ and $e^*_i = \hat{e}_i$. Then (7) is satisfied and furthermore no distortionary bonus/malus payments are required. Since the authority, however, does not know the optimal emission levels $\hat{e}_i$, it has to operate with a (hopefully) convergent sequence of parameters λ_t and e^*_t.

For λ to be constant, $D'(e)$ has to be evaluated at $e(-1)$, the emission levels of the previous period. The environmental authority calculates $\lambda = D(e(-1))$ and the benchmarks e^*_i at the beginning of the period. Next all firms equalize marginal abatement cost to this tax or subsidy rate λ. At the end of the period the firms pay emission taxes if $e^*_i < e_i$ or get a bonus if $e^*_i > e_i$. Then the authority adds up all e_i's and calculates the revised rate λ for the next period. If the damage function and the abatement cost function are well-behaved, this will converge to the tax rate $\lambda = D'(\hat{e})$, where $\hat{e}$ is the socially optimal emission level. This is just the optimal point in the Pigouvian sense. It implies that, in spite of imperfect information on firms' abatement costs the authority can use trial and error methods to reach the Pigovian optimum. This is a different way to reach it than the one proposed by Kwerel, but a reasonable and simpler one. The linear scheme (6) could be modified by setting $e^*_i = e_i(-1)$ implying $e^* - e = 0$ under convergence. The firm will get a bonus if it emits less than in the previous period and it pays a tax for emitting more. (As pointed out by a referee, using the previous period as a benchmark is very risky, because it could lead the firm to raise its emissions prior to the start of the system, in this way reducing its bill (or raising its benefits) over the next year.) Another alternative for e^*_i is average emissions of its co-polluters, i.e.

$$e^*_i = \frac{1}{n-1} \sum_{j \neq 1} e_j, \tag{9}$$

which is a constant for firm i under the Cournot conjecture of zero-reaction of the co-polluters.

Average emission performance as in (9) as a yardstick for a bonus or malus has no effect on the behavior of the firms compared with any other constant e^*_i. Things are different if we introduce a yardstick competition similar to the one by Shleifer (1985) for efforts in cost reduction. Again we define average emissions of the n-1 co-polluters as in (9), so that each firm is measured against the achievement of its average co-polluter with respect to its efforts in pollution control compliance. The parameter λ in the transfer payment rule $f(e_i, \lambda)$ becomes firm specific but independent of e_i if we specify

$$\lambda_i = D'(n \cdot e^*_i) \tag{10}$$

with e^*_i as in (9). λ_i is a constant for firm i if the firms conjecture Cournot behavior. With $f(e_i, \lambda_i) = D'(n \cdot e^*_i)(e^*_i - e_i)$, (4) becomes

$$-\frac{dC_i(e_i)}{de_i} = \lambda_i. \tag{11}$$

Each firm has been assigned its individual parameter, λ_i. If the emissions of firm i are higher than those of an average firm, it has to pay emission taxes at a tax rate λ_i. If it has less emissions than its 'shadow firm', it will get a bonus. By the yardstick rule, the regulator has eliminated the dependence of the firm's tax rate λ_i on its own chosen level of emission. The e^*_i in (10) could be determined by assuming an immediate adjustment of all e_j's at the same time, by giving firms a priority in the sequence of choosing their e_j or by using emissions of the previous period, i.e., $e_j(-1)$. However, according to (2), the yardstick is not an optimal scheme from the point of view of the authority, because (2) does not hold

$$D'(e) \, \Sigma_i \frac{de_i}{d\lambda_i} - \Sigma_i \lambda_i \frac{de_i}{d\lambda_i} + (e^* - e) = 0.$$

If we adopt the assumption that all firms are identical (see Shleifer for this assumption), then we can follow the proof given in Shleifer and conclude that $e_i = e_j$ for all i, j. Hence $\lambda_i = D'(n \cdot e_i) = D'(e)$ and the rule is optimal (see Conrad, 1990).

The standard critique of the tax rule $\lambda = D'(e(-1))$ is that the firms are not supposed to know the tax formula nor are they curious to learn about the mechanism which underlies the change in the tax rate. The firms react myopically to changes in the tax rate due to asymmetric information on the reasons for the size and the change in the tax rate. It is therefore reasonable to ask whether perfect information on the environmental incentive scheme will change the outcome. Does any improvement arise for society or for the firms if the latter were to know the tax formula and the reasons for its change during the adjustment process? We therefore specify now the scheme f as

$$f(e_i, \lambda) = \lambda(e^*_i - e_i), \tag{12}$$

where $\lambda = D'(e)$ is known to the firm as is $e = \Sigma e_i$ and an arbitrary firm-specific constant e^*_i. For λ to be optimal, it has to satisfy (2) (for a proof see the Appendix 1):

$$\Sigma_i D''(e) \, (1 + cv_i) \, (e^*_i - e_i) \frac{de_i}{d\lambda} + e^* - e = 0 \tag{13}$$

because of

$$\frac{de}{de_i} = 1 + cv_i \quad \text{with} \quad cv_i = \frac{d\Sigma_{j \neq i} \, e_j}{de_i}$$

as the conjectural variation of firm i with respect to co-polluters reactions. The cost-minimizing levels e_i follow from (4):

$$-\frac{dC_i(e_i)}{de_i} = D'(e) - (e^*_i - e_i)D''(e) \, (1 + cv_i). \tag{14}$$

There are three possibilities that the scheme (12) is optimal. First, the damage function is linear, i.e., $D''(e) = 0$. Then λ is a constant and we are back to the case considered at the beginning of this section. Second, the firms recognize the public goods property of emissions. To keep the tax rate λ constant, all co-polluters could emit $d(\Sigma_{j\neq i}e_j) = -de_i$ units more if firm i abates de_i units. If a firm conjectures this behavior of its co-polluters then $cv_i = -1$ and (12) is an optimal scheme. Again the e^*_i's have to be adjusted such that they approach the $\hat{e}_i$. And third we could imagine an ad-hoc mechanism with $e^*_i = e_i(-1)$, for instance. Then according to (14) the firm gets a deduction from the uniform emission tax rate $D'(e)$ if $e_i(-1) > e_i$ and it gets an additional tax if $e_i(-1) < e_i$, i.e., if its emission performance got worse. If this scheme converges, then $e^*_i = e_i$ and it turns out to be an optimal one. If none of these three cases holds, then there will be excess abatement effort (if $e^*_i - e_i < 0$) or less effort than optimal (see also Conrad, 1990).

Another scheme with full information on all facts of the scheme is

$$f(e_i, \lambda) = \lambda \cdot (e^*_i - e_i) - \alpha_i[\lambda \cdot (e^* - e) + D(e)] \qquad (15)$$

with $\lambda = D'(e)$ known to all firms. The first part is the usual emission tax or bonus. The second part calculates total tax revenue (if $e^* < e$), subtracts it from total damage in monetary terms and distributes the remainder to the firms according to a distribution parameter α_i, which is different for each firm. In case of a tax ($e^*_i < e_i$) this means that the authority should restore the environment by using the tax revenue. Figure 1 illustrates the situation. Tax revenue ABe*e is higher than the damage caused by e (the area OCBe). The tax bill exceeds the total damage that the industry imposes on society by the amount ABD minus CDOe*. The total levy is thus too high and may induce firms to leave the industry even though their outputs have a net positive value to society.[1] Therefore (15) recommends to repay the excessive fee ABD minus CDOe*. If the damage turns out to be higher than the tax bill (move e^* to be right in Figure 1) then individual tax payments will be increased (second term in (15)).

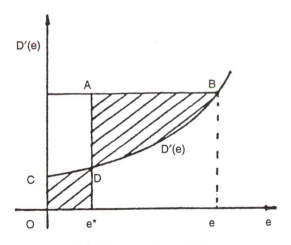

Fig. 1. Refunding excessive emission taxes.

Again, if this scheme is to be optimal, it has to satisfy (2):

$$\Sigma_i\{(e^*_i - e_i) - \alpha_i(e^* - e)\}D''(e)(1 + cv_i)\frac{de_i}{d\lambda} +$$

$$(e^* - e) \cdot (1 - \Sigma\alpha_i) = 0 \tag{16}$$

As before, the scheme (15) is optimal, if the damage function is linear, or if each firm conjectures a public good property ($cv_i = -1$), or if $e^*_i = e_i(-1)$ and the process converges. It is optimal under any conjectural variation if α_i is chosen such that $(e^*_i - e_i) - \alpha_i(e^* - e) = 0$. Since α_i is a parameter in the current period, its size has to be determined from the observed emissions of the previous period:

$$\alpha_i = \frac{e^*_i(-1) - e_i(-1)}{e^*(-1) - e(-1)}. \tag{17}$$

The authority announces that each firm will get back tax expenditure net of damage restoration costs according to its share of non-abated emissions. Firms which have paid higher emission taxes will also get a higher share α_i of the refund.

In practice, regulatory instruments based on the damage function are often considered to be rather useless because a damage function is not known, or if it is, then its value is disputed. It is therefore of interest to extend pricing schemes to simulations where the damage function is unknown to the authority. One good example is the greenhouse effect and the discussion on its damage to the global ecological system. Instead of estimating a controversial damage function, politicians commit themselves to standards at the end of ten or fifteen years and then leave it to the national environmental policy to approach this goal in the years preceding the deadline. An example is the target proposed by a conference in Toronto, 1988. It aims at a 20 per cent reduction of the 1988 levels of CO_2 emissions up to the year 2005. For a growing economy this implies an even higher percentage if energy intensity does not decline at the same rate as output increases. Due to the uncertainty about the consequences of CO_2 taxation for the environment, the authority prefers the introduction of standards and then tightens them in the following years. In the meantime firms can adjust gradually to the more stringent standards and the authority in turn can observe the consequences for the economy and for the environment. We therefore assume that the objective of the authority is to maintain a certain environmental standard e_s at minimal total costs of the bonus/malus scheme. Firms in turn react to that pricing rule by minimizing cost of abatement and emission tax payments.

Instead of (1) the problem of the authority is to find a parameter λ such that

$$\min_{\lambda} \Sigma_i f(e_i(\lambda), \lambda) \tag{18}$$

subject to $\Sigma_i e_i(\lambda) \leq e_s$.

The first-order condition is

$$\Sigma_i \left(\frac{\partial f}{\partial e_i} \frac{de_i(\lambda)}{d\lambda} + \frac{\partial f}{\partial \lambda} \right) + \beta \Sigma_i \frac{de_i(\lambda)}{d\lambda} = 0 \tag{19}$$

$$\beta(\Sigma_i e_i - e_s) = 0 \tag{20}$$

where the Lagrange multiplier β is the shadow price of total emission. By integrating the optimal behavior of the authority and of the firms given by (19) and (5), we obtain

$$\Sigma_i \left(\frac{dC_i(e_i)}{de_i} - \beta \right) \frac{de_i}{d\lambda} = 0. \tag{21}$$

Again cost-effectiveness is a sufficient condition for satisfying this integrated optimal condition. With a transfer payment rule $f(e_i, \lambda)$ as chosen in (6), the parameter λ must be equal to the shadow price β of total emissions. As the true value of β is unknown to the environmental authority, it has to be determined by a trial and error procedure. Figure 2 shows such a procedure. In the first two periods the authority announces $\lambda(-2)$ and $\lambda(-1)$ arbitrarily. When announcing $\lambda(-2)$ it observes total emission $e(-2)$, exceeding e_s, and when raising λ to $\lambda(-1)$, it observes $e(-1)$. The combinations (λ, e) lie on the aggregate marginal abatement cost function[2] $C'(e)$, which is not known to the authority.

The authority can calculate, however, the slope γ of a linear approximation of $C'(e)$. The slope $\gamma = (\lambda(-2) - \lambda(-1))/(e(-2) - e(-1))$ will then be multiplied by the distance $(e_s - e(-1))$ and this change in λ will be subtracted from $\lambda(-1)$:

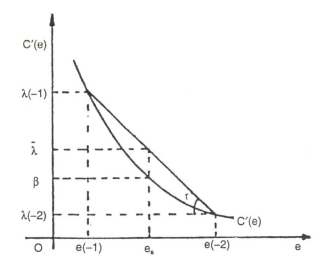

Fig. 2. Determination of the shadow price of emissions.

$$\overline{\lambda} = \lambda(-1) - \gamma \cdot (e_s - e(-1)). \tag{22}$$

This procedure will converge to the Pigouvian tax rate $\lambda = \beta = -C'(e) = C'_i(e_i)$ for all i if the marginal aggregate abatement cost function is well-behaved. In that case the given emission standard e_s is kept with minimal total abatement costs. Especially, if the marginal abatement cost function is linear, the optimum will already be reached after one step.

Table 1 summarizes our four incentive schemes.

Table 1. List of the pricing schemes

Scheme	$f(e_i, \lambda)$	λ_i	e^*_i
1	$\lambda(e^*_i - e_i)$	$D'(e(-1))$	arbitrary
2	$\lambda_i(e^*_i - e_i)$	$D'(ne^*_i)$	$e^*_i = \dfrac{1}{n-1} \sum_{j \neq I} e_j$
3[a]	$\lambda(e^*_i - e_i) - \alpha_i \cdot [\lambda(e^* - e) + D(e)]$	$D'(e(-1))$	arbitrary
4[b]	$\lambda(e^*_i - e_i)$	$\lambda(-1) + \gamma(e_s - e(-1))$	arbitrary

[a] α_i weights with $\Sigma\alpha_i = 1$
[b] $\gamma = (\lambda(-2) - \lambda(-1))/(e(-2) - e(-1))$

If the schemes converge, they are optimal from the point of view of the authority. They satisfy (2), or (19) and (20) respectively, however they are not socially optimal in a Pareto sense. The welfare function (1) or (18) is a special one and does not guarantee the minimization of deadweight loss in the allocation of resources. Hence, as a next step, we have to define a more general welfare function than (1) and (18) in order to find pricing rules f which lead to a social optimum in a broader sense. Under such a family of pricing rules, marginal abatement costs at the social optimum should be the same for all firms.

4. Imperfect Competition, Emission Taxes and Inflationary Pressure

In this section we extend our principal-agent approach by introducing a product market under imperfect competition. We can think of an oligopoly in the chemical market, in the pulp and paper industry, in the energy market (coal, gas, mineral oil), or in some other pollution intensive industries. There is price competition under emission-related transfer payments, which can be influenced by abatement activities. If emission taxes are high, firms will invest in abatement activities and will shift part of the tax and abatement related cost burden to the consumers in terms of higher prices. Hence at the initial stage of the game the authority may prefer a bonus/malus scheme which takes into account the impact of enforcement in environmental policy on prices and on the purchase power of consumers' income. Since a mitigation of the cost-push effect of environmental policy on prices implies higher production levels, this policy is equivalent to a policy of stabilization of consumer surplus and of employment levels.

Since the international competitiveness should not be affected by national environmental policy, instruments should be chosen such that they comply with economic claims. If instruments lead to higher prices, the authority may welcome this effect on the one side because it reduces demand for pollution intensive products and favors substitution. On the other side, however, higher domestic prices will increase imports, decrease exports and, due to lower domestic production, unemployment will raise. Environmental regulation which improves the quality of the environment but not the product itself affects international competitiveness. Domestic prices are higher but the product itself does not reflect a higher technological standard. Examples are air quality regulation for electric utilities, fees for packing material or plastic bottles, the taxation of an input where no abatement possibilities exist (e.g., a CO_2 tax) or a high waste water charge.

Therefore, if pollution intensive firms have to raise their prices under an emission tax, the authority may want to connect its environmental policy with structural policy aspects in order to find an arrangement for the industry's loss in international competitiveness. Such instruments could also cause national structural problems which the government may want to avoid. A carbon dioxide tax, for instance, will increase the price of hard coal more than the price of natural gas or mineral oil because of its higher CO_2 emission coefficient. However, a substitution away from coal is not always what the government had in mind when introducing a CO_2 tax. In Germany, for instance, the coal mining industry is highly subsidized to keep it alive for historical and political reasons and coal-fired power plants are not permitted to substitute natural gas for hard coal.

Furthermore, it has been argued that market oriented instruments like emission taxes could be accompanied by a reduction in taxes on profit or property in so far as they are more costly to firms than standards and controls, as residual emission will also be taxed. Under the latter regulations firms have only abatement costs whereas under market oriented instruments they have to bear abatement costs as well as emission tax expenditures. Hence a rule is required on how to reimburse tax revenues. Our objective is to include this aspect into our transfer payment rule f by linking a refund to the impact of the environmental policy.

In order to determine the parameter vector λ in our extended optimal transfer payment rule f, we assume that the authority maximizes a social welfare function in terms of indirect utility $V(p(\lambda), y)$ less damage, and less bonus/malus payments. The rule f will have an impact on the price vector $p(\lambda) = (p_1(\lambda), \ldots, p_n(\lambda))$ and hence on V with $\partial V/\partial p_i < 0$.

With y we denote the expenditure of consumers for the differentiated products of the industry under consideration; e.g., expenditures for the subgroup 'chemical products' or for 'energy'.

The problem of the authority is:

$$\max_{\lambda} V(p(\lambda), y) - D(e(\lambda)) - \Sigma_i f(e_i(\lambda), p_i(\lambda), \lambda) \tag{23}$$

subject to a restriction on total profit of the industry $(x_i(\cdot): = x_i(p_1(\lambda), \ldots, p_n(\lambda)))$:

$$\Sigma_i^n \; [p_i(\lambda) \cdot x_i(\cdot) - C_i(x_i(\cdot), e_i(\lambda)) + f(e_i(\lambda), p_i(\lambda), \lambda)] \geq \Pi_0 \tag{24}$$

where $C_i(x_i, e_i)$ has the property

$$\frac{\partial C_i}{\partial e_i} < 0 \quad \text{and} \quad \frac{\partial^2 C_i}{\partial e_i^2} > 0. \tag{25}$$

By releasing one more unit of emission, cost of production can be reduced by cutting inputs for abatement activities. Residual profit Π_0 is arbitrary and could be zero, or a certain sum for research and development, or for a stabilization of market exits of firms in the long run. Our formulation of the optimization problem of the authority in terms of minimizing the loss in consumer surplus under a profit restriction is similar to finding Ramsey prices which minimize deadweight loss. For controlling the total emission level e and the price level p we assume that λ consists of two parameters λ_1 and λ_2 the authority wishes to use as instruments. (For the two first-order conditions of problem (23) and (24) see Appendix 2).

Now we turn to the first stage of our game when the firm is confronted with the bonus/malus scheme. Its problem is:

$$\max_{p_i, \, e_i} \Pi_i \; (p_i(\lambda), e_i(\lambda)) + f(e_i, p_i, \lambda), \tag{26}$$

where $\lambda = (\lambda_1, \lambda_2)$ is a vector of parameters.

The first-order conditions are:

$$\frac{\partial \Pi_i}{\partial p_i} + \frac{\partial f}{\partial p_i} = 0, \tag{27}$$

$$\frac{\partial \Pi_i}{\partial e_i} + \frac{\partial f}{\partial e_i} = 0. \tag{28}$$

In designing its optimal parameters λ_1 and λ_2, the authority will take into consideration firms' behavior, i.e., it will use (27) and (28) in deriving λ from its first-order conditions (given in the Appendix 2).

As an example let us consider the following linear transfer payment rule

$$f(e_i, p_i, \lambda) = \lambda_1(e^*_i - e_i) + \lambda_2(p^*_i x^*_i - p_i x_i), \tag{29}$$

where $\lambda_1 = D'(e)$ and

$$\lambda_2 = \frac{\alpha}{1 + \varepsilon} \quad \text{with} \quad \alpha := \frac{\partial V}{\partial Y}$$

and ε the direct price elasticity of demand, which we assumed to be the same across all firms of the industry. If we treat λ_1 and λ_2 as constants, f in (29) satisfies the first-order conditions of the authority's problem (given as (A2) in the Appendix 2) and is therefore an optimal rule. The solution (i.e., $\mu = -1$) implies that profit is added to consumer surplus with equal weights. Again, for λ_1 and λ_2 to be constant, they have to be evaluated at previous period's levels of e and ε.

For determining values of λ_2, the authority can use the profit restriction (24). Inserting f from (29) in (24) results in

$$\lambda_2 = \left[\frac{\Pi - \Pi_0 + D'(e)\,(e^* - e)}{R - R^*} \right]_{t-1}$$

where $R = \Sigma\, p_i x_i$, R* respectively, and $\Pi = \Sigma_i\, \Pi_i$. A bracket with a $t - 1$ means that its term has to be calculated with observations from the previous period.

For an easier interpretation we assume that emissions are not tolerated free of charge (i.e., $e^* = 0$) and that the authority has no special output or price levels in mind ($x^*_1 = 0$ or $p^*_i = 0$). Then the rule f is

$$f(e_i, p_i, \lambda) = -[D'(e)]_{t-1} \cdot e_i + p_i x_i \left[\frac{\Pi_0 - \Pi + D'(e)e}{R} \right]_{t-1} \tag{30}$$

The authority determines the values in the brackets by calculating marginal damage from last year's emissions and by adding up industry's profit published in last year's profit and loss statement. The first term in (30) represents emission taxes and the second term represents the refund aspect. Let us assume that Π_0 was industry's profit before the introduction of f. Since profit Π is industry's profit after the introduction of an emission tax (calculated before subtracting the tax), $\Pi_0 - \Pi$ must be positive. It represents net deadweight loss due to the reduction in output under a tax, but adjusted by that part of consumer surplus which the firms have collected in terms of higher prices.

The scheme f in (30) reflects our idea that it should be in the first place an incentive to abate, and only in the second place an incentive to reduce output and employment as a consequence of higher prices. By refunding emission tax revenues according to revenue shares $p_i x_i/R$, there is an incentive for firms to keep their market shares or to increase output. Since $dR_i/dp_i = x_i(1 + \varepsilon)$, marginal revenue is negative if $\varepsilon < -1$. In this case a firm will reduce its price and the bonus for that action will be a higher share of the refund scheme.

Next we set up the first-order conditions (28) and (29) with respect to p_i and e_i under the rule f in (30):[3]

$$\left(x_i + p_i \frac{dx_i}{dp_i}\right)\left(1 + \frac{\Pi_0 - \Pi + D'(e)e}{R}\right) - \frac{\partial C_i}{\partial x_i}\frac{\partial x_i}{\partial p_i} = 0, \tag{28'}$$

$$-\frac{\partial C_i}{\partial e_i} - [D'(e)]_{t-1} = 0. \tag{29'}$$

From (29') we conclude that our rule achieves cost-effectiveness of abatement because each firm equates its marginal cost of abatement to the uniform marginal damage. Of course, this result could also be achieved by the simple rule $f = -D'(e) \cdot e_i$. However, that rule would not be socially optimal in the sense of (23). Under a simple emission tax rule there will be market exit for those firms with low profit before the introduction of an emission tax. There could also be market exit because the tax bill exceeds the damage (see Fig. 1). Firms have to increase their prices to cover abatement costs and emission tax revenues. It is the task of the refund share in (28') to attenuate the cost push on prices due to environmental policy. It has the effect of a mark-up on marginal revenue and it thus enables the firm to increase prices less than without such a mark-up.

If we neglect the positive term $\Pi_0 - \Pi$ in (28') and (30), the refund part represents a second best approach. A pragmatic reason for omitting $\Pi_0 - \Pi$ would be that it is anyway difficult within a partial equilibrium model to determine the excess burden of taxation for refunding it. A more serious objection against refunding profit reduction $\Pi_0 - \Pi$ is that we are dealing in fact with environmental subsidies which are often not in line with the polluter pays principle. According to this principle the polluter has to bear the costs of keeping environmental quality at some publicly determined level. From a theoretical point of view, subsidies should only be granted to production processes, generating external benefits, or in case of transboundary emission (see Verbruggen, 1990). An alternative within our approach would be to specify e^*_i and x^*_i and p^*_i such that the payment rule is self-financing, i.e., $\Sigma_i f(e_i, p_i, \lambda) = 0$. In that case there is cross-subsidizing within the industry and not a subsidy program financed from taxpayers' money.

Finally, our rule f could be used to regulate excess profit. A zero profit restriction for that industry implies $\Pi_0 = 0$. If the industry makes a positive profit Π, then this profit will be subtracted from emission tax revenue and only the residual amount will be distributed.

Our analysis has shown that a Pigouvian emission tax is only a second best incentive scheme if there is imperfect competition in the industry. The problem with the type of incentive schemes considered is that the firms know the rule but are not permitted to behave strategically. If we want to introduce full information by the firms on λ_1 and λ_2, we would have to proceed similarly as done in Section 3.

5. Conclusion

We have presented environmental policy as a game in two stages within a principal-agent framework. At the outset the authority adopts a transfer payment rule. Then it measures emissions (and residual profit of the industry) and fixes the level of its instruments. Next the firms react by carrying out abatement activities, based on their chosen level of emission and on their output decision. Then the game starts again. It might converge to a Nash equilibrium, might go forever or might explode. Our examples have revealed the problem with the schemes invented. Within the family of optimal rules they are ad hoc. There are several ones with different properties with respect to convergence, smoothness, size of transfer payments and so on. They might converge to the social optimum but there is a family of such schemes with different advantages and disadvantages. There is a need for a normative theory that will derive optimal incentive schemes and study the performance of these schemes. First steps in this direction have been taken by Baron and Myerson (1982) and Laffont and Tirole (1986); for a recent survey see Caillaud, Guesnerie, Rey and Tirole (1988). Our approach also narrows the range of ad hoc incentive schemes by characterizing families of optimal schemes.

Appendix 1

Deduction of Equation (13):
   Since

$$f = \lambda \cdot (e*_i - e_i) = D'(e) \cdot (e*_i - e_i),$$

differentiating partially yields:

$$\frac{\partial f}{\partial e_i} = D''(e) \frac{de}{de_i} (e_i^* - e_i) - D'(e)$$

$$= D''(e)(1 + cv_i)(e_i^* - e_i) - D'(e),$$

$$\frac{\partial f}{\partial \lambda} = e_i^* - e_i.$$

Inserting this in Equation (2) one immediately gets (13).

Appendix 2

For the objective function of the authority (23) subject to the restriction (24) we set up the Lagrange function with μ as the Lagrange multiplier:

$$L = -V(p(\lambda), y) + D(e(\lambda)) + \Sigma_i f(e_i(\lambda), p_i(\lambda))$$
$$+ \mu[\Sigma_i \Pi_i(p_i(\lambda), e_i(\lambda)) + f(e_i(\lambda), p_i(\lambda), \lambda) - \Pi_0]$$

where profit Π_i is $p_i \cdot x_i - C_i$ with the arguments as specified in (24).

The first-order condition is

$$\frac{\partial L}{\partial \lambda_j} = -\Sigma \frac{\partial V}{\partial p_i} \frac{\partial p_i}{\partial \lambda_j} + D'(e) \, \Sigma_i \frac{\partial e_i}{\partial \lambda_j} + \Sigma_i \frac{\partial f}{\partial e_i} \frac{\partial e_i}{\partial \lambda_j} + \Sigma_i \frac{\partial f}{\partial p_i} \frac{\partial p_i}{\partial \lambda_j} + \Sigma_i \frac{\partial f}{\partial \lambda_j}$$

$$+ \mu \, \Sigma_i \left[\frac{\partial \Pi_i}{\partial p_i} \frac{\partial p_i}{\partial \lambda_j} + \frac{\partial \Pi_i}{\partial e_i} \frac{\partial e_i}{\partial \lambda_j} + \frac{\partial f}{\partial e_i} \frac{\partial e_i}{\partial \lambda_j} + \frac{\partial f}{\partial p_i} \frac{\partial p_i}{\partial \lambda_j} + \frac{\partial f}{\partial \lambda_j} \right] = 0.$$

(A1)

for $j = 1,2$.

Appendix 3

In deriving λ from (A1), we employ (27) and (28). This simplifies (A1) to

$$\frac{\partial L}{\partial \lambda_j} = \frac{\partial V}{\partial y} + \Sigma_i x_i \frac{\partial p_i}{\partial \lambda_j} + D'(e) \, \Sigma_i \frac{\partial e_i}{\partial \lambda_j} + \Sigma_i \frac{\partial f}{\partial e_i} \frac{\partial e_i}{\partial \lambda_j}$$

$$+ \Sigma_i \frac{\partial f}{\partial p_i} \frac{\partial p_i}{\partial \lambda_j} + (1 + \mu) \, \Sigma_i \frac{\partial f}{\partial \lambda_j} = 0,$$

(A2)

where we employed Roy's identity, i.e.,

$$-\frac{\partial V}{\partial p_i} = x_i(p, y) \cdot \frac{\partial V}{\partial Y}.$$

Acknowledgements

We have benefited from comments from I.-M. Andréasson, J. B. Opschoor, H. Verbruggen and the other members of the Task Force II: 'Environmental policy instruments' of the European Science Foundation Programme: Environment, Science and Society. Wang acknowledges support from the Deutsche Forschungsgemein-schaft (DFG).

Notes

[1] See Baumol and Oates (1988) on these entry-exit issues (p. 52).
[2] The aggregate abatement cost function $C(e)$ gives minimal costs for satisfying the standard e_s:

$$\min C(e): = \min_{e1, \ldots, e_n} \Sigma_i C_i(e_i) \quad \text{s.t.} \quad \Sigma_i e_i = e_s.$$

The solution implies $C'_i(e_i) = C'(e)$.
[3] We have assumed zero conjectural variation in (28'), i.e., $dp_j/dp_i = 0$ for $j \neq i$.

References

Baron, D. and Myerson, R. (1982) Regulating a monopolist with unknown costs, *Econometrica* **50**, 911–930.

Baumol, W. J. and Oates, W. E. (1988) *The Theory of Environmental Policy*, 2nd edn, Cambridge, Univ. Press.

Caillaud, B., Guesnerie, R., Frey, P. and Tirole, J. (1988) Government intervention in production and incentives theory: A review of recent contributions, *Rand J. Economics* **19**, 1–26.

Conrad, K. (1990) Taxes on emissions, conjectural variations and over investment in abatement capital, *Journal of Institutional and Theoretical Economics* **146**, 281–297.

Dasgupta, P., Hammond, P. and Maskin, E. (1980) On imperfect information and optimal pollution control, *Review of Economic Studies* **47**, 857–60.

Kwerel, E. (1977) To tell the truth: Imperfect information and optimal pollution control, *Review of Economic Studies* **44**, 595–601.

Laffont, J.-J. and Tirole, J. (1986) Using cost observation to regulate firms, *Journal of Political Economy* **94**, 614–641.

Shleifer, A. (1985) A theory of yardstick competition, *Rand J. of Economics* **16**, 319–327.

Verbruggen, M. (1990) Subsidies as an instrument for environmental policy, in R. Gerritse (ed.), *Producer Subsidies*, Pinter Publishers, New York, London.

PART II

Economic Instruments: Empirical Aspects

5. Instrument Choice in Water Pollution Policy in Italy

ANGELA FRASCHINI[1] and ALBERTO CASSONE[2]
[1] *Institute of Economics and Finance, University of Ferrara, Italy*
[2] *Department of Economics, University of Torino, Italy*

1. Water Pollution Policy in Italy

Water pollution control policy in Italy was only fully formulated in the mid 70s with the 'Legge Merli'. This Act had a gestation lag of over a decade; during this period a number of bills had been proposed, sharing the common characteristic of changing the approach toward water resources from one which considered them as free inputs to the economic process, to one which viewed water resources as goods worth protecting.

Water resources regulation before 1976 was characterized by a large number of scattered acts covering public works, health, fishing, agriculture, mining, etc.

As a consequence, the distribution of responsibilities for water resources management was scattered among many different agencies and agents at a national as well as regional and local level. Considering water policy within a principal-agent framework, the fragmented and often overlapping responsibilities turn out to be a cause for more relevant agency problems (moral hazard, adverse selection) and therefore for more expensive and complex institutional arrangements.

The absence of comprehensive legislation and of a definite attribution of responsibilities made it impossible to manage and develop water resources in terms of either quantity or quality.

The current water resources policy is based on the Act 10 maggio 1976, n. 319 (so-called 'Legge Merli' from the name of its rapporteur) and its amendments.[1] Other regulations follow from the implementation of EC Directives.[2]

In January 1992, a bill was drafted by the Government authorizing the issuing of new regulations implementing some EC Directives.[3] However, the new regulations have not yet been defined and, very likely, the process needed to harmonise the Italian and EC legislation will take years.

The main changes the EC legislation will introduce into the Italian system are the following:

(i)   the discharge permit for the polluting plants will be a necessary, prelimi-

Hans Opschoor and Kerry Turner (eds), Economic Incentives and Environmental Policies, 89–112.
© *1994 Kluwer Academic Publishers. Printed in the Netherlands.*

nary condition; the authority issuing the permit will be the 'Provincia', if the discharges are into ground or surface waters; the permit will be temporary and subject to a review every four years;

(ii)   the effluent standards will be related to the total absolute amount of pollutants, so that it will no longer be possible to comply with the standards simply through adequate dilution;

(iii) in order to avoid illegal dilution, the effluent will be measured and controlled at the point of discharge rather than at any downstream point;

(iv)   preventing compliance from the effluent standards through dilution turns out to be an incentive for the recycling of processed water, so reducing the total amount of polluted water.

Generally speaking, water pollution control policy in Italy is characterized by permissive standards, low charges, poor enforcement of pollution control regulation and by large financial aid to private and public agents for the abatement of pollution and for water reclamation.

Taking an extreme view, water pollution is not yet considered (either by law or in public opinion) to be a public offence; rather it is pollution abatement and the compensation for damage caused by pollution that are considered as public goods.

This can be explained, among others, by the following factors:

– environmental quality has entered Italians utility functions only recently (when the Italians have on average reached some private consumption threshold);

– a rent-seeking strategy by polluters who obviously prefer to obtain subsidies for pollution abatement (which entail a reduction in costs and, then, an increase in the size of the output market and/or of the profits) instead of paying charges (which entail an increase in costs and then a reduction in the size of the output market and/or of the profits);

– a rent-seeking strategy by consumers who find that they are more likely to be compensated by the taxpayers than by the polluters, and therefore choose political action instead of legal action;

– a rent-seeking strategy by the policy makers who can enjoy the rent (pecuniary and/or political) stemming from two redistributive processes: one from (many) taxpayers to (few) pollution abating subjects, and the other one from (many) taxpayers to the (few) victims of pollution. The larger size of the group who bear the costs, in comparison with the size of the group who receive the benefits, means that, for the policy maker, the political cost of raising revenue is lower than the political gain of public spending. The consequence is a rising public budget.

Objectives

The purposes of the 'Legge Merli' are stated in the first article, which:

- regulates any effluent discharge to both public and private surface water (inland and sea water) and groundwater, as well as in sewers;
- formulates some general criteria for the use and discharge of water for any kind of settlement;
- organizes public services of water and sewerage systems and purification plants;
- draws up a general plan of water reclamation, on a regional plan basis;
- requires the systematical monitoring of quality and quantity characteristics of the water bodies.

Institutions

The 'Legge Merli' (art. 2–6) amends the previous administrative set-up.

At the national level, at present the Ministry of the Environment[4] has the responsibility to promote, advise, coordinate and direct the relevant public and private activities; to draw up the general plan of water reclamation; to define general criteria in order to ensure a rational and correct use of water resources for all purposes, including drinking water, industrial water, irrigation and recreational uses; to determine general technical rules to regulate the installation and the management of water and sewerage systems and purification plants.

At the regional level (there are 20 Regions in Italy), the Regions (which have the constitutional power to legislate this matter) draw up regional plans for water reclamation, direct the effluent discharge control system, legislate to implement local authorities plans, and monitor the characteristics of the water bodies.

At the local level (there are 101 Provinces and over 8,000 Communes in Italy), the provinces (according to the 'Merli-bis') register public and private effluent discharges in surface water and control the enforcement of the general criteria for a rational and correct use of water. The communes (towns, cities, villages and their associations) control public and private effluent discharges, install the purification plants and can manage them as well as water systems, sewers, drain pipes and water treatment plants. Furthermore, the communes issue the discharge permits.

The overall assignment of responsibilities for water policy among different levels at first seems to be consistent with the general set-up of the Italian political and administrative organization. Actually, in the Italian case, a typical agency dealing with water policy, the River Basin Authority, is provided for, in principle in the legislation, but in fact, these Authorities (provided for in the Act 18 maggio 1989, n. 183 and instituted by decrees (DPCM) of 10 August 1989) are not operating. Therefore, the lack of an authority with a jurisdiction which can encompass the spatial impact of the pollution externalities, is a real problem. The system therefore lacks a mechanism for coordinating activities, redistributing costs, setting up instances for conflict resolutions, etc.

However, the problem of a missing institution is not the most significant issue in a situation characterized, to a large extent, by the malfunctioning of the entire system.

The most relevant problem is the difference between the situation as foreseen in the legislation and the situation actually observed. The reason for this may be identified as a lack of incentives and disincentives capable of influencing the behaviour of the institutions. In other words, the law, often, simply describes the desired outcome, without providing the necessary organizational and incentive devices to produce the actual system required.

If this is typical of an early stage of any legislation, another reasonable explanation may apply in the case of water policy in Italy. A separation between the legal and the observed situation may be the best (i.e., pragmatic) policy in order to maximize overall 'political' acceptance. Thus, stringent legal regulations, to gain the consent of expected beneficiaries of water policies, and permissive practices, to gain the political consent of expected cost bearers does produce a process which is operational. What is needed for this desired (even if schizophrenic) outcome is a malfunctioning or even missing organizational machine.

Instruments

The current legislation (see Appendix I) tries to achieve the goals of water pollution control policy through the application of a set of instruments. The latter can be classified according to the level at which they are applied (national, regional or local level); or in terms of the way in which the desired behaviour of the relevant actors is achieved, i.e., through standards assisted by sanctions or economic and financial incentives or administrative and organizational rules.

From the first point of view, there is no clear-cut top-down hierarchy from national to local instruments. Legal instruments are obviously consistent with the top-down hierarchy: EC Directives are binding for national laws, which are binding for regional laws and the latter constrain local regulations. Administrative and organizational instruments are consistent with a hierarchy conditioned by access to the relevant information.

The lowest level of government (communes) is responsible for the issue of effluent discharge permits, which are the very key of the whole legislation. The higher levels in the system use the information about the permits for planning purposes.

At the intermediate level, the regions are responsible for drawing up the regional plans for water reclamation (which represent the other key feature of the Act 319), whereas the provinces are responsible for the discharges cadastre.

The communes also enter into the planning process as they manage the relevant structures (aquaducts, canalizations, water purification plants) which the regional plan has to assume as a constraint.

The role of the national level in the planning process is apparently limited (assembling the regional plans and checking their compatibility) but, because of the functioning of the regional and local finance in Italy, it is, in the end, crucial as it is the central government that controls almost the whole public budget. Economic instruments, mainly characterized by financial aids from the Government, follow, for this very reason, a top-down hierarchy.

A small number of real incentives for pollution control are set at the local level. In fact they are embodied in the tariffs for water supply, sewerage and purification services.

From the second point of view (the character of instruments as standards, economic incentives and administrative and organizational rules) the present legislation considers charges as a tool mainly intended to finance the provision of public services (sewerage and purification) and only marginally to control pollution. Furthermore, it is not consistent with a strict economic definition of the 'polluter pays principle', because of the uniformity of the rates across large categories of polluters. These economic instruments, developed to support the system of standards and permits, are not very effective because of their design and their application.

The 'Legge Merli' provides financial aids for pollution abatement both to communes and private polluters. The resources needed to finance the purification plants are transferred to the communes or to the firms from the regions; since the regions have no fiscal autonomy, the money distributed is that which is provided by the central government.

At the core of Italian water pollution policy is the system of permits, which are issued by the communes to the polluters. They constitute the administratively necessary and sufficient condition for the discharge.

The permit is granted if, and only if, the polluter observes the law and complies with the effluent standards established in a special table attached to the law. This system of effluent standards and permits is uniform over the national territory and distinguishes receptor bodies (surface water, sewers, sea, rivers, etc.), settlements (industrial and domestic) and the starting date of the effluent discharge (new or existing).

Other minor regulations fix quality standards for water for human consumption or recreational purposes and control the production and use of potentially hazardous substances.

The 'Legge Merli' combines a system of effluent standards and permits (insufficient in itself to directly achieve the optimal level of pollution) with some organizational instruments (the national and regional plans) intended to achieve this goal.

The plans of reclamation define the priorities among different projects, ensure the consistency among sub-projects and, finally, provide economic and human resources to carry out the public works entailed by the projects.

Other acts provide analogous instruments which discipline the activity of the central planner and allocate the resources of the public budget.

Economic Instruments. Economic instruments should provide, for the purpose of environmental improvement, monetary incentives for voluntary, non-coerced action by polluters (see OECD, 1989; on the enforcement of economic instruments for environmental protection see OECD, 1991).

Below, we discuss: (i) effluent charges and user tariffs, and (ii) pollution abatement subsidies.

In the Italian water pollution policy the *effluent charges* are applied together with a user tariff. Both are mainly intended to cover the operating costs of sewerage and purification, as long as the latter is offered. The charges are different for domestic (civil) and productive sources.

The Act 8 ottobre 1976, n. 690 establishes the distinction between productive and domestic (civil) sources: the former concern the production of goods having stable and lasting characteristics; the latter concern dwellings and hotels, tourist, sports, recreational, school, health and service activities or any other activity, included also in productive ones, whose discharges are similar to those of housing. Commercial farms (included fisheries) discharges are also considered to be civil sources.

As far as the domestic sources are concerned, the charge T_1 only depends on the volume of the discharges, both for the sewerage service and for purification, if it exists. The cost coefficients are fixed at the local level, with a maximum set at national level.

The charge is calculated as follows:

$$T_1 = s_1 \ V + p_1 \ 0.8 \ V$$

where s_1 = the cost coefficient for the sewerage service,
        p_1 = the cost coefficient for the purification service,
        V = the quantity (m^3) of water discharged.

The charge clearly has a revenue-raising purpose, since the incentive effect is confined to the quantity of water used. However, the system of collective metering for water supply reduces the charge's effectiveness because of the small individual gain due to individual water-saving behaviour.

Relative to industrial sources, the charge T_2 is calculated according to the following formula:

$$T_2 = F + V[s_2 + dv + K(O_i/O_f \cdot db + S_i/S_f \cdot df) + da]$$

where F = fixed cost depending on the characteristics of the source itself and of the area (total equivalent population and water endowment);

V = quantity (m^3) of the effluent discharged;

s_2 = average cost coefficient for the sewerage service;

dv = average cost coefficient for preliminary and primary purification treatment;

K = parameter measuring the relative costs due to the characteristics of the single source (if the effluents discharged respect the quality standards for the treatment plant, $K = 0$);

O_i = COD of the industrial effluent;

O_f = COD of the overall effluents;

db = average cost coefficient for secondary purification treatment;

S_i = suspended particulates content of the effluent;

S_f = suspended particulates content of the overall effluents;

df = average cost coefficient for treatment and disposal of primary sludges;

da = $[M \cdot (db + df)] /100$, where M is the percentage increase in costs due to the different pollutants costs considered in the parameters db and df.

The cost coefficients are determined as standards according to the total equivalent population and the water endowment of the area. The charges are explicitly intended to finance the public sewerage and purification services. However, the structure of the charge may have incentive effects, both on the decision of where to pollute and on the decision to pollute (or to treat).

In particular, there is an incentive to treat pollutants differently from suspended particulates and reducers and to discharge into public sewers pollutants containing suspended particulates and reducers at a rate equal or lower than that of other sources. However, the current level of the charges, even if they are quite different, are generally low. The lowest and the highest charges range from 1 to 2, parametrically.

As noted earlier, economic instruments, designed primarily to promote a reduction in pollution and not only to finance services as sewerage and purification, play a negligible role (this is underlined also by the low level of the rates).

The 'Legge Merli' provides regional grants and *pollution abatement subsidies* both to the communes and to private polluters for the construction and modernization of purification plants. The amount of grants is fixed by the regions according to the priorities of the water reclamation plans and the budget of the regions themselves.

Other grants available are those transferred from the central government or from the regions to local authorities and other public agencies for the construction and management of pollution abatement devices and reclamation projects. There is, for example, a specific fund (Fondo Investimenti e Occupazione – FIO), financed through general public revenue, created to promote investments of a public good nature and those likely to increase employment. Actually many public works in environmental protection have been (in the 80s) financed in this way. This is the case for most large purification plants in major water reclamation projects, included in the list of the Environmental Protection 3-year Plan.

Non-Economic Instruments. Non-economic instruments are institutional measures which aim to influence directly the environmental performance of polluters. They may seek to regulate both the production process and the products used in the process, thereby reducing hazardous wastes and limiting producing activity to well defined areas and/or periods. They operate via the issuing of permits, setting of standards, zoning, etc.

Non-economic instruments can be classified according to the objects subject to regulation:

(i)   regulations directed at a potential polluter include effluent standards and other specific regulations;
(ii) regulations relating to the social welfare of an integrated river basin include the environmental quality standards;
(iii) regulations directed at public institutions include rules of behaviour and organizing arrangement referring to land planning, industrial and agricultural regulation, regulation of public utilities, etc.

Below, we discuss permits and effluent standards, quality standards, and other regulations.

The key to the Italian water pollution control policy is the general system of *permits* for the discharge of wastes, as 'Legge Merli' (art. 9) reads: 'any discharge must be authorized. The permit is granted by the same authority responsible for the control', i.e., the communes.

The permit is issued only if the discharges comply with the effluent standards defined in specific and detailed tables attached to the act.

An effluent (or emission) standard states that a source cannot emit more than the specified amount over a certain period.

The 'Legge Merli' and its amendments define different standards according to the emitting source (productive or civil, new or existing) and the recipient body (sewers, sea, river, surface water, ground, underground, etc.).

The distinction between industrial and domestic sources is conditioned by the fact that discharges from the latter are always allowed.

As noted above, this distinction is not clear-cut and can be justified only in terms of a distinction between organic and inorganic pollution, and on the basis of the action of powerful lobbies: civil source discharges are always allowed.

All new sources must request a permit. The productive sources can be given a less stringent permit condition for an interim period before tighter conditions are imposed. The distinction made between different receiving media (surface or ground water, sea water, sewerage) implies different issuing authorities (Provinces, Regions, Communes) and more permissive effluent standards in the case of discharges into sewers. The permit can be revoked if the discharges monitored do not comply with the effluent standard. In order to enforce the system of permits and effluent standards the 'Legge Merli' envisages a system of sanctions consisting of the withdrawal of the permits and the imposition of fines.

The system envisaged by the 'Legge Merli' and its amendments has been shown to have many implementation problems such as:

(i)   the controversial nature of the distinction between industrial and domestic sources;
(ii) the exclusion of non-liquid wastes from the regulation, even if they are emitted into a water body;
(iii) difficulties over the measurement of actual emissions and the prevention of dilution practices;
(iv) the granting of more permissive standards if the discharges are emitted into sewers served by waste water treatment plants;
(v)   the fact that the legislation imposes a heavy administrative burden upon local authorities and other public agencies without providing them with the necessary economic, technical and human resources. In particular, the management of public purification plants has been problematic because of the scarcity of required skilled staff, or insufficient revenues to cover costs.

Generally speaking, a system of permits associated with effluent standards is unable to efficiently achieve the optimal level of pollution control because different polluters do not abate emissions at the same marginal cost. Furthermore a uniform effluent standard turns out to produce different levels of environmental quality according to the absorbing capacity of different recipient bodies.

In order to achieve a minimum threshold of environmental quality, some quality standards are needed. Since the 'Legge Merli' did not consider this problem, sub-sequent acts defined water quality standards for specific purposes.

An environmental *quality standard* states the minimum level of environmental quality that the water must meet.

As far as water pollution policy in Italy is concerned, quality standards have been set through acts implementing EC Directives. The quality of bathing water has been defined by D.P.R. 8 giugno 1982, n. 470, D.P.R. 25 giugno 1985, n. 322 and Act 15 luglio 1988, n. 271, following the EC Directive 76/160 with a lag of 6, 9 and 12 years respectively. Quality of water intended for human consumption has been disciplined by D.P.R. 3 luglio 1982, n. 515 and D.P.R. 24 maggio 1988, n. 236, implementing, respectively, EC Directives 75/440 (with a lag of 7 years) and 80/778 (with a lag of 8 years). Quality standards for drinking water or, in general, for human consumption, are often relaxed for specific areas and periods of time, formally because of 'emergency conditions', but in reality because of the chronic pollution of aquifers and surface waters.

Other regulations concern the production, trade, use and disposal of some products which directly or indirectly may pollute the water. Among these, are regulations dealing with the phosphorus content of detergents, used oil disposal, pesticides and other agricultural inputs.

The most important set of indirect regulation in Italy is contained within the plans: the 'Legge Merli' requests regional and national water reclamation plans and the Act 28 agosto 1989, n. 305 establishes the Environmental Protection Three-Year Plan. The regional water reclamation plans are supposed to be, in the spirit of the 'Legge Merli', the instrument able to achieve, through a system of permits and effluent standards, a well-defined quality standard of a specified water body. The regional plans are coordinated at the national level by the national plan. However, the latter has never been completed and the former have been approved only in a few regions.

The lack of a comprehensive policy covering the whole country explains why the recent Act 28 agosto 1989, n. 305 has introduced the conceptual category of 'high environmental risk areas', where public funds are employed as a priority.

Enforcement

The economic and non-economic instruments considered above are assisted, according to the legislation, by a control and sanction system which is not specific to water policy but is the general control and sanction system dealing with public works, health, fishing, agriculture and other matters.

The effectiveness of this control and sanction system is quite poor in the water policy context and for that matter more generally. As in other countries (for instance, the United States – see Portney, 1990), efforts to monitor regulated behaviour appear to have been inadequate and enforcement practices appear not to have been very rigorous. The impression is that the extent of illegal behaviour is quite large: of course there are no reliable figures for the phenomenon, given the obvious inefficiency of the control and sanction system itself.

The quantity and quality of enforcement activity vary significantly across different areas of Italy and in different sectors of economic activity. It depends on both the characteristics of the supply side (the control and sanction system) and the characteristics of the demand side (the balance between the demand from citizen-voters for a clean environment and the demand from firms for permissive practices).

2. Factors Determining the Choice Between Economic and Non-Economic Instruments

Italian politics is still largely dominated by issues relating to unemployment, housing, health and education policies, law and order problems, drug and organized crime.

Pollution and environmental quality have become more of an issue, though still a marginal one for most voters, until very recently. This change coincided with the disappearance of the ideological opposition between centre-right and left parties, which allowed new issues to replace those related to class and strictly political conflicts. Green parties entered local and regional councils for the first time in 1988 and the National Parliament in 1986 (with only a 3% of the votes).

The instrument choice for water pollution policy in Italy can be explained by different models even if their relative contributions are slightly different. It is important to notice that the Italian case seems anomalous (according to conventional analysis) not only in water policy, but also in many other public policies. Actually, there is a strange mix of rigorous legislation and permissive practices: a case of inconsistency in economic policy, not by time, nor by sectors, but by level (or kind) of policy. This requires an explanation.

Why are policy makers willing to pass rigorous legislation and, at the same time, tolerate permissive practices? This schizophrenic behaviour can be explained through a model of one agent serving two principals.[5] Serving two principals means that, for the agent (the legislator), who has his own objective function, there are two optimal contracts. It is a case in which the agent acts, if he can, as a discriminating monopolist.

There are two polarised positions (on the demand-side of the market) in the political arena:

(i)   the environmentally concerned voters, who are dominated by radical green movements. These groups gain benefits from rigorous legislation (of course they have been the more active advocates of it) and a poor enforcement of the legislation itself (they can go on complaining and calling for further initiatives);

(ii) the less conservation minded voters, who are mostly dominated by existing firms. These subjects benefit from rigorous legislation (this can prevent new firms from entering their market, they may also ask for compensation from other public policies) and from a poor enforcement of the legislation itself (they do not bear the costs).

The policy maker, who is on the supply side of the political market, maximizes his gain if he can somehow serve both positions. And he certainly can, as both apparent protagonists are actually demanding the same (albeit contradictory) outcome.

All this crucially depends on the ignorance of the general public (the average voter) who has very little understanding, either of the real significance of a rigorous legislative system or the actual enforcement process which operates. This 'ignorance' is typical of the early stage in the evolution of environmental policy.

In this section we examine different hypotheses which might explain instrument choice. For every hypothesis we will try to evaluate its relevance for the Italian case.

The current water pollution control policy in Italy can be explained by the relative novelty of the issue, the weakness of local governments, the fact that damage functions are not linear in the relevant range, the imperfection of markets, the cost of monitoring and enforcing the legislation, the attitude of citizens about the right to use the environment, the implicit redistribution of wealth associated with different instruments and, last but not least, the external constraints emanating from international legislation.

Water Pollution Policy in Italy Is still in its Infancy

As noted earlier, Italian legislation in the field of water pollution policy is relatively recent.

This means that the implicit environmental quality standards are low and so are the marginal costs of control. Therefore, the conventional cost-effectiveness argument for preferring effluent charges to effluent regulations is weakened.

The obvious policy result is a preference for effluent standards that are more feasible from the political point of view. All this holds also for a transitory period if the effluent standards are becoming more stringent at a very slow rate, as is the case in Italy.

Besides, the Italian water pollution control policy originated in public health and hygiene policies, where direct regulation is the usual and only instrument. This is confirmed by the empirical evidence from the comparative analysis of water pollution policy in other countries, where economic instruments were introduced into existing policy based on direct regulation. As Hahn (1989) points out 'Virtually all environmental regulatory systems using charges and marketable permits rely on existing permitting system. . . . They were grafted on regulatory systems in which permits and standards play a dominant role' (see also OECD, 1989).

Local Governments Have No Fiscal Autonomy and Are Administratively Weak

The choice of non-economic instruments is supported by the fact that the organization of local government in Italy produces a highly centralized pattern, especially in terms of the fiscal relations among different levels of government. In fact, most local expenditures are financed by transfers from central government, often in the form of matching grants and/or specific grants.

Since economic instruments, such as effluent charges, need to be set, adjusted and managed at the relevant local level (for example an integrated river basin), the administrative and fiscal structure of local governments makes economic instruments less desirable.

Non-linearity and Declining Marginal Damage Function

The economic literature suggests that the assumed advantage of an effluent charge vis-à-vis an effluent standard disappears when some restrictive assumptions are dropped. In particular, this happens when the damage function is not linear (Bohm and Russel, 1985) or when a declining marginal damage function is assumed (Rose-Ackerman, 1973). In fact, once uncertainty about the shape of the damage function is allowed, the basic allocational argument in favour of price controls is contingent (Weitzman, 1974). This conclusion is confirmed by the fact that, even if there is uncertainty about the damage function, but it is known that its slope is relatively steep (e.g., in case of strong toxicity or threshold values of ambient concentrations), quantity controls are preferable. A steep damage function exists at the beginning of the water pollution policy, when the regulator tries to control major environmental emergencies.

These hypotheses do not contradict the Italian empirical evidence, but they seem not to provide the most relevant explanation for the preference for non-economic instruments.

Non-Competitive Markets

Another economic explanation for the adoption of direct regulation instead of effluent charges is the fact that the market is not characterized by perfect competition so the informational advantage needed to determine the optimal charge, is weakened (Ebert, 1991). Again, this matches the Italian case, characterized as it is by relatively substantive market imperfections, but, at the same time, it is not the crucial factor explaining the instrument choice.

The imperfection of the market can present an explanation for the choice of a system of permits and effluent standards if we consider the fact that heavy polluters are concentrated in sectors characterized by the presence of large powerful enterprises. In this context a system of non-transferable permits and standards can more easily play the role of a non-tariff barrier.

A similar argument can also be used to explain the preference of other polluters in markets with a lower degree of imperfection, polluters that are able, for some reason (concentration in some specific and small areas, overlapping to a constituency; strong organized national lobby) to control the policy makers. A system of permits and public provision of purification for existing polluters is the best way to keep new competitors out of the market at no cost.

Monitoring and Enforcing Costs

The capacity to monitor and enforce can dramatically affect the choice of instruments (Hahn, 1989, p. 96). In Italy the technology of monitoring and enforcing is quite backward, for a number of reasons: poor level of public officials; long and strong traditions, in most parts of the country, of mismanagement of public affairs; weakness of the local government system; widespread corruption and low reputation for law abiding behaviour. This can explain why economic instruments, which require of effective monitoring and enforcement, are virtually absent.

The non-transferable permits system, the key to water pollution control policy in Italy, can be explained on the basis of costly monitoring and enforcement (Maloney and McCormick, 1982, p. 106–107). Monitoring total emissions is more expensive than monitoring the holdings of the permits.

Beliefs about Property Rights

As pointed out by many studies on positive theories of environmental policy, beliefs in property rights are crucial. Actually, any environmental policy results in a change of the distribution of property rights.

In Italy the situation is perfectly described by the following statement: 'Environmentalists continue to adhere to the symbolic goal of zero pollution. Industry believes and acts as if its current claims on the environment, without any emission reductions, represent a property right.' (Hahn, 1989, p. 110).

The policy makers, implementing a water pollution control policy, have to evaluate the costs and the benefits of the policy itself. Costs and benefits can be measured, for simplicity, in terms of political consent.

The political costs of a system of non-transferable permits and standards are lower than those of a system of effluent charges, because the polluters prefer a more flexible instrument (upon which they can have great influence) to one entailing a definite monetary cost (the effluent charge).

The political benefits of a system of permits and standards are higher than those of a system of effluent charges because environmentalists and other citizens interested in clean water prefer a quantity constraint as they do not like the idea, as they see it, of selling a licence to pollute.

As a consequence, the coalition of polluters and environmentalists asks for the same set of instruments and this set is the one that maximizes the political rent of the policy makers.

This theory seems to fit the Italian experience in water pollution policy: the system of permits was actually much more permissive for existing sources than for new ones and this important feature was inserted again at the request of the same coalition of polluters and environmentalists.

Because of the asymmetry of information between regulator and the regulated, if an effluent standard is set, the polluter has an incentive to declare higher costs of abatement than those actually incurred, in order to obtain a more permissive standard. If an effluent charge is set, the polluter has an incentive to declare lower costs of abatement than those actually incurred, in order to obtain a more favourable rate. In the Italian case, the asymmetry of information results in a preference for the instrument itself, i.e., the system of permits and effluent standards: the polluters – those who have to give up some property rights, when an environmental policy is introduced – prefer to look as if they are giving up more rather than less, as this enables them to request higher levels of compensation.

Redistribution

The non-transferable permits system can also be partially explained on the basis
of the redistribution of wealth inherent in this system (Maloney and McCormick,
1982, p. 107). For the Italian case, heavy polluters, with high value permits (big
companies in basic sectors with strong relationships with the political establishment)
have an interest in preventing others from selling their low value permits, i.e.,
firms with high abatement costs do not want competitors with low abatement costs
to reap the advantages of tradability of permits.

Distributional concerns play an important role in the acceptability of user tariffs
and effluent charges. The revenue from such payments, in Italy too, is earmarked
for environmental activities related to those contributions. This recycling of revenues
underlines the importance of existing beliefs in property rights: those who pay the
user tariffs or the Pigouvian taxes belong to the same group of those receiving the
subsidies.

External Constraints: International and EC Legislation

For the Italian case, external constraints are particularly stringent and international
environmental policy has a significant influence on national policy. Actually, the
Italian legislation must comply with EC Directives and other international regulations, that fix quantity standards, when establishing minimal requirements. However,
the international and EC legislation is usually introduced on an extended timetable
because of other external constraints, related to the assumed relative weakness of
some Italian economic sectors. As such it is assumed that a certain degree of protection for domestic producers is warranted.

3. Concluding Remarks

Reasons why pollution charges and taxes are generally resisted or rejected, include
the following:

- On the side of industry:
    the additional cost burden due to charges being paid on residual pollu-
      tion;
    the impact on competitiveness;
    the loss of bargaining power (as compared with standards) vis-à-vis public
      authorities;

- On the side of public authorities:
    the novelty of the charging systems;
    the fear of losing a grip on polluters in case of charges;
    the alleged loss of predictability of environmental effectiveness;
- On the side of the general public and the environmental pressure groups:
    the sentiment that charges would imply the selling of the 'right to pollute'.

A potential and immediate benefit of a consistent application of charges to administrators at all levels could be that charges provide funds that could be used to finance activities to deal with pollution backlogs. The often alleged efficiency gains should not be expected to arise in the short run, but are likely to become more prominent in the longer term.

These are considerations which have to do with what academically could be expected to be the various positions vis-à-vis water pollution abatement instruments. Let us now turn to what we have observed in the case of the Italian water pollution policy.

To an external observer the overall water pollution policy in Italy looks like a process governed by a reluctant regulator – at the national, regional and local level – constrained by occasional external forces (EC Directives, environmentalists, etc.) trying to translate environmental demands into the means for further political support.

The main features of the water pollution control policy in Italy can be summarized as follows:

(i)   the water pollution policy followed in Italy is still trying to find its definite form;
(ii)   it is almost completely based on non-economic instruments, and in particular on a system of non-transferable permits associated with permissive effluent standards;
(iii)   the few economic instruments applied have no strong incentive functions, as they should have, but they are designed to finance either private polluters, in order to make them comply with the standards, or public agencies with the task of producing more water purification and reclamation;
(iv)   the control and enforcement apparatus is largely ineffective and inefficient;
(v)   the increasing political importance of environmental issues, even if it has not yet produced a comprehensive approach, results in wide policy measures intended to mitigate environmental emergencies: in the case of water pollution policy this can be seen in an increasing regulatory and financial effort for specific areas or sectors;
(vi)   this environmental consciousness pushes policy makers to adopt EC

Directives, even if there is a long time lag compared to other EC members (France or Germany); and to a more extensive use of quality standards;

(vii) the implementation of the 'Legge Merli' has been characterized by continuous downgrading of standards, delays, relaxing of restrictive conditions, progressive assimilation of the restrictive cases into the permissive ones, by-passing of the planning process, etc.

All this can be easily associated with the 'capture' model, where regulated actors 'capture' the regulator to further their own interests (Stigler, 1971). The 'capture' of the Italian regulators by the regulated was possible for the following reasons, among others: the imperfection of the political market, characterized by the relative weakness of the administration; the strong power of organized lobbies; the large ignorance of the median voter; the political choice of allowing the productive system to enjoy the 'positive externality' of a permissive regulation, in order to achieve a high and growing level of economic activity.

The prospects for the near future suggest a change in the whole water pollution policy. In particular:

(i) the process of extending the EC legislation will go on, implying a crucial change also for the administrative procedure;

(ii) the harmonization of the water pollution policy and the full liberalization of the Single European Market will oblige Italian polluters to behave like their European competitors;

(iii) the growing political importance of environmental issues will continue to change the general approach also to water pollution policy: the principle of environmental damage liability has already entered the legislation (see, for instance, the article n. 18 of the Act 8 luglio 1986, n. 349 concerning the institution of the Ministry of the Environment) and will probably be extended in all relevant areas;

(iv) once the principle of environmental damage liability is accepted, the way is paved for introducing economic instruments, allowing polluters to avoid that liability;

(v) the predicament of local communities and the fiscal crisis of central and local governments will probably call for more fiscal accountability at the local level, which implies a larger use of economic instruments;

(vi) this more extensive use of economic instruments, if implemented at a significant extent, will necessarily become a step toward an incentive system, since those who have to bear significant economic burdens prefer avoidable (i.e., incentive) burdens.

Appendix I: List of Acts and Regulations Concerning Water Pollution Control Policy

L. 10 maggio 1976, n. 319 ('Legge Merli' – Norme per la tutela delle acque dall'inquinamento)

L. 8 ottobre 1976, n. 690 (Conversione in legge, con modificazioni, del decreto-legge 10 agosto 1976, n. 544, concernente proroga dei termini di cui agli articoli 15, 17 e 18 della legge 10 maggio 1976, n. 319, recante norme per la tutela delle acque dall'inquinamento)

D.P.R. 24 luglio 1977, n. 616 (Attuazione della delega di cui all'art. 1 della legge 22 luglio 1975, n. 382)

L. 23 dicembre 1978, n. 833 and amendments (Riforma sanitaria)

L. 24 dicembre 1979, n. 650 ('Merli-bis') (Integrazioni e modifiche delle leggi 16 aprile 1973, n. 171 e 10 maggio 1976, n. 319, in materia di tutela della acque dall'inquinamento)

L. 23 aprile 1981, n. 153 (Conversione in legge, con modificazioni, del decreto-legge 28 febbraio 1981, n. 38, recante provvedimenti finanziari per gli enti locali per l'anno 1981)

L. 4 novembre 1981, n. 617 (Conversione in legge, con modificazioni, del decreto-legge 4 settembre 1981, n. 495, concernente provvedimenti urgenti in favore dell'industria siderurgica ed in materia di impianti disinquinanti)

L. 24 novembre 1981, n. 689 (Modifiche al sistema penale)

L. 5 marzo 1982, n. 62 (Conversione in legge, con modificazioni, del decreto-legge 30 dicembre 1981, n. 801, concernente provvedimenti urgenti in materia di tutela delle acque dall'inquinamento)

D.P.R. 8 giugno 1982, n. 470 (Attuazione della direttiva CEE n. 76/160 relativa alla qualità delle acque di balneazione)

D.P.R. 3 luglio 1982, n. 515 (Attuazione della direttiva CEE n. 75/440 concernente la qualità delle acque superficiali destinate alla produzione di acqua potabile)

D.P.R. 23 agosto 1982, n. 691 (Attuazione della direttiva CEE n. 75/439 relativa alla eliminazione degli oli usati)

L. 31 dicembre 1982, n. 979 (Disposizioni per la difesa del mare)

L. 2 maggio 1983, n. 305 (Ratifica ed esecuzione della convenzione sulla prevenzione dell'inquinamento marino causato dallo scarico di rifiuti ed altre materie, con allegati, aperta alla firma a Città del Messico, Londra, Mosca e Washington il 29 dicembre 1972, come modificata dagli emendamenti allegati alle risoluzioni adottate a Londra il 12 ottobre 1978)

L. 22 dicembre 1984, n. 887 (Disposizioni per la formazione del bilancio annuale e pluriennale dello Stato – legge finanziaria 1985)

L. 8 luglio 1986, n. 349 (Instituzione del Ministero dell'ambiente e norme in materia di danno ambientale)

D.M. 16 febbraio 1988, n. 122 (Ammissione al contributo statale di interventi contro l'inquinamento delle acque e fissazione delle procedure e controlli)

D.P.R. 24 maggio 1988, n. 217 (Attuazione della direttiva CEE n. 86/280 concernente i valori limite e gli obiettivi di qualità per gli scarichi di talune sostanze pericolose che figurano nell'elenco I dell'allegato della direttiva CEE n. 76/464, ai sensi dell'art. 15 della legge 16 aprile 1987, n. 183)

D.P.R. 24 maggio 1988, n. 236 (Attuazione della direttiva CEE n. 80/778 concernente la qualità delle acque destinate al consumo umano, ai sensi dell'art. 15 della legge 16 aprile 1987, n. 183)

L. 15 luglio 1988, n. 271 (Conversione in legge, con modificazioni, del decreto-legge 14 maggio 1988, n. 155, recante modifiche al decreto del Presidente della Repubblica 8 giugno 1982, n. 470, concernente attuazione della direttiva CEE n. 76/160, relativa alla qualità delle acque di balneazione)

D.P.C.M. 29 luglio 1988, n. 363 (Piano quinquennale di disinquinamento del bacino idrografico dei fiumi Lambro, Olona e Seveso)

D.M. 13 settembre 1988, n. 413 (Riduzione della percentuale di fosforo nei preparati per lavare)

D.M. 14 febbraio 1989 (Disciplina concernente le deroghe alle caratteristiche di qualità delle acque destinate al consumo umano)

D.P.R. 5 aprile 1989, n. 250 (Approvazione del regolamento di esecuzione della legge 26 aprile 1983, n. 136, concernente la biodegradabilità dei detergenti sintetici, nonchè abrogazione del regolamento di esecuzione della legge 3 marzo 1971, n. 125, approvato con D.P.R. 12 gennaio 1974, n. 238, concernente la medesima materia)

L. 18 maggio 1989, n. 183 (Norme per il riassetto organizzativo e funzionale della difesa del suolo)

D.M. 22 giugno 1989, n. 295 (Regolamento per la disciplina degli interventi di cui ai commi 1 e 2 dell'art. 10 del D.L. 25 novembre 1985, n. 667, convertito, con modificazioni, dalla legge 24 gennaio 1986, n. 7 recante provvedimenti urgenti per il contenimento dei fenomeni di eutrofizzazione)

Decreti ministeriali 14 luglio 1989 (Finanziamento di progetti di risanamento e di protezione ambientale per la regione Campania; per la regione Lombardia (Lambro, Olona, Seveso); per la regione Liguria (Bormida); per la regione Piemonte (Bormida); per la regione Piemonte (Po); per la regione Lombardia (Po); per la regione Emilia Romagna (Po); per la regione Veneto (Po), ai sensi dell'articolo 18, lettera b), della legge finanziaria 11 marzo 1988, n. 67)

L. 4 agosto 1989, n. 283 (Conversione in legge, con modificazioni, del decreto-legge 13 giugno 1989, n. 227, recante provvedimenti urgenti per la lotta all'eutrofizzazione delle acque costiere del Mare Adriatico e per l'eliminazione degli effetti)

D.P.C.M. 10 agosto 1989 (Constituzione dell'autorità di bacino del fiume Po)

L. 28 agosto 1989, n. 305 (Programmazione triennale per la tutela dell'ambiente)

D.M. 4 settembre 1989 (Modificazioni al decreto ministeriale 14 luglio 1989, concernente finanziamento di progetti di risanamento e di protezione ambientale per la regione Lombardia (Po), ai sensi dell'art. 18, lettera b) della legge finanziaria 11 marzo 1988, n. 67)

L. 20 ottobre 1989, n. 345 (Contributo italiano al finanziamento del Piano di azione per il Mediterraneo per il biennio 1988–1989)

D.M. 12 dicembre 1989 (Concessione di finanziamento per l'adeguamento degli impianti di depurazione delle acque reflue urbane nelle aree costiere adriatiche e piano di riparto dello stanziamento)

L. 19 marzo 1990, n. 57 (Istituzione dell'Autorità per l'Adriatico)

D.P.C.M. 23 marzo 1990 (Atto di indirizzo e coordinamento ai fini della elaborazione e della adozione degli schemi previsionali e programmatici di cui all'art. 31 della legge 18 maggio 1989, n. 183, recante norme per il riassetto organizzativo e funzionale della difesa del suolo)

L. 5 aprile 1990, n. 71 (Conversione in legge, con modificazioni, del decreto-legge 5 febbraio 1990, n. 16, recante misure urgenti per il miglioramento qualitativo e per la prevenzione dell'inquinamento delle acque)

L. 9 aprile 1990, n. 97 (Ratifica ed esecuzione dell'accordo tra il Governo italiano ed il Consiglio federale svizzero per iniziative comuni a difesa dall'inquinamento delle acque, firmato a Roma il 13 novembre 1985)

L. 7 agosto 1990, n. 253 (Disposizioni integrative alla legge 18 maggio 1989, n. 183, recante norme per il riassetto organizzativo e funzionale della difesa del suolo)

D.P.C.M. 1 marzo 1991 (Ripartizione tra i bacini di rilievo nazionale, interregionale e regionale dei fondi disponibili nel periodo 1989–93 da destinare all'attuazione degli schemi previsionali e programmatici per il riassetto organizzativo e funzionale della difesa del suolo)

D.M. 26 marzo 1991 (Norme tecniche di prima attuazione del decreto del Presidente della Repubblica 24 maggio 1988, n. 236, relativo all'attuazione della direttiva CEE n. 80/778, concernente la qualità delle acque destinate al consumo umano, ai sensi dell'art. 15 della legge 16 aprile 1987, n. 183)

D.M. 8 maggio 1991 (Disciplina concernente le deroghe alle caratteristiche di qualità delle acque destinate al consumo umano)

D.M. 1 luglio 1991 (Disciplina concernente le deroghe alle caratteristiche di qualità delle acque destinate al consumo umano)

D.M. 23 dicembre 1991 (Disciplina concernente le deroghe alle caratteristiche di qualità delle acque destinate al consumo umano)

D.P.R. 7 gennaio 1992 (Atto di indirizzo e coordinamento per determinare i criteri di integrazione e di coordinamento tra le attività conoscitive dello Stato, delle autorità di bacino e delle regioni per la redazione dei piani di bacino di cui alla legge 18 maggio 1989, n. 183, recante norme per il riassetto organizzativo e funzionale della difesa del suolo)

D.P.C.M. 14 gennaio 1992 (Costituzione dell'Autorità di bacino pilota del fiume Serchio)

Acknowledgements

The research was carried out with the assistance of Dr. Alessia Grosso.

For their helpful comments on an earlier draft we are grateful to Prof. Hans Opschoor and Dr. Alexander de Savornin Lohman. We are, of course, responsible for any shortcomings.

Notes

[1] The amendments of the 'Legge Merli' are:
(1) L. 8 ottobre 1976, n. 690
(2) L. 24 dicembre 1979, n. 650 ('Merli-bis')
(3) L. 23 aprile 1981, n. 153
(4) L. 4 novembre 1981, n. 617
(5) L. 24 novembre 1981, n. 689
(6) L. 5 marzo 1982, n. 62

(7) L. 2 maggio 1983, n. 305
(8) L. 22 dicembre 1984, n. 887
(9) L. 8 luglio 1986, n. 349
    1–9 concern minor or non-essential aspects of the 'Legge Merli' as they change the composition of some administrative committees, terms of compliance and provide financial resources and coordinate the Act 319 with the new legislation.
[2] Among those:
    (1) D.P.R. 8 giugno 1982, n. 470 (EC Dir. 76/160) concerning the quality of bathing water
    (2) D.P.R. 3 luglio 1982, n. 515 (EC Dir. 75/440) concerning the quality of surface water intended for drinking purposes
    (3) D.P.R. 23 agosto 1982, n. 691 (EC Dir. 75/439) concerning the disposal of used oil
    (4) D.P.R. 25 giugno 1985, n. 322 (EC Dir. 76/160) concerning the quality of bathing water
    (5) D.P.R. 24 maggio 1988, n. 217 (EC Dir. 86/280) concerning the limit values and quality standards for some hazardous substances
    (6) D.P.R. 24 maggio 1988, n. 236 (EC Dir. 80/778) relating to the quality of water intended for human consumption
    Other EC Directives have not yet been implemented.
[3] Many EC Directives are still waiting to be included into the Italian legislation, among them those concerning the quality of fresh water for fish life (78/659), specific discharges (82/176, 83/513, 84/156, 84/491, 88/347) and underground water (80/68).
[4] The Ministry of the Environment was established by the Act 8 luglio 1986, n. 349. The same Act attributed to the new ministry the functions that according to the 'Legge Merli' were previously carried out by the Ministry of Public Works and an interministerial committee, constituted by the Ministries of Public Works, Health and the Merchant Navy.
[5] The principal-agent literature does not consider the problem, but the Italian 'commedia dell'arte' (art comedy) does: Harlequin is a typical character in this context.

References

Baumol, W. J. and Oates, W. E. (1988) *The Theory of Environmental Policy*, Cambridge University Press, Cambridge.

Bohm, P. and Russel, C. S. (1985) Comparative analysis of alternative policy instruments, in A. V. Knees and J. L. Sweeney (eds), *Handbook of Natural Resource and Energy Economics* 1, North-Holland, Amsterdam, Ch. 10.

Buchanan, J. M. and Tullock, G. (1975) Polluters' profits and political response: Direct controls versus taxes, *Amer. Economic Rev.* 65(1), 139–147.

Conrad, K. and Wang, J. (1991) *On the Design of Incentive Mechanisms in Environmental Policy*, Mannheim University, Discussion Paper No. 451–91.

Dales, J. (1968) *Pollution, Property and Markets*, Toronto University Press.

Dewees, D. N. (1983) Instrument choice in environmental policy, *Economic Enquiry* 21, 53–71.

Downing, P. B. (1984) *Environmental Economics and Policy*, Little, Brown, Boston, Toronto.

Ebert, U. (1991) *Pigouvian Tax and Market Structure: the Case of Oligopoly*, Report No. V-70-91, Dept. of Economics, University of Oldenburg, Germany.

Hahn, R. W. (1989) Economic prescriptions for environmental problems: How the patient followed the doctor's orders, *J. Economic Perspectives* 3(2), 95–114.

Hahn, R. W. (1990) The political economy of environmental regulation: Towards a unifying framework, *Public Choice* 65, 21–47.

Maloney, M. T. and McCormick, R. E. (1982) A positive theory of environment quality regulation, *J. Law and Economics* 25, 99–123.

Nelson, R. H. (1987) The economics profession and the making of public policy, *J. Economic Literature* 21, 49–91.

OECD (1989) *Economic Instruments for Environmental Protection*, OECD, Paris.

OECD (1991) *Politique de l'environment: comment appliquer les instruments économiques*, OECD, Paris.

Portney, P. R. (ed) (1990) *Public Policies for Environmental Protection*, Resources for the Future, Washington.

Rose-Ackerman, S. (1973) Effluent charges: A critique, *Canadian J. Economics* **6**, 512–528.

Stigler, G. J. (1971) The theory of economic regulation, *Bell J. Economics and Management Science* **2**, 3–21.

Weitzman, M. (1974) Prices vs. Quantities, *Review of Economic Studies* **41**, 477–491.

6. Carbon Taxation and Global Warming: Domestic Policy Aspects

DIEGO PIACENTINO
University of Urbino, Italy

1. Introduction

Aims of the Study

This chapter is concerned with the possible use of carbon (dioxide) taxation measures in the context of domestic policies directed at the prevention of global warming. As such, it represents an attempt to expand analysis of issues which have started to attract attention only recently.[1] Domestic policy aspects of carbon taxation have tended to be overlooked, as long as the discussion about global warming policy addressed more general issues, such as the general principles of carbon taxation,[2] or the potential role and implications of an international carbon tax.[3]

However, more attention for the domestic aspects of carbon tax policy seems to be warranted – indeed it seems to represent a natural development which follows from the analysis of the more general, global issues. In the first place, if carbon taxation appears to be, in principle, a policy instrument with favourable properties, and one that might have a role in international negotiation about global warming, it is nevertheless the case that it will have to be put into practice, in general, at the domestic policy level. In this respect, it is hardly conceivable that a carbon tax of some significance could be levied at the international level (by an international agency). This would imply surrender of national tax power and revenue – a very unlikely event. A more likely perspective is that international negotiation leads to national commitments, that in turn must be translated into national policies, perhaps involving carbon taxation. In the second place, national (unilateral) commitments and actions can be easily conceived of, and are already being undertaken by a number of countries (notably by Norway and Sweden, but also, on a more limited scale, by Finland and the Netherlands).[4]

Furthermore, focusing on the domestic policy aspects of a carbon tax also has the advantage of bringing into the foreground a number of policy issues and alternatives covering both the choice of instruments and their design.

Hans Opschoor and Kerry Turner (eds), Economic Incentives and Environmental Policies, 113–128.
© 1994 *Kluwer Academic Publishers. Printed in the Netherlands.*

Analytical Approach

For the purposes of this study, it will be assumed that the decision (analysis) on if and how to implement carbon taxation can be effectively separated from the decision (analysis) on what goals it is worthwhile pursuing in the field of global warming policy. In other terms, global warming policy goals will be taken as given, i.e. as decided upon at some previous stage.

This is a debatable assumption at the level of principles – which would require that the aims and instruments of policy be decided at the same time, as the outcome of what has been called a meta-cost-benefit analysis.[5] But it is nevertheless an assumption which is usually difficult to do without in practice, and that can also be defended by reference to concrete policy contexts, where the goals tend to be decided first, and then the policies. In the case of carbon emissions, indeed, most of the discussion, both at the international and the national level, focuses on emission volumes and on stabilization/reduction goals.

It is the main contention of this chapter that a case in favour of a carbon tax can be made, but that this has to be accompanied by a number of qualifications. The basic case rests on a single principle – the cost-effectiveness property of the instrument – but this argument has to be qualified by the consideration of distributional implications and of economic effects generally; furthermore, practical implementation issues are such as to constrain significantly the choice of tax instruments.

Following these introductory remarks, the exposition will be organized as follows. In the first place, an attempt will be made (in Section 2) to characterize the policy framework that is likely to materialize under different assumptions, in particular with regard to the nature of the commitment (unilateral or deriving from an international agreement), and the aim of policy (financing global warming policy or reducing carbon emissions). Then (in Section 3), the case for the use of carbon taxation will be expounded; in Section 4, issues of tax design will be discussed; in Section 5, a brief reference will be made to complementary measures. Finally (in Section 6) some concluding comments will be offered.

2. The Domestic Policy Context

In the domestic policy context, the question of whether or not a carbon tax should be adopted, can be examined in a variety of different circumstances.

(1) In the first place, a commitment to a global warming policy can be made as a national, unilateral, decision, or it can emerge from participation in an international agreement. In principle, an unilateral decision allows for the

widest freedom as to the choice and design of policy instruments, but in practice it will have to take into account, and will be constrained by, what has been called the single country problem. That is, the decision will be constrained by a concern not to impair the country's competitive position. Typically, in this case, the decision problem will present itself as a problem of avoiding (minimizing) damage to the domestic industrial sector. If a country is party to an international agreement, implications of and constraints on domestic policy will depend on the nature of the agreement. The agreement might simply commit participating countries to reduce emissions in some proportion.[6] Countries would then be free to decide their most preferred policy, and the policy situation would not differ much from that arising out of a unilateral decision. The international competition constraint would, however, be less binding, given simultaneous action on the part of a – perhaps large – group of countries. Alternatively, an international agreement might commit countries to take specific, harmonized measures, of which a carbon tax could be one. This is perhaps an unlikely outcome, as long as negotiation at the global level is concerned, but it is not necessarily so at a regional negotiation/organization level, like the European Community.[7]

(2) In the second place, carbon taxation can be conceived of as an instrument which can perform either or both of two tasks. It can induce a reduction in the volume of emissions, and it can bring in a revenue that can be used (not necessarily in its entirety) to finance emission-reducing activities. Of course it is the first task that has usually been emphasized in the literature, but the revenue-raising property should not be overlooked. Revenue raising, is, however, a double-edged process. It can make the tax appealing to governments experiencing financial difficulties; it can mobilize resources that can be usefully directed to the funding of public policy aimed at mitigating global warming; but also, as it will be seen below, it can give rise to difficult distributional problems.

Indeed, it is precisely on the basis of apprehensions with regard to these problems that now and then the idea surfaces to make the carbon tax an exclusively revenue-raising device: to levy the tax only to the extent that additional resources are needed, e.g. to subsidize scientific research and technological innovation, or to finance the costs of information-shedding.[8]

(3) In the third place, the taxation measures that can be considered may be characterized by widely differing tax rates and revenues. Most of the following discussion will focus on the case of substantial tax rates, i.e., on tax rates capable of generating a significant impact on incentives and choices.

(4) In the fourth place, the question of a carbon tax can be discussed in terms of a piecemeal/comprehensive approach to global warming policy. Here it is assumed that a commitment to abatement of carbon emissions is an essen-

tial, though generally not the sole, component of any global warming policy. A second tenet is that the problem of carbon emissions can be dealt with, to a large extent, separately from problems of reducing other types of emissions.

3. The Case for Taxation

The case for taxation must ultimately rest on the cost-effectiveness of this instrument – but it must also take into account other aspects relating to its distributional implications and, more generally, its economic effects.

Cost-effectiveness of Taxation

If the question were only one of efficiency, the answer could be simple and straightforward: in the case of carbon emissions, reduction can be best achieved (i.e. at minimum cost) by just such a tax, for various reasons.

(1) A carbon tax is technically and administratively simple. The carbon content of fuels is stable and known, and carbon dioxide emissions from burning correspond fairly precisely to content,[9] as no economically viable ways exist for abating or sequestering emissions after combustion. This means that a carbon tax would in practice be a product (excise) tax, with rates proportional to carbon content of fuels. From this point of view, it is hard to find emissions, other than carbon emissions, that lend themselves to taxation with greater ease.[10]

(2) A carbon tax has the property of inducing emission reductions at minimum cost, through energy switching (e.g. from fossil fuel to solar energy), fuel switching, and energy saving; and, at the same time, it stimulates activities in the field of R&D, with respect both to efficiency of combustion processes and emission-sequestering technologies. From this point of view, taxation qualifies as a truly general approach to reduction of carbon emissions.

(3) Tradable permits (which share with taxation the cost-minimizing property) do not seem to be, in this case, a realistic option. The complexity of the relevant relationships, and the very large number of the actors involved, are formidable obstacles to the use of permits. Two basic permit schemes can be singled out, one distributing permits in the form of fuel allowances to final consumers, and the other to producer firms. The first scheme would work like a war-time rationing system; the second scheme would amount

to a licensing system with respect to admissible fuel use on the part of firms in their plants. To a large extent, this would mean a licensing system with respect to scale of output. Both schemes would involve farreaching government planning and control, and would translate into substantial interference with private decision making and with the working of markets.

Here it can also be noted in passing that a parallel with the US experience in the field of tradable permits, as developed in the field of air pollution and more recently expanded to CFCs, should not be drawn, because of contextual differences. Emissions which are dealt with in the air pollution scheme can be reduced by means of technologies, already available or being developed; in this case, interference with decisions of firms is limited. Such interference, on the contrary, is pronounced in the case of CFCs (quantitative limits are placed on output of producer firms), but this is warranted in relation to the policy goal of fully phasing out production in a short span of time.

(4) Subsidization (of alternative energy sources, like solar and wind; of insulation of buildings; of afforestation; of R&D; of information to consumers) can undoubtedly contribute to a reduction of emissions. However, it is a policy approach that can be implemented only in certain cases, for example when zero pollution activities are available as substitutes for emitting ones.

(5) In the case of carbon emissions, regulation via uniform standards is an inherently inefficient approach, which has severe limitations from the point of view of impact. It is perhaps in the field of electricity generation that it might find application, e.g. in the form of prescriptions with regard to technology of new plants and fuel use in existing ones. But standards for construction, the car, and electrical appliances industries might have little or no effect on the intensity of use; furthermore, their direct effects on fuels use could be partly offset by second round effects induced by income effects.

Distributional Considerations

Questions about the distributional consequences of taxation and the disposal of its revenue are important and must be addressed.

(1) First of all, it should be recalled that most proposals with regard to global warming policy refer to quite large emissions reductions: e.g., stabilization of emissions, at some future date (end of this century or earlier decades of the next), at the present level; or reduction of emission levels of 20–50% with respect to projected values for similar future dates. But achieving such goals, given the presumably low elasticities of demand for the various fuels,

would require quite substantial tax rates. This, given the size of tax bases, would result in substantial revenues – perhaps in the range of 1–4% of GNP, according to some estimates based on a plausible range of tax rates.[11] Exclusive recourse to carbon taxation for the reduction of emissions would then have far-reaching implications in terms of redistribution and for public budgets.

(2) In addition, given the structure of final consumption by income groups of energy products, carbon taxation is likely to produce undesirable distributional consequences.

Only a few studies are available on this aspect, mostly with reference to the UK.[12] There (but this is likely to be a general feature at the international level), an increase in energy prices, as would follow the introduction of a carbon tax, would be especially resented as far as domestic energy use is concerned: low income groups (as well as other vulnerable groups such as the old and the young) spend substantial amounts on domestic energy, and furthermore spending across income groups rises much less than income; as a consequence, the tax burden on those groups would also be substantial, and its overall impact would be regressive. The distributional implications of a carbon tax appear to be less critical when applied to transport fuels. These rise steeply with income, in such a manner as to make the tax broadly progressive; however, low income car owners are liable to considerable burdens. Finally, if the two aspects are considered at the same time, the regressivity of effects of taxation of domestic energy prevails over the progressivity of effects of taxation of transport fuels, making the tax on direct energy expenditure regressive.

Indirect distributional effects of this tax, as levied on energy inputs used in industry and shifted on to final product prices, remain fairly obscure. Modelling exercises of these effects are just beginning, and reliability as yet is low.

An attempt to extend analysis to direct spending on energy in other European countries has also been made,[13] showing evidence of spending patterns that are different from those referred to above: approximately proportional and not regressive. This was, however, a very first attempt, and further, less aggregate analysis is required.

(3) A substantial carbon tax rate is bound to increase prices and reduce demand with regard to products and sectors (especially coal and steel) which have an important position in many or most national economies, and a very delicate position from the point of view of employment.

This problem must be considered in relation to the fear that energy intensive productive activity can be relocated to countries not committed to global warming policy. In this case imports would substitute for domestic production: the domestic costs in terms of lost production would be significant, and the final gains in terms of reduction of emissions would be small.

(4) These considerations tend to suggest the need, or the advantage, of a pragmatic, but at the same time comprehensive approach to the design of carbon taxation measures. The overall taxation level should be determined in such a way as not to cause unmanageable stress via budgetary redistribution activities. It is to be accepted, as a consequence, that taxation may not result in the full control of emissions; a special, more favourable, tax treatment of some products or consuming sectors might be considered; and finally, re-channelling of revenue to the economy may be necessary to soften unfavourable distributional consequences.

(5) A corollary of this will be, then, that if carbon taxation is not carried out up to the overall level needed to obtain the emissions reduction which is deemed necessary and planned, further measures will have to be devised – complementing and completing the carbon tax.

Economic Effects of Taxation

Various calculations have been made of the costs of carbon taxation – both macroeconomic (in terms of GNP reduction) and microeconomic (in terms of deadweight loss).[14] While these calculations are legitimate, and are indeed an essential input for deciding if a policy of reducing emissions is warranted, and on which scale, it is doubtful that they can be relevant for the case for (or against) taxation. If the cost-minimisation property of taxation is believed to be founded, then it is to be accepted that the instrument cannot be improved upon: the resulting costs are, simply, the costs that must be incurred, in the most favourable case, for achieving a given goal in terms of emissions reduction and environmental improvement. However, in the present context, there are other economic effects that are more relevant, notably those on demand and prices. Taxation may depress the former and stimulate to a rise of the latter.

Consideration of these effects suggests, in the first place, that revenue generation and use should be integrated with overall budgetary policy in such a way as not to result in undue pressure on the fiscal policy stance. From the macroeconomic point of view, a carbon tax, by reducing demand, would have a contractionary effect on the level of economic activity; therefore, offsetting measures would be in order – most obviously reductions of other taxes, but also, perhaps, as will be seen below, measures involving greater expenditures.

In the second place, carbon taxation could initially involve low tax rates, to be increased subsequently in a progressive manner, thus allowing a smoother adjustment on the part of agents in the economy.[15]

4. Issues of Tax Design

Various issues about tax design need to be discussed, starting from choice of the
tax base and the tax point, and then proceeding to the treatment of imports and
exports, the possibility of tax differentiation and exemptions, integration with the
existing systems of energy taxation, and finally use of revenue.

Choice of the Tax Base

What to tax – production or consumption – is a question that has been considered
(among others by Whalley-Wigle, 1991) in the context of an internationally agreed
carbon tax. This choice is the exact equivalent of that between the origin principle or the destination principle in relation to indirect taxation.

Taxation of consumption is the most likely option to emerge, both from unilateral policy decisions and from an international agreement. Not only is this type of
taxation widely used, and therefore familiar to tax administrations;[16] it is also a
type of taxation that allows some 'insulation' of national economies and, therefore, national discretion in tax policy.

Choice of the Tax Point

The question of the choice of tax point then arises, given that fuels undergo, from
production (or import) to final use (or export), a complex process involving transportation, transformation, and marketing. Two main options exist: taxing fossil
fuels during production at oil wells and mines and when imported; or taxing refined
and derived products during processing, in refineries and electric generation plants
(in both cases, exemption from, or rebate of, tax for exports should be allowed).
Other possibilities, which could be thought of,[17] are more apparent than real: taxation
during transport (upon consignment or delivery), or taxation at the wholesale
level. Both tend to be indistinguishable from the previous options, and when
distinguishable, to be more cumbersome. In turn, taxation of sales to the final
consumers may not be a realistic option, as it would involve a very large number
of agents, and an even larger number of transactions, and in the end assessment
of tax bases and liabilities might become unnecessarily costly (if feasible at all).

If considered in isolation (i.e., without consideration of connections with other
aspects of tax design), the problem of choice between the two main options would
be a difficult one of balancing opposing considerations. On the one hand taxation
of primary fossil fuels when produced or imported could be advocated on the basis

of two considerations: the number of the taxpayers and activities which have to be monitored for taxation purposes would be kept to a minimum, constraining enforcement costs; at the same time, taxation would thus appropriately, hit fuel use occurring before or in the course of final processing.[18]

On the other hand, however, two reasons could be found, for moving the point of taxation downstream. The first has to do with the fact that an identical specific rate on carbon content translates into different *ad valorem* tax rates when hitting different stages of the production/marketing process: from this point of view, taxation at an earlier stage means higher *ad valorem* rates, more likely to be resented and resisted (and maybe evaded). The second reason is linked to uncertainties about the final economic incidence of taxation (as opposed to initial, formal incidence). Mark-up (full-cost) pricing, if present in the economy, could operate in such a way as to amplify the effect of taxes levied at an early stage, but this effect would be avoided by taxing a later stage.

However, there is one consideration that seems capable of shifting judgement decisively in favour of taxation at the later stage of processing. This is that the possibility of differentiating rates and exemptions becomes more feasible. Lighter tax treatment or exemption of some products or end uses may be allowed on distributional grounds. Exemption is in any case warranted for non-energy uses of fuels – e.g., when used as raw materials in the production of plastic materials, man made fibres and lubricant oils.

Furthermore, with reference to the Western European context, this case can be reinforced by the fact that taxation of energy is an absolutely common practice, enacted on the basis of an analogously common choice of taxing refined products. From this point of view, abandoning the present system, and switching to taxation at an earlier stage, would be warranted only in the case (to be proven) that this can bring about substantial advantages.

Tax Treatment of Imports and Exports

Taxation of imports and exemption of exports are general features of existing excise tax systems, and have implicitly been assumed above as features of the attempt to design a carbon tax.

Taxation of imports and exemption of exports can be applied at two different levels. On one level, imports and exports of fuels would be taken into account, but not imports and exports of goods into whose production fuels have entered as intermediate goods. At the other level, imports and exports of both fuels and goods produced with use of fuels would be taken into account.

The first approach underlies the present practice in the field of excise taxes, having been resorted to for practical reasons, as international trade in fuels can be easily subjected to border controls. The second approach makes sense in economic policy terms, as it avoids undue damage to the competitive position of the domestic economy in the international trade context. But can this last approach be made operational? Poterba (1991, p. 89–90) believes that, to a large extent it is (with reference to the US situation, but his remarks could be easily generalized). As he sees it three classes of imported/exported goods are characterized by a high energy content – steel, cars and chemicals; and he concludes that imports and exports of these goods could be respectively exempted and taxed on the basis of average energy use incorporated in domestic production. But steel is present in a great variety of products, and so are important classes of chemicals, like textile fibres, and, especially, plastics; chemicals themselves, furthermore, come in many forms, and are continuously changing. This seems to translate into significant practical difficulties.

In the case of cars, difficulties arise from different circumstances. It would perhaps be possible to determine an (very approximate) energy content of cars, e.g. based on weight. But then a new problem arises: that of accounting for the energy content of imported parts entering national production.

Perhaps a stronger case in favour of the solution advocated by Poterba can be made with reference to another product, electricity. The primary energy content of electricity (in case of thermal generation) is substantial, and the uniform nature of the product greatly facilitates the measurement of international trade flows for taxation purposes.

Rate Differentiation and Exemptions

If rate differentiation and exemptions are considered legitimate features of carbon taxation, the question arises as to their practical feasibility.

Obviously, the more complex the differentiation scheme, the more complicated and costly the enforcement process. However, this is a problem that should not be exaggerated. The present excise tax systems manage without apparent stress, to differentiate rates and to grant exemptions, in such a way that it is not at all uncommon that the same product is taxed differently when put to different uses (and bought by different classes of users). In European countries, diesel fuel used in the transport sector is taxed more heavily than diesel fuel used for heating. It is possible to single out two conditions that can greatly facilitate this: the existence of physical connections linking suppliers and users, as in the case of electricity and natural gas; and, secondly, the separation of distribution networks directed at different classes of users.

Carbon Taxation and Existing Excise Taxes

It appears that carbon taxation can operate in very much the same way as excise taxes levied on energy products.

As a consequence, the introduction of a carbon tax could, to a large extent, rely on technical solutions and administrative procedures which are already in use. This remark, however, does not apply to taxation of coal, as international experience in this field is limited (Finland, Japan and Sweden are the OECD countries which tax coal). In principle rate differentiation would be required, to take account of the differing carbon content of different grades of coal; in practice, however, it may be necessary to ignore this, in order to have a simpler tax.

Another question that might arise is whether the carbon tax rates should simply be an addition to the existing excise tax rates. This is not strictly necessary, in the sense that high tax rates levied at present on some products and in some countries[19] could be reduced to accommodate (at least in part) the new tax. This, however, would weaken the overall impact of taxation, and should be balanced against tax differentiation and exemptions, which have a similar effect.

Use of Revenue

Finally, the question of the use of the tax revenue has to be touched upon briefly. Reference is made to the case of a substantial tax. A fraction of the revenue from the tax may be used to finance environmental expenditure; another fraction might be channelled to finance international initiatives in the environmental field; but it is unlikely that these uses can exhaust the entire revenue.

The main question is, then: could the revenue of carbon taxation be considered as freely available to government, for financing new expenditures, or reducing a deficit? Here the answer is likely to be in the negative, even without the hostility to increases in taxation which seems to be, in a variety of countries, a pronounced feature of social attitudes. In part, this negative answer can be justified by reference to the constraints on choices deriving from the need to avoid adverse macroeconomic effects, as indicated earlier. At least as important, however, is the fact that the use of revenue can perform an essential function – and will therefore be constrained – if negative distributional consequences of the carbon taxes are to be corrected. Expenditures, as well as tax relief, can be directed to the population (low income) groups who are to bear a disproportionate share of the tax burden. The choice of specific measures will involve questions of the adaptation of social policy instrumentation and of tax reform.

5. Carbon Taxation and Complementary Measures

A final set of questions can now be considered, with regard to the relation of carbon taxation to the overall global warming policy effort. What further measures are needed, in addition to carbon taxation, to reinforce the effects of this type of taxation with respect to carbon emissions, and/or to address (in a more comprehensive fashion) emissions of other greenhouse gases? A related problem is that of coordination among the various measures.

A case has been made for addressing the problem of global warming policy in terms of a fully comprehensive approach – i.e. of an approach embracing at one time all emissions of greenhouse gases, and all sources and sinks.[20]

But while this is undoubtedly an intellectually appealing approach, and one which is useful in order to think of the main available options and linkages, it is nevertheless not very pragmatic when questions relating to choice and design of concrete policy measures are addressed. Policy goals and costs, with reference to the various sources, will have to be compared, and trade-offs calculated. But the policies themselves will have to be designed to deal with each source separately.[21]

Complementary policies addressing carbon emissions will be required if taxation measures result in outcomes which fall short of overall reduction goals. Subsidies and regulating measures should be designed in such a way as to bring about additional benefits on top of those resulting from taxation.

When the question arises of the advantage/necessity of addressing, in terms of policy intervention, emissions apart from carbon, CFCs are of course the first candidate, as their global warming potential is high, their overall contribution to the risk of global warming large, and their sources well known.

A policy for the reduction of CFCs emissions into the atmosphere is, however, already under way in many countries, as a follow-up of the Montreal Protocol and subsequent agreements, relating to substances that deplete the ozone layer.

The question might arise, whether it would be worthwhile to make a greater effort than planned until now in the reduction of CFCs emissions, in such a way as to gain leeway as far as carbon emissions are concerned. This is a question the answer to which could come only from careful cost-benefit analysis. But the possible advantages of this strategy are limited by the proximity of the phasing-out deadline for CFCs, and the rapid development of appropriate policies that this requires.

Methane emissions are large contributors to the risk of global warming, but it seems unlikely that they can be targeted by means of systematic policy measures, given that sources are various and, in nearly all cases, uncontrollable.

One exception to this is emissions of methane resulting from leakages in the course of extraction and transport of natural gas. These can be significant, and, in this case, can present a significant source of greenhouse gases to be reduced.[22] However, such leakages tend to be much lower, in relative terms, in western, industrialized countries, i.e. in those countries which are more likely to adopt global warming policies. Thus the problem is, above all, one of international action, and of effectively inducing reduction of leakages in poorer (developing and Eastern European) countries.

Emissions of nitrous oxide are most unlikely to lend themselves, at least for the time being, to reduction measures. The chemistry of the generating process is not well understood, to a point that large uncertainty remains with regard to the global size of the emissions and, specially, the contributory role of some sources, such as nitrate and ammonium fertilizers.[23] In addition, the largest anthropogenic source, biomass burning, can hardly be controlled.

Finally, forestry is often cited as one sector offering especially favourable conditions for greenhouse policy. Deforestation could be stopped (or slowed), and afforestation activated, at relatively low cost. However, this is again a policy area which requires international action, given that it is only in a few, most of which are relatively poor countries, where most of the costs of policy action would be felt.

6. Concluding Comments

The first main conclusion that can be derived from the previous discussion is that the simple idea of taxing carbon emissions, when reflected upon, is not likely to be translatable into practice by means of a simple tax formula.

It is the ability of a tax on carbon emissions to potentially produce a substantial revenue which is the main relevant factor: a substantial revenue implies in turn substantial distributional impacts, which are bound to hit with particular strength, and to be particularly resented by, some income groups and productive sectors.

Thus, the design of a carbon tax must incorporate as a basic constraint the avoidance of excessive burdens on vulnerable social groups and energy intensive sectors in terms of loss, respectively, of purchasing power and of competitiveness. This, in turn, opens the way and offers justification for measures of tax differentiation and exemption, with regard to different categories of energy uses and/or users.

However, further constraints are met at this point, arising from the fact that tax differentiation and exemptions imply on the one hand a more complex management of the tax, and, on the other hand, a weakened impact on the level of emissions. As a consequence tax differentiation and exemptions may well fall short of achieving the smoothing of distributional impacts that is regarded as necessary or desirable.

In addition, at the macroeconomic level, the dampening effects of taxation on demand and economic activity must be offset, and this brings into the picture a constraint of another sort.

These considerations lead to a second main conclusion, namely that the introduction of a carbon tax is more likely to be normatively acceptable (and politically feasible) if it is part of a wider policy package, involving modification of other taxes as well as expenditure measures. Smoothing of distributional impacts can, indeed, be achieved by lowering the tax burden on persons and companies, by directing specific income support measures to some social groups, and (perhaps) by targeting subsidies on some industrial sectors; and these are also measures which are unlikely to intensify the adverse macroeconomic effects of the imposition of the tax.

Acknowledgements

I wish to thank for their comments and suggestions all the members of the European Science Foundation Task Force devoted to the economic evaluation of environmental policy instruments, and especially the Editors of the present volume, Hans Opschoor and Kerry Turner, and my discussant, Lex de Savornin Lohman. In addition, I wish to thank an anonymous referee, Emilio Gerelli, Camille Langlois, Ernesto Longobardi, and Vincenzo Patrizii, who have commented on an initial version, and Robin Pemberton, who helped to improve my English.

Notes

[1] See Cnossen-Volleberg (1992); Montgomery (1991); Osserwaarde *et al.* (1991); Poterba (1991); Victor (1991).
[2] See, e.g., Barrett (1991a, specially pp. 73–85; 1991b); Pearce (1991).
[3] See, e.g., Whalley-Wigle (1991).
[4] See Schmidt (1991).
[5] See Bohm-Russell (1985), p. 397.
[6] This would follow the model of the agreement reached with regard to CFCs' emissions: for which see, e.g., Benedick (1991).
[7] Indeed this is exactly the arrangement envisaged by the recent EC proposal for a carbon tax: see EC Commission (1991; 1992).
[8] It is possible to note in passing that most international experience, in the field of environmental taxation, has developed around revenue raising aims: see OECD (1989).
[9] Emissions of carbon monoxide due to incomplete combustion of fuel can occur, involving, in particular, combustion engines: but this must be neglected, as no practical ways exist to proceed with measurement.
[10] Not even CFCs emissions can be equated from this point of view. CFCs can be recovered and recycled, and in case of taxation this would make assessment of tax liabilities more complicated. This has led Bohm (1988) to propose recourse to a deposit-refund system.
[11] See, e.g., Poterba (1991).
[12] See Pearson-Smith (1990); Johnson-McKay-Smith (1990); Pearson-Smith (1991).
[13] See Pearson-Smith (1991).
[14] See, e.g., Poterba (1991).
[15] This is, incidentally, a feature of the EC Commission proposal already referred to; see EC Commission (1991; 1992).

[16]   See OECD (1988).

[17]   See Victor (1991), p. 5.

[18]   This would not take care, however, of accidental leakages and spills, which give rise to environmental problems of their own, to be treated in specific manner. In the global warming context,
mention must be made at least of natural gas leakages into the atmosphere, which are quantitatively
and qualitatively significant: see below, p. 124–5.

[19]   An obvious example of this is taxation of petrol in France, Italy or Portugal, with taxes higher
than in any other industrial country, and exceeding 70% of final prices. See IEA (1991), Table 1,
p. 276.

[20]   This case is forcefully made in US Department of Justice (1991).

[21]   For a similar position, with reference to international policy action, see Schelling (1991), p. 197–8.

[22]   Estimates are quoted in US Department of Justice (1991, p. 51), according to which leakages of
natural gas might be in the range of 1–10%, depending on countries and technologies.

[23]   See Watson et al. (1990), p. 25–27.

References

Barrett, S. (1991a) Economic instruments for climate change policy, in *Responding to Climate Change:
Selected Economic Issues*, OECD, Paris, 51–108.

Barrett, S. (1991b) Global warming: The economics of a carbon tax, in D. Pearce (ed), *Blueprint 2:
Greening the World Economy*, Earthscan, London.

Benedick, R. E. (1991) *Ozone Diplomacy: New Directions in Safeguarding the Planet*, Harvard U.
P., Cambridge, Mass.

Bohm, P. (1988) *Economic Instruments for Reducing CFC Emissions*, Nordic Council of Ministers,
Copenhagen.

Bohm, P. and Russell, C. S. (1985) Comparative analysis of alternative policy instruments, in A. V.
Kneese and J. L. Sweeney (eds), *Handbook of Natural Resource and Energy Economics* 1, North-
Holland, Amsterdam, 395–460.

Cnossen, S. and Volleberg, H. (1992) Towards a global excise on carbon, *National Tax Journal* 45,
March, 23–36.

EC Commission (1991) *A Community Strategy to Limit Carbon Dioxide Emissions and to Improve
Energy Efficiency: Communication from the Commission to the Council*, Brussels.

EC Commission (1992) *Proposal for a Council Directive Introducing a Tax on Carbon Dioxide
Emissions and Energy*, Brussels.

International Energy Agency (1991) *Energy Prices and Taxes*, 2nd quarter.

Johnson, P., Mckay, S. and Smith S. (1990) *The Distributional Consequences of Environmental Taxes*,
Institute for Fiscal Studies, London.

Montgomery, W. D. (1991) Designing fees on greenhouse gases, OECD (mimeo), Paris.

Organization for Economic Co-operation and Development (1988) *Taxing Consumption*, OECD, Paris.

Organization for Economic Co-operation and Development (1989), *Economic Instruments for
Environmental Protection*, OECD, Paris.

Osserwaarde, M., de Savornin Lohman, A. F. and van der Burg, T. (1991) The use of charges for the
reduction of greenhouse gases: Designing the charge, OECD (mimeo), Paris.

Pearce, D. (1991) The role of carbon taxes in adjusting to global warming, *Economic Journal* 101,
July, 938–48.

Pearson, M. and Smith, S. (1991) *The European Carbon Tax: An Assessment of the European
Commission's Proposals*, Institute for Fiscal Studies, London.

Poterba, J. M. (1991) Tax policy to combat global warming: On designing a carbon tax, in R. Dornbusch
and J. M. Poterba (eds), *Global Warming: Economic Policy Responses*, MIT Pr., Cambridge,
Mass., 1991, 71–98.

Schelling, T. C. (1991) Economic responses to global warming: Prospects for cooperative approaches,

    in R. Dornbusch and J. M. Poterba (eds), *Global Warming: Economic Policy Responses*, MIT Pr.,
    Cambridge, Mass., 197–221.
Schmidt, K. (1991) How industrial countries are responding to global climate change, *International
    Environmental Affairs* 3(4), Fall 1991, 292–315.
US Department of Justice (1991) *A Comprehensive Approach to Addressing Potential Climate Change:
    Report of the Task Force on the Comprehensive Approach to Climate Change* (mimeo), Washington
    D.C.
Victor, D. G. (1991) Practical aspects of implementing greenhouse taxes: Issues for OECD countries,
    OECD (mimeo), Paris.
Whalley, J. and Wigle, R. (1991) The international incidence of a carbon tax, in R. Dornbusch and
    J. M. Poterba (eds.), *Global Warning: Economic Policy Responses*, MIT Pr., Cambridge, Mass.,
    233–63.
Watson, R. T., Rodhe, H., Hoeschger, H. and Siegenthaler, U. (1990) Greenhouse gases and aerosols,
    in J. T. Hougton,-G. J. Jenkins and J. J. Ephraus (eds), *Climate Change: The IPCC Scientific
    Assessment*, Cambridge U.P., Cambridge, pp. 1–40.

7. Environmental Policy Instruments for Controlling Air Pollution: An Applied General Equilibrium Modelling Approach for Quantifying their Efficiency and Effectiveness

KLAUS CONRAD and MICHAEL SCHRÖDER
University of Mannheim, Germany

1. Introduction

Since the beginning of the 1970s, environmental regulation of air pollutants has increased in Germany. The goal of all environmental laws has been to protect people and the environment against damage from negative externalities. For an economically rational environmental policy, it is necessary to know the costs of the negative externalities from pollution as well as the economic costs caused by environmental policies. Given the resistance to more restrictive environmental regulation by some groups of society, it is becoming more and more important to quantify the costs of such a policy. Before considering, however, an enforcement in regulation, the first important questions as a guide for policy are: given the present quality of the air, what are the costs in resource allocation by employing a command and control policy instead of price instruments? How much growth can we achieve by cost-effectiveness in environment policy? Which policy instruments should be used? Are emission taxes more cost-effective than subsidies for abated emissions? And if yes, by how much in terms of additional growth in GDP?

At present, reduction in greenhouse gas emissions has a high priority in environmental policy. However, politicians as well as the public have to be aware that there might be a trade-off problem between reducing greenhouse gas emissions and stability in growth and employment. Announcing an impressive rate of CO_2 reduction by the year 2005 for vote-maximizing behavior and not carrying out this policy for the same reason is a consistent strategy in politics. It is therefore a policy-relevant objective to quantify the economic impact of committing a country to a CO_2 reduction agreement. We will calculate the economic costs of the Toronto commitment of reducing CO_2 emissions to the year 2005 by 20% based on the 1988 CO_2 level. Important questions are not only the impact on growth and unemployment, but also on the structure of the economy (energy intensive industries, motor-vehicle industry, export-intensive industries).

Hans Opschoor and Kerry Turner (eds), Economic Incentives and Environmental Policies, 129–151.
© 1994 *Kluwer Academic Publishers. Printed in the Netherlands.*

The purpose of this chapter is to employ an applied general equilibrium model (AGE-model) with an input-output matrix, extended by emission coefficients, and with abatement technologies for the industries in order to quantify the impact of different environmental policy instruments on the economy. Obviously, such an analysis of the effect of emission control costs cannot be carried out within a partial equilibrium framework. An environmental policy aimed at significantly reducing the emissions of major air pollutants such as SO_2, NO_x and CO_2 will have general equilibrium effects on the structure of prices, on the structure of the economy and on growth and employment. Environmental policy may result in a service orientated industrial structure and in a lower weight for the pollution intensive raw material industries. Hence the net impact on growth and employment can only be analyzed in an interindustry general equilibrium framework. Such an approach is also required for an analysis of the cost-effectiveness of different instruments in terms of economic costs if sub-optimal environmental policy instruments are introduced.

In order to evaluate the economic impact of alternative environmental policy approaches we employ a dynamic AGE-model of a region (state) in Germany. By using a regional model, we can analyze the impact of environmental policy on structural changes with regional characteristics such as coalmines, heavy industry or industries depending on waterways. The results obtained from using this regional model however, can, easily be generalized and quantified for countries and regions with a similar structure of production and consumption. In the following section, we present a short description of the structure and main characteristics of the AGE-model used for our environmental policy simulations. In the section thereafter, we outline how the cost of abatement and the instruments of environmental policy have been implemented in the AGE-model. Subsequently, we carry out an analysis of cost-effectiveness and efficiency of different instruments in environmental policy. The last section summarizes our experience with AGE-modelling for evaluating environmental policy proposals.

2. A Dynamic Temporary AGE-Model

In recent years, there has been an increasing number of papers utilising a AGE-approach which present the economic impacts of environmental policy proposals. Willett (1985) developed a static AGE-model based on the activity analysis related to different processes for producing goods. The input structure also includes the costs of the abatement activities and the derived output of emissions. The model has been employed by Shortle and Willett (1986) in an economic evaluation of U.S. emission standards for waste water. Jorgenson and Wilcoxen (1990a, b) constructed a dynamic AGE-model based on econometrically estimated translog functions for producer and consumer behavior. The model calculates the cost of environmental regulation in terms of lower U.S. growth rates. Instead of abatement functions for the polluting industries the authors assign published abatement costs to each of the industries. Stephan (1989) looks into the short- and long-run adjustment processes under environmental policy by using a neo-Austrian vintage capital approach. The model contains abatement functions for waste water treatment and presents the growth of global GDP and water quality without and with regulation. Bergman (1991) analyses the effect of regulation of air pollution on the Swedish economy. Abatement activities for SO_2 and NO_x are part of the model and the main purpose of the paper is to explore the slope of the marginal cost function for reduction in CO_2 emissions. Whalley and Wigle (1991) used a single-period computable general equilibrium model to evaluate the possible effects of alternative CO_2 emission reductions, and Manne and Richels (1991) examine alternative strategies to limit global emissions using their analytical framework 'global 2100'.

In this section, we will present the main characteristics of our dynamic AGE-model. The model will be applied to the regulation of air pollutants under alternative instruments in environmental policy. The present standards for emissions of SO_2, NO_x and particulates have been integrated into a base simulation of the performance of the economy and the environment. The state of the environment in the base run will be kept constant for all simulation studies in order to permit an analysis of the cost-effectiveness of alternative policy instruments like emission taxes or abatement subsidies. With a given quality of the environment, the economic impacts under alternative simulations can be compared directly. The main advantage of this approach is that there is no need for a monetary evaluation of different states of the environment. The application of AGE-models in terms of a comparison of the performance of the economy without and with environmental policy, as analyzed in the AGE-models mentioned above, does not permit a direct comparison and ranking, since the quality of the environment is different.

Our AGE-model is a temporary equilibrium model. In such a model the unrealistic assumption that all variables adjust immediately to their long-run optimal values is relaxed. We treat capital as quasi-fixed in the short-run so that the economy is in a short-run equilibrium, different from the long-run equilibrium. This case may occur when an ecologically orientated tax reform leads to under- or over-utilization of capacity. We will not set out in detail the framework and specifications of our temporary equilibrium model. This has already been done in several other papers where this approach has been adopted to quantify the economic impact of tax and energy policy proposals.[1] Here we want to present the modifications and extensions required to incorporate the impact of intermediate input and capital demand by abatement activities, to model the trade-off between tax payments for emissions and between abatement costs, to emphazise the role of consumer durables in environmental policy, and to specify abatement technologies.

Figure 1 presents the structure of the model and its solution process. The core of the temporary equilibrium model is the input-output matrix for the State Baden-Württemberg[2] containing twenty industries, a system of twenty prices as the solution of a simultaneous equation system of average cost functions, and a price-dependent input structure. Each industry uses energy, non-energy inputs, capital and labor to produce its output. The energy aggregate consists of nine energy components and the non-energy aggregate of eleven material components. In modelling pollution, a detailed disaggregation of the energy inputs is absolutely necessary since most of the pollutants originate in the burning of fossil fuels. The input-output

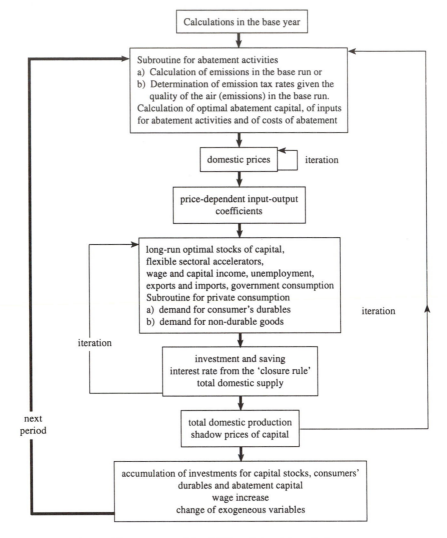

Fig. 1. The structure of the AGE-model and its solution process.

table has been enlarged by a 4×20 sub-matrix containing emission coefficients of four air pollutants (particulates, SO_2, NO_x and CO_2). Additional columns in the input-output matrix represent the abatement activities. These activities are, however, an integral part of the production decision of each industry and hence integrated into the structure of input demand of each industry.

Our model of producer behavior integrates factor demand with an explicit optimization of factors which are fixed in the short-run, but variable in the long run. In this dynamic cost of adjustment model the modification of the stock of quasi-fixed factors is assumed to be costly. By such an approach we consider the fact that increases in energy saving and pollution abating technologies to their new long-run optimal levels result in a loss of productive efficiency. The speed of adjustment is endogenous and will be derived from dynamic cost minimization behavior including transaction costs. The point of departure for considering trans-action costs is the assumption, that the introduction of a high tax on emissions will increase marginal cost depending on the speed of adjustment. This in turn implies a delay in the modification of quasi-fixed factors like the capital stock.[3]

We characterize the technology of a cost minimizing firm by a variable cost function VC.

$$VC = (x, K, \dot{K}, q, q_L, t), \qquad (1)$$

where x is output, q is the price vector of intermediate inputs, q_L is the price of labor and t represents technical change. The quasi-fixed factor capital K is given at the beginning of the period and its change $\dot{K}$ is an argument of the variable cost function, resulting in a loss of productive efficiency; hence $VC_{\dot{K}} > 0$. Since the base year need not be a year of a long-run equilibrium, base year adjustment costs are included in the observed variable costs $VC = \Sigma q_i v_i + q_L \cdot v_L$ where v_i are the n intermediate inputs.

From Shephard's lemma we derive short-run demand functions as variable input coefficients:

$$\frac{v_i}{x} = \frac{\partial vc}{\partial q_i}, \qquad i = 1, \ldots n, L, \qquad (2)$$

where $vc = VC(1, K/x, \dot{K}, q, q_L, t)$ is the average variable costs with $VC = x \cdot vc(K/x, \dot{K}, q, q_L, t)$ due to our assumption of constant returns to scale (CRTS) of VC in x and K. We assume separability of the overall production function in energy, non-energy, capital and labor inputs and choose a CES-specification of the overall cost function in corresponding prices and in the corresponding x and K term. For the sub-functions in the energy components and in the non-energy components we have also chosen CES-specifications. The distribution parameters can be derived from base year input coefficients, and values for the elasticities of substitution can be different for different industries. Assuming profit maximization under perfect competition ($p = VX_x$), Euler's Theorem implies zero profit under the ex post price of capital q_K ($q_K = -VC_K$):

$$px = VC(x, K, \dot{K}, q, q_L) + q_K \cdot K, \qquad (3)$$

or

$$p = vc(1, K/x, \dot{K}, q, q_L) + q_K(K/x) \qquad (4)$$

This 'price equal total average cost'-condition can be employed to determine the system of n output prices. Since the price vector q of intermediate inputs in exactly the price vector ($p_1, \ldots, p_n$) of output prices, equation (4) for industry i is:

$$p_i = vc_i(K_i/x_i, \dot{K}_i, p_1, \ldots, p_n, q_L) + q_{K,i}(K_i/x_i). \qquad (5)$$

Hence we can solve this system of n prices, given the beginning of year capital stock and the price of labor.

We next turn to the derivation of the optimal path of the quasi-fixed capital stock. Modifications of this incur costs to the firm. Under the assumption of static expectation the firm minimizes the present value of variable costs and capital costs:[4]

$$\min_{K, \dot{K}} \int_0^\infty e^{-rt}\{VC(x, K, \dot{K}, q, t) + p_K \cdot K\}dt \qquad (6)$$

where $p_K = p_I(r + \delta)$ is the ex ante price of capital, p_I is the investment goods deflator, r is the nominal rate of return and δ is the rate of replacement. The problem of the firm is to choose the time path of $K(t)$ and $\dot{K}(t)$ which minimizes the present value of total costs.

The Euler first-order condition of (6) in the steady state ($\dot{K} = 0$) is:

$$-\frac{\partial VC(x, K^*, q, q_L)}{\partial K} = p_K. \qquad (7)$$

Given the expected ex ante price of capital, this envelope condition has to be solved for the long-run optimal capital stock K^*. As was shown by Lucas (1967) and Treadway (1974), the short-run demand for the quasi-fixed capital input determined by (7) as a desired stock can be approximated around the long-run equilibrium by the solution of a linear differential equation

$$\dot{K} = m \cdot (K^* - K) \qquad (8)$$

where m is an adjustment coefficient which is an increasing function of r and mainly determined by the curvature of the variable cost function with respect to K and $\dot{K}$. Finally, r changes over time in order to equate the ex post identity of investment and saving. If final demand exceeds total income, r will increase and investment will go down as K^* decreases in $p_K = p_I(r + \delta)$.

The aspect of quasi-fixity of goods in the short run is also incorporated in our model of consumer behavior. Environmental regulation affects the use of consumer durables like cars, electric appliances, and heating. Hence our model of a representative consumer integrates the demand for non-durables and for services from the quasi-fixed durables, with the investment demand for modifying the stock of consumer durables towards their long-run optimal levels. This approach permits us to model the impact of an emission based motor-vehicle tax or of a higher tax on gasoline.

In order to develop a dynamic model of consumer behavior we make use of the similarity between the dual concept in the theory of cost and production, and between the dual concept of utility and expenditure functions. Our objective is to develop an integrated framework of consumer demand for the 20 non-durable goods like food and services, and for our three durable goods: cars, heating and electric appliances. Since non-durable goods like gasoline or electricity are linked to durable goods such as cars and electric appliances, we will state some prices in terms of cost prices which will include all costs of using durables.

We begin with the notion of a variable expenditure function $e(u, p, z)$ which gives minimal expenditure for non-durable goods given the utility level u, the price vector p of the non-durable goods and the vector z of the quasi-fixed stock of durables. Since expenditure refers only to non-durables, its value is $e = \Sigma p_i x_i$, where x is the optimal consumption plan for non-durable goods of quantity x_i. The expenditure function $e(\cdot)$ has the following properties $(i = 1, \ldots, 20; j = 1, 2, 3)$:

$$\frac{\partial e(u, p, z)}{\partial p_i} = x_i, \quad \frac{\partial e}{\partial z_j} < 0, \quad \frac{\partial e}{\partial u} > 0 \tag{9}$$

and $e(\cdot)$ is convex in z.

The first property is Shephard's lemma and the second one states that the purchase of durables will reduces expenditures for non-durables given the standard of living u. If the consumer buys more units or higher quality units of durables, he has to cut back expenditures for non-durables like restaurant meals, entertainment or textiles.

The optimal stock of the durable can be derived from an intertemporal minimization of expenditures (see Conrad and Schröder, 1991d. These expenditures consist of expenditures for non-durables, of purchases of new durables as net investment $(p_{I_j} \cdot \dot{z}_j; p_{I_j}$ is the acquisition price of durable $j)$, of purchases for replacement $(p_{I_j} \cdot \delta_j \cdot z_j; \delta_j$ is the rate of replacement), and of taxes on durables like a motor vehicle tax $(p_{I_j} \cdot \tau_j \cdot z_j; \tau$-tax rate on property of durables).

The long-run optimal stock z^* of consumer durables follows from:

$$p_{zj} = -\frac{\partial e(u, p, z^*)}{\partial zj}, \quad j = 1, 2, 3, \tag{10}$$

where $p_{zj} = p_{I_j} (r + \delta_j + \tau_j)$ is the ex ante user cost of the durable good, and r is the interest rate on government bonds. Net investment in the stock of durables will be a fraction of the difference $z_j^* - z_j$ and private consumption will be the sum of variable expenditure for non-durables and the service flow of old and of new durables. Hence savings will be influenced by the decision to buy durables. Saving is equal to disposable income minus consumption C and it affects the level of the interest rate r via the ex post identity of savings and investment.

For a specification of our demand system we choose the linear expenditure system. Since gasoline, electricity, and heating energy are linked to the stock of durables, we use a composition of these goods into a linked part and into a disposable part (see Conrad, 1983, 1984). The idea behind such a composition is that demand for gasoline (x_G) is linked to the use of the stock of automobiles (z). Or, in algebraic terms, $x_G = \propto_{G, z} \cdot z + \tilde{x}_G$ where $\propto_{G, z}$ is yearly gasoline consumption per unit of purchase price of the car and $\tilde{x}_G$ is gasoline consumption from fast driving or bad maintenance of the car. This implies a cost price $\tilde{p}_z$ of the services of an automobile which is the user cost of capital p_z plus the cost of gasoline, i.e., $\tilde{p}_z = p_z + \propto_{G, z} \cdot p_G$. The introduction of a tax on CO_2 or NO_x will therefore increase the price of gasoline, hence the cost price of a car, and demand for new cars will decline. Under a carbon dioxide tax, for instance, the cost price of a car is $\tilde{p}_z = p_z + \propto_{G, z} (P_G + t_{CO_2} \cdot e_{CO_2})$ where t_{CO_2} is the tax rate and e_{CO_2} is the emission coefficient. Again, most of the parameters will be estimated from base year data. Other parameters like income elasticities will be taken from other studies.

The models of producers' and consumers' behavior constitute the main parts of the interindustry model with final demand for consumption and investment goods. Total supply for intermediate and for final demand will be determined by the Leontief inverse; this generates also income from labor and capital. The wage rate is however not an equilibrium price but determined from inflation and productivity changes in the previous year; unemployment therefore is an endogeneous residual in our model.

3. Costs of Abatement and the Effect of Environmental Policy Instruments on Prices

Polluting firms can react to standards and/or emission taxes either by factor substitution or by abatement activities or by both. They have abatement cost functions and determine the level of the abatement activity by equating marginal cost of abatement to the uniform tax rate on emissions. Abatement activities also imply demand for intermediate goods, for capital and for labor.

In our model abatement decisions are an integral part of firms' decision making. The abatement technology is characterized by high fixed costs due to the capital intensity of abatement measures. A special feature of abatement technologies is a drastic increase in costs if the degree of abatement is increased. The reason for that is that abatement technologies are designed for a certain degree of abatement. We will therefore assume constant returns to scale (CRTS) in abated emissions for a firm's aggregated abatement technology but will assume that costs per unit of abated emissions are convex in the degree of abated emissions. This aspect, however, will only influence the capital part of abatement costs.

We first specify the abatement cost function. The use of inputs entails total potential emission TE; and abated emissions AE will depend on the degree of abatement, i.e., $AE = ae \cdot TE$. The degree ae is either legally determined or a decision variable of the firm if confronted with an emission tax. With $u_i = a_i \cdot AE$ ($i = 1, \ldots, n$, L, K) as the input quantities for abatement as a function of ae, we have the following abatement cost function $c_u(q, ae, TE)$ which is convex in ae (the coefficients a_i are in [input in DM/tons of abated emissions]):

$$c_u = (\Sigma q_i \cdot a_i + q_K \cdot a_K(ae)) \cdot AE \qquad (11)$$

with $a_K(ae) \to \infty$ for $ae \to 1.$[5]

We will distinguish abatement cost functions with respect to the type of emissions and in some cases with respect to the industry. For solid waste we assume the same abatement cost function for all industries. For SO_2 we distinguish between electricity and the non-electricity industries as well as between old and new installed technology. The same has been done for NO_x but here we additionally differentiate between the type of input used (coal, natural gas, or fuel oil).

In order to demonstrate the effect of different environmental policy measures on output, input and abatement decisions of a profit maximizing firm we concentrate on a case with two inputs where only the first input causes emissions. For this case total potential emissions are $TE = e_1 \cdot v_1$ where e_1 is an emission coefficient [tons of emission/input in base year DM].

The abatement cost function is:

$$c_u(q, ae, TE) = c_u(q, ae) \cdot AE = c_u(q, ae) \cdot ae \cdot e_1 \cdot v_1 \qquad (12)$$

where the unit cost function $c_u(q, ae)$ is the term in the round bracket given in (11).

Case 1: A regulated degree of abatement ae

The current environmental policy regulates the quality of air in the air quality act of 1986 (TA-Luft 86). User of furnaces have to adhere to limits of emissions which can be interpreted in terms of our model as a minimum degree of abatement $\overline{ae}$. Hence the problem of the firm is:

$$\max_{x} p \cdot x - C(x, \tilde{q}_1, q_2) \qquad (13)$$

where the price of the first input $\tilde{q}_1 = q_1 + c_u(q, \overline{ae}) \cdot \overline{ae} \cdot e_1$ has increased by the shadow price of the standard $\overline{ae}$, i.e., the cost of regulated abatement per unit of this input. Under CRTS of C in x, the price will be equal to average cost and will include the cost of abatement.

Case 2: A tax on emissions

If a tax on emissions is introduced, the problem for the firm is:

$$\max_{x, \, ae} p \cdot x - C(x, \tilde{q}_1, q_2) - t_1 \cdot (1 - ae) \cdot e_1 \cdot v_1 \tag{14}$$

where again $\tilde{q}_1 = q_1 + c_u(q, ae)ae \cdot e_1$, but the degree of abatement ae is now a decision variable. Since the emission tax increases the price of input 1, (14) is equivalent to

$$\max_{x, \, ae} p \cdot x - C(x, \tilde{\tilde{q}}_1, q_2) \tag{15}$$

where $\tilde{\tilde{q}}_1 = \tilde{q}_1 + t_1 \cdot (1 - ae) \cdot e_1$. Again, under CRTS, price will be equal to average cost including abatement, and output x will be determined as part of the inter-industry input-output solution.

Case 3: A subsidy for abated emissions

If the firm gets a subsidy s per unit of abated emissions, its objective is:

$$\max_{x, \, ae} p \cdot x - C(x, \tilde{q}_1, q_2) + s \cdot ae \cdot e_1 \cdot v_1. \tag{16}$$

Since the subsidy reduces the total unit cost of using input 1, (16) is equivalent to

$$\max_{x, \, ae} p \cdot x - C(x, \tilde{\tilde{q}}_1, q_2) \tag{17}$$

where $\tilde{\tilde{q}}_1 = q_1 + (c_u(q, ae) - s) \cdot ae \cdot e_1$. The effect of a subsidy is to reduce the cost of abatement and hence the price of the product. Whereas in our model an emission tax permits a lump sum transfer to consumers in order to compensate for higher prices, the subsidy requires a lump sum payment for financing it.

Case 4: Regulated abatement for SO_2 and a tax on CO_2 (without abatement possibilities)

Let input 1 (e.g., coal) causes two types of emissions: SO_2 which can be abated and CO_2 which cannot be abated. Then, if a tax t_2 on CO_2 emissions is introduced additionally to the standard $\overline{ae}$, the problem of the firm is:

$$\max_{x} p \cdot x - C(x, \tilde{q}_1, q_2) - t_2 \cdot e_2 \cdot v_1. \tag{18}$$

Since the CO_2 emission tax increases the price of input 1, (18) is equivalent to

$$\max_{x} \; p \cdot x - C(x, \hat{q}_1, q_2) \tag{19}$$

where $\hat{q}_1 = \bar{q}_1 + t_2 \cdot e_2$. A CO_2 tax will enhance substitution and will also reduce SO_2 emissions.

4. The Impact on the Economy and on the Environment under Alternative Environmental Policy Approaches

The final goal of our modelling effort is to evaluate quantitatively the economic consequences of environmental policy measures. An obvious measure of the welfare change involved in moving from a base case with prices p^0 to an economy with emission taxes with prices p^1, and income y^1 is the difference in indirect utility. As the money equivalent we choose the money metric utility function as a measure of utility differences. We will employ Hick's measure of equivalent income variation (EV), defined as

$$EV = e(u^1, p^0) - e(u^0, p^0). \tag{20}$$

It gives the income change at the base case prices that would be equivalent to the policy implied change in utility. If $EV < 0$, welfare after the policy measure is lower than in the base case. The consumer would be willing to pay the maximum amount EV at the fixed budget level $y^0 = e(u^0, p^0)$, to avoid the decline of utility from u^0 to u^1. Similarly, if $EV > 0$, the consumer would be willing to pay the maximum amount EV to see the change in environmental policy implemented.

The Cost-Effectiveness of Market Instruments in Environmental Policy

For measuring the cost-effectiveness of a change in environmental policy we have first produced a base run from 1985 to 1996. It is based on the present emission standards given by the air quality acts TA-Luft and GFAVO.[6] The standards define the emissions permitted per m^3 of used air. These emission standards can be converted into the permitted emissions per unit of input. The regulated inputs are hard coal and different types of fuel oil, and gas. We consider emissions of sulphur dioxide, nitrogen oxides, and particulates. The emission standards are valid for new vintages only. The older vintages have to be adjusted within a given time period. For the electricity sector we assume the years from 1985 to 1988 as adjustment period. After 1988 the emission standards are kept constant for the rest of the simulation period. For the industrial sectors regulated by the air quality acts the adjustment period starts in 1988 and ends in 1991.[7]

Simulating the Economic Impact of Policy Instruments

Our first simulation will show the economic impact of an efficient environmental policy where all industries are confronted with uniform emission tax rates differentiated only in terms of specific air pollutants. The magnitude of each emission tax rate has been computed so as to guarantee exactly the air quality under the base run with standards. Marginal cost of pollution avoidance for each pollutant will now be equal to the uniform tax rate across industries and abatement costs will be minimized given the quality of the air from the base run.[8] For an easier welfare comparison of the two simulations, tax revenues have been redistributed to the consumer as a lump sum transfer.

In a second simulation we have reduced the possibility of substitution. The overall elasticity of substitution among the aggregates energy, non-energy and labor is equal to 0.75 in all our simulation studies. In this second simulation the elasticity of substitution among the energy aggregate and among the non-energy aggregate in the input structure of the industries is set equal to zero (Leontief assumption of fixed input coefficients). In the first simulation these elasticities have been 1.0 for the energy aggregate and 0.85 for the non-energy aggregate. Since many AGE-studies are based on the assumption of fixed coefficients, this simulation can show whether this assumption matters.

In a third simulation we will evaluate the economic impact of another market instrument as an economic incentive – a subsidy for abating emissions. The rates of subsidy per unit of abated emissions will be calculated such that the air quality of the base run is achieved. For a welfare comparison we keep the government budget constant and introduce a lump sum payment for consumers to finance the subsidy.

Since a CO_2 levy is at present under consideration in several countries we will analyze in a fourth simulation its effect.[9] In order to prevent a drastic change in the global climate the conference at Toronto in 1988 on the world climate agreed upon a recommendation that all industrial nations should reduce their CO_2 emissions up to the year 2005 by 20 percent based on the 1988 CO_2 levels. This proposal implies a yearly reduction of 1.17 percent from 1989 on. We have taxed all sources of CO_2 emissions, i.e., all industries and private households to a level such that the CO_2 emission limit is met but not exceeded. For that purpose we have introduced a tax on CO_2 emissions with a tax base $e_{CO_2, i} \cdot v_i$, where $e_{CO_2, i}$ is the CO_2 emission coefficient of fossil fuel of type i, where i is hard coal, mineral oil, and natural gas. As shown in (19) in section 3, the unit cost of those inputs will increase by at least $t_{CO_2} \cdot e_{CO_2, i}$. Consumers cause CO_2 emissions by using gasoline for their cars and by burning fossil fuel in their heating systems. According to our approach to modelling consumer behavior, a CO_2 emission tax will raise the price of gasoline G by at least $t_{CO_2} \cdot e_{CO_2, G}$. Since the use of a car is linked to gasoline, our new user-cost price of a car will also be higher. Hence the desired stock of cars will decline. This will reduce the purchase of new cars and, due to the now lower stock of cars, also the CO_2 emissions caused by cars.

Results of the Simulation

In Table 1 we present the impact on the economy under alternative environmental policy measures. Our welfare measure (equivalent variation) permits a ranking of these measures. The best policy is an emission tax and the second best one is a policy with abatement subsidies. In this ranking the assumption of the flexibility of the economy matters because the welfare measure in 1996 under emission taxes and low possibility of substitution is smaller (1529) than the welfare measure under abatement subsidies (1781). Obviously, all policy approaches are better than the command and control approach used as the reference case. GNP will be higher by 0.2 to 1.3 per cent in 1996, depending on the policy approach, and unemployment will be reduced in the range of 2.3 to 40 per cent. Real consumption and investment will increase but prices will also be higher under market instruments as incentive schemes. As was shown earlier, emission taxes increase the price of an input, they increase the prices of emission intensive intermediate goods, and the resulting higher level of production increases the marginal productivity of capital and hence the price of capital.

The last two columns show the economic impact of a CO_2 tax. We observe a decline in GDP growth and in spite of the cost push of a CO_2 tax, a decline in the price level. The main reason for that is the drop in the price of capital due to a low capacity utilization. The welfare figure of −59 bill. DM in 1996 means that the household sector would have paid this amount at the most in order to avoid the lower utility level in economic terms. One reason for our pessimistic growth scenario under a CO_2 tax is that in order to keep the 1.17 per cent reduction per year on the 1988 CO_2 emission base, an increasing tax rate is required due to the steady increasing CO_2 emissions in the base simulation. In 1996, for instance, 30 per cent and not the 9.4 per cent of the 1988 based CO_2 reduction had to be achieved. Another reason is the declining growth of the stock of automobiles with its direct and indirect effect on production. In Conrad and Schröder (1990 b) we presented a less pessimistic scenario which took into account energy saving technical change. But most CO_2 tax simulations published in the literature, show that the economic costs of keeping the Toronto agreement are very high indeed. Our calculations imply a rate of DM 177 per ton of CO_2 ($100) in 1990 and DM 1360 in 1996. Since a car produces about 3.5 tons of CO_2 each year, a car owner would have to pay DM 620 in 1990 as a carbon tax and DM 4760 in 1996. An effective control of CO_2 emission would therefore require a general tax reform with lower value added taxes, for instance. It is to be expected that in

Table 1. Cost-effectiveness of environmental policy

	Emission standards		Emission taxes (high subst.)		Emission taxes (low subst.)		Abatement subsidies		CO_2 taxation	
	1990	1996	1990	1996	1990	1996	1990	1996	1990	1996
Real GNP (bill. DM)	233.7	303.6	+0.2	+0.6	+0.2	+0.3	-0.08	+0.2	-0.04	-7.5
Unemployment (10^3)	156.3	122.0	-5.2	-14.0	-3.5	-2.3	-6.1	-14.8	311.0	894.0
Production (bill. DM)	477.4	617.8	+0.0	+0.4	+0.0	+0.1	+0.04	+0.5	-4.0	-18.6
Investment (bill. DM)	48.9	84.8	+1.0	+1.6	+0.9	+0.7	+0.0	+1.3	-2.4	-33.2
Consumption (bill. DM)	127.6	171.8	+0.3	+0.8	+0.3	+0.4	+0.08	+0.5	-3.0	-18.6
Welfare (mill. DM)	0.0	0.0	623	2765	528	+1529	121	1781	-5200	-59000
Trade balance (bill. DM)	55.0	42.2	-0.5	-4.5	-0.8	-1.0	-0.9	-5.7	10.7	145
GNP price index	1.516	1.916	+0.5	+0.5	+0.3	0.0	+0.06	+0.4	-2.4	-15
Capital price inded	1.282	1.659	+0.5	+0.2	0.0	-0.5	+0.5	+0.7	-7.4	-22.8
Emission tax revenue (in mill DM; if negative: subsidies)	0.0	0.0	+707	+986	+778	+1168	-133	-156	12700	90000

The results of the base run are in constant prices of 1978; the price index is 1.0 in 1978. The results of the simulation runs are given in terms of percentage changes from base run values or indexes, respectively. The welfare measure and emission tax revenues are given in absolute figures. Columns 5 and 6 refer to a somewhat different base run with lower elasticities of substitution not presented here. The increase in unemployment under a CO_2 corresponds to an unemployment rate of 7.7 in 1990 and 20.9 in 1996.

the near future government may wish to reconsider their commitments to the Toronto agreement.

The Impact of Policy Instruments on Substitution and Abatement

Table 2 shows the differences in substitution and abatement behavior under environmental policy approaches. If substitution possibilities are high, the air quality from the base run will be achieved by taking advantage of substitution and by reducing costly abatement activities (use of end-of-pipe technologies). Under emission taxes, emission-intensive inputs like hard coal or oil become more expensive than under emission standards. Hence the increased substitution of these inputs causes less emissions. The conclusion from this is that an environmental policy with emission taxes induces a less emission-intensive production structure whereas an environmental policy with emission standards induces more abatement activities.

If the possibility of substitution is low, the ratio of reducing emissions by substitution and by abatement is about the same as in the base run. Compared with the simulation under high substitution possibilities the degree of abatement must be higher to compensate for the inflexible input structure. This requires higher rates of emission taxes in the low substitution case. The NO_x tax rate in 1990 for the high substitution case is 1600 DM/per ton and for the low substitution case it is 2500 DM/per ton.

The structure of substitution and abatement in order to keep the given air quality is quite different under the abatement subsidy simulation. Depending on the degree of abatement chosen by an industry, the cost-price of emission-intensive inputs can now be even lower than under the base run with regulated degrees. Compared to the emission tax simulation, those inputs will become less expensive and demand will be higher. Hence substitution towards the wrong input structure requires higher abatement efforts in order to keep the base run quality of the air. The subsidy rate for SO_2 in 1990 is 2870 DM per ton and higher than the tax rate of 2350 DM per ton under the emission tax run.

Under a CO_2 tax the reduction in fossil fuel consumption results also in less emissions of the other air pollutants. The last two columns permit a comparison of the reduction in the taxed CO_2 emission with the reduction of the other pollutants, regulated by their degree of abatement. The lower consumption of carbon intensive fossil fuels in production and private households explains the considerable reduction of particulates, SO_2 and NO_x emissions.

Table 2. Emission of air pollutants and abated emissions

	Emission standard (base run)		Emission taxes (high subst.)		Emission taxes (low subst.)		Abatement subsidies		CO_2 taxation	
	1990	1996	1990	1996	1990	1996	1990	1996	1990	1996
Particulates	35.9	44	–	–	–	–	–	–	–12.5	–34.1
Abated partic.	11.8	16.6	–9.3	–9.6	+1.7	+0.0	+44.3	+38.7	–25.9	–60.2
SO_2 total	342.5	439.0	–	–	–	–	–	–	–19.9	–58.4
abated	37.2	50.3	–76.1	–64.6	–1.6	–1.8	+84.6	+68	–5.4	–38.8
NO_x total	386.5	520.1	–	–	–	–	–	–	–12.8	–45.1
abated	374	50.5	–11.2	–8.1	+0.9	+1.7	+59.0	+58.6	–9.9	–46.1
CO_2 total	81435	96474	–	–	–	–	+2.3	+2.2	–12.2	–31.4

The figures in column 1 and 2 are in thousand tons. All other figures are in percentage change to the base run. Column 5 and 6 show the percentage change to a base run which is different from the base run given in columns 1 and 2 for the case with high elasticities of substitution.

The Impact of Policy Instruments on the Economic Structure

In Table 3 we present the impact on the structure of the economy as a result of the effect of our environmental policy approaches on unit costs and hence on prices. We first compare the emission tax simulation with the base run. Total production in 1996 is higher by 0.4 per cent (see Table 1), but growth is different at the sectoral level. Electricity increases by 0.8 per cent in 1996 but other pollution intensive industries like chemicals, mineral oil or pulp and paper decline in output. The reason for this (relatively low) change in the structure of production is that under uniform emission taxes the burden of abatement activities will be better allocated among industries. The electricity industry does not carry the main burden but other industries also have to abate more to contribute to the given air quality level. With lower substitution possibilities total production increases by only 0.1 per cent in 1996 (see Table 1). Therefore the deviation of the figures in column four of Table 3 will be smaller and hence the change in the structure of the economy. We therefore do not present the case of emission taxes under low substitution.

Under abatement subsidies weighted growth in production in 1996 is higher by 0.5 per cent. On the sectoral level we see that pollution-intensive industries have growth rates above average (electricity: 3.4; iron and steel: 2.0; pulp and paper: 0.9). We conclude from those figures that abatement subsidies are not an instrument for a structural policy towards an energy saving and less pollution-intensive structure of the economy.

The fourth column of Table 3 shows the economic impact of a CO_2 tax on the industry structure and on prices. Whereas domestic production is lower by 18.6 per cent in 1996, output of services declines by only 17 per cent but output of iron and steel or of mineral oil declines by about 28 per cent. The general price level is lower by 15 per cent in 1996, but for motor vehicles it is lower by 22.4 per cent and for electricity it is higher by 15 per cent. For all industries we observe a decline in growth of sectoral production. For some industries this implies zero growth from 1988 on (electricity, machinery, motor vehicles), for some industries the level of production in 1996 will be below the 1988 level (chemicals, mineral oil, iron and steel, pulp and paper), and for services growth will still be about 2 per cent per year under a CO_2 tax. Except for electricity, prices decline in spite of the cost-effect of the CO_2 tax due to the decline in the demand for capital. Since we have linked the wage rate to inflation, the price of labor also declines.

We finally have simulated the performance of the economy without any enforcement of environmental policy. The installed equipment represents the state of the art of technology but there are no additional regulations. Emissions are now higher so that a cost-effectiveness analysis is not possible. However, the effect on growth and the structure of the economy can be evaluated. For 1990 total output is higher by 0.8 per cent and for 1996 it is higher by 5.6 per cent compared to production

Table 3. Impact on the structure of the economy under alternative environmental policy approaches

Industry	Emission standards (base run)		Emission taxes ($g_x = 0.4$)		Abatement subsidies ($g_x = 0.5$)		CO_2 tax ($g_x = -18.6$)		No environmental policy ($g_x = 5.6$)	
	1990	1996	1990	1996	1990	1996	1990	1996	1990	1996
Output, real:										
Electricity	7.7	9.7	+0.8	+0.8	+3.1	+3.4	-3.8	-20.4	+4.4	+9.0
Chemistry	19.7	23.9	-0.4	-0.1	+0.3	+0.5	-5.5	-20.8	+0.4	+3.5
Mineral oil	8.1	10.4	-2.8	-2.0	-0.0	+0.5	-10.5	-27.9	+0.5	+6.1
Iron & steel	13.5	17.1	-0.1	+0.2	+1.8	+2.0	-9.5	-28.3	+3.3	+7.4
Machinery	43.4	54.1	+0.0	+0.2	+0.5	+0.7	-5.5	-18.9	+1.1	+4.4
Motor vehicles	39.6	50.1	+0.0	+0.2	+0.2	+0.4	-4.8	-19.5	-0.6	+3.8
Pulp & paper	6.6	8.0	-0.4	-0.1	+0.7	+0.9	-7.1	-23.0	+1.2	+4.2
Services	127.4	172.3	+0.2	+0.7	+0.0	+0.4	-2.9	-17.0	+0.7	+6.3
Price index:										
Electricity	14.9	1.87	-0.3	+0.2	-3.4	-2.5	+5.3	+15.0	-2.0	+3.0
Chemistry	1.52	1.89	+1.0	+0.9	-0.1	+0.3	-6.1	-8.9	+0.8	+4.7
Mineral oil	1.27	1.67	+1.3	+1.4	+0.0	+0.0	-4.0	-10.1	+0.5	+3.8
Iron & steel	1.58	1.98	+0.7	+0.7	+0.0	+0.2	-1.5	-11.6	+1.0	+5.1
Machinery	1.61	2.0	+0.4	+0.5	+0.1	+0.4	-2.4	-15.0	+1.0	+5.0
Motor vehicles	1.63	2.2	+0.6	+0.8	+0.1	+0.6	-3.7	-22.4	+1.3	+11.3
Pulp & paper	1.59	1.98	+1.1	+1.0	+0.0	+0.3	-1.3	-10.0	+0.9	+4.7
Services	1.46	1.86	+0.5	+0.3	+0.2	+0.5	-4.0	-20.4	+1.3	+6.6

g_x = average growth rate of aggregate output in 1996.

in the base run. These are much higher growth rates than the rates presented in Table 1, row 3. The last columns of Table 3 indicate the energy- and pollution-intensive industries will grow above the average if there is no change in environmental policy. Since growth and employment is higher under a simulation of the economy with no enforced environmental policy we conclude that environmental policy may not have the often emphasized positive effect on employment. The main reason for this result is that investment in pollution control devices crowds out investment for capital accumulation which reduces economic growth under environmental policy.[10]

5. The Effectiveness of Additional Environmental Policy Measures

One can imagine several environmental policy measures which, when introduced, would support the effectiveness of the present environmental policy. Here we will simulate the effect of two technical changes in pollution intensive processes and the effect of cooperative behavior in international environmental policy. The technical changes are the installation of a catalytic converter into private automobiles, and the introduction of fluid-bed combustion to coal-fired power plants. Under each measure average emission coefficients will change over time. The level of total emission as calculated in the base run will be achieved via the use of emission taxes.

Catalytic Converter

The installation of catalytic converters is supposed to reduce emissions of oxides of nitrogen (NO_x) of a car by about 80 per cent. We therefore have reduced the emission coefficients of those cars by 80 per cent. The percentage of cars of a certain vintage with a catalytic converter installed is: assumed to be 0 per cent before 1985, 1 per cent in 1985, 10 per cent in 1986, 23 per cent in 1987, 34 per cent in 1988, 55 per cent in 1989, 77 per cent in 1990, and 100 per cent from 1991 on. Replacement of old cars and purchases of new cars change the average emission coefficient of cars owned by private households.

Fluid-bed Combustion

The fluid-bed combustion is a combustion process in coal-fired power plants which significantly reduces the emissions of sulfur dioxide and nitrogen oxides below those of conventional power plants. We assumed for the electricity industry that from 1985 on new investments in coal fired combustion processes are of the fluid-bed type.

Since their emission coefficients of NO_x and SO_2 are identical to the emission standard imposed by law, no additional abatement activities are required. For particulates, however, abatement efforts have to be intensified because the emission coefficient of particulates will increase by a factor of four under fluid-bed combustion.

International Cooperation in Introducing Emission Taxes

In order to simulate the effect of a reduction in foreign emissions by international cooperation we suppose that fifty per cent of emissions are exchanged by air transportation. Instead of assuming the status quo in environmental policy abroad, we introduce the same regulation for air quality in European countries as simulated in our base run. This will reduce transborder emissions into our state country and therefore more can be emitted by the national industries while still keeping the air quality of the base run. We assume that a reduction in foreign emissions by 10 per cent reduces ambient emission by 5 per cent in our state. Hence national emissions can be increased by 10 per cent without violating the base run target because 5 per cent will cross the border.

Simulation Results of Additional Measures in Controlling Air Pollution

As shown in Table 4, all three environmental policy measures augment the positive economic effects obtained from introducing emission taxes. Compared with the results given in Table 1, growth in GDP, consumption and investment is higher, and unemployment is less. The welfare measure, which exceeds, of course, its value in Table 1, permits again a ranking of the three measures: cooperation in environmental policy, then catalytic converters and finally the fluid-bed combustion.

The impact on the environment is shown in Table 5. Since emissions of NO_x have decreased because of the installation of catalytic converters, the industry can emit more NO_x without violating the given limits of the base run. This means that the electricity industry and other industries have to abate less NO_x than they had to in the simulation run with emission taxes as presented in Table 2. Without the introduction of catalytic converters end-of-pipe abatement activities for particulates and SO_2 declined more because of greater substitution in energy inputs than in the present case with converters. The reason for that is that the low tax on NO_x reduces the incentive for substitution among pollution intensive energy inputs. This implies an increase in emissions of particulates and SO_2 which then have to be abated.

The installation of fluid bed combustion results in less emissions of SO_2 and

Table 4. The effect of additional environmental policy measures: catalytic converters for auto-mobiles, fluid-bed combustion for coal-fired power plants, and emission reduction by international cooperation

| | Emission taxation and | | | | | |
| | Catalytic conv. | | Fluid-bed comb. | | Intern. coop. | |
	1990	1996	1990	1996	1990	1996
Real GNP	0.2	1.0	0.3	0.7	0.3	1.3
Unemployment	−7.7	−16.0	−5.2	−21.0	−5.2	−40.0
Production	0.1	0.9	0.1	0.7	0.2	1.3
Investment	1.0	3.4	1.6	2.3	3.5	4.6
Consumption	0.4	1.5	0.3	1.1	0.5	2.0
Welfare (mill. DM)	743	5202	623	3673	978	6908
Trade balance	−0.9	−11.0	−0.7	−7.3	−1.4	−15.0
GNP price index	0.6	1.4	0.4	0.7	0.6	1.5
Capital price index	0.5	1.3	0.5	0.7	0.8	1.6
Emission tax revenue (mill. DM)	683	977	638	911	644	956

The results are presented as differences in percentage from the base run figures; welfare and tax revenues are in mill. DM.

NO_x but more emissions of particulates. Lower tax rates for SO_2 and NO_x, and a higher tax rate for particulates are the consequences. As seen in Table 5, abatement of particulates increases and for SO_2 and NO_x it decreases more than those in the third and fourth columns of Table 2.

The final two columns of Table 5 show the increase in national emissions permitted under the given ambient quality levels because of international coopera-

Table 5. Emission of air pollutants and abated emissions under additional environmental policy measures

| Type of air pollutants | Emission taxation and | | | | | |
| | Catalytic conv. | | Fluid-bed comb. | | Intern. coop. | |
	1990	1996	1990	1996	1990	1996
Particulates	–	–	–	–	11.7	15
Abated partic.	−5.8	−0.4	74.5	155	−67.3	−37
SO_2 total	–	–	–	–	4.9	6.8
abated	−72.1	−49.3	−81.0	−82	−100	−94
NO_x total	–	–	–	–	4.0	6.0
abated	−68.7	−100	−24.6	−27	−40	−40.2
CO_2 total	0.1	0.6	0.3	0.4	0.4	0.1

The results are presented as differences in percentage from the base run figures.

tion in environmental policy. Correspondingly, abated emissions can be reduced for all three air pollutants. In the case of SO_2, substitution induced through emission taxes even suffices to achieve the SO_2 emission level in 1990 without abatement efforts.

6. Concluding Remarks

It is well known from the literature that environmental regulation by standards (command and control) is less efficient than regulation by market instruments. With fiscal measures that contribute to the efficiency of a program to control externalities, optimal resource allocation could allegedly be achieved. However we know that we are still very far from being able to construct from empirical information the required general equilibrium model in the detail needed to calculate optimal tax rates.

The purpose of this paper was therefore not to compute optimal emission tax rates but to demonstrate the usefulness of AGE-analysis as a device for evaluating alternative environmental policy approaches. Although models of this type cannot be used for economic forecasting, they are indispensable for ranking alternative policy measures. Using general equilibrium theory economists very often can get a good idea of the welfare effect and the qualitative results of a change in a given policy instrument. However, the ranking of the welfare effects of different policy instruments requires AGE-models.

Notes

[1]   See Conrad (1982), Conrad and Henseler-Unger (1986), Conrad and Schröder (1988, 1991 a, b, c). A detailed presentation of the model and its application to environmental policy are given in Schröder (1991).
[2]   See 'Baden-Württemberg in Wort und Zahl', Heft 7, 1985, pp. 248–253.
[3]   The theoretical foundation of dynamic models of firm behavior with adjustment costs stems from Lucas (1967), Lau (1976), and McFadden (1978).
[4]   See Lau (1976) or McFadden (1978) on normalized restricted or variable cost functions.
[5]   For details see Conrad and Schröder (1991 a, b).
[6]   'Technische Anleitung Luft' from 1986 and 'Großfeuerungsanlagen-Verordnung' (GFAVO) from 1983.
[7]   These industries are: chemicals, mineral oil refining, pottery & glass, iron & steel, machinery, motor vehicles & equipment, paper & pulp and leather & clothing.
[8]   The term 'pollution avoidance' includes all activities that are able to reduce emissions in our model. These are: substitution of emission-intensive inputs and the installation of end-of-pipe technologies. With 'pollution abatement' only the latter is meant.
[9]   For more details see Conrad and Schröder (1991 b).
[10] See also Jorgenson and Wilcoxen (1990 a) on that point.

References

Bergman, L. (1991) General equilibrium effects of environmental policy: A CGE modelling approach, *Enviromental and Resource Economics* **1**, 67–85.

Conrad, K., Cost prices and partially fixed factor proportions in energy substitution, *European Economy Review* **21**, 299–312.

Conrad, K., Konsumnachfrage, Folgekosten und Kostenpfeise (1984) *Zeitschrift für Wirtschafts- und Sozialwissenschaften* **104**, 251–268.

Conrad, K. (1982) Die Anpassung der Volkswirtschaft beim Übergang zu neuen Energieversorgungs- systemen: Die theoretischen Grundlagen eines Energiemodells für die Bundesrepublik Deutschland, in H. Siebert (ed), *Reaktionen auf Energiepreis-steigerungen*, Frankfurt, Lang, 1–37.

Conrad, K. and Henseler-Unger, I. (1986) Applied general equilibrium modelling for longterm energy policy in the Fed. Rep. of Germany, *Journal of Policy Modelling* **8**(4), 531–549.

Conrad, K. and Schröder, M. (1988) Effekte einer Emissionssteuer auf sektorale Produktionsstrukturen am Beispiel Baden-Württembergs, in H. Siebert (Hrsg.): *Umweltschutz fü Luft und Wasser*, Springer Verlag Heidelberg.

Conrad, K. and Schröder, M. (1991a) An evaluation of taxes on air pollutants emissions: An AGE- approach, *Schweizerische Zeitschrift für Volkswirtschaft und Statistik* **127**, 199–224.

Conrad, K. and Schröder, M. (1991b) The control of CO_2-emissions and its economic impact, *Environmental and Resource Economics*.

Conrad, K. and Schröder, M. (1991c) Controlling air pollution: The effect of alternative policy approaches, in H. Siebert (ed), *Environmental Scarcity: The International Dimension*, Tübingen, 35–53.

Conrad, K. and Schröder, M. (1991d) Demand for durable and non-durable goods, environmental policy and consumer welfare, *Journal of Applied Econometrics*.

Jorgenson, D. W. and Wilcoxen, P. J. (1990a) Environmental regulation and U.S. economic growth, *The Rand Journal of Economics* **21**, 314–340.

Jorgenson, D. W. and Wilcoxen, P. J. (1990b) The cost of controlling U.S. carbon dioxide emissions, *Harvard Institute of Economic Research*, Discussion Paper.

Lau, L. J. (1976) A characterization of the normalized restricted profit function, *Journal of Economic Theory*, 131–163.

Lucas, R. E. (1967) Adjustment costs and the theory of supply, *Journal of Economic Theory* **7**, 17–39.

Manne, A. S. and Richels, R. G. (1991) Global CO_2 emission reductions – the impact of rising energy costs, *The Energy Journal* **12**, 87–108.

McFadden, D. (1978) Costs, revenue and profit functions, in M. Fuss and D. McFadden (eds), *Production Economics: A Dual Approach to Theory and Applications* **1**, Amsterdam.

Schröder, M. (1991) Die volkswirtschaftlichen Kosten von Umweltpolitik: Kosten-Wirksamkeitsanalysen mit einem Angewandten Gleichgewichtsmodell, Diss. Univ. Physika-Verlag, Heidelberg.

Shortle, J. S. and K. D. Willett, The incidence of water pollution control costs: Partial vs. general equilibrium computations, *Growth and Change* **17**, 32–43.

Stephan, G. (1989) *Pollution Control, Economic Adjustment and Long-Run Equilibrium; A Computable Equilibrium Approach to Environmental Economics*, Springer Verlag.

Treadway, A. B. (1974) The globally optimal flexible accelerator, *Journal of Economic Theory* **7** 17–39.

Whalley, J. and Wigle, R. (1991) Cutting CO_2 emissions: The effects of alternative policy approaches, *The Energy Journal* **12**, 109–124.

Willett, K. (1985) Environmental quality standards: A general equilibrium analysis, *Managerial and Decision Economics* **6**, 41–49.

8. Regulating the Farmers' use of Pesticides in Sweden

ING-MARIE GREN
Beijer International Institute of Ecological Economics, Stockholm, Sweden

1. Introduction

Since the earliest times, farmers have used pest management practices which were largely biological in nature, involving the use of crop rotation and timing of planting. The introduction during the 1940s of chemical pesticides led to a rapid dissemination of the biological methods in the postwar era. During this period, farmers experienced high increases in yield due to the new production technologies. However, at the beginning of the 1960s attention was drawn to the negative environmental impact of the use of pesticides (DDT) by, among others, Rachel Carson in Silent Spring (1962). Today, no one in the industrialized countries should have any doubt about the disadvantages of the overuse of pesticides. The main purpose of this paper is therefore to find the minimum cost for reducing the environmental damage caused by the use of pesticides. Another related purpose is to compare the performance of different policy instruments aimed at implementing a certain pesticide reduction.

The distorted market for agricultural products is one important reason for the excess use of inputs. Due to subsidies on outputs, farmers' use of inputs is higher than it would otherwise have been, see, e.g., Nutzinger (1992). A decrease in the prices of outputs and/or an increase in the price of pesticides would thus have a negative impact on the use of pesticides. In this paper, increases in the prices of pesticides are considered.

It is, however, a well-known fact that the existence of risk plays a role in production decisions. One important factor is the stochastic nature of weather conditions. This is the main source of risk in many industrialized countries where prices of outputs and inputs are determined by negotiations at a national level. Pesticides are perceived to be a risk-reducing mechanism and are therefore partly used for insurance purpose, see, e.g., Moffit (1986), Antle (1988). Another way of reducing the use of pesticides is then to improve the insurance system, which is the second type of measure included in this study.

So far, we have considered only measures reducing the farmers' use of pesticides.

Hans Opschoor and Kerry Turner (eds), Economic Incentives and Environmental Policies, 153–173.

The damaging effects caused by the use of pesticides can also be reduced by mitigating the impact of pesticide residues on surrounding fields. One way to do this is by the use of the so-called eco-technologies which make use of nature's self-regulating capacity (Mitsch and Jörgensen, 1991). The third type of measure investigated in this study is another way in which residue transfer can be contained in protection zones around crop fields, i.e., marginal lands along the borders of the fields are left untreated.

It should be noted that a switch from current practice in agriculture to a agricultural system which does not depend on either chemical fertilizers or pesticides would require the application of many types of eco-technologies. In this paper, however, such a large-scale technological change is not considered. Instead, only relatively small changes within the current system are considered. It should also be noted that when evaluating alternative controls on the use of pesticides only short-term impacts are calculated.

Given that we have estimates of cost functions for all of the candidate type of mitigation measures, a cost efficient allocation of pesticide reductions among these measures can be found. It would then be possible to choose the most appropriate policy instrument or combination of alternative policy instruments. Three different policy instruments are compared in this chapter; command and control, charges and a permit market. It should be noted that there is an extensive literature on this topic encompassing a range of evaluation criteria; see e.g., Bohm and Russel (1985) and Tietenberg (1984). The comparison of policy instruments in this paper is, however, very brief and the only criteria considered are cost effectiveness and income distribution effects.

The paper is organized as follows. First, a brief description of farmers' use of pesticides and its environmental impact is given. Then, the farmer's choice of pesticides is modelled. The next section contains estimates of the costs of the three different types of measures. In Section 5, the minimum costs for alternative pesticide reductions are calculated and different policy instruments are compared. The paper ends with a summary.

2. Use of Pesticides and Environmental Impacts

In the introduction, the term pesticides has been used to cover all types of pesticides. In practice, hundreds of different types exist. They are usually divided into three classes; herbicides, fungicides and insecticides. Since their introduction in the 1940s the total use of pesticides has increased. However, the composition of pesticides has changed. The use of herbicides accounts for the largest increases, see Figure 1. It should, however, be noted that during this period not only has the use composition of pesticides changed but also their qualities. Further, changes in

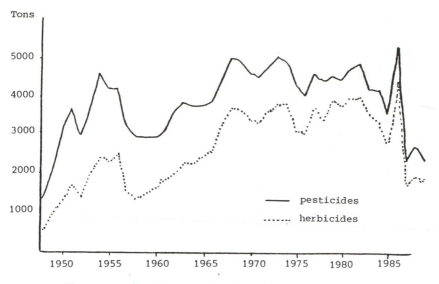

Fig. 1. Use of pesticides and herbicides in Sweden, 1948–1989.

application technologies have influenced the use of pesticides. Smaller doses are now required in order to obtain the same effect. The quantities in Figure 1 are measured in the so-called active substances. See Appendix for a description of the data.

Since the 1960s the increasing degree of social concern has resulted in a reduction in the use of damaging pesticides in Sweden. This has been achieved by the banning of the most toxic types of chemical agents such as DDT. In the beginning of the 1980s the government declared that its aim was to reduce the use of pesticides by 50%. This target was supposed to be achieved by a combination of command and control, i.e., the banning of certain agents, and the use of economic instruments. A charge on pesticides equivalent to 10–20% of the input price was therefore introduced in 1985. The effect of this combination of policies can be seen from Figure 1. In 1984 there was a sudden increase in the use of pesticides, which was probably due to hoarding. The use of pesticides then declined drastically in 1985 and it seemed as if the government's declared objective of reducing the use of pesticides by 50% was achieved. In 1990, the government once again announced its intention to decrease the use of pesticides by 50%. An investigation committee was therefore appointed, the aim of which was to find the most appropriate measures to achieve this reduction. The results of this investigation have not yet been presented.

Today, the total cost of using pesticides ranges between 5% and 10% of total variable costs. The variation depends on type of plant and on region. In general, the cultivation of oil seeds (especially the spring varieties) is critically dependent on insecticides and the cultivation of grain requires the application of all types of pesticides. The use of pesticides is more intensive in the south of Sweden than in the northern regions due to differences in climate and cultivation systems.

Herbicides are used to stop weeds from maturing and thereby increasing the seed population in the soil. The application of herbicides in one season affects the growth conditions for several subsequent seasons. The reason for this is that if herbicides are not applied during one season the seed bank in the soil increases which implies that it becomes more difficult to curb the spread of weeds in subsequent seasons. In practice, farmers apply herbicides routinely every year.

Fungicides and insecticides are applied when it is recognized that the weather conditions are such that there is an enhanced risk of pest attacks leading to significant yield damage. Ideally, the farmer has the knowledge and equipment necessary to apply the right dose at the right time. In practise, however, it is not likely that the farmer has the appropriate amount of knowledge or the right equipment. Further, it is often the case that insecticides are applied during windy conditions. It should be noted that there is a wind drift problem even under favourable weather conditions. About 0.1–0.5% of the applied pesticides are found in areas located at least 100 m from the treated fields (Fogelfors *et al.*, 1991).

The negative impacts of pesticides can be classified into three categories (Fogelfors *et al.*, 1991):

- Health risks associated with the treatment and transport of pesticides
- Residues of pesticides in drinking water and food
- Direct and indirect impact on the ecosystems

At the global level, about 20 000 people are killed every year when working with pesticides. However, most of these deaths occur in the third world where there is very little or no information on the proper handling of pesticides. In Sweden, some evidence for an increase in the risk of cancer was detected related to the types of pesticides and handling procedure which occurred during the 1950s. Better education and information on the safe handling of pesticides in recent years has meant that the associated health risks should now be almost eliminated (Fogelfors, 1991).

According to tests of surface and ground water done for several regions in Sweden, the maximum residues limit (MRL) of 0.1 $\mu/1$ has not been exceeded, except for the island of Gotland (Lantbruksstyrelsen, 1991). Residues above the MRL level are, however, found in crops and vegetables. Most of the unacceptable levels of residues are found in imported food (Anderson *et al.*, 1991). The content of synthetic pesticides in food compared to the 'natural' pesticides is thought to be relatively low (Fogelfors, 1991).

Pesticides residues can be transported to ecosystems outside the treated fields in three ways: via evaporation, water and wind. Wind drift is considered to be the most significant transfer function for pesticides (Fogelfors, 1991). The negative impacts of pesticides on surrounding ecosystems have been documented in several studies; see, e.g., Hansen *et al.*, 1991 and Lankbruksstyrelsen, 1991. It has been shown that the biodiversity in areas close to treated fields has decreased and that certain species have been brought close to extinction. Further, the specific characteristics of several types of species have changed such that their resistance to pesticides has increased. It is feared that these effects will be more damaging in the future when new types of pesticides are introduced which are more specialized than those of today (Fogelfors, 1991).

Our brief survey has indicated that the main negative impacts of pesticides are on the ecosystems surrounding the treated fields. The point of departure in this study is therefore that the aim of pesticide control policies is to improve the natural environment. This can be achieved in two ways; (i) by a decrease in farmers' use of pesticides and (ii) by the establishment of protection zones, i.e., leaving about 5–10 m along the borders of the fields untreated.

3. The Farmer's Input Choice

Farmers' use of pesticides can be reduced in two ways; by increasing the price of pesticides and by improving the insurance system. The costs of reducing the use of pesticides by an increase in the input price are measured as the associated decrease in the expected utility of profits. The cost of improving the insurance system is measured by means of the risk premium. The risk premium is defined as the amount of money a farmer is willing to pay for a guaranteed given expected level of income.

It is assumed that the farmer makes his decision on the use of pesticides prior to any information on pest attacks. This is true for herbicides which accounts for about 50% of the total expenditures on pesticides. The application of insecticides and fungicides should be applied after the forecasted onset of weather conditions which favour pest attacks. Thus, the assumption of pure uncertainty seems to be irrelevant. However, it is doubtful whether or not the farmers have the necessary knowledge to apply insecticides and fungicides properly (Fogelfors, 1991). In the following analysis, the farmer's use of insecticides and fungicides are therefore treated in the same way as herbicide application.

In order to determine the relevant cost functions, the farmer's decision problem is formulated as follows. The prices of inputs and the output are given to the farmers. On the basis of a production function $Q = f(X, Z, \Theta)$, where $X = [X^1, X^2, \ldots, X^h]$ is a vector of variable inputs, $Z = [Z^1, Z^2, \ldots, Z^j]$ is a vector of fixed factors of production and Θ is the random parameter, the farmer is assumed to choose variable inputs such that the expected utility of profits is maximized according to

$$\text{Max } E[U(\pi)], \qquad X \qquad\qquad\qquad\qquad\qquad\qquad\qquad\qquad (1)$$

where E is the expectation operator and $\pi = pQ - \Sigma_i v^i X^i$ is the random benefits minus the total cost for variable inputs. The cost of reducing the use of an input by increasing the input price from v^{i0} to v^{i1} is measured as the associated decrease in expected utility of profits, C^i, according to (2)

$$C^i = \int_{v^{i1}}^{v^{i0}} \partial E[U(\pi)]/\partial v^i \, dv^i, \qquad\qquad\qquad\qquad\qquad (2)$$

where v^i is the price of input. However, the cost as defined in (2) is expressed in utilities. In order to find a measurement of the welfare change in money terms, the certainty equivalent is required. The certainty equivalent, CE, corresponds to the expected profits minus the risk premium. The risk premium or insurance cost is defined as the maximum amount of money the farmer would be willing to pay in order to obtain a given profit with certainty instead of facing the risk. It then follows that R satisfies

$$U(E[\pi] - R) = E[U(\pi)]. \qquad\qquad\qquad\qquad\qquad\qquad (3)$$

Thus, the utility of obtaining π with certainty less the risk premium, or insurance cost, equals the utility of the risky project. The certainty equivalent, CE, is then equal to

$$CE = E[\pi] - R = U^{-1}(E[U(\pi)]). \qquad\qquad\qquad\qquad\qquad (4)$$

The certainty equivalent is the amount of money that the farmer requires if he or she was insured against the risk. Since CE is a welfare measure in money terms, choosing X to maximize CE is the same as maximizing $E[U(\pi)]$ as long as U^{-1} is positive.

Note that $E[\pi] = p\Omega - \Sigma_i v^i X^i$, where $\Omega = E[Q]$. The first-order condition for maximizing CE can then be written as

$$\partial CE/\partial X^i = p\Omega_x - v^i - R_x = 0. \qquad\qquad\qquad\qquad\qquad (5)$$

where subscripts denote partial derivatives. Note that if the risk premium is independent of X^i, the input choice problem would be the same for a risk-neutral and a risk-averse farmer, i.e., the expected value of the marginal product is set equal to the factor price. However, if the choice of input affects the risk premium, i.e., $R_x \neq 0$, the optimal choice of X^i would be higher (lower) than in the risk-neutral case for R_x is negative (positive). Following Pope and Kramer (1979), the input is defined as marginally risk-increasing (reducing) if the risk-averse firm uses less (more) of it than the risk-neutral firm. Thus, for our purpose, an input is defined as risk-decreasing when $R_x < 0$.

By applying the envelope theorem to (4), a money measure of the cost for reducing the use of pesticides by increasing the price from v^{i0} to v^{i1} is found, $C^{i\prime}$, which is expressed as

$$C^{i\prime} = \int_{v^{i0}}^{v^{i1}} - (X^i + R_v)\, dv^i \qquad (6)$$

Thus, the cost of reducing the use of pesticides by increasing the price from v^{01} to v^{10} is divided into two parts: the value of the decrease in yield and the change in the risk premium. The cost $C^{i\prime}$ is calculated by means of estimated pesticide demand functions, which is carried out in Section 4.

A measurement of R is found by a second-order Taylor expansion of the utility function. The risk premium can then be expressed as

$$R = -(U''/2U')\, \text{Var}(\pi) \qquad (7)$$

Note that $R = g(p, v, \Theta)$. The sign of R_x is determined by the Arrow-Pratt measure of absolute risk aversion, $\text{AP} = (-U''/U')$, and by the production risk which is measured as $\text{Var}(\pi)$. The derivative of R with respect to X^i is

$$R_x = 1/2((\partial \text{AP}/\partial \pi)(\partial \pi/\partial X^i)\, \text{Var}(\pi) + (\partial\, \text{Var}(\pi)/\partial X^i)\text{AP}) \qquad (8)$$

According to (8), X^i is a risk reducing factor of production when the first term is negative and when the variance in profits is decreasing in X^i. A reduction in the variance will then reduce the use of X^i, see e.g., Pope and Kramer (1979). An improvement of the insurance system which reduces the variance in income then implies a reduction in the use of pesticides. The associated insurance cost, C^R, for reducing the use of pesticides by increasing the price from v^{i0} to v^{i1} is measured as

$$C^R = \int_{v^{i0}}^{v^{i1}} R_v\, dv^i \qquad (9)$$

A measurement of R_v is found by means of econometric methods which are described and applied in Section 4.

4. Estimation of Costs for Different Measures

In this section, the results from the calculations of cost functions for different measures reducing the use of pesticides are presented. Changes in producer surplus due to increases in the prices of pesticides are measured by means of pesticide demand functions. A measurement of the cost of insurance is found by estimating the Arrow-Pratt measurement of absolute risk aversion.

It should be noted that the econometric estimates of these two types of regression equations are based on quite different data sets. Since prices of inputs and outputs are the same everywhere in Sweden, time-series data are needed to estimate the pesticide demand functions. However, the quality of pesticides have changed rapidly so time-series data do not measure the same inputs in all time periods. Since times-series data on prices of inputs and outputs are not required to estimate risk attitudes, the disadvantage with time-series data can be avoided. Cross-section data for all counties in Sweden are then used to estimate risk attitudes.

When estimating the cost of creating protection zones engineering data is used. These data are based on field experiments carried out at the Swedish University of Agricultural Sciences.

Pesticide Demand Functions

As mentioned in the introduction of this paper, different types of pesticides are used for quite different purposes. In this section, demand functions are therefore estimated for three different types of pesticides; herbicides, insecticides and fungicides. The specification of the regression equations is based on eq. (2).

It should be noted that the use of the different types of pesticides may be interrelated. For example, the use of herbicides may be positively related to the demand for both insecticides and fungicides. The cross effects between these inputs must therefore be accounted for. Other variable factors of production included in the regression equations are labour and nitrogen fertilizers. The supply of land is considered as a fixed factor of production. The regression equations are similar for all types of pesticides. The demand equation for herbicides, H, is expressed as

$$H = f(k^H, k^F, k^I, g, w, p, A) \tag{10}$$

where k^H = price of herbicides, k^F = price of fungicides, k^I = price of insecticides, p = weighted price of outputs, g = price of nitrogen fertilizers, w = wage and A = supply of land. A time variable, T, was included in order to account for the monotonic change in technology. The same variables are included in the regression equations for insecticides and fungicides, I and F respectively.

In order to account for correlation in disturbances between the three equations, they were estimated jointly by using the SUR-estimator (Seemingly Unrelated Regressions). The estimation period is 1948–1989. The functions were assigned a logarithmic form. The estimation results are presented in Table 1. Numbers within parentheses denote t-statistics.

According to the results presented in Table 1, the own-price elasticities for all pesticides are negative and significantly different from zero. The results indicate that

Table 1. Regression results for pesticide demand functions

	C	k^H	k^I	k^F	g	w	p	A	T	R	DW
Herbicides	4.79	−0.93	0.03	0.23	−0.05	0.52	0.01	0.01	0.46	0.87	1.38
	(3.01)	(8.00)	(0.58)	(3.31)	(0.22)	(3.16)	(0.09)	(0.93)	(7.04)		
Insecticides	5.40	−0.37	−0.52	0.11	0.76	−0.23	0.04	−0.02	0.05	0.86	2.05
	(2.02)	(1.93)	(4.06)	(0.94)	(1.94)	(0.80)	(0.57)	(0.91)	(0.46)		
Fungicides	2.02	−0.31	−0.01	−0.39	1.07	0.11	−0.02	−0.01	0.42	0.79	1.95
	(1.24)	(2.59)	(0.13)	(5.32)	(4.41)	(0.65)	(0.33)	(0.92)	(6.47)		

nitrogen fertilizers and insecticides and fungicides are substitutes. This is not in accordance with expectations since in general an increased use of nitrogen makes the crops more sensitive to attacks of insects and fungi, thereby increasing the demand for fungicides and insecticides.

The estimated cross-price coefficients between insecticides and fungicides are not significant and the levels are relatively low. The cross-price coefficients of herbicides are significant but not symmetrical with respect to sign. In the calculations of costs presented in Section 5 therefore only the own-price elasticities are used. It should be noted that the own-price elasticities presented in Table 1 are comparatively high in terms of the results from other studies, such as Dubgaard (1987) and Johnsson (1991). A sensitivity analysis is therefore carried out in Section 5.

During the estimation period, there has been a rapid change in the qualities of different pesticides. Part of this effect is accounted for by the time variable. However, if, as seems to be the case, the change has been more rapid during the last 10–20 years the estimated parameters may not be stable over the entire time period.

A Chow-test was undertaken for each of the regression equations in order to test for stability in the parameters. Estimation of the regression equations was therefore undertaken for two sub-periods 1948–1968 and 1969–1989. According to the results of the Chow-test, the hypothesis confirming stability in the parameters during 1948–1989 could not be rejected for any regression equation. The estimated own-price elasticities presented in Table 1 will therefore be used in Section 5 where total costs for different pesticide reductions are calculated.

Estimations of Risk Attitudes and Risk Premium

Following Antle (1988), the moment-based approach is used to estimate risk attitudes and to measure the risk premium. All analysis in this section is to a large extent based on Antle (1988). The farmer's objective function is then specified as a function of the moments of the random variables in the utility function according to

$$EU[\pi] = u[\mu^1, \mu^2], \tag{11}$$

where μ^1 and μ^2 are the first two moments of the profit function, i.e., the mean and the variance. The first-order condition for maximization of expected utility of profits with respect to X^i is

$$\partial EU/\partial X^i = (\partial u/\partial \mu^1)(\partial \mu^1/\partial X^i) + (\partial u/\partial \mu^2)(\partial \mu^2/\partial X^i) = 0, \tag{12}$$

which can be written as

$$\partial \mu^1/\partial X^i + r(\partial \mu^2/\partial X^i) = 0, \tag{13}$$

where $r = (\partial u/\partial \mu^2)/(u/\partial \mu^1)$. It is assumed that the distribution of r in the population can be written as

$$r = \beta + \phi \tag{14}$$

where ϕ is the error term. The regression equation for the estimates of risk attitudes is then based on (13) and (14), and is written as

$$D_1 = -\beta D_2 + \sigma, \tag{15}$$

where σ is the error term, $D_1 = \partial \mu^1/\partial X^i$ and $D_2 = \partial \mu^2/\partial X^i$. Given a certain specification of the production function, which is estimated below, data on the variables D_1 and D_2 are obtained from the observed data.

In order to interpret r and consequently β it is assumed that expected utility can be expressed as a second-order Taylor expansion of the utility function.

$$E[U] = U[\mu^1] + U''(\mu^1)\mu^2/2. \tag{16}$$

Differentiation of (16) with respect to μ^2 and μ^1 gives

$$\partial E[U]/\partial \mu^2 = U''(\mu^1)/2, \tag{17}$$

$$\partial E[U]/\partial \mu^1 = U'(\mu^1) + U'''(\mu^1)\mu^2/2 = E[U'(\mu^1)]. \tag{18}$$

Thus, r in Equation (13) can be written as

$$r = U''(\mu^1)/2E[U'(\mu^1)]. \tag{19}$$

This measure of r comes very close to the Arrow-Pratt (AP) measure of absolute risk aversion, $-U''/U'$. Using $E[U'(\mu^1)]$ as a first-order approximation of U', -2β can be interpreted as the AP measure of absolute risk aversion. The risk premium is then calculated as

$$R = \beta \mu^2. \tag{20}$$

When calculating the cost for an insurance system it is assumed that the absolute risk aversion is constant in profits. When inserting (20) into (9) the estimated insurance cost for a certain reduction in the use of pesticides is expressed as

$$C^R = \int_{v^{i1}}^{v^{i0}} \beta(\partial\mu^2/\partial v^i) \; dv^i. \tag{21}$$

In order to find measurements of D_1 and D_2 in (15), a production function must be estimated. The data used for the estimation of a production function and of risk attitudes are cross-sectional, and include observations for all 24 Swedish counties, for the years 1989 and 1990. During this short period there should not have been any significant changes in the qualities of different pesticides. However, the counties are very different with respect to soil fertility and farm sizes. In general, these differences are correlated such that large farms operate on fertile soils. The observations were therefore divided into three groups according to the farm sizes as measured by the holdings of land. Two dummy variables were therefore added to the production function.

The OLS estimator was used to estimate several specifications of the production function where, among other things, a distinction between pesticides was made which was identical to that used when estimating the demand equations. The results were however poor. In most of the estimates, the result failed to show a positive marginal product for the pesticides. A simple functional form was therefore chosen, which resulted in

ln Y = −25.4 + 0.76 ln X + 1.20 ln N + 1.74 ln L + 1.77 ln A −
     (−1.43) (2.29)   (4.03)   (0.73)   (1.03)

−0.08 ln P·ln N − 0.15 ln L·ln A − 0.66 DUM1 − 0.29 DUM2 +
  (−1.91)   (−0.72)   (−2.95)   (−1.97)

+0.20 DUM3
  (0.29)

where Y = weighted output including wheat, barley, ray, oats and oil plants where the output prices serve as weights, X = pesticides, N = nitrogren, L = labour, A = area of land, DUM1 = dummy farm size 20–40 ha, DUM2 = dummy farm size < 20 ha, DUM3 = dummy for the year 1990. Numbers within parentheses denote t-statistics.

When estimating risk attitudes it is obvious from Equations (14) and (15) that the error term in (15) is related to the dependent variable. The instrumental variable estimator is therefore used to estimate this equation. Output is used as an instrument. The estimation result is

D_1 = −0.000015 D_2
   (6.42)

Although the regression coefficient is negative its value is too low to reject the hypothesis that farmers are risk-neutral. When this estimated value of β is inserted in Equation (20) the calculated value of the relative risk premium, i.e., the risk premium as a percentage of profits from crop production, is only 0.5%. This result is surprising since the empirical results from several studies indicate that farmers are risk averse; see e.g., Lin *et al.* (1974) and Moscardi *et al.* (1981). According to the empirical results in Antle (1988), the farmers' use of insecticides is influenced by their risk averse attitude.

It should be noted that the estimation of risk attitudes in the above mentioned studies are based on observations of individual farmers. The data used in this study is on a county level and can therefore be interpreted as representing the average farmer in each county. The wide range of input rates between farmers that may exist is probably not captured by the data used here. Another reason for the low value of the risk premium may be that the aggregate of pesticides is used as an independent variable. As mentioned in Section 2, different types of pesticides are used for different purposes. A division between herbicides, insecticides and fungicides might have changed the result. But, as mentioned above, the regression results of the production function were very poor when such a division was carried out. Because of the results from the risk attitudes estimation analysis, the measure involving a decrease in production risk is not included in the calculations of the total costs for pesticide reductions, see Section 5.

Costs for Protection Zones

In Sweden and in several other countries field experiments have been carried out for different types of protection zones. Swedish field studies have been undertaken involving two types of protection zones; fixed and variable border zones (Lankbruksstyrelsen, 1991). A fixed zone implies that the areas left untreated remain constant and a variable zone changes its dimensions according to its location. For both types of zones there are three kinds of costs; value of reduced yield, increased cost for controlling pests and increased cost of harvesting. These costs vary for herbicides, insecticides and fungicides. According to results from field experiments, the cost corresponding to a reduction in yield is highest for all pesticides and accounts for at least 60% of total costs.

The cheapest type of border zone is the variable zone, the average cost of which amounts to SEK 800/ha border zone (1 ECU = 9.01 SEK, Jan. 18, 1994). It is then assumed that the border zone corresponds to 5% of the arable land. If it is further assumed that the use of pesticides is reduced by the same percentage, the constant marginal costs for protection zones correspond to the following costs for reducing the use of different pesticides: SEK 127/kg herbicides, 222/kg insecticides and 80/kg fungicides. The cost functions for protection zones used in the next section are thus linear.

5. Cost Efficiency and Farmers' Income Reductions

There is an extensive literature, theoretical and empirical, on the comparison of policy instruments; see e.g., Baumol and Oates (1971), Tietenberg (1984), Bohm and Russel (1985), and Opschoor (1990). Common criteria of comparison are cost efficiency, technological development, income distribution effects and certainty in reaching the target level. In the empirical literature the costs of a system based on economic instruments have often been compared with the costs of a command and control system. It has then been shown that the efficiency losses, costs in excess of the minimum cost, of a quota system can be very high (Tietenberg, 1984). Sometimes income distribution effects have been included as a criterion of comparison and a general result is that the regulated firms' income reductions are highest under a charge system. In this section, the quota, charge and permit market systems are compared with respect to cost efficiency and farmers' income reductions.

Because of the results presented in Section 4, the measure involving an improved insurance system is excluded. The measures included when calculating costs are therefore pesticide reductions under current production technology and the creation of protection zones. The optimal allocation of these measures among different pesticides occurs where their marginal costs are equal. The minimum cost and the allocation of pesticide reductions depend on the required level of total reduction. Thus, in the first part of this section a cost curve is calculated. The cost curve shows the minimum cost for different reductions in the total use of pesticides. Next, it is assumed that the objective of the environmental agency is to reduce the use of pesticides by 50% which corresponds to the declaration made by the government in 1990. Different policy instruments aiming at achieving this objective are then compared. The policy instruments analyzed are the quota, charge and permit market systems. All values presented refer to 1990.

It should be noted that when calculating costs it is assumed that the environmental damage of all types of pesticides are the same. In practice, however, it is most likely that the environmental impacts differ across different pesticide types. It is further assumed that the environmental damage of one unit of pesticide is the same regardless of where in Sweden it is deposited. However, the damage is likely to vary between regions due to differences in application technologies and climate. A third critical assumption concerns the 'translation' of the creation of protection zones into pesticide reductions. The corresponding pesticide reduction is proportional to the average application rate, which corresponds to 5% of total use of pesticide prior to any regulation. Note that it is thus assumed that the environmental improvement of 5% reduction in the use of pesticides is the same as the creation of a corresponding scale of protection zones. All these assumptions are questionable but unfortunately unavoidable since there exist no measurements of the differences in the environmental damage which can be used for the calculations of costs.

Minimum Costs for Alternative Pesticide Reductions

The minimum costs for different reductions in the use of pesticides are found by solving the following non-linear programming problem.

$$\underset{X^{ig}}{\text{Max}} \quad \Sigma_i \Sigma_g \ C^{ig}(X^{ig})$$

$$\text{s.t.} \quad \Sigma_i \Sigma_g \ X^{ig} \geq X^* \tag{22}$$
$$X^{ig} \leq X^{ig'}$$

where $C^{ig}(X^{ig})$ represent cost functions for the different measures, $g = 1, 2$ are the reduction technologies; pesticide reduction and creation of protection zones and $i = 1, 2, 3$ are the three types of pesticides. The required reduction in the total use of pesticides is X^*, $X^{ig'}$ is the maximum possible reduction by measure ig. Six types of measures are included; reductions in the use of the three types of pesticides and creation of protection zones for the same three types of pesticides. The cost functions for reductions in the use of pesticides are calculated by integrating the inverse of the demand functions estimated in Section 4. The cost functions for creation of protection zones are linear as described in Section 4.

A cost curve showing the minimum cost for different reductions in the total use of pesticides is found by solving (22) for different values of X^*. It should be noted that the cost curve shows the reductions in the social net value of yield, i.e., the yield is measured at world market prices. The result is presented in Figure 2.

As mentioned in Section 2, in 1990 the government announced an objective to reduce the total use of pesticides by 50%. According to the curve in Figure 2, the associated minimum cost amounts to 94 million SEK. However, the government did not include the possibility of creating protection zones. The cost of reducing the use of pesticides by 50% without creation of protection zones would amount to 126 million SEK. Thus, by including the possibility of reducing the impact of pesticides on the environment via protection zones, the total cost is reduced by 25%.

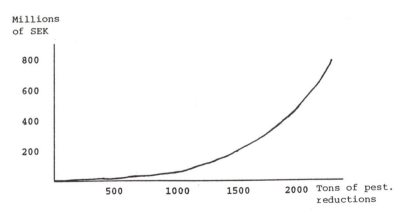

Fig. 2. Minimum costs for alternative pesticide reductions.

Comparison of Policy Instruments

All policy instruments compared are assumed to reduce the use of pesticides by 50%, i.e., by 1195 tons. In order to compare their performance with respect to cost efficiency and income distribution effects certain assumptions concerning the design of the policy instruments must be made. Thus, before presenting the results, a description of the policy instruments is given.

A quota system is defined here as a system where each farmer is allowed to use 55% of his previous application of pesticides prior to the regulation. The reduction requirement for each farmer is then assumed to be the following: every farmer is supposed to create protection zones which correspond to a 5% reduction in his use of pesticides; then, each farmer has to reduce the use of pesticides by 45% of the level used prior to the regulation.

However, in order to calculate the costs of such a quota system, estimates of pesticide demand functions for every farmer would be required. Such estimates are not available. Instead, it is assumed that the use of each type of pesticide, i.e., herbicides, insecticides and fungicides, is reduced by 45%.

Under a charge system, an efficient charge is implemented. This charge is found from the marginal cost curve. The marginal cost for different pesticide reductions is obtained from the dual values of (22). The marginal cost curve is shown in Figure 3.

When the aim is to reduce the use of pesticides by 50%, i.e., 1195 tons, the charge should amount to SEK 257/kg pesticide. This level of the charge implies an increase in the price of herbicides, fungicides and insecticides by 97%, 99%, and 17% respectively.

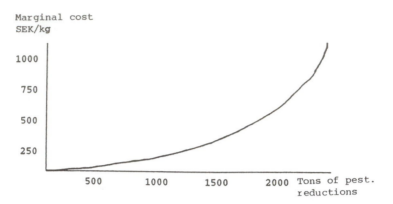

Fig. 3. Marginal costs for alternative pesticide reductions.

However, if these price increases are implemented without any consideration for the creation of protection zones, such zones will not be created. The farmers must have an economic incentive in order to create the zones. If such an incentive is not implemented the final reduction in the use of pesticides will be 45% and not the required 50%. It is therefore assumed that the farmers receive a subsidy when they create protection zones. In order to obtain a cost-efficient outcome, the level of the subsidy should correspond to the level of the efficient charge, i.e., SEK 257/kg.

A permit market is a combination of the charge system and a quota system. The similarity with the quota system is that the total reduction in the use of pesticides is determined in physical terms. Permits to use pesticides which do not exceed the total required level, i.e., 1195 tons, are then distributed among the farmers. It is assumed that these permits are distributed so that each farmer receives permits to use 50% of the pesticide used prior to the regulation. The difference with a quota system is that these permits can be traded among the farmers. A permit market is then established where the equilibrium price of permits is determined. It is assumed that the permit market is efficient which implies that the equilibrium permit price equals the efficient charge; see e.g., Tietenberg (1984).

A further assumption under a permit market system is that the initial permits corresponding to 50% of the use of pesticides prior to the regulation are distributed free of charge. The farmers receive additional permits conditional upon their creation of protection zones. Given all these assumptions concerning the design of the policy instruments, the results of the calculations of costs and farmers' income reductions are presented in Table 2.

Note that the reductions in yields due to a decrease in the use of pesticides are evaluated at the world market prices when estimating net value of yield losses and at the prices paid to the farmers when estimating farmers' income reductions.

Table 2. Net value of yield losses and farmers' income reductions different policy instruments, millions of SEK

	Quota	Charge	Permit market
Net value of of yield losses	138	94	94
Income reductions	184	440	133
% of total income	5	11	3

The prices paid to the farmers are on average about 25% higher than the world market prices.

Under both the charge and permit market systems a pesticide reduction by 50% is obtained at minimum costs. The costs of a quota system are almost 40% higher due to the efficiency losses under this system. The income losses for the farmers are highest under a charge system and correspond to a reduction in total income, including income from animal and crop production, of 11%. The reduction in farmers' incomes is smallest under a permit market system. It should however be noted that if the initial permits were distributed at the equilibrium permit price the reductions in incomes would be the same as under a charge system.

Sensitivity Analysis

It was mentioned in Section 4 that the estimated price elasticities of pesticides are high as compared to other studies. According to Dubgaard (1987) the price elasticity of herbicides is about −0.5 and results from Johnsson (1991) show that the price elasticity of insecticides is about −0.3. In both studies the price elasticity of fungicides is close to the result of this study, i.e., about -0.4. It should however be noted that the results in Dubgaard (1987) and Johnsson (1991) are based on field experiments and not on farmers' actual behaviour.

However, the difference in price elasticities is large and a sensitivity analysis is therefore carried out in this study. The costs for different policy instruments are then estimated for values of price elasticities of herbicides and insecticides which correspond to half of values of price elasticities estimated in this study. Thus, the price elasticity of herbicides is assumed to be −0.47 and the price elasticity of insecticides is assumed to amount to −0.25. The social net value of reductions in yields and farmers' income reductions increases for all policy instruments, see Table 3.

The minimum cost for reducing the use of pesticides by 50% or 1195 tons of active substance increases by about 50% from 100 million SEK to 147 million SEK.

Table 3. Net value of yield losses and income farmers' income reductions when the price elasticities of herbicides and insecticides decrease by 50%, millions of SEK

	Quota	Charge	Permit market
Social net value of yield losses	197	147	147
Income reductions	258	858	196
% of total income	7	21	5

Since the costs for reducing the use of herbicides and insecticides are increased, farmers are assumed to adjust their use of fungicides to a greater extent.

The level of the charge is now SEK 553/kg active substance as compared to SEK 257/kg active substance when the price elasticities are higher. The income distribution effects, i.e., the farmers' reduction in incomes, under a charge system are thus higher, 21% as compared to 11%. The social net value of yield losses, i.e., when the yield is evaluated at the world market prices, increases by about 50% under all policy instruments.

Thus, this simple sensitivity analysis indicates that the income distribution effects of a charge system are quite sensitive to different levels of the price elasticities of herbicides and insecticides. The farmers' reductions in incomes are doubled when the price elasticities decrease by 50%. The impact under the quota and permit market systems is lower. The social net value of yield losses and income distribution effects then increase by about 50%.

6. Summary

The purpose of this chapter has been to estimate the costs for reducing farmers' use of pesticides. It was assumed that farmers partly use pesticides in order to avoid large income losses caused by pest attacks. Three different types of mitigation measures were then considered; i) reductions in the use of pesticides under current production technology, ii) improvement of the insurance system, and iii) creation of protection zones, i.e., marginal land along the borders left untreated. Different policy instruments designed to reduce the use of pesticides by 50% were then compared with respect to cost efficiency and farmers' income reductions.

In order to estimate the costs of the first two types of measures, econometric estimates of pesticide demand functions and risk attitudes were carried out. According to the results, the price elasticities for herbicides, insecticides and fungicides were -0.93, -0.52 and -0.39 respectively. Since the results from estimating risk attitudes did not verify the hypothesis that farmers are risk averse improvements of the insurance system were not included in the subsequent cost calculations and comparisons of policy instruments.

According to the results from the calculations of total costs, the minimum cost for reducing the use of pesticides by 50% was 94 million SEK, which correspond to 3% of farmers' total incomes. The creation of protection zones for all types of pesticides was included in the cost efficient solution. This so-called eco-technology was not mentioned in the government's advice issued to guide the appointed investigation. The results in this study indicate that the total cost of achieving a reduction corresponding to 50% of the current use of pesticides is decreased by 25% when this eco-technology is included.

Under the charge and permit market systems the required pesticide reduction was obtained at the minimum cost. The cost of a quota system was 40% higher than the costs of the charge and permit market systems. The farmers' income losses were highest under a charge system, 10% of total incomes; and lowest under a permit market system, 3%. According to the results of a sensitivity analysis, when the price elasticities of herbicides and insecticides are decreased by 50%, farmers' income losses under a charge system are doubled.

It should be noted that the farmers' income reduction under a permit market system is strongly dependent on the initial distribution of permits. In the analysis presented above the initial permits were assumed to be distributed free of charge. When the initial permits are distributed at the equilibrium permit price, the income losses under a permit market are the same as under a charge system. Another noteworthy factor concerns the limitations of the policy instruments included. If information on a proper treatment of pesticides is combined with the implementation of a quota, charge or permit market system, the costs and income losses under all these systems are probably reduced.

In this study we have not analysed the policy instruments with respect to their incentives to create fraud. If surrounding countries do not introduce any controls on pesticides it is relatively easy for Swedish farmers to buy pesticides at a lower price abroad. According to a theoretical comparison of profits from violating policy instruments, the incentives to violate a permit market system may be the smallest (Andréasson-Gren, 1992). The reason is that the occurrence of illegal use of an input affects the market clearing price of permits. This, in turn, may reduce the economic incentives to violate regulations of a permit market system.

Appendix: Description of the data

Time-series data:

Prices of inputs and outputs during 1948–1989 are found in the Yearbook of Agricultural Statistics.

Quantities of herbicides, insecticides and fungicides are measured in active substance. Measurements of active substances are available from 1975. The proportion of active substance of total quantities was therefore assumed to be the same during 1948–1974 and correspond to the proportion in 1975.

Quantities of nitrogen fertilizer, labour and arable land during 1948–1989 are found in the Yearbook of Agricultural Statistics.

Cross-section data:

Quantities of herbicides, insecticides and fungicides are given in active substance in 'Use of pesticides in agriculture', SM 9101 and 9102, Statistics Sweden.

Quantities of nitrogen fertilizer, arable land, labour and yields from wheat, grain, oats, ray and oil plants are found in Statistical Yearbook. Prices of crops in 1989 are used as weights when constructing the output index.

Acknowledgement

I am indebted to Hans Nutzinger, Hans Opschoor and to other members of the ESF Task Force II for their valuable comments. Comments from Karl-Göran Mäler, Henry Tulkens, Hans Andersson and Bertil Johnsson are also gratefully acknowledged.

References

Andersson, A., Pålsheden, H. and Bergh, T. (1991) Pesticide residues in fruits and vegetables – 1990, *National Food Administration*, Rapport 5, Uppsala.
Andréasson-Gren, I-M. (1992) Profits from violating controls on the use of a polluting input, *Environmental and Resource Economics* **2**, 1–11.
Antle, J. M. (1988) Pesticide policy, production risk, and producer welfare. An econometric approach to applied welfare economics, *Resources for the Future*, Washington, D. C.
Baumol, W. J. and Oates, W. (1971) The use of standards and prices for protection of the environment, *Swedish J. Economics* **73**, 42–54.
Bohm, P. and Russel, W. C. (1985) Comparative analysis of alternative policy instruments, in A. V. Kneese and J. L. Sweeney (eds), *Handbook of Natural Resource and Energy Economics*, Elsevier.

Dubgaard, A. (1987) Anvendelse of afgifter til regulering af pesticidforbruget, *Statens Jordbrugsökonomiske Institut*, Rapport 35.

Fogelfors, H., Johnsson, B., Pettersson, O and Petrini, F. (1991) Miljövänlig bekämpning i jordbruket – en diskussion av möjligheter och konsekvenser, Research paper. Department of Economics, The Swedish University of Agricultural Sciences, Uppsala.

Hansen, P. E. and Jörgensen, S. E. (1991) Introduction to environmental management, Elsevier.

Johnsson, B. (1991) Kostnader för begränsad användning av kemiska bekämpningsmedel, Research paper. Department of Economics, Swedish University of Agricultural Sciences, Uppsala.

Lantbruksstyrelsen (1991) Problemområden i yttre miljön vid kemisk bekämpning – Förslag till åtgärder, Rapport 1991: 2.

Lichtenberg, E., Parker D. D. and D. Zilberman (1988) Marginal analysis of welfare costs of environmental policies: The case of pesticide regulation, *American J. Agricultural Economics* **70**(4), 866–874.

Lin, W., Dean, G. W. and Moore, C. V. (1974) An empirical text of utility vs. profit maximization in agricultural production, *American J. Agricultural Economics* **5**.

Mitsch, W. J. and Jörgensen S. E. (1989) Ecological engineering, *An Introduction to Ecotechnology*. John Wiley & Sons.

Moffitt, L. J. (1986) Risk-efficient thresholds for pest control decisions, *J. Agricultural Economics*.

Moscardi, E. and de Janvrey J. E. (1981) Attitudes toward risk among peasants: An econometric approach, *American J. Agricultural Economics* **59**, 710–716.

Nutzinger, H. G. (1991) Economic instruments for environmental protection in agriculture: Some basic problems of implementation, Research paper, University of Kassel, Germany.

Oos┅┅oor, J. B. (1990) Environmental policy instruments – experiences with economic incentives, in ┅. Andersson and U. Svedin (eds), *Towards Ecologically Sustainable Economy*, Swedish Council for Planning and Coordination of Research, Report 906.

Pope, R. D. and Kramer, R. A. (1979) Production uncertainty and the factor demands for the competitive firm, *Southern Economic Journal* **60**, 425–435.

Tietenberg, T. H. (1984) Marketable emission permits in principle and practice, presented at the Economics of Energy Environmental Policies conference, Stockholm School of Economics.

9. Economic Instruments for Environmental Protection in Agriculture: Some Basic Problems of Implementation

HANS G. NUTZINGER
University of Kassel, Germany

1. Economic Instruments: Foundations, Classification and Implementation

Frequently, environmental policy is perceived as a problem of choice between different policy instruments. In this context, environmental policy instruments are sometimes subdivided, as a first approximation, into three broad, sometimes overlapping categories: *regulatory instruments, economic instruments* and *moral suasion.*

But before addressing the application of these different instruments, a more basic choice problem has to be resolved: *first*, it has to be decided which elements of the economic sphere are to be considered as constituent parts of the economic system,[1] and hence are a precondition of the economic process.[2] These constituent parts are not subject to economic evaluation but are determined on the basis of fundamental principles, such as preservation of human life and dignity or – in the case of insufficient knowledge – the precautionary principle (cf., Pearce, Turner, O'Riordan, 1992). For example, in the case of highly toxic and dangerous pollutants (such as PCPs) we have good reasons to exempt those elements from any economic evaluation and to forbid them outright.[3] The specification of those constituent parts of the economic system should not be regarded as part of the regulation process, but as a necessary element in the original problem formulation.

This leads to a *second* step: after the basic elements of the economic system have been properly defined – but only then – the question of the choice between different instruments of environmental policy arises in a meaningful sense.[4] Of course, the theoretical formulation (and the practical realization) of the economic system has its implicit impact on the economic process and the evaluations taking place within this process.

As our discussion of economic instruments will make clear, we have good arguments for preferring economic instruments to regulatory ones, if the institutional and legal order is reasonably specified by excluding, *inter alia*, imminent threats

Hans Opschoor and Kerry Turner (eds), Economic Incentives and Environmental Policies, 175–193.
© 1994 *Kluwer Academic Publishers. Printed in the Netherlands.*

to human life or nature.[5] But even then, in some cases (e.g., the transaction costs of implementing those economic instruments or problems of imperfect information)[6] practical considerations can militate against the use of economic instruments, not because there is an imminent threat to human life or nature, but because the costs of applying market-oriented instruments can sometimes be higher than the benefits accruing from the choices and the decentralized evaluations generated by those economic devices.[7] As we will see, both kinds of considerations have to be taken into account when we consider the implementation of economic instruments for environmental policy related to agriculture. Before doing that, we will look more closely into the three types of environmental policy instruments:

(1) The traditional instruments of environmental policy are of the *regulatory* or of the *administrative type, and they can best be described as*

> institutional measures aimed at directly influencing the environmental performance of polluters by regulating processes or products used, by abandoning or limiting the discharge of certain pollutants, and/or by restricting activities to certain times, areas etc., through licensing, setting of standards, zoning, etc. (Opschoor and Vos, 1989, p. 12).

Within the limits set by the regulatory instruments, utilisation of the environment is normally free of charge, whereas any transgression of the limits is considered to be a legal offence subject to judicial or administrative penalties. Therefore the polluter's room for manoeuvre is limited, and, above all, he is not directly confronted with prices for his use of the environment. In terms of comparative systems, this regime is very close to *central planning* (cf., Nutzinger, 1974, section III.2; 1988, section 3), at least as far as the utilization of the environment is concerned. Broadly speaking, the right to use environmental resources is not allocated according to each potential willingness to pay, but rather through devices of governmental *command and control.*

(2) In contrast to the first category, instruments are labeled *economic* if

> they affect estimates of costs and benefits of alternative actions open to economic agents, with the effect of influencing decision-making and behaviour in such a way that alternatives are chosen that lead to an environmentally more desirable situation than in the absence of the instrument (Opschoor and Vos, loc. cit.).

Within this broad category at least three different subdivisions have to be considered (relating to different theoretical or practical justifications):

(1) We speak of market-oriented instruments, such as taxes, charges, certificates (including the 'bubble' and the 'offset' policy practised in the US), liability rules etc. if they try to apply the economic 'polluter pays principle (PPP)' based on environmental damage costs.[8] In the language of welfare economics, these instruments aim at internalizing the negative externalities of production and/or consumption upon the environment.

(2) It is also possible to impose taxes or charges on the use of exhaustible resources, such as energy taxes, which try to telescope the future shortage of these limited resources into the present time by putting a 'surcharge' (user cost) on current prices. From the perspective of future generations, who are the prospective victims of today's excessive use of those resources, these taxes can also be seen as an application of the 'polluter pays principle' in a broader sense: in this case, the *user* has to pay.

(3) Commonly used *subsidies* are economic instruments only insofar as they influence the cost-benefit ratio of certain activities in the direction of a reduced use of the environment, but normally they cannot be regarded as an application of the 'polluter pays principle'.[9] Their practical justification lies in their function as a 'lubricant' to facilitate desired changes in economic behavior.

(3) A third category of instruments is *moral suasion*, whereby some political and public pressure is used in order to bring about a 'voluntary' change in the behavior of economic agents. Basically this involves the internalizing of

environmental awareness and responsibility into individual decision-making by applying pressure and/or persuasion either indirectly or directly (e.g., in negotiations aimed at 'voluntary' agreements or convenants between industry and governments, on environmental issues) (Opschoor and Vos, 1989, p. 13).

The moral suasion approach has characteristics in common with both the regulatory and the economic instruments as it uses the threat of possible regulations in order to bring about 'voluntary', more flexible settlements and behavioral changes, often supported by economic incentives and disincentives.

Whereas it is correct to state that regulatory instruments – in contrast to economic ones – do not directly encompass the use of the environment in prices, this does not mean that they will not affect costs. On the contrary, in general the costs of meeting the regulatory standards will *ceteris paribus* be higher than with economic instruments, as the standards affect all producers in the same way regardless of their specific abatement cost conditions. Therefore, whenever there are cost differences among producers, a desired average level of environmental quality will be achieved with higher costs as no individual trade-offs between costs and benefits of the use of the environment are allowed under a regulatory scheme.[10]

As noted above, this broad theoretical classification is less clear-cut in reality and very often instruments of environmental policy may combine elements of the regulatory, economic pricing and suasion approaches. We will not go deeper into the theoretical classifications and foundations (for this, see Endres (1985) and Opschoor and Vos (1989, chapters 2 and 3)).

2. The Basic Elements of the Agricultural 'Market' in European Countries

The question of the use of economic instruments in environmental policy can only be raised properly after a prior specification of the constituent parts of the economic system. Therefore, a brief look into specificities of the agricultural 'market' is needed.

In practically all European countries, and particularly in those within the European Community, agriculture is largely exempted from the normal market mechanism.[11] Usually, the following three types of arguments are raised in order to justify this market-constraint policy:

(1) Securing a stable food supply involves providing for basic human needs.
(2) Without a specific agricultural policy, farmers' incomes cannot be stabilized at a socially acceptable level.
(3) Agriculture does not only mean the production of food, but also implies the cultivation of landscape as a by-product.

Based on those general arguments, practical agricultural policy inside, but also outside the European Community, is generally characterized by a series of interventions and specific programs whereby agricultural prices have largely lost the function of harmonizing supply and demand, and have instead assumed the role of maintaining a socially acceptable level of farmers' incomes. This shift in the role of prices does not fit into the normal functioning of mixed market economies, and therefore it comes as no surprise that long sequences of specific measures, interventions and counter measures have had to be introduced without resolving the basic problem – the disequilibria on agricultural markets brought about by the agricultural policy of the European Community and most other OECD countries.

Guaranteeing agricultural prices in order to maintain a certain income level for farmers only makes sense if these prices are fixed above the market level; and this is exactly the case for numerous agricultural product prices within the European Community and also in non-EC countries such as Sweden, Austria and Switzerland. The consequences of this approach are obvious:

– International agricultural markets have to be protected against foreign competition via tariffs and/or import quotas.[12]
– As prices are guaranteed above the market level, there is a constant incentive for farmers to produce even more agricultural surpluses.
– These surpluses in turn absorb many financial and material resources for storage, transportation, processing for non-agricultural purposes, export subsidies, disposal as manure, etc.
– In order to limit resource misallocation related to those activities, production quotas (e.g., for milk or sugar-beets) are assigned to individual farmers,

and financial incentives for early retirement or for temporary non-use of arable land are also applied. In EC countries, for some products, such as cereals, milk and sugar, there is also an indirect taxation of production via the so-called 'joint responsibility charges'[14] which in turn decrease farmers' incomes without increasing consumer demand.

- As a consequence of this intensive overproduction, there is a corresponding excess use of inputs, fertilizers and pesticides which has caused serious negative effects on the environment, especially on soil and water.

To sum up: considered from a welfare economics viewpoint, relative prices in agriculture have ceased to reflect the relevant scarcities. High guaranteed prices tell the farmers that there is a high demand for their products (whereas, in fact, more and more surpluses are generated); production quotas, 'joint responsibility charges' and incentives for early retirement as well as temporary non-use of arable land (*land set-aside programs*) indicate the contrary: that there is in fact an excess supply of agricultural goods. This system of contradictory economic incentives has been widely criticized[14] and there are also attempts at explaining the 'political economy' which leads to this rather confusing situation. I do not want to go deeper into this discussion; instead I would like to focus on those characteristics of the regulated agricultural market which are relevant for the question: What kind of economic and regulatory instruments for environmental protection can be applied to the agricultural sector?

3. Applying Economic Instruments for Environmental Protection to the Agricultural Sector: A Perspective of Comparative Systems

The characteristics of the EC agricultural order belong more to the type of indirect central planning (through fixed non-market prices) than to normal market mechanisms; even some elements of direct physical planning are applied by means of a purchasing quota for some agricultural goods. The basic consequences of this situation are twofold: on the one hand, they affect the production processes in farming and, on the other hand, they influence the applicability and efficiency of economic instruments for environmental protection in agriculture:

(1) State-guaranteed prices for agricultural goods above the market level do not only provide incentives for surplus production, they also lead to a distortion between output and input prices, thereby inducing an excessive use of capital and material inputs, such as fertilizers and pesticides;[15] those inputs are relatively cheap compared with the artificially high commodity prices. This is one of the basic reasons why in most developed countries, capital and material intensive ways of farming have become dominant.[16]

(2) The theoretical idea of internalizing negative externalities via a Pigouvian
     tax does not make much sense in a world of seriously distorted commodity
     prices, especially if they are fixed for the sake of income stabilization.[17]

While it is true that even under conditions of central price planning – be it in specific
sectors, such as agriculture, or in whole economies – economic instruments can
be (and have been) applied,[18] they seem less suited to induce fundamental ecological improvements. The reason for this reduced efficiency of economic instruments
under a regime of fixed prices, and hence in most branches of agriculture in EC
and other European countries, can be briefly summarized as follows (cf., Nutzinger,
1991, p. 32):

– As centrally planned or exogenously fixed prices are largely biased and
   frequently inconsistent, the imposition of 'ecological duties' (e.g., through
   environmental taxes) onto these prices will be less effective than they should
   be because the underlying price base is already inappropriate.[19]
– Due to the misallocation of resources, based on distorted relative prices, there
   is a tendency for excessive application of material inputs, such as fertilizers
   and pesticides (with accompanying negative effects on air, soil, water and
   food).[20] This tendency is very difficult to counteract by means of specific input
   charges because the income losses generated by those taxes would provide
   strong incentives for further increases in state-guaranteed commodity prices
   which, in turn, would lead again to intensified application of pesticides and
   fertilizers. In order to counteract this tendency, specific compensation schemes
   which are not related to the (former) application of fertilizers have to be
   implemented.[21]
– If input and output prices are increased in the same proportion, we should
   not expect any significant change in agricultural output and in the use of
   non-labor inputs but an increase in farm income, as the costs of non-labor
   inputs are only a part of farmers' gross income. Hence, farmers' income can
   be held constant if the increase in input prices is higher than the increase in
   output prices. In this case, input use and physical output are both reduced,
   but the former reduction is greater than the latter. This effect will be dominant if the expenditure on a specific input is only a small fraction of
   farmers' gross income. Therefore, taxation of minor inputs is probably not
   an effective instrument to reduce agricultural production, whereas taxation
   of outputs will normally not lead to important reductions in the use of fertilizer inputs.[22]
– The effectiveness of economic instruments in agriculture will be further
   reduced by the fact that they have to be embedded in a very complex, if not
   confusing network of purchasing quotas, 'joint responsibility charges',
   economic incentives for temporary non-use of arable land (*land set-aside*

programs) and for early retirement of farmers, combined with a host of specific national, regional and sectoral programs.

This reduced efficiency of economic instruments for environmental protection in agriculture does not necessarily mean that regulatory instruments would do any better. The basic problem is agricultural surplus production in response to artificially high state-guaranteed prices. Therefore, economic instruments can be considered in a more favorable perspective if they seem suited for reducing both environmental destruction *and* agricultural overproduction. For this reason, we will now discuss the practical applicability of economic instruments for environmental protection in European agriculture taking the examples of a nitrogen tax, a pesticide tax and a specific water charge. Finally, I would like to summarize the preliminary results in order to indicate broadly the general direction in which the agricultural sector has to be restructured in order to meet both economic and ecological requirements.

4. Three Practical Examples

The Case of Nitrogen Taxes

As indicated in the previous section, agricultural policy in developed countries has contributed to intensive and spatially concentrated agricultural production. Relative to the high and guaranteed commodity prices, most material factors of production are too cheap; this is particularly true for yield-increasing inputs such as pesticides and nitrogen.

The excessive use of nitrogen is a particular problem in terms of contamination of ground water, rivers and lakes; the concentration of nitrate is contributing to the eutrophication of coastal waters and is thus posing a threat to the diversity of species. This intensive agricultural system while providing relatively cheap foodstuffs also contributes to an excessive separation of cattle breeding (including intensive livestock production, e.g., pigs and poultry) on the one hand and plant cultivation on the other hand, and thus supports an ecologically dangerous specialization between different farms and different regions; the accompanying tendency to monoculture is also threatening the bio-diversity in these areas. For example, liquid manure from cattle is frequently diverted away from its former disposal outlet in plant cultivation; instead, excessive 'free disposal' of liquid manure by cattle breeders concentrated in their small areas of land takes place and this effluent loading is added to by the increased application of artificial nitrogen fertilizers by plant cultivators. Moreover, the excessive use of nitrogen favors a simpler crop rotation which is less resistant to external influences and therefore more dependent upon an increased use of pesticides.

For these reasons, nitrogen could be regarded as the central input for an economic *and* ecological policy of cost internalization and of extensification in agriculture (cf., Binswanger *et al.*, 1990, section 2.3). Due to the decisive role of nitrogen fertilizers, a rise in their price may lead to a strong reduction in fertilizer application, much stronger than would be the case with lower product prices; furthermore, the resulting income losses will be relatively smaller.[23]

It is very difficult to calculate the quantitative impact of a nitrogen tax on the use of this and other inputs, on agricultural output and on farmers' incomes. Most German studies[24] agree that a considerable reduction in agricultural production can only be expected if current nitrogen prices are increased by about 100%. The estimated results of this doubling vary considerably according to the quality of soil and the farm size; moreover, farms concentrating on plant cultivation are much more sensitive to increases in nitrogen prices than cattle breeding farms which can partially compensate for the price increase through intensified utilization of their own liquid manure.[25]

Given the variety of conditions and the range of differing estimates, the following figures (cf., Weinschenck, 1989; Binswanger *et al.*, 1990; Dubgaard, 1990) are only intended to give a rough idea of the magnitude of the probable impact of a nitrogen tax.[26] Based on 1989 prices it can be expected that a doubling of nitrogen prices (i.e., a 100% nitrogen tax rate) will reduce nitrogen use in plant cultivation on average by about 20%.[27] This reduction will probably not lead to important yield reductions, given present levels of fertilizer input. Both from an ecological viewpoint (which would require a dramatic decrease in nitrogen use) and from an economic viewpoint (which would favor significant reductions of agricultural surpluses) this is far from being sufficient. Either consideration would call for dramatic price increases in the range of 300–400%, i.e., a nitrogen tax rate of about 200–300% added to current prices. At least for the time being, such increases are not acceptable for political, social and technical reasons. Therefore, more time for the necessary adjustment processes has to be granted, and the nitrogen tax has to be implemented in a stepwise fashion, starting with a tax rate of about 100% (amounting to about 1 DM per kg pure nitrogen). In order both to facilitate the adjustments in crop cultivation and to induce early changes in long-run decisions (e.g., related to investments in farming and to the development of technical progress in agriculture), a definite plan for achieving the final level of the nitrogen tax should be agreed, indicating the time span and the single steps in the increasing tax rate schedule. In this way, the costs of any necessary adaptations would be minimised, and the efficiency of nitrogen taxation would be greatly improved. In this longer perspective, there is also a dynamic taxation effect involved: the more profitable it seems to reduce or maybe even to eliminate the input for fertilizers and pesticides, the faster alternative ways of farming will be developed.

The final nitrogen tax rate would lead to a considerable decrease in agricul-

tural production; this reduction of supply would in turn contribute to an elimination of agricultural surpluses and probably also to a moderate commodity price
increase. Of course, as long as there is no world-wide agreement on nitrogen taxes,
the corresponding import protection levels for agricultural goods have to be main-
tained by the European Community in order to prevent imports from intensive
farming aboard. In this case, part of the income losses due to higher fertilizer costs
would be compensated for by probably slightly higher prices for agricultural
commodities.

If we start with a nitrogen tax rate of about 100%, then initially product prices
are unlikely to rise. It would be possible to compensate for this income loss by paying
back revenues to farmers in the form of a fixed amount per hectare.[28] Technically,
there are only two ways legally to enact the proposed combination of a special
duty on nitrogen and compensation for the consequent income losses. Either the
nitrogen tax is passed on as a special *charge*, or there is a political obligation on
both Parliament and the administration to grant income compensations when the
nitrogen tax law is passed.[29]

After the nitrogen tax rate has reached its final target level, there will be a
strong economic incentive for farmers to use less intensive production methods in
agriculture. As nitrogen fertilizers have become more costly, there has been an
incentive to use liquid manure in a more economical way, which would reduce
'free disposal' on small parcels of land and would contribute to a re-integration
of cattle breeding and plant cultivation. In addition, more natural ways of crop
rotation would become competitive, and hence the dependency on pesticides would
decrease. Therefore, positive consequences can be expected from a nitrogen tax both
on environmental grounds and via the reduction in agricultural surpluses.[30]

As stated earlier, the forecasted effects of a nitrogen tax differ considerably
between plant cultivation and cattle breeding, between various qualities of soil,
and across various farm sizes within a single country. Furthermore, differences in
the own-price elasticities of nitrogen can be expected between various countries.
Therefore, the analysis above should be viewed as an illustration of the general
procedure through which the nitrogen tax instrument can be implemented, what kind
of compensation schemes should be added, and what kind of qualitative effects
can be reasonably expected. As there is a broad range of probable quantitative
impacts on various groups of farmers according to the criteria mentioned above,
some accompanying measures will be necessary in order to avoid harmful social
effects and to bring about the desired changes even for those farms and those farming
methods which are only slightly affected by taxation alone. For example, it will
still be necessary to limit the intensive rearing of animals by specific regulations
which tie the number of animals to the available farm land (1.5 to 2 large animal
units per hectare).[31]

In order to develop more concrete tax proposals, more detailed studies and calculations for the different cases might be necessary. Another or complementary approach could be based on some kind of trial and error procedure, whereby the different steps in the nitrogen taxation schedule would be adjusted according to the observed empirical results of each successive tax increase. In any case it would not be reasonable to postpone nitrogen taxation for a long time just because of the absence of full knowledge of all quantitative effects; alternative regulatory measures also have their side effects on costs, prices and income which are not fully known to the administrators whenever they implement those devices. For the reasons given at the beginning of this section, a nitrogen tax appears to be an appropriate starting point – not a panacea – in order to initiate the necessary economic and ecological changes in European agricultural policy. At the same time it is obvious that supplementary measures, partly of the administrative type, will also be necessary.

The Case of Pesticide Taxes

As already indicated in note 16 above, the risk-reducing properties of pesticides could lead to an anomalous impact on pesticide applications in the wake of a specific tax on this input. Clearly this effect would not count in favor of a pesticide tax. There are, however, even more compelling arguments against this instrument: the impact of different pesticides on the environment varies widely, and very often we do not have sufficient knowledge of their specific consequences. Therefore, a general tax or charge on pesticides does not make sense, given their large number and variety, unless we can find a common denominator in terms of toxicity.

As there is no clear correlation between the toxicity of pesticides and their prices, it might well be the case that cheaper pesticides are even more detrimental to the environment than more expensive ones. So, neither price nor sheer quantity would give an environmentally reasonable tax base. Moreover, the share of pesticides in total production costs is, in general, rather low so that significant changes in usage rates can reasonably be expected only at very high (and politically unacceptable) tax rates. Therefore, it is perhaps impossible to solve the problem of pesticide application by changes in relative prices. If so, we have a case which requires physical regulation of agricultural production. Tough licensing procedures where the burden of the environmental proof rests on the pesticide supplier and strict application controls for licensed pesticides are then called for. Here, we have a good illustration of the possibility that – contrary to prevalent a priori reasoning of naive economists – economic instruments are not always superior to regulatory devices. Under certain specific conditions, there is not much ecological room for economic choices, and in this case the regulatory instrument is superior.

Whether the conditions are favorable for pesticide taxation or not, cannot be decided on theoretical grounds. As Ing-Marie Andréasson-Gren (1992) argues, it is possible to take account of the differing toxicity of various pesticides by relating it to some physical measure such as kilogram of active substance. If this measure is a sufficiently reliable indicator of the respective toxicity, then (but only then) the use of economic instruments, such as charges (or permit markets) makes sense. Additionally, one can think of detailed rules for and some random controls of pesticide application.

The Wasserpfennig in the German Federal State of Baden-Württemberg

In protected ground water zones, there are specific restrictions on the use of fertilizers and pesticides as well as on crop cultivation. Compared with a restriction-free situation this means yield and income losses for the farmers concerned. One German Federal State, Baden-Württemberg, has introduced a particular compensation scheme for farmers, based on a specific water charge (*Wasserpfennig*).

The principle of this charge is as follows: pumping water in this state carries a certain duty (the *Wasserpfennig*) which has to be paid by enterprises and public water utilities. This charge is passed on to the users of water (households, etc.) via higher water tariffs so that, finally, every user of water has to carry the charge. Of course, by making the use of water more expensive, some incentives to save water are provided.[32] The revenues arising from this charge are distributed to the farmers affected who then have to reduce the intensity of their agricultural practices in certain areas in order to improve the quality of surface and ground water reserves.

There has been some discussion whether this *Wasserpfennig* can be regarded as an application of the 'polluter pays principle'. In a technical sense, farmers' intensive use of land is the cause of the strain on surface and ground water, and therefore it seems inappropriate to compensate (or to subsidize) them for reducing their activity levels in protected water zones. However, as e.g., Bonus (1987) has argued, the *Wasserpfennig* can also be considered as an application of the *Coase* (1960) *Theorem*: both water users and farmers are competing for the utilization of scarce resources; the excessive zoning and the high quality level needed for surface and ground water is also a result of permanent increases in household demand for drinking water.[33] Therefore not only farmers but also consumers are contributing to the problem.

Nevertheless, there are also good reasons for rejecting this instrument. If farmers are not expected to reduce their production, even in protected water zones – because the misguided agricultural policy outlined above gives them the wrong incentives –, then such compensation payments should be financed for a transitional period out of general taxation, and not by the users of water. The basic problem is the European agricultural policy which favors intensive farming methods, and under these conditions, the application of a water charge is more a treatment of symptoms. Whereas from a welfare economics viewpoint it is not correct to say that the *Wasserpfennig* turns the 'polluter pays principle' upside down, there are practical arguments against it. Acceptance of this combination of an environmental charge and the subsidization of affected groups, carries with it the danger that more and more compensation claims will be put forward whenever a reduction in polluting activities is required. This could lead to a serious financial constraint on the implementation of environmental policy.

Therefore the *Wasserpfennig* might be considered as a pragmatic solution under the specific conditions of a German Federal State. It should not be taken as a starting point for a generalized scheme of environmental charges for the compensation of people affected by environmental policy. Moreover, as indicated above, the basic problem is agricultural policy in the EC.

5. Final Remarks on Economic Instruments in Agriculture

The discussion of three possible economic instruments for environmental protection in agriculture was an attempt to illustrate the kind of practical considerations which have to be taken on board when we leave the ideal world of general competitive equilibrium prices and enter a sector such as agriculture which is characterized by lots of already existing regulations and government interventions on the one hand, and by a variety of technical and social problems on the other hand. We have tried to show that even under these conditions, the application of economic instruments can be helpful in terms of a 'second best' solution.

This is particularly true in the case of a nitrogen tax which can contribute to a reduction in overproduction due to price fixing, and hence in the long run, can contribute to the restoration of market equilibria in agriculture; at the same time, it can support more natural and extensive ways of farming which are less detrimental to the environment. If combined with appropriate compensation schemes, it can also alleviate social problems for the people working and living in the agricultural sector.

It should also have become clear that a nitrogen tax cannot be considered as the panacea for all the economic, social and ecological problems of farming, but rather as a reasonable point of departure. Of course, it has to be supplemented and accompanied by a series of other measures, both of the economic and of the regulatory type. In the long run, even the more fundamental questions of the national and international economic system have to be addressed.[34] This goes far beyond the scope of this paper.

The discussion of the pesticide tax was presented as an illustrative example of a context in which regulatory instruments could prove superior. Here, the crucial question is whether we can relate the tax rate (or the price of a permit) to a sufficiently reliable measure of toxicity. In any case, detailed rules for (and some random controls of) pesticide application seem to be necessary. Under these conditions, a pesticide tax could contribute considerably to reducing the environmental damages associated with its application.[35] It will probably not contribute much to reducing the agricultural surpluses due to the fact that in most cases the share of pesticide costs in total production costs is rather low (even after imposing an additional charge on pesticide prices).

So far we have not addressed the question whether economic instruments for environmental protection in agriculture should be applied by single countries or by the EC as a whole. There are good reasons – such as unbiased competitive conditions between member states – for favoring an EC-wide solution. This is particularly important if we value the side-effect of a reduced surplus production very highly.[36] There is, however, an even more compelling argument for a common environmental EC policy in agriculture (Dubgaard, 1990, pp. 135–136). The supranational nature of the common agricultural market enables a member state to transfer most of the marginal costs of its own contribution to agricultural surpluses to the other member states. This 'free rider' problem has a clear impact on national environmental policies for agriculture. Member countries will not attach much importance to savings on the EC budget due to reduced agricultural surpluses. Their national agricultural policies will be guided by internal EC prices, and the resulting costs in terms of surplus administration will be largely neglected.

For these reasons, in each single EC member country the negative output effects of reducing agricultural intensity will be overvalued. Environmental damages associated with surplus production and intensive farming will be consequently undervalued in relation to possible income losses in agriculture. Therefore, at a national level the less efficient subsidization of environmentally favorable practices in agriculture which violates the polluter pays principle has become predominant. Hence Dubgaard (1990, p. 136) summarizes correctly: 'For the EC as a whole it is a rather inefficient way of dealing with agricultural pollution. There is a need, therefore, to establish a common input pricing policy for EC agriculture using levies to ensure that prices paid by farmers for environmentally damaging inputs will cover environmental as well as private costs.' As a nitrogen tax also contributes to the reduction of surpluses in the common agricultural market (which is less probable in the case of a pesticide tax or of a water charge), it can be considered as a valuable economic instrument which helps to bring about, at least in the long run, the desirable economic *and* ecological changes in agriculture.

In the last example of a specific water charge, there were good economic reasons for both its implementation and for its rejection. The main criticism which was raised against it was its 'embeddedness' in a misguided agricultural policy. The competing (and conflicting) claims on the use of ground water by both farmers and non-farmers cannot be reasonably harmonized within the context of a European agricultural price policy which favors intensive ways of farming. Therefore, the *Wasserpfennig* could only be regarded as a transitional solution, and not as a substitute for the necessary change in agriculture policy.

In contrast to this, the nitrogen tax could be considered as an instrument which helps to bring about the necessary long run changes in agriculture. But accompanying regulations will be needed for political and social reasons. This reminds us of a general problem of the 'second best' world in which we live: very often, both inside and outside agriculture we are faced with conditions where the theoretical superiority of economic instruments is superseded or at least modified by the specific conditions of the case in question. Therefore, in many cases a combination of regulatory and economic instruments will prove to be the realistic optimum choice.

Acknowledgements

For helpful comments and suggestions I would like to thank especially Ing-Marie Andréasson-Gren (The Royal Swedish Academy of Sciences, Stockholm), Hans Opschoor (Raad voor het Milieu- en Natuuronderzoek, Rijswijk, and Free University of Amsterdam), R. Kerry Turner (CSERGE, University of East Anglia, Norwich) and Rolf Werner (University of Hohenheim, Stuttgart). I am also indebted to Alex Dubgaard (The Royal Veterinary and Agricultural University, Frederiksberg, Copenhagen), Ulrich Hampicke (University of Kassel), Angelika Zahrnt (BUND, German Environmental Association, Neckargemünd) and an anonymous reviewer for their valuable suggestions and support.

Notes

[1] Following Walter Eucken (1975), in the German discussion the notion of *Rahmenordnung ('frame order')* is used in order to describe the constituent parts of the economic system.

[2] In this context, Eucken (1975) distinguishes between the shaping of the 'frame order' (*Rahmenordnung*), which he calls *Ordnungspolitik ('order policy')*, on the one hand, and government attempts at influencing the economic process which takes place within this prespecified 'frame order' on the other hand; the latter is called *Prozeßpolitik ('process policy')*.

[3] Unfortunately, PCPs are forbidden only in some countries, such as Germany. Another example of a strict ban would be the highly toxic pollutant dioxine; however, for practical reasons (dioxine cannot be completely removed from the atmosphere in the short run) we must confine ourselves to very restrictive upper limits. The general reasoning, however, is the same as in the case of PCPs.

[4] Of course, this two-step procedure of first defining an economic system and then choosing the appropriate instruments is an oversimplification; in reality, this procedure will take place as an iterative process where certain experiences with the implementation of policy instruments can be

used in order to redefine the underlying economic system. But this realistic feedback does not essentially change the basic choice problem discussed above.

[5] In the case of unknown risks, the necessary specification can only be based on pragmatic considerations given the uncertainties present.

[6] For instance, administrative costs of applying economic instruments might be prohibitive, or in a realistic world of imperfect knowledge and corresponding uncertainties in the application of instruments, mistakes in indirect price planning might have very severe consequences (Weitzman, 1974, pp. 485–487).

[7] In a fundamental theoretical contribution concerning the relative merits of price versus quantity planning, Martin L. Weitzman (1974) has illustrated this theoretical 'second best' problem by using the example of air pollution whereby both costs and benefits of a certain level of air cleanliness are not fully known to the controlling agency. In his model, there are good arguments for preferring indirect price planning to direct quantity planning if the benefit function is closer to being linear than the cost function. However, if marginal costs rise very steeply around the target level, the difference between controlling by price or quantity instruments is diminished. Moreover, if the cost function is closer to being linear than the benefit function, the consequences of price planning will then be inferior and in some cases even disastrous. So, in a realistic world with incomplete information about costs and benefits of certain environmental activities, there can be sound arguments for direct quantity planning, depending on the curvature of the relevant cost and benefit functions.

[8] In practice, PPP has been interpreted such that it includes the imposition of regulatory measures (standards, permits etc.) forcing the polluters to take concrete measures, the costs of which they have to bear themselves; but no costs are imposed for any residual pollution beyond the limits of the regulation. For the development and the meaning of the PPP principle in the context of the OECD see Opschoor and Vos (1989, chapter 1 and chapter 2, sections 2.3 and 2.5).

[9] There might be good theoretical reasons for subsidies in support of basic environmental research. Arguments for subsidies related to the so-called *Coase Theorem* will be discussed later on in section 4.3 in the frame of German water charges. See also OECD (1992).

[10] If for some reason – e.g., in order to avoid dangerous local concentrations of toxic material ('hot spots') – standards have to be set at the enterprise level, then of course there is no room for individual trade-offs, and in this case physical regulation might be more appropriate than economic instruments.

[11] The different devices which are applied in order to exempt the agricultural market from the usual price mechanism are listed in section 3 below. They can be considered as illustrative examples of *policy failure* which *add* to the traditional *market failure* described above (divergence between social and private costs of production). Instead of correcting market failure, this kind of policy increases ecological and social problems associated with farming.

[12] This statement does not imply that the present agricultural world market prices are to be considered as the correct ones. On the contrary, they are seriously distorted because transportation costs usually fail to reflect the accompanying environmental damages. In addition, the social and ecological conditions of agricultural production in most countries, especially in the Third World, give rise to serious doubts whether there is not a big gap between social and private costs of farming with the corresponding distortions of agricultural prices.

[13] In addition to these measures at the EC level, there are numerous specific agricultural programs within each single member country at national, regional and sectoral levels. This makes the situation even more complicated (if not confusing), but we omit these specific programs as they do not change the basic line of our argument.

[14] For a comprehensive critique from a liberal viewpoint, see, e.g., the evaluation of the Frankfurter Institut: *Argumente zur Wirtschaftspolitik* 18/April 1988. – For the reasons indicated in notes 13 and 35 I do not agree to the liberal proposals for changes in European agricultural policy whereas I share the liberal critique of the *status quo* in agriculture.

[15] If fertilizer and pesticide prices are relatively low, farmers may have an additional incentive to

overapply them in order to increase the security of reaching the target level; with low marginal costs of fertilizer and pesticide application, a certain amount of overdosing can be considered as some kind of risk premium against possible yield reductions 'in the worst case', following the dictum: if overdosing does not benefit much it will at least do no harm.

[16] Certain anomalies in the application of economic instruments in agriculture, such as the possibility of *increased* use of pesticides in response to an increase in pesticide prices (e.g., brought about by a pesticide tax) can be traced back to a combination of two features: first, to the incentive for an excessive use of pesticides and fertilizers as a consequence of artificially high commodity prices, and second, to the risk-reducing – and therefore yield stabilizing – properties of pesticides; this leads under some specific assumptions about risk behavior to an anomalous reaction similar to the classical Giffen case in consumption. For this see Antle (1988), and Andréasson-Gren (1992). According to German studies (Krayl, Leibfried and Werner, 1990; Hanf and Hilbert, 1991), the use of pesticides as an insurance against the yield risk leads to a high level of pesticide application, but not to an anomalous price reaction. See also section 4.2 below.

[17] Remember that Pigou's (1920) original tax approach was based on the assumption of equilibrium prices under perfect competition in all markets. Even for more modest attempts, such as the standard price approach by Baumol and Oates (1971), there is no arbitrary room for commodity price fixing: The intention of the latter is to stabilize farmers' incomes, and this function would be hampered by the application of input taxes which do not only lead to desired allocative effects but also to an undesired negative impact on farmers' incomes. As long as the goal of stabilizing farmers' incomes via state-guaranteed agricultural prices is not abandoned, there will generally be a strong incentive for further increases in output prices (in order to compensate for the tax-generated income losses) which in turn will counteract the intended reduction of pesticides and fertilizers in agriculture. This, however, is not inevitable; for alternative compensation schemes see note 21 below.

[18] They may be applied either in the form of environmental taxes and subsidies, or licenses, and/or in form of changed liability rules, sometimes combined with additional administrative regulations; for East Germany see Leipold (1983).

[19] The basic problem can be sketched as follow: If we impose ecological taxes or charges on distorted prices, we will undoubtedly create incentives for reduced production (and for reduced environmental damages); however, relative prices both of taxed and non-taxed commodities remain distorted with further consequences for the size of the sectors involved and the use of inputs in different branches of production. Assume, for example, we have two ecologically dangerous inputs A and B, let the price P_A be too low compared with P_B. If we now impose an eco-tax at the rate t on both inputs, there is an incentive to reduce both inputs in production, but the relative share of input A still remains too high. Therefore, the notion of correcting taxes cannot be applied properly in this context. For a general welfare economics discussion of the problem see Sohmen (1976, chapters 5 and 7), and for a brief discussion in a planning context cf., Nutzinger (1988, section 4; 1991, p. 32–33) – For an empirical comparison and evaluation of environmental policy between West and East Germany see Leipold (1983).

[20] For a comprehensive survey on the consequences of intensive farming for the environment see Rat von Schverständigen für Umweltfragen (1985, chapters 3 and 4). This report focuses on the German situation but both the description of the present state and of the perspectives of agriculture apply in a qualitative sense more or less to most European countries.

[21] Exactly for this reason, the German *Rat von Sachverständigen für Umweltfragen* (1985, pp. 364–366) has proposed to use the receipts of a nitrogen tax (see section 4.1 above) for farmers' compensation in the form of a fixed lump sum payment per hectare of arable farm land, and not related in any way to the (former) use of nitrogen. These lump sum payments should not be considered as subsidies conflicting with the 'polluter pays principle' but rather as a payment for landscape cultivation.

[22] This will be illustrated below by comparing the case of a nitrogen tax with a taxation of pesticides.

[23] The underlying theoretical reasoning for this is described in the preceding section.

[24] For a survey and a tentative evaluation of German research studies up to 1985 see Rat von

Sachverständigen für Umweltfragen (1985, pp. 363–365). For the Danish experience see Dubgaard (1987, 1990, 1991(a), 1991(b)).

[25] For a detailed quantitative estimate based on a German cluster sample see Weinschenck (1989, pp. 152–155).

[26] In the following example, the own-price elasticity of nitrogen is assumed to be –0.2. According to a survey (Burrell, 1989) the elasticity may vary between –0.15 and –2.1.

[27] According to Dubgaard (1990), a levy of 150% on the present Danish nitrogen price would reduce the use of inorganic nitrogen by 20 to 25%. The corresponding output reduction is estimated to range from 5 to 10%. This fall in crop production would lead to an appreciable alleviation of EC surplus problems (cf., note 36 below) although it is less than what would be needed to remove the total agricultural surplus even after the reductions of agricultural guaranteed prices agreed upon by the EC Council of Ministers in May 20, 1992; whereas these EC decisions do not remove completely agricultural surplus production, they will help to decrease it and hence support the reduction effect of nitrogen taxation. See also von Urff (1992).

[28] This compensation per hectare could also be justified as a payment for the positive externalities of landscape cultivation. Another possibility for compensation has been proposed by Dubgaard (1990, p. 131): 'The income effects of nitrogen tax could be reduced significantly by combining taxation and quota regulation, for example by allocating a tax-free quota of nitrogen to farmers and taxing only additional nitrogen purchase.' This idea has the additional advantage of transforming liquid manure from an undesirable waste of cattle-breeding into a valuable agricultural input which then should be used in a more economical *and* ecological manner, at least within the limits of the tax-free allowance of nitrogen for each farmer. Strong incentives for the transport or the processing of manure can be expected.

[29] In this respect, the proposal of a nitrogen tax has some parallels with Dutch government plans for a high energy charge coupled with reimbursing certain affected groups.

[30] Additional positive effects can be brought about if there are economic incentives related to alternative land use which reduces the dangerous nitrogen leakages into ground water, such as forestry, wetland and catch crop cultivation.

[31] For a good survey of the qualitative effects of nitrogen taxation and the necessary accompanying measures see *Rat von Sachverständigen für Umweltfragen* (1985, section 5.7.4).

[32] Other Federal States in Germany are considering the introduction of a comparable water charge, but so far they have not yet come to a final decision.

[33] In Coase's (1960, p. 2) original example, a crop-growing farmer and a cattle raiser are competing for the use of land; he speaks of 'the reciprocal nature of the problem'. However, by addressing himself mainly to the question of the cattle raiser's or the farmer's liability for the damage caused by the straying cattle and to the compensation payments taking place between both producers, Coase does not make sufficiently clear that the competition for the use of a scarce resource (land) lies at the heart of his problem. Of course, only in this generalized sense can the *Wasserpfennig* be considered as an application of his famous theorem. – See also Endres (1976).

[34] The current attempts at a worldwide liberalization of agricultural markets, for instance, seem to be misguided, for the reasons indicated above (note 12), as agricultural world market prices do not reflect the full social and environmental costs of farming and transportation; therefore, currently they cannot be taken as a point of reference for liberalization of agricultural markets which might be desirable in the long run.

[35] For a detailed description of the negative impacts see the paper by Andréasson-Gren (1992).

[36] Following Dubgaard (1990, p. 135) the tentative estimate that a 30% reduction in the use of nitrogen in commercial fertilizer (due to a tax rate of about 150%) could lead to a 5 to 10% fall in total crop production. As for the EC as a whole, grain surplus is about 15% of total production and a 5 to 10% fall in EC crop production would result in an appreciable alleviation of agricultural surplus problems.

References

Andréasson-Gren, Ing-Marie (1990) Costs for reducing farmers' use of nitrogen in Gotland, Sweden, *Ecological Economics* **2**, 287–299.

Andréasson-Gren, Ing-Marie (1991) Regional management of nitrogen polluted water: The Swedish case studies, Swedish University of Agricultural Economics, Department of Economics, Discussion Paper No. 42, Uppsala.

Andréasson-Gren, Ing-Marie (1992) Regulating the farmers' use of pesticides in Sweden, Beijer Discussion Paper Series No. 10, Beijer International Institute of Ecological Economics, Royal Swedish Academy of Sciences, Stockholm.

Antle, J. N. (1988) *Pesticide Policy, Production Risk and Producer Welfare, An Econometric Approach to Applied Welfare Economics*. Resources for the Future, Washington, D.C.

Baumol, W. J. and Oates, W. E. (1971) The use of standards and prices for protection of the environment, *Swedish J. Economics* **73**, 42–54.

Binswanger, H. C., Nutzinger, H. G. and Zahrnt, A (1991) *Umwelt(-)Steuern*. Bonn: Bund für Umwelt und Naturschutz Deutschland e.V. (BUNDargumente) (English translation: *Ecological Taxes*. Bonn: Bund für Umwelt und Naturschutz Deutschland e.V. (BUNDzargumente).

Bonus, H. (1987) Wider die Vulgärform des Verursacherprinzips, *Neue Zürcher Zeitung* 11–12.

Burell, A. (1989) The demand for fertilizer in the United Kingdom, *J. Agricultural Economics* **40**, 1–20.

Coase, R. (1960) The problem of social cost, *J. Law and Economics* **3**, 1–44.

Dubgaard, A. (1987) Reconciliation of agricultural policy and environmental interests in Denmark (regarding controls on nitrogen fertilizer), in M. Merlo, G. Stellin, P. Harou and M. Whitby (eds) *Multipurpose Agriculture and Forestry*. Proceedings of the 11th Seminar of the EAAE, April 28–May 3, 1989, Wissenschaftsverlag Vauk, Kiel, pp. 535–544.

Dubgaard, A. (1990) The need for a common nitrogen policy in the EC, in R. Calvet (ed) *Nitrates – Agriculture – Eau* (International Symposium, Nov. 7–8, 1990), Institut National de la Recherche Agronomique, Paris, pp. 131–136.

Dubgaard, A. (1991a) Pesticide regulation in Denmark, in N. Hanley (ed) *Farming and the Countryside*: An Economic Analysis of External Costs and Benefits. CAB International, Oxon, pp. 48–58.

Dubgaard A. (1991b) The Danish nitrate policy in the 1980s, Statens Jordburugsokonomiske Institut, Rapport nr. 59, Copenhagen.

Endres A. (1976) *Die pareto-optimale Internalisierung externer Effekte*, Frankfurt/M. -Bern: Lang.

Endres, A. (1985) *Umwelt- und Ressourcenökonomie*, Darmstadt: Wissenschaftliche Buchgesellschaft.

Eucken, W. (1975) *Grundsätze der Wirtschaftspolitik*, 5th ed., J.C.B. Mohr, Tübingen.

Frankfurter Institut (1988) Die Agrarpolitik der Europäischen Gemeinschaft. Die Reformbeschlüsse von 1988 und ihre Bewertung. *Argumente zur Wirtschaftspolitik* **18**.

Hanf, H. C. and Hilbert, D. U. (1991) Beziehungen zwischen Riskoeinstellung und Umweltgefährdung durch Stickstoffdüngung, *Agrarwirtschaft* **40**, 117–122.

Krayl, E., Leibfried R. and Werner, R. (1990) Einfluß der Risikoeinstellung von Landwirten auf Betriebseinkommen und Umweltgefährdung durch Stickstoffdüngung, *Agrarwirtschaft* **39**, 175–186.

Kumm, K. I. Incentive policies in Sweden to reduce agricultural water pollution, in J. B. Braden and S. B. Lovejoy (eds) *Agriculture and Water Quality, International Perspectives*, Lynne Rienners Publ., Boulder, London, pp. 105–116.

Leipold, H. (1983) Planversagen versus Marktversagen, in H. Hamel (ed), *Bundersrepublik Deutschland – DDR. Die Wiertschaftssysteme*, 4th ed., Beck, Müchen, pp. 199–261.

Nutzinger, H. G. (1974) *Die Stellung des Betriebes in der sozialistischen Wirtschaft*, Herder & Herder, Frankfurt-am-Main, New York.

Nutzinger, H. G. (1988) Eigentumsrechte und Umweltschutz: Überlegungen zu einer systemvergleichenden Analyse, Research Paper, University of Kassel, Department of Economics.

Nutzinger, H. G. and Zahrnt, A. (eds) (1989) *Öko-Steuern*, Umweltsteuern und -abgaben in der Diskussion. (Alternative Konzepte 73). C. F. Müller, Karlsruhe.

Nutzinger, H. G. (1991) Environmental policy in a comparative systems perspective, in H. G. Nutzinger (ed) *Social Policy and Environmental Policy in a Comparative Perspective*, Department of Economics, University of Kassel, Kassel, pp. 29–33.

OECD (1992) *Environment and Economics: A Survey of OECD Work*, OECD, Paris.

Opschoor, J. B. and Vos, H. B. (1989) *Economic Instruments for Environmental Protection*, OECD, Paris.

Pearce, D. W., Turner, R. K. and O'Riordan, T. (1992) Integrating quantity and quality in energy planning, CSERGE Working Paper, GEC-92-05 CSERGE, University College London and University of East Anglia.

Pigou, A. C. (1920) *The Economics of Welfare*, 4th ed., 1950, Macmillan, London.

Rat von Sachverständigen für Umweltfragen (1985) Umweltprobleme der Landwirtschaft, Sondergutachten (Special Report), March 1985 (Drucksache 10/3613) Kommissionsverlag Heger, Bonn.

Sohmen, E. (1976) *Allokationstheorie und Wirtschaftspolitik*, J.C.B. Mohr, Tübingen.

von Urff, W. (1992) Die Besteuerung von landwirtschaftlichen Betriebsmitteln als Konzept einer Agrarreform, Research Paper, Lehrstuhl für Agrarpolitik, Technische Universität München-Weihenstephan.

Weinschenck, G. (1989) Nitratsteuern zur Umwelt- und Marktenlastung, in Nutzinger/Zahrnt, pp. 147–159.

Weinschenck, G. and Werner, R. (1991) Agrarpolitik für eine umweltverträgliche Pflanzenproduktion, Konsequenzen unter zukünftigen Rahmenbedingungen, Research Paper, University of Hohenheim, Department of Farm Economics, Stuttgart.

Weitzman, M. L. (1974) Prices vs. quantities, *Review of Economic Studies* **41**, 477–491.

Werner, R. (1991) Trade, environment and sustainable farming, Research Paper, University of Hohenheim, Department of Farm Economics, Stuttgart.

Werner, R. (1991) Policies for Environmentally Sound, Economically Efficient and Sustainable Agriculture, Research Paper, University of Hohenheim, Department of Farm Economics, Stuttgart.

Werner, R. (1991) Sicherung der bäuerlichen Familieneinkommen – ein Widerspruch zur Senkung der Intensität? Research Paper, University of Hohenheim, Department of Farm Economics, Stuttgart.

White Paper of the European Environmental Organisations (1991) *The European International Market and the Environment, Towards Sustainable Development in the EC, Brussels*, European Environmental Bureau.

PART III

Product Cycles, Innovation and the Design of
Economic Instruments

10. Chain Management in Environmental Policy: Analytical and Evaluative Concepts

HANS OPSCHOOR
Free University, Amsterdam, The Netherlands

1. Introduction

In many industrialised economies, environmental policy is moving into a new phase in terms of both strategies and policy instruments.

The strategic focus is shifting to *prevention* of environmental pressure. That is, environmental policy is promoting the development and implementation of basic technological innovations at source, rather than relying mainly on measures on the effect's side. This requires an understanding of the environmental systems in order to properly link effects to the points (sources) where materials are being released into these systems: critical loads need to be translated into emission standards and targets. This 'systems approach' leads to an interest in *materials flows* through natural environments.

Moreover, there is a growing recognition of the 'interwoveness' of environment and the economic process: environmental pressure is now regarded as the result of a multitude of decisions taken at the micro level. In order to affect environmental pressure, policy will have to understand and address the environmentally relevant actors (or agents) in the economy and how these agents are related e.g., through supply-demand or input-output relationships. The 'actors orientation' thus recognises the need for a '*product life cycle*' approach and this in turn leads to an interest in aspects of industrial organisation or economic structure in relation to environmental degradation.

The interest in policy instruments is shifting as well. Traditionally, environmental policy instruments were of the 'command-and-control'-type: direct regulation through e.g., permits, zoning and standards. Once policy takes the prevention-oriented approach as outlined above, then instruments based on incentives operating through the market or through direct bargaining contacts with actors, are much more appropriate (see also chapter 1).

In addressing the issue of instruments choice, economic theory has often disregarded the intricacies of the environmental and economic processes that

Hans Opschoor and Kerry Turner (eds), Economic Incentives and Environmental Policies, 197–228.
© 1994 *Kluwer Academic Publishers. Printed in the Netherlands.*

environmental policy has to face, including those captured by materials flows and product life cycle models. Hence, environmental economics still falls short in appropriately accommodating the environmental side of the interactions. In order to contribute to the development of environmental policy, environmental economics will also have to draw more on one particular subbranch of economics-industrial organisation or industrial relations.

This chapter searches for economic methods to analyse environmental policy instruments as applied to specific materials or product chains.

Section 2 looks at economy-environment interactions by incorporating into the analysis materials flows and product cycles.

Section 3 extends this by developing the notion of chain management and associated instruments.

In Section 4 a simple first simulation model is used to evaluate some economic instruments in relation to manipulating the PVC-subchain.

In Section 5 some conclusions are drawn.

2. Chain/Cycle Analysis and Modelling

Environmental degradation can manifests itself as: pollution, resource depletion and the structural alteration of ecosystems. These manifestations can be interrelated: pollution may lead to effects in ecosystems and both pollution and changes in ecosystems may affect adversely the regenerative properties of the systems reproducing resources. In this chapter we are interested in instruments for source manipulation as a policy response to pollution and depletion. But in this section we shall look into environmental degradation and its links with economic processes (2.1), some examples (2.2) and how to analyse and model these economy-environment links (2.3).

2.1. *Materials Flows and Product Chains: concepts and definitions*

Environmental degradation is linked with a range of features, processes and agents in the natural environment and in society:

(i)   sources of environmental pressure (economic activities),
(ii) receptors of environmental degradation (ecosystems, cultural objects, people),
(iii) 'intermediate' environmental processes linking sources to receptors (transportation/dispersion, transformation/decomposition, accumulation etc., in the various environmental subsystems/compartments),

(iv)   feedbacks, or responses by social agents, to environmental degradation ('spontaneous' or endogenous responses and/or exogenous policy responses) addressed at (i) through (iii), or even at

(v)   the societal 'determinants' of economic activities (e.g., pollution growth, etc).

This chain of human activity-induced sequential events and interventions is called: *the environmental intervention chain* (Figure 1). Within that chain there are several interfaces between the environment and the economy, specifically (i): sources related environmental pressure, and (iv): pressure related responses.

It is important to note that the box labelled 'activities' in Figure 1 represents a multi-dimensional reality in itself, namely that of networks of specific activities within the various economic (sub)sectors, e.g., input-output relationships or product cycles (see below).

Ignoring this feature for the moment, we assume 'activities' to capture a certain distribution of (levels of) production and consumption. As such, these activities are sources of pollution and waste generation, and they are generators of resource demands. That is, they bring about environmental pressure in the form of a kind of metabolism between the economy and the environment: materials flows. Natural processes link these materials flows with stocks, sinks and with other processes. Once materials enter the system, they trigger sequences of events and processes,

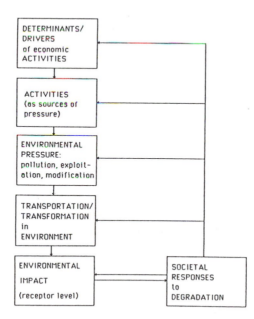

Fig. 1. Environmental intervention chain.

leading to changes in stock/sink levels and in the productivity of these environmental processes or the general environmental quality (i.e., the box 'environmental impact' in Figure 1).

Figure 2 represents the feature neglected above, i.e., economic relations. If the diagram were to do justice to the economy as a whole, it should show all relevant input-output relationships within the economy. However, the industrial relations are presented here, *pars pro toto*, as one consumption-oriented (material or physical) product cycle: primary production – secondary (and tertiary, etc.) production – consumption – waste processing. Each of the activities can be regarded as generating flows through the system, and as inducing stockpiling at several points within the system. The activity 'waste processing' includes any type of action dealing with waste, from allowing it to pile up somewhere, via illegal dumping, to all kinds of deliberate activities such as reusing, recycling, controlled storage, incineration, etc.

By definition, at each level (economic or ecological) the systems as represented by Figures 1 and 2 are linked to each other; they are subsystems in a more elaborate economy-environment system. In addition, each subsystem is an open system, which allows for imports and exports of economic as well as environmental flows from other 'economies' and 'environments'.

The relationships in Figures 1 and 2 are expressed in different units.

At the economic level (Figure 2) the appropriate units are numbers of 'products'

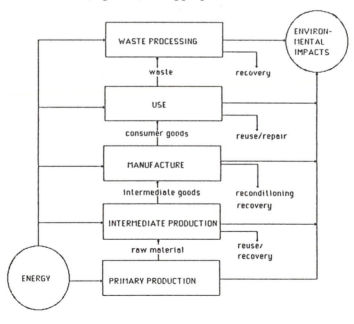

Fig. 2. Product cycle and environmental change (pollution and resource exploitation only).

(normally expressed in aggregated terms, via their market values). Products are organically and functionally linked in a product cycle, where extraction and processing of materials, product manufacturing and consumption are logical main units. Products move from activity to activity until they enter the waste sink; meanwhile these activities (and the waste sink) give rise to residuals that are emitted into the environment. Products may also pile up earlier in the economic process, due to certain properties of productive and consumptive activities.

At the environmental level however, products are not the most appropriate units of analysis: they are merely bundles of materials or compounds that *as materials or as compounds* exert influence on environmental processes and stocks. The logic in the processes here follows physical, chemical and biological laws rather than economic ones.

In order to proceed with a clear set of concepts definitions will be presented for: materials cycles and materials balances, product cycles and materials-product chains (MP chains).

Materials cycles are:

flows through economy-environment systems structured along origin-destiny lines, i.e., as flow charges, with mass/time as the basic dimensions of single compounds (e.g., chlorine, CFC's) or of complex aggregates of compounds, or materials (e.g., plastics, wood (cf. Olsthoorn, 1991)).

These cycles ideally trace the sequences of events or 'fate' of compounds and materials in both the economic and ecological subsystems. That is, mechanisms of push and pull through the economy (spatially disaggregated) as well as production functions at all levels, and of transport and transformation in the environmental compartments, are described. Basically, Lavoisier's law of conservation of mass holds for these cycles (Olsthoorn, 1991). *Materials balances* represent a bookkeeping approach to mass flows in materials cycles.

In practice, however, it turns out to be very difficult to capture the entire system of stocks and flows for any material and hence most materials cycles or materials balances are either very abstract representations of the underlying real flows, or they focus on one aspect (the environmental or the economic one) only.

Product cycles are:

representations of flows of products through the economic process, from primary production through waste treatment, as well as their related joint products in terms of environmental pressures (cf. Van Weenen, 1990).

Product cycles could, as a first approximation, be seen as very complex heterogeneous materials cycle. But they have a different structure and basic dimensions (mass being replaced by number of units of products) and events in both economy and environment would be included but with emphasis on the economic level (Figure 2; see also Figure 4).

MP chains can be defined as:

subsets of linked materials and product cycles, demarcated so as to best suit a pre-determined purpose or application (cf. Olsthoorn, 1989, 1991; ADCI, 1991).

The need for some pragmatic process of truncation in MP chains is obvious: in reality each and every substance, or product, will turn out to be linked to, say, 80% of all other products and materials, once they are analysed fully. Economically this is reflected in the notion of an input-output matrix with mostly nonzero coefficients.

MP chains can show several types of links between their elements (Olsthoorn, 1991):

(a) *chemical linkage*, due to the occurrence of a certain chemical in several compounds and the heterogeneity of compounds as such; thus, the cycles of chlorine, fluorine and bromine are linked through the chemical composition of CFCs.

(b) *technological linkage*, due to technological coefficients or (joint externalities) in production processes; thus, the materials flows of SO_2 and NO_x are linked by the coal combustion technology;

(c) *economic or functional linkage* (e.g., complementarities and forward/ backward linkages in economic activities, and substitutability between products and inputs). Thus, SO_2 emissions and radiation are linked by the possibility of substituting nuclear for coal technologies in electricity generation; flows of glass and plastics are related by the demand for packaging.

AS MP chains are pragmatically truncated materials/product cycles, the principle of conservation of mass no longer applies. One chooses a relevant subset, depending on the application intended. If the application is an environmental regulation, then the materials incorporated will be environmentally relevant pollutants, product inputs, substitutes, alternative products, etc. Thus, a materials balance of cadmium includes flows of fertilizers, PVC batteries, etc.; these individual cycles can be aggregated in a Cd-chain (see Huppes, 1987; see also Klepper and Michaelis, 1991). Other examples are 'pollutant flow analyses' looking at the specific flows of e.g., phosphates through a given region (Nijkamp and Vohwahsen, 1990), or Halon 1301-flows through the economy and into the environment (Olsthoorn, 1991). Since 1988 Ayres and Stigliani *et al.* have used the materials balance approach to model the Rhine river system (Ayres *et al.*, 1989).

2.2. *Example of a MP chain*

We shall illustrate some of the above concepts and relationships by the so-called chlorine chain as it manifests itself in the economy of the Netherlands. We begin by looking at chlorine itself, and then look at some detailed MP chains: PVC and Halon 1301. Chlorine-related environmental impacts have led to a desire by environmental authorities to manage the chlorine chain at least to the extent that the leakage of chlorine is controlled, and if this fails, to substitute chlorine by other chemicals.

Chlorine is one of the basic substances used in a series of economic processes leading to a very wide range of final products (see e.g., Yanowitz, 1989). Figure 3 provides the chlorine MP chain for the situation in the Netherlands (1989) mostly in qualitative terms and ignoring pollution aspects. At present, Dutch chlorine production is about 670 kilotons per annum, 88% of which are destined for domestic use or processing. The price of chlorine is in the Dfl 300/ton range. On the basis of the annual production value of appr. MDfl 200,000, an impressive chemico-economic structure has been erected, with a substantial overall economic significance. Figure 3 traces produced Cl through its various intermediate products to derived final products; the percentages presented in the figure indicate the shares of the chlorine flow accounted for (as % of the 670 kilotons).

Chlorine is produced by the electrolysis of salt in water. In this process sodium hydroxide is also formed, which is another chemical feedstock. This chemical linkage is ignored here, but it is pointed out that lowering chlorine production (e.g., for environmental reasons) would have significant chemical supply feedbacks elsewhere in the economy, unless other (available, but more expensive) processes of sodium hydroxide production were used. An environmentally important technical linkage is that of the energy demands of the electrolysis process: per ton of chlorine, 31–3900 kWh is required. In the phase of primary chlorine production, the market structure is as follows: 1 producer (AKZO) accounts for appr. 75% of produced Cl, and 2 others produce the remainder (Solvay: 21% and General Electrics: 4%).

We now move to the phase of intermediate production. Some important applications of chlorine are:

(a) direct use as Cl (appr. 5%); in water purification and in bleaching processes in the paper and pulp industry;

(b) 1,2 dichloro-ethane (over 50%); this is used in the production of vinylchloride (VC, 44%), per (1%) and ethylene-amines (6%);

(c) phosgene (7–8%) used to produce polyurethane and polycarbonate;

(d) dichloromethane (7%), the input for producing tetra and chloroform, both mainly used as basic material for CFCs, solvents and cleansers;

(e) epichlorohydrine (ech) (2.5%) used to produce epoxyresins;

(f) pesticides (1–4%).

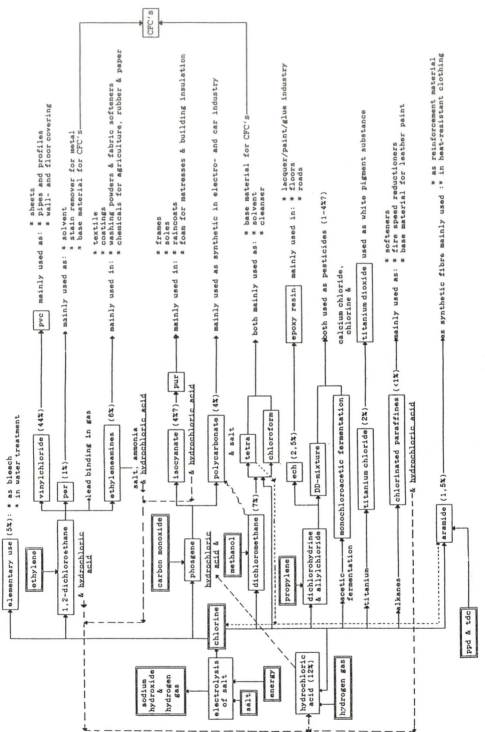

Fig. 3.

In terms of industrial organisation and market structure, our (incomplete) information shows that approx. 70% of the primary production by AKZO is internally processed (AKZO, 1990).

The processes described in Figure 3 result not only in intermediary or final chlorine-based products but also in discharges of residuals into the environment with very different environmental impacts. Before listing these it is to be noted that chlorine as such is a quite common phenomenon in the natural environment: as chloride in salt it is abundant, not only in sea water but also in the form of deposits in soils. The environmental significance of chlorine derivatives or joint products in the form of pollution and wastes, varies tremendously. The impact in the form of chloride is rather small, assuming that this material enters the environment in places where it occurs naturally (e.g., the sea). But chlorine itself is a very aggressive element and so are many of its derivatives.

Some very significant environmentally hazardous chlorine related emissions are:

(i)   Releases of persistent pollutants such as dioxines, phenoles, furanes in bleaching processes;
(ii)   Emissions of 1, 2 dichloroethane especially in relation to the production of vinylchloride, with carcinogenous and mutagenous properties;
(iii)   Releases of perchloroethylene and tetra (from e.g., solvents) which is carcinogenous after chronic exposure; losses of solvents related to pharmaceutical processes are particularly problematic;
(iv)   Emissions of CFCs with impacts on ozone layer and atmospheric warming;
(v)   Releases of epichlorohydrine to air with organic impacts and carcinogenic and possibly mutagenic consequences;
(vi)   Pesticides residuals and metabolites entering the environment through a range of pathways, leading to e.g., accumulation in drinking water reserves, and in fatty tissues of organisms.

We shall now look at two components of the chlorine chain: PVC and Halon 1301. The former is chosen for its relevance to waste flow management and a first and preliminary version of a model to evaluate alternative PVC-chain management tools will be presented in section 4 below. The latter is selected for its environmental significance: its role in the expansion of the hole in the ozone layer.

The production of PVC involves 44% of the annual chlorine flow in the Netherlands (see Figure 3), through the production of VC, the feedstock, in PVC production (see Figures 3 and 4). AKZO produces 500 kilotons of VC p.a., which is turned into 400 ktons of PVC powder by 2 companies. PVC accounts for 23% of total plastics consumption, especially in the sector of durable applications (e.g., 50–60% PVCs are used in the construction industry (Cesar, 1990). The annual turnover (1988/89) almost reached Dfl 4 billion and employment was approx. 7,500 (ibid.), giving the sector an economic significance in the order of 1% of GNP and 0.1% of total employment. Figure 4 presents the product chain of PVC.

One particularly important property of PVC is its durability: more than 60% of PVC applications have a lifespan of over 15 years; profiles and pipes have a lifespan of 35 and 50 years respectively and a high potential for recycling. Apart from these there are a number of other environmentally relevant aspects of PVCs:

(i)   pollution and wastes associated with the production of VC: 3–3.5% of VC production, much of that in the form of (carcinogenous) chlorinated hydro-

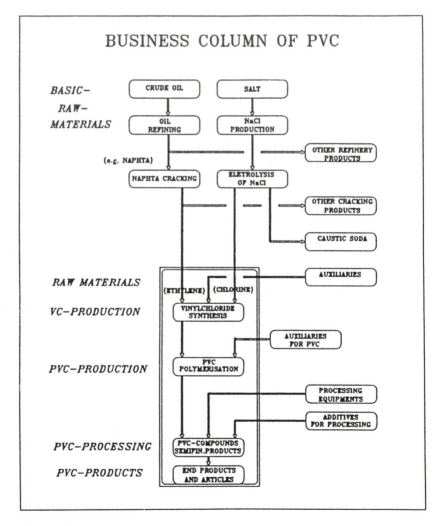

Source: Cesar.

Fig. 4. PVC product chain.

carbons; some of these (over .08% of produced VC) into air and water; some as solid wastes to be incinerated;

(ii)   emissions and wastes related to the polymerisation to PVC: VC losses (90 ton p.a.), PVC solid waste (150 ton PVC p.a.) and releases (110 PVC p.a.);

(iii) emissions resulting from the incineration of PVC (e.g., dioxines, hydro-chloric acid, metabolites of additives such as heavy metals, and of pigments);

(iv)   the Cl-immobilising aspect of PVC (a dubious argument); and the energy saving properties of PVC in comparison to other hard plastics.

Halons (see Olsthoorn, 1989, for further details) are chemicals comparable to CFCs; they contain bromine as well as chlorine and fluorine. As chemicals that deplete the ozone layer they fall under the Montreal Protocol. Halons are almost exclusively used as fire extinguishers. All halons used in the Netherlands are imported; Figure 5 provides a materials chain for Halon 1301. The environmental impacts of using Halon 1301 are:

(i)   halons discharged in testing, maintenance and repair: 30 tons p.a.;

(ii)   halons released in use: 20 tons p.a.;

(iii) halons released through accidental triggering: 15 tons p.a.

Sales of halons containing equipment are to terminate before 2000; sales of halon to replenish existing equipment will continue. The development of emissions over time will then depend on the rate of replacing equipment and on the release of halons at the time of scrapping.

2.3. *Chain Analysis and Modelling*

MP chain analysis (*chain analysis* for short) aims at linking the materials approach and the product approach as defined above, in an application oriented, policy relevant fashion. The typical approach in chain analysis is, to extend economic product cycle analysis with an environmental phase, but to restrict the analysis along the entire sequence of events to the more relevant components. That is: to strongly linked products and materials and to events in certain environmental compartments within certain regional boundaries.

Chain analysis draws much of its relevance from the fact that for many features of MP chains, alternatives are available such that economic agents within the chain, chain managers and even environmental policy makers, are able to make choices between them. Figure 6 visualises this. Product demand is taken as the point of departure, but even here, substitute products can meet the underlying needs,

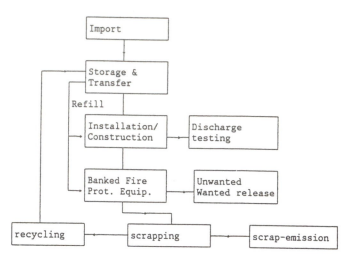

Source: Olsthoorn 1989.

Fig. 5A. Materials chain of halon 1301 (The Netherlands 1986).

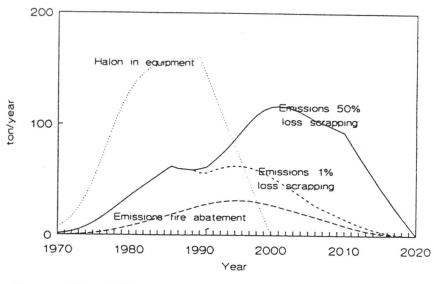

Source: Olsthoorn 1989.

Fig. 5B. Halon emission scenarios.

thus indirectly linking specific MP chains to potentially very different ones. Demand for a product may be met by producing it with either standard technology or alternative technologies (e.g., agricultural products based on traditional farming methods or on the so-called biological methods). These various technologies draw on dif-

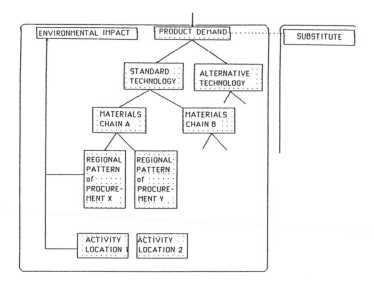

Fig. 6. MP chains as bundles of choices.

ferent, technology-specific, materials cycles and these may give rise to alternative patterns of procurement and spatial configurations of implied materials production, each with different environmental repercussions.

In the context of chain management alternative chains may have to be evaluated and compared. Certain elements or modules of these chains could be substituted by others e.g., by environmentally more appropriate ones. Examples of this are the change to environmentally friendly substitute product, alternative technologies, substitute materials, alternative patterns of procurement and production in Figure 6. Another example is: a recycling module to be injected in traditional chains between the consumption module and the waste module.

It is extremely difficult to combine, in one information system or one forecasting model, the full range of subchains and alternatives as indicated in Figure 6. Thus, in reality, there is a tendency to focus either on the top half of the chain in the diagram from product demand down to materials chains A or B, or to the bottom half, with a focus on actual environmental repercussions. The analysis presented here indicates how both halves of Figure 6 can be better integrated by beginning at the product demand stage and encompassing all successive stages down to environmental media impacts.

How should complex systems such as the ones addressed here be modelled in order to understand their behaviour and to predict and evaluate alternative ways of manipulating them from an environmental policy perspective? Two approaches traditionally used in applied environmental economics will be briefly introduced:

materials balances and input-output analysis. Finally, a new approach based on system dynamics and simulation will be outlined.

The *materials balances* tool has been suggested for application at the level of regional and national economics as long ago as 1969 (Ayres and Kneese, 1969) and was subjected to much discussion subsequently (Perrings, 1989; see also Opschoor, 1974 and 1991). Basically, material flows between the economy and the environment are accounted for in the model, and reference is made to the law of conservation of mass as a point of departure (see above). The problems with this approach are those of modelling vast and very complex systems and of inadequate data; neither of these problems has been fully tackled since, but much progress has been made in terms of data (e.g., on environmental impacts, on environmental processes, on source-emission relationships) and on tools (e.g., simulation models).

Input-output analayis links the various economic activities through a normally linear approach to deliveries of goods and services from one activity or sector to the others. Integrated input-output analysis attempts to augment this by adding resource inputs (e.g., energy) from the environment and joint outputs of the economy (in terms of wastes) into the environment. From empirical work along these lines we know that this would typically involve a large number of economic sectors or activities and a frustratingly large number of materials or compounds. Furthermore, input-output analysis is restricted to part of the product cycle only: from primary production to consumption. The waste processing phase and the environmental events phase are normally excluded (see e.g., Hordijk *et al.*, 1979, James *et al.*, 1978).

From these early attempts at linking environmental processes and economies in policy-oriented modelling, one may learn that analysing and describing complete chains at any level of detail, turns out to be too unwieldy; analytical solutions to these systems may not be known or may be non-existent (see e.g., Van den Bergh, 1991). An alternative is, to develop a simulation model focusing on the main features of very specific subsystems such as particular MP chains only. One theoretical attempt to develop a dynamic chain simulation model is Howe's model for resource/commodity/toxins simulation in a 2-sectoral economy (Prince *et al.*, 1990). However, this again appears to be rather too abstract for concrete policy oriented application. Research along such lines must continue but in order to be of some policy relevance, environmental economies should accept that ad hoc, 'casuistic' simulation models are very appropriate alternatives or substitutes in the short and medium term.

Olsthoorn (1991), Olsthoorn *et al.* (1991) and Herwijnen *et al.* (1991) at the Institute for Environmental Studies in Amsterdam (Free University) have developed dynamic models coupled with information systems for simulating environmental impacts coupled to alternative policy strategies/scenarios.

Their menu-driven system has the following structure:

(a) a module with exogenous economic developments and their implications for levels of production throughout the chain, and market prospects of the materials under study;

(b) a module with information on the applications of wastes and residuals of the materials under study, including scenarios for the development of preferences for the treatment of these residuals;

(c) a module with materials balances scenarios, 'driven' by (a) and (b);

(d) emissions functions quantitatively linking the various production and treatment options with emissions and discharges; here residence times and rates of release of substances play a crucial role;

(e) emission scenarios, driven by (c) and (d).

With this model, scenarios can be constructed to include materials production, emissions, treatment, etc. over very long periods; applications of this model for flyash have produced forecasts over a 60-year period. Another long-term oriented application of this system has been to halons (Olsthoorn, 1989, 1991), see Figure 5. Scenarios for halons were based on a strategy of banning and phasing out halon-using equipment and assumed scrapping practices. No use of economic incentives is considered, nor are alternative technological paths compared in terms of economic implications.

It is important to note that market developments and treatment/reuse preferences are exogenously determined and are in no way linked through an economic module. This prevents endogenous adaptions to changes in relative scarcities or in relative prices and hence this model is not suited for an analysis of chain management options or alternative instruments for chain management from an economic perspective. Similar 'physical' chain management models have been developed of some chlorine parts of the chemical industry by ADCI: HCFC-22 as a substitute for CFC replacement in refrigerators, control of dichloromethane emissions by Dutch pharmaceutical industry, environmental impacts of PVC window frames and alternatives (ADCI 1991).

A more generic model for chain management simulation is DESC (Decisions Environmental Strategies of Corporations) by Krozer (unpubl. 1991). DESC distinguishes a number of sectors (currently 30) that are linked through a 'basic input-output table'. From that basic table, relevant product chains can be derived and modelled. Alternative environmental constraints are then imposed and transformed into a set of sufficient technological responses, the economic impacts of which (in terms of, e.g., costs, levels of production and levels of employment) can then be calculated. Presently, some 40 groups of pollutants have been incorporated, as well as appr. 1,000 environmental measures and their costs, in relation to several hundreds of technologies used in the various sectors. Measures may lead to modified input-output relationships. Secondly, the environmental and economic repercussions of corporate strategies and product chain strategies can be predicted: extending product lifetimes, altering products' materials composition, etc. Repercussions are predicted both for the sectors of prime concern and for the linked sectors. The notion of a chain approach is thereby given substance. In principle, DESC can calculate abatement cost levels that could be used to set effluent charges. For some materials input or product charges have been analysed in a chain context (e.g., paints/coatings). But basically it is a policy and technology driven model derived from an input-output table; the latter feature may obscure a number of environmentally relevant features of the specific MP chains under consideration. And furthermore, DESC currently tends to disregard economic (as opposed to technological) feedbacks such as the implications for demand levels of alterations in relative prices.

It appears that there is scope to extend MP chain simulation modelling and to improve it. It is potentially rewarding to develop appropriate simulation models for a range of environmentally relevant specific products, against a background of shared economic and chemical linkages as encapsuled by input-output models. The latter would enable a common empirical framework; the former might lead to a learning process in terms of how to model specific aspects of chain management efficiently.

3. Chain Management

In this section we shall firstly describe some new directions in environmental policy development as backgrounds to the concept of MP management (3.1). Then we shall try to develop that notion analytically (3.2) in order to move to the main focus of this section: instruments for chain management (3.3).

3.1. *Policy Context*

One of the most important principles underlying environmental policies in OECD countries, is the 'Polluter Pays Principle' (PPP); this principle is likely to be applied to a much wider geographical arena, if – as is expected – institutions such as GATT and even the UN are to adopt it. Principles such as these are used to legitimise certain rules on the allocation and distribution of environmental costs PPP (OECD, 1972) basically was (and is) a 'no subsidy' principle prescribing the polluter to pay for the costs of meeting environmental standards. PPP as currently implemented suffers from several deficiencies: it may create insufficiently strong feedbacks from effects to polluters, it does not systematically lead to a regulatory impact on behaviour, it does not stimulate process-integrated measures, the principle does not generate cost covering revenue flows, and it focuses too much on pollution, ignoring aspects such as resource depletion and structural ecological degradation. In several countries discussions are thus taking place on how better to apply the underlying notions (e.g., by extending PPP to the area of resources through a 'User Pays' variant) and on the need for complementing PPP by *inter alia*, a principle of 'Chain Liability' or 'Chain Accountability' (CAP). CAP operates on the notion of legally extending liability for environmental aspects of products along the product chain. One way to implement this is to impose an obligation to take in and recycle or reuse certain products.

An example of policy (ref)formulation in terms of chain-related concepts is provided by Dutch environmental policy (NEPP, 1990). NEPP defines environmental policy objectives in terms of:

- 'closing' cycles (i.e., reducing outflows such as pollution, waste by applying residuals levers and reuse levers);
- 'extensification' of cycles (i.e., reducing the amount of materials and energy per unit of 'product');
- enhancing the quality of the products (in economic terms, as well as in environmental ones; the latter is achieved by e.g., enhancing recyclability or extending the product's life span).

The core concept of the NEPP is, that source oriented measures and feedback mechanisms must be directed at, *inter alia* integrated life cycle management (including product life cycle management). Efforts are aimed at saving in the order of tens of percents in the use of raw materials in 2010 as compared with 1985 and at emission reductions of 75–100%.

The Dutch policy proposal on waste management renders the producer or importer of a product responsible for the product's fate in the waste stage. It is analogous to the German packaging policy (the Töpfer plan, adopted in November 1990). The Dutch policy proposes suppliers of products to have the obligation to recollect all wastes the origin of which can be traced in cases where the waste is separable from the general waste flow. It proposes a prescription on reuse and/or materials recovery for e.g., batteries, electrical equipment, cars, etc. And it suggests the use of financial incentives (refunds, charges on primary materials, etc.). The new policy proposes the introduction of 'return systems' in which suppliers either recollect themselves or collectively organize a separate recollection infrastructure. It further proposes: product assessment, environmental labelling, information, bans, etc.

A bottom-up variant of this product-cycle approach to managing the environmental implications of production and consumption, is the notion of 'product stewardship' which has emerged in certain sectors of industry, especially in the chemical branches. Product Stewardship can be defined as the systematic corporate effort to reduce product environmental risks over all or significant segments of a product life cycle (Dillon and Baram, 1991). It covers the initiatives to redesign a product for safety or environmental reasons, and the transfer of knowledge about the safe handling, use and disposal of products. In a more advanced form, it may also cover responsible care for procurement and even 'co-makership': concern over and/or responsibility for the environmental quality of products (and their packaging) and even of processes 'upstream' in the product cycle. This is stimulated by implicit or expected economic returns (quality improvement, enhanced consumer demand, liability reduction etc.). Dillon and Baram (1991) identify some policy measures that would support private initiatives along the stewardship line: identify and remove obstacles to technology transfer and technology change, identify product sectors or life cycle phases that could benefit most from technology transfer and technological change, and additional incentives or regulations to stimulate further environmental risk reduction. CAP could be one of those additional regulations.

In the rest of this chapter we shall look at prospects for economic incentives in the context of chain management.

3.2. *The Concept of Chain Management*

Chain management can be defined as:

the manipulation of MP chains so as to optimise the environmental impact of these chains, or so as to achieve a certain accepted environmental impact at least social cost.

The notion of chain management implies that the environmental agency does have ways to effectively influence decisions within the chain. In order to have that, the environmental agency must have *leverage*, to be applied at effective *leverage* points (see also Bertolini's contribution to this volume). In abstract terms, leverage may be sought in terms of:

(i)   alternative inputs/products, and/or
(ii)   alternative processes, and/or
(iii) alternative behavioural options, and
(iv)   alternative institutional arrangements capable of enhancing (if not enforcing) chain management (Opschoor, 1991).

As potential leverage points chain management can consider those parts of the chain at which management may wish to exert influence on decisions given the availability of environmentally relevant alternative courses of action. See again Figures 1, 2 and 6 for indications of where these leverage points might be. Looking again at the product cycle (Figure 2) there are several types of leverage to consider. Firstly, at each stage in the cycle, an activity can be controlled in terms of its level of output (*product* or *output* leverage). Then, one may wish to manipulate the process inputs (*input* leverage). If pollution or waste flows are to be addressed directly, one could apply *residual leverage*. Finally, *reuse leverage* may be considered for stimulating recovery, repair, reuse and the various ways of disposing the remaining fractions of residuals (including landfill, incineration and illegal dumping).

Here we are not interested in developing theories of chain management in general, but more specifically in the development and evaluation of policy instruments and management tools; that is: the application or implementation of levers.

We distinguish between leverage to be applied in four stages relevant to product's environmental significance in a product cycle context: the (product and process) *design* stage, the actual *production* stage and the processes used therein, the *marketing* stage and the *use/waste* stage (see Table 1, vertical entry). In these stages several strategic options exist, as well as barriers to effectively implement these (Table 1, middle columns). Instruments or levers actually applied to overcome barriers at these points, can be of three types: regulatory, economic and suasive instruments (see Chapter 1 and Table 1, last column).

Influencing the *design of products and processes* is one of the most crucial activities in a prevention-oriented, product chain based environmental policy strategy. In designing products, criteria must be applied taking into account environmental impacts at all levels of the cycle, with special emphasis on the 'front end' (primary production of main materials) and the 'back end' (waste related) aspects (Van Weenen, 1990).

The next important stage is that of enhancing the *adoption of new technologies and products*. In a context of uncertainty, innovation depends heavily on a firms' market based interactions with others (clients, suppliers, etc.) (Dosi *et al.*, 1988; Georg and Jorgensen, 1990:6). The actual impact of charges and other economic incentives on the rate and direction of innovation is mainly unknown. Both Georg and Jorgensen (1990) and Opschoor and Vos (1989) conclude that the complexity of the process of innovation precludes simple, broad-brush preventive solutions; rather, context-specific and often complex (i.e., mixes of elements of command and control, incentive and suasive natures) approaches will have to be developed.

Skipping the stage of marketing, we reach the *prevention of waste flows*. This can take the form of materials savings by promoting less consuming lifestyles, or the longer and more intensive use of materials through repair, recycling etc.

Looking at materials or product chains from an economic point of view one perceives that going from one stage of the product cycle to the next, there may be differences in market structure or industrial organisation-related aspects, *inter alia*:

- market form and structure (e.g., numbers of actors, access, market power),
- elasticities (income, price and substitution),
- degree of internationalisation of the market

These factors influence the extent to which cost increases as a consequence of

Table 1. Options, barriers and instruments for chain management

	Options	Barriers	Instruments	Type[a]
Design	Green designing	Current attitudes	Design criteria	R/S
			Training research	S
	Increasing level of information	Accessibility of information	Dissemination of information	S
Production/ technology	Clean/input saving processes	Lack of (competitive) options, lack of information	Stimulate innovation	E/S
			Stimulate diffusion	E/S
			Subsidise adoption	E
			Disseminate info	E
		Attitudes	Train management	S
			Charges (emission or inputs)	E
			Permits/bans on Emissions/materials	R
Marketing	Production information	Attitudes	Education	S
			Promotion	S
			Green labelling etc.	S
			Product bans	R
	Green consumerism/ product policies	Purchasing power	Deposit refunds	E
			Charges/subsidies	E
		Competitiveness	Harmonisation of tariffs and duties	E
			EC policies	R/E
Use/waste	Materials saving	Attitudes	Education	S
			Input charges	E
	Repair/reuse	Attitudes	Promotion	S
		Costs	Subsidies	E
			Return systems	R/E
	Recycling	Lack of infrastructure	Market support	R/E
			Subsidies	E
			Return systems	R/E

[a] R = direct regulation; E = economic incentive; S = suasion/communication; for explanation: see Chapter 1.

environmental measures can be passed on to buyers, that is to the next set of agents in the product chain. It is in this context that, especially in open economies, there is much concern over the impacts of (national or regional) environmental policies on the competitive positions of firms. Much more empirical work is needed in order to incorporate these aspects in descriptive/predictive models of economic responses to environmental policy, and to evaluate models for instrument choice.

Many chains spread over more than one nation. This frequently implies that chains extend over the borders of the administrative powers of environmental agencies:

there may not be one single regulatory body to oversee the entire chain. In such cases, full chain management is impossible and the actual environmental performance of the chain is likely to be sub-optimal (RMNO, 1991).

One example of this phenomenon is the difficulty in applying regulatory energy charges in countries or even blocks of countries. Unless there were a system of global charges, there would always be regions where energy would be available relatively cheaply compared with the region where a charge would be applied. For example, substantial energy charges (25% or more ad valorem) in the Netherlands alone, would drastically impair the competitive position of a substantial number of Dutch energy-intensive industrial sectors (Wolfson et al., 1992).

3.3. *Instruments for Chain Management*

What levers or instruments exist for chain management and in which policy contexts can they be expected to be effective? These questions will be addressed now. Table 1 (last columns) provides a number of examples of instruments according to various points in the design, production, marketing and use of stages as distinguished above. We shall elaborate on some of them by approaching them from the vantage point of the type of leverage to apply; given the interest in chain management, the emphasis is on residual, input and reuse leverage.

Residual leverage. Incentives to reduce emissions/discharges aim at promotion good housekeeping measures, inplant collection or treatment and process innovation. Such incentives include:

- emission charges and user charges,
- (environmental) damage liability,
- subsidy/financing facilities for installation of clean technologies
- marketable emission permits

Charges will create obvious opportunities for reducing negative cash flows through emission reduction in the plant. Generally speaking, charges can be efficient incentives in cases where sources are stationary, potential exists for technological innovation, substantial differences occur in marginal abatement costs; water pollution and noise are the more promising policy fields (OECD, 1991:82).

Liability will affect the firm's balance sheet and financing opportunities unless counteracted by insurance; the insurance premiums will then affect firms' behaviour as do charges.

Marketable emission permits have been applied especially in the US (e.g., air and water pollution) but are increasingly being considered for use elsewhere. Marketable permits can be efficient instruments in cases where there are differences in marginal compliance costs, large numbers of (preferably stationary) sources, and implementation can be relatively cheap; especially air pollution could be dealt with this way (OECD, 1991). Applications could perhaps be envisaged in other policy fields as well (e.g., trading in permits of PVC containing packaging in the area of waste policy).

Input and reuse leverage. Incentives to reduce materials throughputs may also aim at a change in technologies towards materials saving alternatives, and/or at increased recycling of materials once they have been introduced into the economic cycles.

Such instruments include (Turner, 1990; Huppes, 1988; Opschoor and Vos, 1989):

- levies or charges on primary (virgin) materials,
- product charges,
- deposit-refund systems and return premiums.

The first two of these generate net revenue flows; the latter does not. Additional instruments for encouraging reuse are:

- user fees for waste collection, landfill, incineration of waste, etc.
- bottom price guarantees on secondary resource markets (e.g., paper).

Materials charges (e.g., on: aluminium, steel, glass, plastics, paper/board) may help to reduce the use of exhaustible resources, encourage recycling and hence discourage spillage. In addition, they generate funds that might be considered for earmarking for encouraging specific innovations or activities in the area of chain management (e.g., market support for secondary materials sectors, subsidies for speeding up technological innovation, funding waste treatment facilities).

Product charges (e.g., on packaging materials) would also support recycling and waste minimisation and would also generate funds. A disadvantage compared with materials charges may be their relatively high administrative and transaction costs (Turner, 1990).

Deposit-refund systems (e.g., on plastic or glass containers, paper, packaging materials) involve no net revenue flows and hence there will be no distributional impacts.

In terms of environmental impact, in principle these instruments favour recycling and waste minimisation. In addition to these points, Turner (1990) mentions the risk of competitive distortion on international markets. See also his contribution elsewhere in this volume (Chapter 12). Such systems can be appropriate when there are serious disposal problems, recycling or reuse are feasible, cooperative behaviour of agents is to be expected and administrative costs are low; the most promising field is that of waste management (OECD, 1991).

A new instrument yet to be tested empirically would be the Materials Deposit-

Refund. If the production of a certain product involves the use of certain materials or chemicals, this use could be the basis of a deposit claimed at the production stage or at the point of importation, and returned when that product is exported or offered for waste treatment (Huppes, 1988). The amount of the material would have to determine the sum to be deposited. In this way, only the polluter/user of the material would pay. Preliminary desk research on such systems has produced the following conditions: stable, non-volatile materials or equally undesirable metabolites, concentrations of material in products easily measured. Likely applications include: heavy metals, sulphur, compounds of N and P, halogenised hydrocarbons (including CFCs) (Huppes, 1988).

Output leverage. This type of leverage is normally implemented by using non-economic instruments such as direct regulation, zoning, structural sector-policies, etc. Products could also be subjected to a tax (or a subsidy); then, of course the effectiveness would depend on the tax rate and the price elasticity of demand. In areas such as transportation, a variety of economic incentives exist, all aimed at affecting the relative prices of using modes of transport, demand at specific times or in specific regions etc.

4. Evaluation of Chain Management Instruments: a Pilot Study of PVC

From an economic perspective it is important to be able to evaluate alternative instruments for chain policy in terms of their performance vis-à-vis a set of appropriate criteria. Amongst these are: environmental effectiveness, economic efficiency (both in the allocative sense and in terms of its including technological innovation), distributional impacts, administrative feasibility and costs, legitimacy (in terms of overall policy objectives or formal and informal conventions), political acceptability (Opschoor and Vos, 1989; OECD, 1991; Chapter 1 of this volume). It is important to be able to assess instruments impact along the entire MP chain under study and this again poses the question of how to model these chains (see Section 2.3).

Below, we wish to point out certain possibilities for evaluating alternative instruments in MP chain management on the basis of simulation with MP chain models. This is a tool yet to be developed, and the presentation is a very preliminary one only. The empirical area chosen for this pilot study is that of the PVC-oriented part of the chlorine chain.

Plastics are major contributors to waste problems in the Netherlands. At present, appr. 60% of all plastics including PVCs end up in landfills; this has to be reduced to 20% in 2000. Recycling is an important means to achieve that objective, although the avoidance of particular materials uses giving rise to this waste flow would be even more effective. In a waste prevention oriented environmental policy there will, at least as an intermediary step, be a need for enhancing the reuse of materials in the product life cycle. Reuse is to grow from the present 10% to 35% in 2000.

Sophisticated reuse strategies may have to be considered, e.g., the so-called 'recycling cascades' in which materials are recycled in a sequence of phases by using them as inputs for products where the quality requirements decrease with each subsequent phase. PVC and PVC substitutes provide examples of this: PVC can be collected and cleaned to form an input for PVCs used in less demanding applications in materials for pipes and floors; less pure collected PVCs can be reused for lower grade secondary or tertiary end-products such as pallets, garden seats etc; finally, unclean PVC, often mixed with other plastics will be incinerated, with heat as a side product. PVC as a packaging material could be replaced by the environmentally less damaged polyethene and polypropylene.

PVC chain management can be looked at from two perspectives: strategies and notions of the sector itself, and the governmental position; the latter was, in general terms, described in Section 3.1. In terms of instruments a range of options exist (see Table 1) ranging from bans of certain products such as chlorine or of emissions such as VC, to persuasive tools such as product labelling; here we shall confine ourselves to some economic instruments.

The PVC industry itself regards as its objectives (Caesar, 1990; AKZO, 1990): the management of the chain as such, and the minimisation of environmental objections to PVC. In terms of strategies, industry focuses on technical abatement of VC emissions, responsible incineration of the so-called 'heavy ends', the substitution of environmentally undesirable additives, the support of new recycling projects, and the reconditioning of retrieved plastics, etc.

In terms of specific instruments, industry is against charges and prefers a gentleman's agreement type of approach to reuse, etc. In addition, it is in favour of a low VAT tariff for recycled/reconditioned products. In line with industry's general attitude, the PVC industry demands that any measures taken and instruments applied, in concordance with EC regulations.

Looking at the PVC chain (Figures 3, 4) possible economic instruments for controlling the PVC chain include:

(1) a charge on chlorine,
(2) a charge on vinylchloride,
(3) a product charge on PVC,
(4) an emission charge,
(5) a deposit-refund system on chlorine,
(6) a deposit-refund system on PVC,
(7) tradable Cl emission rights

First, an *ex ante* evaluation will be attempted in general terms. Out of the list of potential economic instruments the following ones have been selected as candidates for a further analysis: 2, 3, 4, 5, 6. The chlorine charge has been excluded because of its impacts on environmentally acceptable applications; tradable Cl rights have been excluded because of the market structure and the considerations discussed in Section 3.3.

A VC charge would favour plastics without Cl; a PVC charge would be a direct alternative to this. An emission charge would discriminate between alternative processes within the PVC chain. A chlorine deposit-refund system would discriminate against PVC applications where the chlorine is gradually released into the environment, and would make alternatives without chlorine attractive from a cashflow perspective; it would also favour reuse, as collection of PVC is stimulated. A PVC deposit-return system would operate in very much the same fashion.

A qualitative comparison of instruments by assessing their performance in terms of various criteria (such as environmental effectivity, economic efficiency, acceptability) is all that policy making is normally based on. Implicitly or explicitly, this amounts to deciding on the information as contained in a matrix of instruments-by-criteria such as shown in Table 2 for PVC chain management instruments (Hanemaaijer, 1991, unpubl.). In Table 2, a tentative and very preliminary evaluation has been given for the 5 instruments considered, in terms of:

(i)   their environmental effectiveness (i.e., the environmental improvements to be expected),
(ii) their economic efficiency (i.e., the economic losses relative to these environmental improvements),
(iii) their acceptability (as indicated by the expected loss in international competitiveness) and
(iv) their compatibility with PPP (see 3.1 above).

Such a matrix could be subjected to multicriteria analysis in order to reduce its complexity, but clearly decision making would be helped substantially by enhancing the information content of such a matrix, e.g., by searching for more quantitative and objective alternative approaches.

Simulation of some economic and environmental repercussions of applying these instruments in a model built on the PVC chain would potentially generate such a more solid decision support base for instrument selection.

A dynamic simulation model is being developed (in Stella) that will eventually capture the essentials of the PVC chain as described above (Figures 3 and 4). At present the middle segment of the product cycle of Figure 4 (i.e., from NaCl electrolysis to PVC polymerisation) as well as some features of PVC recycling have been modelled in separate modules.

Table 2. Tentative performance scores (− − to + +) of 5 instruments in PVC chain management

Criteria:[a] Instrument:	Environm. effectiveness	Economic effectiveness	Acceptability	PPP-conformity
VC charge	+	+	− −	−
PVC charge	+	+	−	−
Emission charge	+	+	+	0
C12 return	+ +	0	−	+
PVC return	+	0	+	+

[a] Criteria as defined in main next.

The first module models part of the PVC product cycle, prices and costs (of energy, ethane, NaCl, Cl, VC, PVC) as well as a demand function for VC. At present, two economic instruments have been incorporated in the model: a charge on Cl and a charge on energy. Figure 7 presents the model in a diagrammatic form; Figure 8 gives results of some runs. The model uses as much as practicable information on chemical and functional links (see sections 2.1 and 2.2), as well as real prices and costs. Explicit functions are introduced to describe VC demand as a function of price, and to postulate a time path for introducing levies or charges on chlorine and energy.

Assuming an exogenous growth tendency for PVC demand of 9% p.a. (2% in the model runs illustrated in Figure 8) and the postulated (as yet hypothetical) demand function, actual demand for VC is derived. Demand for VC in period t is assumed to determine production levels in the next period. The possibility of substitution of other products for VC is allowed for, i.e., up to 90% of present VC consumption (for appr. 10% of current applications no substitutes are available). The model's initial values are set to represent the 1988 situation and to produce price and demand levels for subsequent years. Alternative paths for introducing charges etc. can be modelled; in the runs behind Figure 8, a Cl charge gradually building up to a doubling of the Cl price in 5 years was modelled. A 2-step increase in the energy price was incorporated by first equalling energy prices of large consumers with those of smaller energy consumers (i.e., a 55% charge in period 1) and by subsequently introducing an overall regulatory energy charge (in period 6). Technical linkages between the various stages in the product life cycle have been modelled on the basis of the underlying chemical infrastructure of Olsthoorn's method (see above). Figure 8 (a and b) presents the resulting (hypothetical) patterns for price and demand for VC.

This simulation model is only a first step toward MP chain model for PVC. To begin with, the various applications of VC in PVC products and their markets

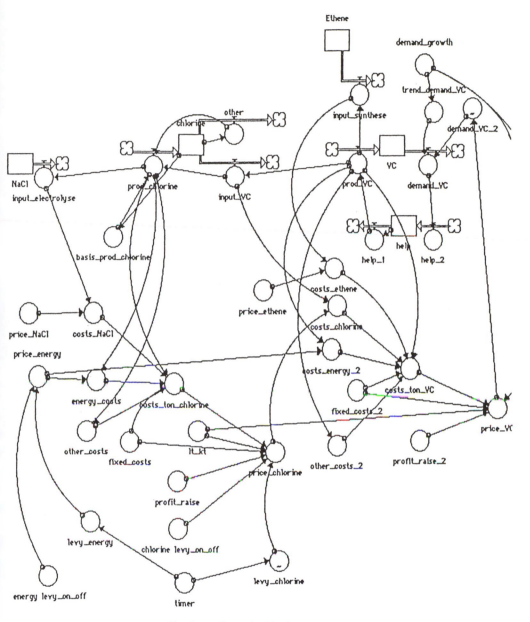

Fig. 7. A dynamic (P)VC chain model.

need to be modelled. The process of substituting for VC and PVC must also be modelled more explicitly in order to do justice to some of the elements in the upper half of Figure 6. Deposit-refund systems can be modelled in relation the recycling cascade. In order to be a fully integrated MP chain model, the spatial

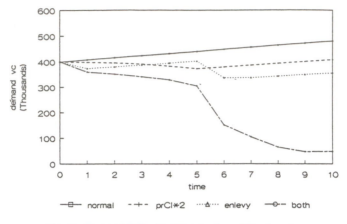

Fig. 8. Demand VC with 2% growth and fixed costs.

and associated ecological aspects would have to be taken into account. This latter step is beyond the scope of current research but the former modifications are being considered.

Beyond the production of PVC products, there is the waste/recycling stage to be modelled with various options for reuse of PVC through a 'cascade' ending ultimately in the incineration of plastics. This work has led to an as yet incomplete module for tracing the impacts of economic incentives on PVC recycling capacity. The module focuses on a specific subsidy scheme on PVC pipes recycling. Recycling options are constrained initially by a low initial collection as well as recycling capacity; the latter will grow as a function of expected future differences between recycling costs and virgin prices, under conditions of decreasing costs in relation to capacity. Recycling options are also constrained by a technical limit to the number of times PVC can in fact be recycled; beyond that level, the only option available is incineration with heat recovery. Figure 9 presents some typical runs of this module.

Under the assumption made, the module predicts a logistical growth in the capacity for recycling PVC and a decline (to technically determined minimum levels) of landfilling. If the module parameters were to match empirical values, calculations could be made of the net present values of the subsidy scheme in terms of the induced flows of costs (of recycling, incineration and landfilling, as well as the subsidy) and benefits (in terms of reproduced PVC and reclaimed energy).

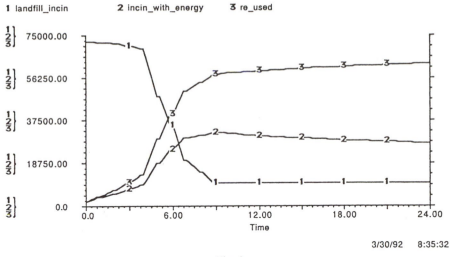

Fig. 9.

5. Summary and Conclusions

Environmental policy is developing a materials and products orientation, and an interest in the notion of 'chain management'. Chain management is the manipulation, from an environmental perspective, or 'materials-products chains' so as to optimise the environmental impact of these chains, or so as to achieve a certain accepted environmental impact at least social cost. This approach requires an understanding of *materials flows* and *product life cycles*. Materials flows are (mass) flows of materials through economy-environment systems structured along origin-destiny lines; materials balances account for these flows. Product cycles show flows of products through the economic process from primary production through waste treatment, as well as the related joint products in terms of environmental pressures. They have a different structure and basic dimensions. Materials product chains or MP chains are specific subsets of linked materials and product cycles.

Chain management requires instruments to effectively influence decisions within the chain. Table 1 presents a range of chain management instruments and some of their features are discussed. In order to assist in properly evaluation the various new instrumental and strategic options environmental economics needs to develop an appropriate understanding of the processes it attempts to influence. This point is elaborated by analysing the chlorine chain and some associated MP chains (Halons, and, particularly PVC) in the (Dutch) economy environment- system.

Attempts to analyse and describe complete chains appear to be too unwieldy; analytical solutions to these systems may not be practicable or may be non-existent.

Ad hoc, 'casuistic' simulation models are very appropriate alternatives or substitutes in the short and medium term. It appears that there is ample scope to extend MP chain modelling and to improve it in terms of applicability in ex ante evaluative research; even if one restricts it to the technological and economic aspects of MP chains. A dynamic simulation model is being developed (in Stella) that will eventually capture the essentials of the PVC chain; some modules and several model run results are presented. Various additional modules are to be developed and to be linked to the present model.

A process of learning through developing ad hoc MP chain models is required in order to improve the input of environmental economics into environmental policy oriented decision support. Such ad hoc models could be developed against the background of 'shared' input-output relations between the various product groups and economic sectors, both in terms of financial and material flows.

References

AKZO (1990) *Chloor en de samenleving: de rol van AKZO (Chlorine and Society: AKZO's Role)* AKZO-Hengelo.

ADCI (Association of the Dutch Chemical Industrial) (1991) *Integrated Substance Chain Management*, Leidschendam.

Ayres, R. U. and Kneese, A. V. (1969) Production, consumption and externalities, *Am. Ec. Rev.* **59**, 282–297.

Ayres, R. U., Norberg-Bohm, V., Prince, J., Stigliani, W. M., Yanovitz, J. (1989) Industrial metabolism, the environment and application of materials balance principles for selected chemicals, Report RR89-11, IIASA, Laxenburg (Austria).

Barde, J.-Ph. (1991) Economic instruments for controlling PMPs: A comment, in J. B. Opschoor and D. W. Pearce (eds), *The Economics of Persistent Micro Pollutants*, Kluwer Academic Publishers, Dordrecht, pp. 177–182.

Bergh, J. C. J. M. van den (1991) Dynamic models for sustainable development (PhD thesis), Tinbergen Institute, Free University Rotterdam.

Cesar, H. M. (1990) *PVC en Ketenbeheer (PVC and Chain Management)*, Nederlandse Federatie van Kunststoffen, Woerden.

Coase, H. (1960) The problem of social costs, *J. Law and Economics* **3**, 1–44.

Dales, J. H. (1968) *Pollution, Property and Prices*, Un. of Toronto Press, Toronto.

Dillon, P. S. and Baram, M. S. (1991) Forces shaping the development and use of product stewardship in the private sector, *The Greening of Industry* conference, 17–19 Nov. 1991, Noordwijk.

Dosi, G. (1988) The nature of the innovative process, in C. Freeman, R. Nelson, G. Silverberg, and L. Soete (eds), *Technical Change and Economic Theory*, pp. 221–238. Pinter Publishers, London/New York

EPA (1991) Economic incentives: options for environmental protection, USEPA, Policy, Planning and Evaluation PM-220, 21P2001, Washington, DC.

Georg, S. and Jorgenson, U. (unpubl., 1990) Clean technology: Innovation and environmental regulation. Paper presented at the Venice Conference of the European Association of Environmental and Resource Economists, Venice.

Hanemaayer, A. (1991) Het beheersen van de PVC-keten door het gebruik van financieel regulerende instrumenten (Managing and controlling the PVC chain by using economic instruments), unpublished thesis, Fac. of Economics, Dept. of Regional and Environmental Economics, Free University, Amsterdam.

Herwijnen, M. van, Koppert, P. C. and Olsthoorn A. A. (1991) Lange termijn mileubelasting en gebruik bulkafvalstoffen (Long term environmental burdens and the use of bulk residuals) IVM E–90/01, Free University, Amsterdam.

Hordijk, L., Jansen, H. M. A., Olsthoorn, A. A. and Opschoor, J. B. (1979) *Economische Structuur en Milieu* (Economic structure and environment), Min. of Envir. Management, VAR-series Nr. 7, Leidschendam.

Huppes, G. (1988) Principles van een stofstatiegeldsysteem: met een toepassing op Cadmium (Principles of a materials deposit refund system: With an application on Cadmium Policy), in H. Bezemer, W. T. de Groot and G. Huppes (eds), *Instrumenten voor Milieubeheer* (Instruments for Environmental Policy), Samson/Tjeenk Willink, Alphen a/d Rijn, pp. 103–112.

James, D. E., Jansen, H. M. A. and Opschoor, J. B. (1978) *Economic Approaches to Environmental Problems*, Elsevier Scientific, New York, Amsterdam.

Klepper, G. and Michaelis, P. (1991) Cadmium in West Germany: How much do we know about stocks and flows? Unpublished paper, Kiel Institute of World Economics.

Krozer, J. (1991) Decision model for environment strategies of corporations, Unpublished internal document, Institute for Applied Environment Economics, The Hague.

Mekel, O. C. L. and Huppes, G. (1990) *Environmental Effects of Different Package Systems for Fresh Milk*, CML-Communications Nr. 70, Centre for Environmental Studies, Leiden.

Neth. Min. of Environment (1990) *Nationaal Milieubeleidsplan: Afvalproblematiek* (National environmental policy plan: The waste problem), Tweede Kamer 1990/91, 21 137, nr 49.

Nijkamp, P. and Vohwachsen, A. (1990) New directions in integrated regional energy planning, *Energy Policy* (Oct. 1990), 764–773.

OECD (1991) *Guidelines for the Application of Economic Instruments in Environmental Policy*, Env Committee Meeting (Min. Level). 30–31 January 1991, Background Document No. 1. OECD, Paris.

Olsthoorn, A. A. (1989) Voorstudie Schone Technologie en Ketenbeheer (Pilot study clean technology and chain management), Inst. Envir. Studies (internal document) Report, VROM-project 262705-01. Free University, Amsterdam.

Olsthoorn, A. A. (1991) Sources of persistent micro pollutants: Analysis with dynamic materials balances, in J. B. Opschoor and D. W. Pearce (eds), *Persistent Micro Pollutants*, Kluwer Academic Publishers, Dordrecht, pp. 9–19.

Olsthoorn, A. A., van Herwijnen, M. and Koppert, P. C. (1991) Ketenbeheer van Vliegas met Dynamische Materiaalbalansen Chain management of flyash with dynamic materials balances, *Milieu* 1, 7–11.

Opschoor, J. B. (1991) Economic instruments for controlling PMPs, in J. B. Opschoor and D. W. Pearce (eds), *The Economics of Persistent Micro Pollutants*, Kluwer Academic Publishers, Dordrecht, pp. 163–176.

Opschoor, J. B. and Vos, H. B. (1989) *Economic Instruments for Environmental Protection*, OECD, Paris.

Perrings, Ch. (1987) *Economy and the Enviroment*, Cambridge University Press.

Pigou, A. (1920) *The Economics of Welfare*, London, MacMillan, 1962.

Prince, R. Butler, P. and Howe, Ch. W. (1990) Incentive for improving pollution control technology in a single internal market: a comparison of simple and combinative abatement policies, Paper presented at the 1990 Conference of the European Association of Environmental and Resource Economists, Venice.

RMNO (Raad voor Milieu en Natuuronderzoek) (1991) *Naar een Duurzaam Grondstoffenbeheer* (Towards a substainable management of resources), Signaaladvies, Rijswijk.

Turner, R. K. (1990) *Funding Mechanisms for Improved Recycling of Packaging Materials in Europe*, ERRA (Eur. Recovery and Recycling Ass.), Brussels.

Weenen, J. C. van (1990) *Waste Prevention: Theory and Practice*, Ph.D-thesis, Delft Technical University.

Wolfson (Stuurgroep Regulerende Energieheffingen) (1992) *Eindrapportage Stuurgroep Regulerende Energieheffingen* (Final Report by Steering Group Regulatory Energy Charges). Ministry of Economic Affairs, The Hague.

Yanowitz, J. (1989) Chlorine: Anthropogenic Sources and Flows, in R. U. Ayres, V. Norberg-Bohm, J. Prince, W. M. Stigliani, J. Yanovitz (eds), Industrial metabolism, the environment and application of materials balance principles for selected chemicals, Report RR89-11, IIASA, Laxenburg (Austria).

11. Wastepaper Cycle Management: Incentives and Product Chain Pressure Point or 'Leverage Point' Analysis

GERARD BERTOLINI
Centre National de la Recherche Scientifique, University of Lyon I, France

1. Introduction

In the paper product chain, a policy aimed at the substitution of secondary materials for virgin materials (cellulosic fibres) arguably combines environmental safeguards with positive macroeconomic effects, i.e., conservation of forests; savings on inputs and reduction of the pollution associated with the use of energy, water, and chemicals; savings on capital costs; savings on the financial and environmental costs of waste disposal; the creation of new resources and opportunities for economic development.

However, a number of caveats to this general proposition also need to be mentioned:

- is recycling merely an inferior economic substitute (an 'Ersatz') for consumption reduction measures? Such source reduction measures reduce overall materials usage via reduced packaging and product redesign or bans;
- how environmentally 'friendly' is recycling? The virgin pulp industry has reduced its consumption of energy, water, chemicals and the environmental damage which is associated with their use.[1] It contributes to the maintenance of some forests and also uses wood by-products from the forestry and wood industries, and other cellulosic products and by-products. Wastepaper can be incinerated with energy recovery, or turned to compost. On the other hand, wastepaper collection for recycling consumes in some cases a large amount of energy, and the disposal of sludges from de-inking processes is often not satisfactory;
- the viewpoint of countries exporting wood, virgin pulp or paper may be different (see infra);
- other restrictions and side or lateral effects are related to import-export of wastepaper (see infra).

Hans Opschoor and Kerry Turner (eds), Economic Incentives and Environmental Policies, 229–249.
© 1994 *Kluwer Academic Publishers. Printed in the Netherlands.*

More generally, how are the benefits distributed? It is also, of course, necessary to consider the microeconomic implications at all different stages – production
of paper products, distribution, consumption, recovery or disposal – in terms of:

- technical possibilities (substitutability);
- prices (differential costs) and qualities; competitiveness of the substitutes
  (recycling must compete simultaneously with primary manufacturing and
  with traditional disposal options);
- specific preferences.

The policy options and the tools used to enable an extension of wastepaper
recycling will be constrained by:

- the nature (technical, economical, etc.) of the barriers to the reuse of wastepapers;
- the different stages, or 'the links in the chain';
- the different types and grades of paper products and wastepaper (the qualitative aspects);
- the environmental and economic 'profiles' of the countries, and their (cultural,
  legal, etc.) background.

Figure 1 presents the paper cycle and distinguishes 4 'pressure blocks', or a set
of 'pressure points' for policy to target:

Block No. 1 – Final demand-oriented policy: pressure (incentives) to use recycled
    paper.
Block No. 2 – Recycled paper supply-oriented policy, or wastepaper demand-
    oriented policy: pressure (incentives) to produce recycled paper, or to use
    recovered fibres.
Block No. 3 – Wastepaper recovery supply-oriented policy: pressure (dis-
    incentives) towards disposal. However, this block could be split up into two
    blocks.
Block No. 4 – Pressure (disincentives) towards the use of virgin materials.

This chapter reviews policy and instruments options at each of these pressure
blocks, and attempts a first comparison of these options in terms of their economic
and environmental repercussions, given the structural features of the markets concerned and other contextual characteristics. In order to compare alternative
configurations of flows of wastes of different grades through the subsectors of the
wastepaper market, a concept of entropy within the waste flow system is developed. Furthermore, the recycling rates and recovery rates in different countries
and over time are calculated and compared to obtain a first impression of the scope
for policies to boost recycling and reuse in European countries; and to understand
countries' behaviour in international wastepaper trading.

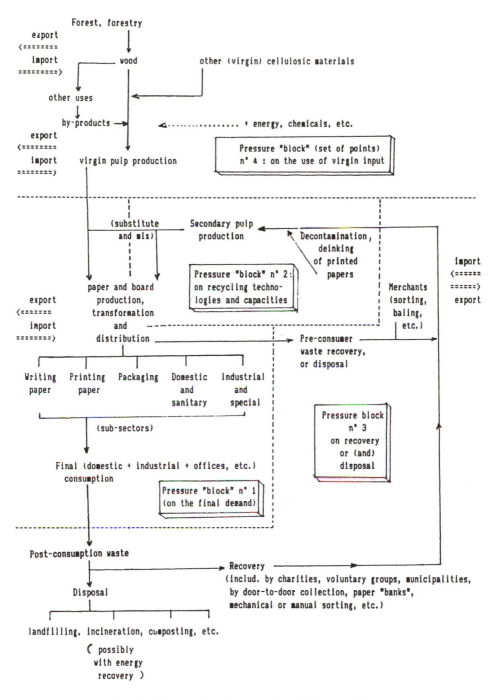

Fig. 1. Paper cycle and pressure 'blocks' for a policy.

Finally, the economics of recovery, recycling/reuse and trade of incinerating/ landfilling recovered materials is analysed.

2. Final Demand-Oriented Policy: Pressure (Incentives) to Use Recycled Paper

The preferences of the purchasers of wastepaper are related to:

(a) availability of supply;
(b) adequacy of the recycled paper and board for the end-use in mind (quality and technical performances criteria);
(c) relative prices of wastepaper and virgin pulp and pulp-based products;
(d) psycho-sociological factors;
(e) degree of environmental awareness.

The relative importance of these factors depends on the exact category of purchaser – households, public and private agencies, printers, industrial and commercial purchasers (with intermediaries, i.e., distributors and designers) – and the corresponding categories of paper products: writing paper, domestic and sanitary paper, copier paper, printing paper, packaging. Factors (d) and (e) relate mainly to the households.

For products such as envelopes, cards, notepaper, pads etc., the initial demand came from 'green consumers' and these items were sold by 'green shops' and networks. But the market was constrained by problems of availability and delivery guarantees. The price of the product was high, because the overall size of the 'green market' was not sufficient to allow volume-related price reductions (however cooperative purchasing agreements have since been developed). Product marketability was further inhibited by some quality deficiencies such as sizing, calendering, fluffing, yellowing and ageing. It was an example of a 'captive (green) market'.

Largely because of a greater degree of environmental sensitivity, the demand for recycled paper has been higher in W. Germany and other countries than in France. As a side-effect, France is now a major importer of secondary paper products. In France, households collect wastepaper largely for export and purchase imported recycling paper. The question then is should demand to be encouraged only if there is a domestic supply? Over the short run there is a possible conflict between the global environmental viewpoint and some national economic viewpoint.

For some environmentally conscious buyers, the recycled paper is (was) a 'superior' product, regardless of its texture or colour ('if it's grey, it's green'). But other buyers demanded bright white paper, especially for domestic and sanitary products; whiteness in this context, seemed to be associated with cleanliness and purity (a point reinforced by advertising).

In France and in the EC, product standards (NF and ISO) have been revised so as to eliminate references to the fibre composition (which were considered discriminators). A French law prohibits advertisements which highlight the virgin fibre composition of the product. An 'adequate for the purpose' grading system would be sufficient. But some consumers have higher or different 'quality' standards which recycled products cannot meet, and the vendors prefer to sell those products with the highest profit margins. Moreover, the photocopier and printing papers sector of the market needs information services, technical assistance and adaptation of some equipment, before recycled paper can make inroads. Ecolabelling is another potential option to distinguish and discriminate in favour of recycled paper products.

However, problems of terminology, definition and standards, all combine to constrain the market for 'recycled paper'. How much recycled fibre needs to be contained in a recycled product – 100%? For newspaper and domestic and sanitary papers, a mix of virgin pulp and recycled pulp will be required with the exact proportions being dependent on production (including decontamination) technology and innovation.

To develop the demand of recycled paper, the government may also use instruments such as tax incentives or disincentives; as well as restrictions, including an obligation to incorporate recycled fibres in certain paper products (i.e., the French law of 15 July 1975, Title V, art. 17 contains this provision, but it has not been implemented).

Furthermore, public agencies, in their role as major paper purchasers, may set an example and 'prime the pump' for market development. Thus in the U.S.A., for example, the Resource Conservation and Recovery Act imposed a general obligation on federal agencies to purchase items from recycled materials. EPA was to issue guidelines to assist them in carrying out this task but took a long time to do so. However, in the U.S.A. like in other countries, the actual results have been disappointing.

3. Policy and Pressure (Incentives) to Use Recovered Fibres

At this level in the product chain, the producers (the papermills) are the pivotal point of the system; hence pressure is likely to be best exerted on these mills, or incentives offered to them. There are two aspects to take into account:

- technical substitutability (of secondary/virgin fibres); and
- comparative production costs.

In order to mitigate the technical problems which inhibit the use of secondary fibre inputs, the types of incentives available are: R and D programmes, R and D subsidies, technical feasibility studies, technical assistance, loans, tax exemptions, tax credit programmes, etc. De-inking and decontamination (problems from gummed labels, adhesives, glued binders, waxes, rubber, etc.) continue to present technical difficulties. Thus, the use of some inks, contaminants or contraries could be prohibited provided adequate substitutes were available. In France, from 1978 to 1988, investment in de-inking to produce printing papers and corrugated cardboard was actively encouraged. The aim was to achieve:

- a capacity expansion of 700 000 tons at least; with
- a total investment of 371 million FF, in addition
- to public funds from the Waste Agency (67 million FF.)
    + other public aids from the Water agencies, the R and D Agency and the Ministry of Industry.

Substitution is partly a technical problem, partly an economic problem. Comparative production costs (recycled versus primary price inputs) give the ceiling price of the recovered wastepapers.

Some statistical data are required in order to anlayse the structure of the wastepaper market. In particular we need to know:

(a)   the recovery (or collection) rate;
(b)   the recycling (utilisation) or reuse rate;
(c)   the imports and exports of wastepaper.

The definitions of these concepts are given in Figure 2. Statistical information on recovery and recycling in the EC countries is presented in Tables 1 and 2.

Table 3 presents recycling rates for different grades of paper and board in France.

Differences in the structure of the paper and board industry across countries explain some of the variance in their global recycling rates. Clearly it is easier to have a high recycling rate in a country producing large quantities of corrugated cardboard than in a country producing mainly writing and printing papers.

Furthermore, it is also necessary to consider more qualitative factors, and to relate the paper and board types with wastepaper grades, using an input-output matrix, see Table 4. It is possible to calculate technico-economic coefficients (related to a price structure), to try to concentrate the main values on a diagonal or to obtain a triangular form (by order inversion – possibly aggregation – of lines and columns), in order to calculate a coefficient of 'entropy' for this material system (sorting, decontamination and de-inking are upgrading or 'neg-entropic' factors) see Table 5.[2] It is also possible to use this analysis to examine the effects of some structural changes.

The wastepaper grades 4, 5, 6, 7, 8 are used partly by A + B, F + G and C + D + E, whilst the grades 1, 2, 3 are not used by A + B and are used mainly by C + D + E.

Moreover, A + B involves, after use ('consumption'), the recovery ('produc-

The basic idea of a recycling rate is given by the ratio:

$$R = \frac{\text{tonnage recycled annually}}{\text{annual tonnage available for recycling}}$$

But in practice availability is a fuzzy concept and international trade in secondary materials complicates matters. This gives us a paper recovery (or collection) rate, which is a measure of an economy's 'domestic' (national recycling effort. Thus,

$$R_R = \% \ \frac{\text{domestically collected paper and board}^1}{\text{apparent consumption of paper and board}^2}$$

It also gives us a paper utilisation (or recycling/reuse) rate, which is a measure of an economy's recycling 'activity' level. Thus,

$$U_R = \% \ \frac{\text{apparent consumption of waste paper}^3}{\text{total fibre usage by paper and board industry}^4}$$

R_R and U_R are usually calculated on a national and an annual basis. It is also necessary to consider production growth and stock variation.

Notes:
[1] imports of waste paper are excluded; incineration/compositing activities excluded;
[2] production plus imports, minus exports (also complicated by the fact that the lifetime of some paper products is longer than one year);
[3] international trade in wastepaper included in the statistics;
[4] use of fibres in other sectors, e.g., construction, insulation, moulded products and animal bedding excluded.

Fig. 2. Recycling activity and effort rates.

Table 1. Wastepaper recovery rates (%) of the EC countries, 1960 to 1990

	1960	1965	1970	1974	1980	1985	1987	1988	1989	1990
Belgium + Luxembourg	26	27	30	30	29	33	33	36	35	33
Denmark	21	13	18	26	27	31	33	33	33	33
France	27	27	28	28	30	35	35	34	34	35
Ireland	8	10	9	22	24					
Italy	15	17	21	28	29	30	23	28	26	26
The Netherlands	34	34	42	46	45	46	53	54	49	51
United Kingdom	28	29	29	28	32	29	30	30	30	33
West Germany	27	27	30	32	35	40	40	41	43	44
Spain	25	28	28	32	37	41	42	41	39	39
Greece	34	21	19	11	18		26			
Portugal							44	39	39	40

tion') of 4, 5, 6, 7, 8 and partly 1, while C + D + E involves, after use, 2, 3 and partly 1.

So it is possible to appreciate the entropy of the system, or alternatively, closed cycles, self-replenishment, recycling loops. In fact, entropy implications have to

Table 2. Wastepaper recycling rates (%) of the EC countries, 1960 to 1990

	1960	1965	1970	1974	1980	1985	1987	1988	1989	1990
Belgium + Luxembourg	30	28	22	18	28	27	25	28	22	22
Denmark	34		32	47		60	64	65	71	80
France	28	31	35	36	36	41	42	45	46	47
Ireland	29	42	35	66						
Italy	22	25	29	41	45	44	42	42	48	46
The Netherlands	20	23	34	43	50	61	68	69	66	65
United Kingdom	32	36	38	46	53	56	55	47	58	59
West Germany	40	46	44	45	42	44	44	45	45	48
Spain	28	32	30	38		57	59	54	61	64
Greece	33	31	29							
Portugal		21	5	11		34	42	39	40	41

Table 3. Recycling rates for different types of paper and board productions and their evolution, in France

Type of products, sub-sectors	1976	1982	1986	1987	1988
Newsprint			27.2	30.0	42.8
	4.0	5.7			
Other printing and writing paper			7.6	9.4	9.6
Paper for corrugated (fluting)	72.0	85.6	82.4	82.2	85.9
Other packaging	23.4	32.5	30.7	34.4	37.3
Boards	83.9	73.5	81.3	80.2	79.1
Household and toilet tissue (domestic and sanitary paper)	38.5	28.1	31.3	29.9	35.6
Industrial and special paper	5.3	5.2	15.1	21.9	23.5
Total (average)	36.0%	38.3%	41.1%	42.2%	44.5%

be viewed directly and narrowly (i.e., via the recycling rate), but also indirectly and extensively (i.e., recycling in the same or different subsector, with different kinds of recycling 'cascades'). Thus for writing and printing papers (A + B), the recycling rate is low (13.9%). The recovered fibres are used not only within the subsector but also by the other sectors. Moreover, within the sector, the de-inking process can be considered as a 'neg-entropic' factor.

On the other hand, the recycling rate for the packaging sector is high (77.1%) and the recovered fibres are all used internally within the sector.

From a policy intervention viewpoint the pressure points or blocks (1) and (2), the limiting factors and the appropriate incentive points all depend on the types of wastepapers under consideration. Thus, old corrugated containers and other kraft qualities are supply-side limited, while old newspapers and magazines are demand-side limited (see Table 6).

It is also interesting to set the recycling rate against the recovery rate for different countries, and track the outcome over time, see Figure 3 and Table 6.

Table 4. The structure of a national wastepaper market. Example: France, 1988. Wastepaper Consumption (KT = 1000 Tons). By subsectors (columns) and wastepaper grades (lines)

Subsectors / Grades	A News-print	B Other printing + writing	C Paper for cor-rugation	D Other packag-aging	E Boards	F Household and sani-tary (tissue)	G Indus-trial and special	Total
1. Mixed	–	–	228,1	8,1	107,3	–	–	343,4
2. Old corrugated containers (boxes)	–	–	1301,2	47,7	167,0	4,8	23,7	1546,4
3. Kraft qualities, sacks, etc.	–	–	17,5	21,6	1,6	4,4	6,5	51,6
4. Newspapers	11,7	8,4	0,4	3,2	54,4	3,0	1,8	82,9
5. Pamphlets and magazines	7,7	43,7	27,4	19,3	42,2	8,2	2,8	151,3
6. = 4 + 5 (mixed)	135,2	23,8	8,5	10,0	62,4	44,3	12,9	297,1
7. High grades	3,8	36,6	12,4	7,5	32,2	18,3	1,4	112,2
8. Highest grades (from chemical pulp; "best white")	1,6	127,5	6,9	49,0	12,2	23,1	6,7	227,0
Total paper and board	160,0	240,0	1604,4	166,3	479,3	106,1	55,8	2811,5
Recycling rates	42,8%	9,6%	85,9%	37,3%	79,1%	35,6%	23,5%	44,5%

Table 5. Aggregation, inversion of lines and columns, and calculation of % in lines and in columns

Subsectors / Grades	B + A Writing and printing	F + G Dom., San., Ind., Spec.	C + D + E Packaging	Total KTons %
8 + 7 + 4 + 5 + 6	46% / 400 / 100%	14% / 123 / 76%	40% / 348 / 15%	100% / 871 / 31%
3 + 2 + 1	0% / 0 / 0%	2% / 39 / 24%	98% / 1902 / 85%	100% / 1941 / 59%
Total	14% / 400 / 100%	6% / 162 / 100%	80% / 2250 / 100%	100% / 2812 / 100%
(Recycling rates)	(13.9%)	(30.3%)	(77.1%)	(44.5%)

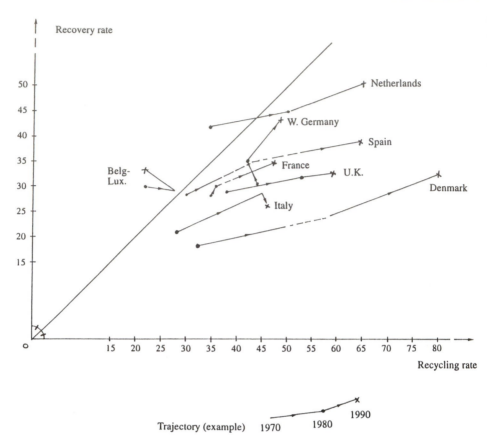

Fig. 3. Recycling rates and recovery rates of EC countries, and their evolution 1970, 1980 and 1990 (trajectories).

Table 6. Limiting factors and incentive points

Materials	Limiting factors		Appropriate incentive points		
	Supply	Demand	Collection processing	Mills	Industrial/ commercial consumers
Old newspapers		X		X	X
Old corrugated containers	X		X	X	
Office papers	X		X		
Mixed papers		X		X	X

Source: Franklin Associates Ltd 'Economic Incentives and Disincentives for Recycling of Municipal Solid Waste', contract prepared for U.S. Congress, Office of Technology Assessment (Prairie Village, KS: 1988).

In 1990, the recycling rate of the EC countries – except Belgium – was superior to their recovery rate (particularly for Denmark, and also UK and Spain). The Netherlands, and to a lesser extent Spain, combine a high recycling rate with a high recovery rate. A high recovery rate means collection from domestic households. The recovery rate is high in the Netherlands, and in Germany and Spain; but it is very low in Italy. Other countries have high recycling rate but a relatively low recovery rate (Denmark, and to a smaller extent UK). France is situated approximately in a 'medium' position. From 1970 to 1990, the recycling rates increased generally more than the recovery rates, except in Belgium and in W. Germany.

Table 7 examines these changes in more detail for just two countries – W. Germany and France. A recycling rate which is higher than the recovery rate implies a net import of wastepaper. The EC is a net importer and Figure 4 presents a diagrammatic analysis of the international wastepaper trade (1990) with a focus on EC countries.

The volume of trade in wastepaper has increased significantly over time. The exports of North America to EC represent rapidly growing streams, 738,000 tons in 1990, while the exports of the EC to the USA are very low. More globally, the USA is the main exporter worldwide, its exports have increased from 400,000 (short) tons in 1960 to more than 6.5 million tons in 1990.

The selling prices for the US exported wastepapers are low. This is because the domestic demand is relatively small and the freight tariffs for export are very low. It might be argued that at times US wastepaper is being 'dumped' on the world market.

However, the use of wastepaper to produce newspaper is growing rapidly in North America. In the USA expected growth is 3 million tons at the end of 1990 to 5 million tons (project) at the end of 1992. In Canada, expected growth is from 300,000 tons (one plant) at the end of 1990 to 1.5 million tons (12 plants) at the end of 1993 (including increasing wastepaper imports from the USA).

Trade between the EC and the rest of the world is relatively low and most of the activity is related to intra EC wastepaper flows which are considerable – see Tables 8 and 9.

France was a net exporter but has now turned into a net importer, while the reverse is true for W. Germany.

For a given country, if the recycling rate is inferior to the recovery rate (for some grades) it is likely that a policy of export promotion will be favoured, e.g., W. Germany and to an even larger extent the USA. Conversely, if the recycling rate is superior to the recovery rate (for some grades), it is likely that a policy of export-substitution will be favoured. Some countries have tried to limit the export of wastepaper, e.g., Switzerland (by taxes), and France, some years ago, with restrictions concerning exports (notably of old corrugated containers) to Spain.

Some countries, like Sweden, which are net exporters of pulp and paper products

Table 7. Evolution: comparison W. Germany/France

	1970	1965	1970	1974	1980	1985	1988	1989	1990	Comments
W. Germany										
recycling rate (A)	39.9%	45.6%	43.8%	45.2%	42.2%	43.5%	45.3%	45.1%	48.3%	relatively high in 1965 then stagnant
recovery rate (B)	29.6%	27.4%	30.0%	31.9%	34.5%		40.6%	43.0%	43.5%	increases (recently)
A – B	+13.2%	+18.2%	+13.3%	+7.7%			+5.3%	+2.1%	+4.8%	going to an equilibrium
France										
recycling rate (A)	28.2%	30.9%	34.5%	36.0%	36.0%	41.3%	44.5%	45.7%	46.7%	has reached recently W. Germany level
recovery rate (B)	27.1%	26.8%	27.5%	30.6%	30.4%	35.2%	34.2%	34.4%	34.7%	increases more slowly
A – B	+1.1%	+4.1%	+6.0%	+5.4%	+6.4%	+6.1%	+6.3%	+11.3%	+12.0%	the difference increases recently

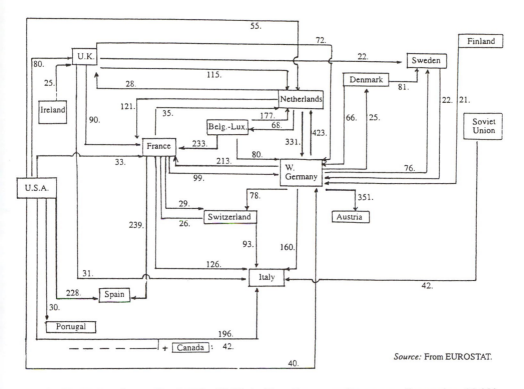

Fig. 4. Wastepaper international trade (1990) in West Europe; major streams (larger than 20,000 tons).

could only achieve a high recycling rate by importing increasing amounts of wastepaper. One can also mention that Italy, Spain and Portugal have 'invisible' exports of corrugated cardboard boxes (mainly produced from wastepaper). These containers are used for vegetables which are exported and therefore lost to the domestic economy.

Table 8. Intra and extra EC wastepaper exchanges (million tons)

1990	Intra EC	Extra EC	Total
Exports	2.8	0.9	3.7
Imports	3.0	1.1	4.1

Table 9. Details on exports from EC countries

From	To	1986	1990
W. Germany	The Netherlands	239 KT	423 KT
	Austria	298 KT	351 KT
	France	55 KT	213 KT
	Italy	129 KT	160 KT
Belgium and Luxembourg	France	140 KT	233 KT
	The Netherlands	130 KT	177 KT
	W. Germany	60 KT	80 KT
The Netherlands	W. Germany	205 KT	331 KT
France	Spain	222 KT	239 KT
	Italy	131 KT	126 KT

4. Wastepaper Recovery Supply-Oriented Policy: Disincentives Towards Disposal

The low prices for wastepapers give them a competitive edge over virgin fibres, but only some mills have the required technical flexibility. Other mills would have to invest in new equipment with all the attached risks.

While the comparative production costs (virgin/recovered fibres) provide a ceiling price – at least in the medium run – on the demand side, the floor price is given (in principle) on the supply side, by the costs of recovery, transportation cost, baling cost, sorting cost, collection cost, minus disposal cost.

Transportation costs depend on tariffs and on distance. Tariff policies (and also taxes and other restrictions) may encourage or discourage imports or exports. Some regional policies have been designed to develop local use: regional cooperation and agreements between mills and collectors, long-term contracts (some with guaranteed prices).

More ambitious attempts have been to accumulate, at a regional or a national level, flexible stocks to limit market fluctuations. The results of such schemes have, however, been poor.

Collection cost depends on the source of the different grades of wastepaper (from mill broke and printers' trimmings to post-consumer papers) and on the methods of collection and types of organisation (i.e., door-to-door collection, selective or separate, 'Grüne Tonne', 'bag + bag', containers, paper 'banks' and other facilities; or Municipal Solid Waste (MSW) sorting plants). In the EC countries, wastepaper represents approximately 40% of the MSW, by weight.

Experience in a number of countries has shown that when attempts are made to increase the collection rate the marginal costs increase while the value of the corresponding collected material decreases, that is to say a 'scissors' effect' is present.

In fact, the price elasticity of the supply is low (Turner, 1986; Edwards, 1979) and influenced by the grade structure. The supply of high grades is quantitatively limited, while the supply of low grades (newspapers, magazines, mixed paper) is related to the prevailing waste management policy. Local authority organised collection systems need time to set up and reach full potential but are not easy to stop once established and supported by local communities.

In W. Germany, the amount of wastepaper collected increased by 1,300,000 tons from 1982 to 1987 and the contribution made by household waste increased from 600,000 tons to 1,500,000 tons by 1987. In France, however, collection from households is stagnant at 150,000 tons, that is to say a recovery rate of 3%.

Some wastepaper is exported by W. Germany to France, with a negative price at the origin point. France and the 'Bureau International de la Récupération' have complained to EC about W. Germany subsidisation of wastepaper collection.

The main explanation for this practice is cost-avoidance; disposal costs in Germany are high.

The choice between recovery and disposal brings together two opposing forms of logic. The logic of recovery has been one of classical market-economy (with decreasing returns to scale) for a selective and extensive secondary materials collection service. On the other hand, the logic of disposal is one of public service (with increasing returns to scale up to some limit), for an exhaustive collection. Public officials had tended to argue that recycling must be profitable while at the same time sanctioning disposal subsidies.

To reach a financial optimum (cost minimisation), and also to restore fair competition, a payment (a 'pay-back solution') to the recovery sector is required. Moreover, recovery and disposal can be considered as functions to be integrated into an overall management system. The recovery function may be integrated by the disposal sector (e.g., in France, the largest disposal company – 'Compagnie Générale des Eaux' – has taken control of the largest wastepaper recovery company 'Etablissements Soulier').

It is also necessary to consider the competition between fibre recovery and incineration with energy recovery or composting, as different ways to 'recycle' wastepapers.

5. Household Refuse: Recovery or Disposal?

When the refuse recovery rate increases, one can realistically assume that:

(1) the marginal cost of collection will increase, and

(2) the value of the corresponding (marginal) recovered materials will decrease
     (lower grades, more contaminated materials, and so on).

For an illustration at a micro-economic level, with a fixed price for each specified quality of the recovered materials, see Figure 5. In that diagram, the quantities
are arranged in order of decreasing benefit to the collectors.[3] Revenue minus the
cost is the benefit (or 'rent') if the collectors are not required to pay a fee in order
to collect the material; if they have to pay, the benefit will be lower and can be equal
to zero.

In Figure 6, a similar analysis is provided for disposal. Here the assumption is
made that average and marginal costs of disposal decline with economies of scale.

Figure 7 summarises Figures 5 and 6 by bringing recovery and disposal together.
This figure has to be read from left to right for the recovery sector and from right

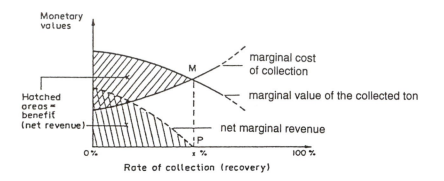

Fig. 5. Recovery: variation of the costs, revenues and benefits with the quantities (rate of collection)
and equilibrium point (M or P).

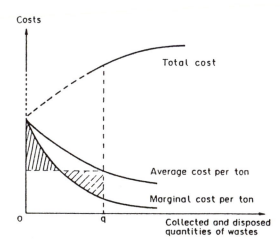

Fig. 6. Disposal: variation of the costs with the collected and disposed quantities of waste.

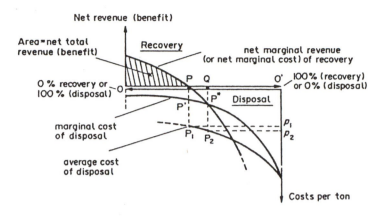

Fig. 7. Optimal recovery and disposal.

to left for the disposal sector. The first 'view' is one of complementarity, i.e., recovery as far as P (where net revenue or benefit is not negative), and disposal of the remainder. However at P, or in the neighbourhood of P, there is a jump from a zero cost for the community to a relatively high cost (or negative price): P′ or P_1. Is this situation financially optimal for the community and is it 'fair'? The disposal sector provides a new frame of reference for the recovery sector, viz that recovery reduces the need for the cost of disposal. It is therefore a substitute and may be paid for as a service, so the recovery sector would operate on a dual (mixed or combined) basis:

(1) recovered materials sold on the market(s), and
(2) payment (pay-back) for the service.

This question or dilemma may be considered for all the recovered quantities but, from a practical point of view, it is more useful to consider it only from or beyond P. Beyond P, the marginal cost of recovery is higher than the marginal value of the recovered ton, but the recovery option is less costly than the disposal option. For the municipality, the financial optimum (minimising the total cost) is for recovery until point Q; at this point the net marginal cost of recovery is equal to the marginal cost of disposal.

This defines the optimum for the quantities, but it does not quantify payments. The payment to the recovery sector as far as Q (from P to Q) will be framed between the area PP*Q and the area PP′P*Q (the corresponding saving on disposal) in Figure 7.[4] However, the disposal sector has to be paid for on the basis of the average cost P_2 for the disposal of the remainder.[5]

Higher fees or charge for landfilling and incineration – and the pay-back solution which is justified by the cost avoidance – will be favourable to the development of the recovery option. However, in some contexts, a side-effect could be the development of illegal dumping.

The fees for landfilling or incineration are at least twice as high in W. Germany than in France. Some countries, such as the USA, combine mandatory recycling with disincentives, i.e., product disposal (waste-end) taxes and product charges, to contribute to the disposal costs. Other countries, e.g., Sweden, W. Germany, Denmark, have introduced other restrictions on disposal. Another way is to revise the practical rules of auction and bidding on municipal contracts, to bid out segments of the waste stream.

However, one may have doubts about the effects on the wastepaper market of a generalisation of the 'pay-back solution'. There is a risk of excess supply and glut on the market. In an over-supply situation the risk is that some separately collected tonnages of wastepaper will be diverted to landfills or incinerators.

6. Minimising the Use of Virgin Materials

The inefficiency lies in the lack of or incomplete internalisation of environmental externalities which result from partial primary resource costing.

One can in principle apply pressure or (dis)incentives:

(1) towards other materials, e.g., plastics (with high energy consumption and disposal costs); or
(2) towards the use of virgin cellulosic fibres (e.g., taxes on wood, virgin pulp and paper consumption or importation, on energy, water, chemicals etc. or removal of subsidies.[6]

In the case of exporting countries, recycling reduces the demand of virgin fibres, but these countries have to consider, over the long run, the depletion cost of the resource. Some exporting countries operate an integrated recycling policy. Thus, Sweden, while it exports 90% of its pulp production and 75% of its paper production, has increased its domestic collection of wastepaper (350,000 tons in 1979 to 900,000 tons in 1989) and its recycling rate to 11%. But the rate remains comparatively low as a result of the importance of the pulp and paper exports; imports of wastepaper (in 1989, 220,000 tons were imported and 150,000 tons were exported); and the mixing of wastepaper pulp with virgin pulp.

It is necessary to consider the effects of several cycles on the quality of the fibres; some technical research effort has been directed at the problem of reducing the 'entropy' of the material system.

7. Conclusions

Wastepaper recycling can provide an answer to concerns of environmental conservation, from forestry to waste disposal. The objective would be to limit the entropy of the material system. Recycling may combine environmental protection with positive macroeconomic effects. There are some restrictions, for wood and virgin pulp and paper exporting countries, but the EC is a large importer. Moreover, a final demand-oriented policy (pressure or incentives) may involve conflicts between a global environment viewpoint and some national economic viewpoints, when recycled paper is imported.

The answer lies in a R and D policy to widen technical substitutability (recovered/virgin fibres) and to fund expansion in recycling manufactures, with complementary programmes to develop wastepaper collection from households.

Qualitative aspects have been introduced to consider limiting factors and appropriate incentive points, depending on the wastepaper grades and the relevant paper subsectors.

However, a side-effect of expanded recycling capacities may be an increase in wastepaper imports, instead of domestic collection, when the disposal costs are higher in other countries.

Another way to stimulate recycling activity involves the application of disincentives towards the use of virgin materials, but with other possible side-effects.

To avoid some side-effects and to avoid possibly going from one bottleneck to another, there is a need to combine policy instruments, and to develop an overall interactive chain management strategy. However, some iterative adjustments are not excluded.

In 1973, after the Kipur war, recycling was considered by EC countries not principally as an environmental challenge but as an economic and industrial objective with positive environmental side-effects. Efforts have been made to develop demand for recycled paper, and to provide the industrial infrastructure by developing recycling technologies and capacities (e.g., de-inking plants).

Public environment pressure has increased but it varies in degree from one country to another. Paper markets have been affected by this public pressure.

Recycling constraints (mixing virgin and secondary pulp) remain a major limiting factor, but pressure for recovery – instead of waste disposal – is growing and represents a form of 'backward inducement' to the paper market.

As a consequence of increasing costs and other restrictions and rules concerning waste disposal, in some countries, the supply of low grades wastepaper is rapidly increasing. Therefore their prices will stay low in the short and medium run with potential gluts on national wastepaper markets.

The problem of choosing the correct balance between recycling and disposal is complicated by the following factors:

(a) imperfect competition between virgin and secondary fibres (which are partly substitutable) and wastepaper prices which are defined by reference to the prices of the virgin fibres;

(b) different grades of wastepaper, which are partly substitutable in the paper and board sub-sectors; the limiting factor and the appropriate incentive points depend on the type of wastepapers;

(c) recovery as a substitute for disposal, depending on the cost of disposal and on the wastepaper prices etc.

Moreover, it is necessary to examine how the environmental and economic advantages are distributed. At the global level, the recovery rate coincides with the recycling rate. But does it have to coincide in every country? Specialisation or self-reliance of the EC countries?

While the paper and wastepaper market is international, with prices defined in this framework, one can observe large differences between countries concerning disposal costs. As a consequence, some countries with high disposal cost (i.e., West Germany) export excess recovered quantities at low prices (negative prices at the point of origin) and this hinders the development of recovery efforts in some other countries (e.g., France).

A basic problem is one of definition of waste, in order to distinguish it from secondary materials. If the price at the point of origin is negative, does wastepaper then have to be considered as a waste? If this is the case, wastepaper trade would have to respect the EC rules concerning waste import-export, including a special authorisation and the application of the principle of proximity. The rules may be applied only for extra EC exchanges or also for intra EC exchanges. However, an EC dilemma remains between the opening of the frontiers and restrictions justified by a waste management policy. The US 'dumping' practice also needs to be discussed and negotiated further, notably in the context of GATT (General Agreement Tariffs and Trade).

Notes

[1] For example, in France, the pulp and paper industry has signed with the Ministry of the Environment, for the period 1972–1976, a contract (an engagement) to invest 300 million FF – with financial incentives (mainly from the water agencies) to abate pollution and to develop cleaner technologies.

[2] The concept of entropy for materials is derived from its definition for energy:

 – The first basic physical law for energy is the conservation of the energy quantity, in its different forms. It is the same for matter; 'nothing disappears, nothing is created, all is converted', and the materials or mass balances have to be in equilibrium.

 – The second basic law for energy, which is known as 'entropy law' is one of degradation of the usable energy, from a (more) concentrated to a (more) dispersed form. It is the same for materials which are dispersed or which lose (some of) their original qualities.

However, it is possible to limit or to slow down the degradation, as 'neg-entropy'.

[3] Figure 5 may also correspond to an urban area, from the central, dense and richest parts of the town (on the left) to the less dense and poorer outskirts (on the right).

[4] The solution with be PP*Q notably if there is competition between collectors for recovery. Otherwise it will be the result of agreement.

[5] We have seen that a payment on the basis of the marginal cost leads to a deficit. In Figure 5 the value of the recovered materials is decreasing, but this has been considered as the result of decreasing qualities and not as the effect (or combining the effects) of the recovered quantities (supplied on the market) on their price. If there were only one quality the corresponding curve would have been a horizontal straight line.

[6] For example, in the US the elimination of tax subsidies for the timber industry has been estimated to have increased the use of wastepaper by 0.04% to 0.6% (Ruston and Dresser, 1988).

References

Bertolini G. (1987) Household refuse: Recovery or disposal? Research for a new economic optimum, *Conservation and Recycling* **10**(4), 321–330.

Deadman, D. and Turner, R. K. (1981) Modelling the supply of wastepaper, *J. Environmental Economics and Management* **8**, 100–103.

Edwards, R. (1979) Price expectations and the supply of wastepaper, *J. Environmental Economics and Management* **6**, 332–340.

Grace, R., Turner, R. W. and Walter, I. (1978) Secondary materials and international trade, *J. Environmental Economics and Management* **5**(2), 172–186.

Office of Technology Assessment (OTA), Congress of the United States (1989) Facing America's trash.

Massus, M. Wastepaper inputs into paper and board products (matrix), COPACEL, France.

Opschoor, J. B. (1994) Chain management in environmental policy: Analytical and evaluative concepts, chapter 10 in this volume.

Opschoor, J. B. and Vos, H. B. (1989) *Economic Instruments for Environmental Protection*, OECD, Paris.

Ruston, J. and Dresser, S. (1988) Policy options for developing secondary materials markets, *J. Resource Management and Technology* **16**(2), 52–64.

Turner, R. K. (1986) Recycling futures: Market prospects for wastepaper in the EEC, 1980–1990, *Resources and Conservation* **12**, 261–279.

12. The Role of Economic Instruments in Solid Waste Management Policy

R. KERRY TURNER[1] and DAVID PEARCE[2]
[1] CSERGE, University of East Anglia, Norwich, England
[2] CSERGE, University College London, England

1. Introduction

The generation and disposal of municpal solid waste (MSW) appears to have become an important policy problem in all industrialised economies. The OECD Member countries produced, according to official statistics, 420 million tonnes of MSW annually in the late 1980s. The precise composition of this waste varied from country to country, but in most countries packaging, it has been claimed, has become a significant proportion of the total (15%–50%). Table 1 presents estimates of the total amount of packaging waste in the EC and the level of recycling activity. Waste disposal practices also vary both between countries and across regions within countries. But with some exceptions (e.g. Japan, Denmark and Switzerland) a majority of industralised economies dispose of the bulk of their MSW via landfill.

Policymakers, and to a more limited extent society in general, have become more concerned about MSW, especially in metropolitan areas, as existing landfills have closed or have approached full capacity and resistance (on social acceptability grounds) to sitting new disposal facilities has intensified (i.e., the NIMBY SYNDROME).

Table 1. Estimates of packaging waste in the EC (late 1980s)

Sector	Total	Non recycled	Recycled	% waste recycled
		(m. tonnes)		
Domestic	25.0	22.5	2.5	10
Commercial	15.0	12.5	2.5	17
Industrial	10.5	6.0	4.5	43
All	50.5	41.0	9.5	–

Hans Opschoor and Kerry Turner (eds), Economic Incentives and Environmental Policies, 251–273.
© 1994 *Kluwer Academic Publishers. Printed in the Netherlands.*

2. Impediments to Rational Waste Management Policy

However, although waste management issues have acquired a higher political and social profile in recent years, efficient decision making – i.e., the achievement of the least-cost method or combination of methods for managing MSW in a given community (Turner, 1991) – as well as equitable decision making (i.e., the avoidance of overly regressive policy impacts) has been constrained by a series of 'failures' (Turner and Powell, 1991).

At a fundamental level databases on waste generation and disposal are deficient (information failure). While there is a variety of sources of data on MSW and other waste flows, most countries lack a single database that is national, comprehensive and current. Further, few countries have agencies which have taken an overall systems perspective when dealing with waste planning and management, and the lack of economic cost-benefit thinking has also been commonplace (analytical failure).

Even with better data collection and analysis, however, more efficient waste management would still be impeded by market failure. The authorities have failed to correctly price MSW collection and disposal services. The underpricing of MSW services (i.e., failure to reflect the full social costs of collection and disposal) leads to too high an aggregate level of MSW in a market economy and too low a level of recycling or source reduction measures. The causes of the throwaway society lie in the distorted market incentives that affect both consumer and producer behaviour. The result according to some analysts is product design, product choice and disposal decisions that are overly resource intensive (Menell, 1990). Too much waste is produced and additionally, the product-mix will not be optimal. It will not reflect that combination of products with the least-cost net environment impact.

3. Economically Optimal Level of Waste for Disposal

Figure 1 shows stylised costs and benefits of preventing MSW from reaching final disposal. The optimal level of waste for disposal to final environments is given by W*, where the marginal benefits of reducing waste (= the marginal damage avoided) are equated with the marginal costs of preventing waste reaching final environments (land, water or air).

More formally, we define

$$NBWR = B(WR) - A(WR)$$

where

$NBWR$ = net benefits of waste reduction

B(WR) = benefits of waste reduction

A(WR) = costs of waste reduction

Thus the optimal waste disposed of to final environments is given

$$B'(W^*) = A'(W^*)$$

or

$$-D'(W^*) = A'(W^*)$$

where D(W) is damage from final disposal.

Since all industrialised countries already engage in some recycling of components of MSW, we show actual recycling and source reduction measures (e.g., product redesign to achieve less resource intensive production) as W_0-W_1, i.e., W_0 would be the amount of waste being disposed of to final environments if there was no

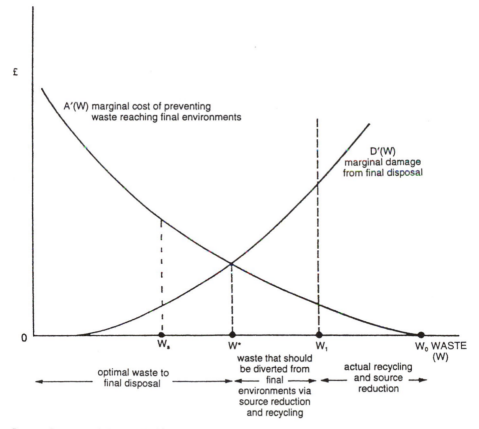

Source: Pearce and Turner (1993).

Fig. 1. Optimal disposal of waste to final environments.

recycling or source reduction activity. $W_0 - W_1$ is the waste already recycled or subject to source reduction.

In the absence of any government intervention, $W_0 - W_1$ is the financially optimal level of recycling and waste reduction – i.e., the level that will occur because of market forces. But because of the 'failure' phenomena outlined in section 2 the economically optimal level of recycling and waste reduction $W_0 - W^*$ is in excess of the current level, $W_0 - W^*$. Intervention policies are required in order to increase recycling and source reduction activity to the level $W_0 - W$.

4. Waste Management Policy Instruments: Command-and-Control Versus Economic Instruments Approaches

Regulatory Command-and-Control Approach

Environment (including waste management) policy has traditionally been secured (with varied success) through the use of the *command-and-control* regulatory standard approach. Under this approach the regulatory authority sets an environmental standard (target) and the polluter is required to honour the standard, under the threat of some penalty system. Table 2 summarises some of the waste recycling standards that have recently been adopted, or are under consideration, in industrialised economies.

This targets setting process is well-meaning but may not always represent a feasible policy objective because of information deficiencies and the lack of a proper 'systems' perspective. In the USA, Alter (1991) has concluded that a proper analysis of the MSW data that are available suggests a future decrease in the amount of recyclable items in MSW, hence a change in the economics of recycling. He further claims that an analysis of the intensity of waste generation (similar to materials intensity of Gross National Product calculations, Evans and Szekeley, 1985) questions whether the generation rate of MSW in the USA is likely to increase as the economy grows. Even if recycling scheme participation rates and collection system efficiency improve, Alter believes that national recycling targets much in excess of 25% of MSW are unobtainable.

In any case we would argue that neglect of the economics of waste management could lead to the setting of environmental targets that, although feasible possibilities, would still not induce net reductions in total waste flows.

In terms of Figure 1 suppose an environmental target W_s is set. The move from W^* to W_s would involve a net loss of economic welfare to society. The costs and benefits of moving from W^* to W_s may be written as,

$$\Delta NB = B_m + B_{nm} - C_m - C_{nm}$$

Table 2. Examples of the regulatory approach to waste recycling

Country	Regulatory standard (target)
Austria	Has passed a regulation which mandates the following refilling/recycling rates for glass and cans: Beer: glass 70% by 1992; cans 90% by 1994; Carbonates: glass 60% by 1992; cans 80% by 1994; Juices: glass 25% by 1992; cans 40% by 1994.
Belgium	Target level of 30% of waste to be recycled by 1995; the balance to be incinerated; landfill to be used only as a last resort.
Canada	National Packaging Protocol adopted in 1990, aims to reduce packaging in the MSW by 20% (from 1998 levels) by 1992 and by 50% by the year 2000.
France	50% recycling target (undated), either involving materials recycling or energy production.
Germany	64% recycling target by 1995, bias towards materials recycling rather than energy production.
Holland	10% reduction in all waste target; 50% minimum reuse/recycling target for MSW, up to 30% of which could be for energy recovery; landfill to take a maximum of 10% of waste by the year 2000 (intermediate targets to be achieved by 1994).
Italy	Legislation has laid down a 50% recycling target for both glass and cans, to be achieved by the end of 1992. From April 1993, containers which have not met this target will have a penalty tax imposed on them.
Switzerland	Legislation has laid down that the amount of beverage packaging in the waste stream must not exceed 10% by the end of 1993. PVC bottles are banned, and a 50% recycling rate for aluminium beverage cans must be met by the end of 1991.
United Kingdom	50% of recyclables (25% of total MSW) to be recycled by the year 2000.
United States	1988, EPA National goal of reducing waste disposal by 25% by 1992 via recycling and source separation.
EC	Packaging Directive is under consideration; proposals include a packaging waste 'standstill principle' which would operate 5 years after adoption and be related to a 1990 base level. After five years materials recycling should encompass 60% of waste, with a maximum of 30% as energy recovery and a maximum landfill requirement of only 10% of total waste.

where the subscript m refers to monetised benefits/costs, and nm refers to non-monetised benefits/costs. If we think of non-monetised costs and benefits as being purely 'psychic' there need be no *physical* resource flow associated with these gains and losses. For monetised costs and benefits, however, there are likely to be physical resource counterparts. Thus, associated with ΔNB is a resource flow of

$$r_1 B_m - r_2 C_m$$

where r_1, r_2 is the coefficient relating resource use to monetary flows of benefits and costs, i.e., the *amount* of resources per £1 of benefit or cost.

If we assume $r_1 = r_2$, then, if $B_m < C_m$ in going from W* to W_s, the resource use involved in the move is

$$R = r(B_m - C_m) > 0$$

There will be a waste flow W_R associated with this resource flow, where

$$W_R = R = r(B_m - C_m) > 0$$

by the laws of conservation of mass.

Thus, whereas the move from W* to W_s in Figure 1 involves a waste *reduction* of W* − W_s, it also entails a corresponding increase in waste of $r(B_m - C_m) =$

$$r\{[A(W^*) - A(W_s)] - [B(W^*) - B(W_s)]\}$$

$$= r\{\Delta A(W) - \Delta B(W)]$$

Thus the non-optimal move from W* to W_s involves *net* physical resource reductions of:

$$[W^* - W_s - r[\Delta A(W) - \Delta B(W)]$$

The sign of this expression is not obvious. It cannot therefore be concluded that recycling targets 'beyond the optimum' are legitimate even in terms of overall waste reduction expressed in physical terms.

Menell (1990) has concluded that although policies such as mandatory separation of household waste and product bans respond to some of the symptoms of the MSW problem, they fail to systematically address the causes of the problem. They do not remedy the distorted incentives that underlie consumer and producer behaviour. Product choice, as well as the disposal decision determines the social costs of MSW. Focusing solely on the separation decision (e.g., via mandatory separation) can lead to perverse results

Economic Instruments Approach

The economic approach to environmental policy has now been generally accepted (at least in principle) in most industrialised countries. It stresses the advantages of economic instruments (Els) which seek to modify human behaviour through the price mechanism (Opschoor and Vos, 1989). The basic idea is that Els would be deployed in the economy in order to correct for market failure. Els have the further advantage that they fit neatly into the cost-benefit approach and principle of management. Els do not, however, in themselves mitigate the problem of information failure and they will also require careful deployment, with due regard to system-wide effects and the need for integrated management.

A range of different EIs could potentially be deployed (see Table 3), including the so-called product charges, waste disposal taxes, and deposit-refund systems (in essence a combined tax and subsidy system). Administrative charges (covering among other things disposal site licensing), recycling credits (money paid to agencies responsible for recovering elements of MSW and equal to disposal costs saved by the disposal authority), and material levies, all represent steps in the direction of the EI approach. A system of marketable permits has also been suggested as a mechanism for boosting waste paper and board recycling (Dinan, 1990). EIs are now very much in favour in EC Commission circles and we can expect to see pressure building up in Europe for their more widespread application in the waste management system of the future.

EIs could be applied in the waste management system in order to raise finance and/or stimulate prescribed behaviour via incentives. Financing charges (user charges) have been used to facilitate the collection, processing and storage of waste, or the restoration of old hazardous waste sites. Incentive charges can be used to achieve multiple objectives such as, waste minimisation, source reduction and increased reuse/recycling. In this paper only EIs which are *directly* aimed at MSW reduction and/or recycling (reuse) will be covered. We therefore neglect the use of emission charges to air and water, resource extraction taxes and user charges, even though *indirectly* they will serve to reduce the overall generation of waste.

Table 3. Examples of the use of economic instruments in the management of packaging waste

Country[a]	Type of economic instrument[b]	Application: in use (u); under study/proposed (p)
Austria	deposit-refund	refillable plastic beverage containers subject to mandatory deposit of ÖS 4 (u)
		non-returnable beverage containers: ÖS 0.5 to 1 per container
	product charge	
Belgium	waste charges (incentives)	MSW (u)
Canada	deposit-refund	beer and soft drinks containers
		non-refillable containers
	waste charge	
Denmark	deposit-refund	refillable beer and soft drinks containers
		beverage containers, pesticides in small containers (u)
	product charge	various packaging products
	waste charge (incentive)	

Table 3. *(Continued)*

Country[a]	Type of economic instrument[b]	Application: in use (u); under study/proposed (p)
Finland	product charge	non-returnable beverage (carbonated) container (u)
		refillable beverage (carbonate) containers (u)
	deposit-refund	
Germany	deposit-refund	plastic beverage containers (u)
		extension to other packaging[c]
Italy	product charge	non-biodegradable plastic bags (u)
Netherlands	waste charge (incentive)	MSW (p)
	product charge	non-recyclable packaging (p);
		products with short live PVCs (p)
		products containing aluminium and long life-cycle PVC (p)
	deposit-refund	
Norway	product charge	disposable carbonate drinks containers (u)
		refillable beverage containers (u)
	deposit-refund	
Portugal	deposit-refund	metal cans (p)
Sweden	product charge	beverage containers (u)
	deposit-refund	aluminium cans (u)
	waste charge (incentive)	not-specified (p)
Switzerland	product charge	disposable beverage containers (p)
United Kingdom	recycling credits	MSW (u)
USA	deposit-refund	beverage containers (u)
	marketable permits	newsprint (p)
	waste charges	unseparated waste (u)

Source: Pearce and Turner (1992b).

[a] Some instruments apply at state, province or regional level only.

[b] User charges for collection and treatment of MSW are applied in almost all industrialised countries; taxes on the use of virgin materals have been implemented in Denmark and have been proposed in the context of sand and gravel resources in Finland.

[c] A 'Dual System' has been introduced (1991), it involves mandatory take-back requirements throughout the supply chain which can only be replaced by industry established separate waste collection and recovery systems (outside of normal municipal system). The Dual System would be financed by a 'Green Spot' approval systems, where verification and approval of a package's recyclability will have to be obtained. A payment (user charge of 0.02 DM per package will be imposed, depending on size, to cover the costs of collection and crude separation. A further fee to the form of a recycling subsidy is also being considered.

5. Criteria for Choosing Between Economic Instruments

According to OECD Guidelines for the application of Els (1991) a number of general
criteria can be listed against which the various Els can be evaluated:

(a) the chosen El should be able to mitigate the range of pollution and resource
     usage impacts associated with packaging. This is the *environmental effec-
     tiveness* principle.
(b) the El should provide a continuous incentive for seeking least-cost solutions.
     This is the economic *efficiency* (static and dynamic) principle.
(c) the impact of the El should not be significantly regressive, i.e., should not
     confer a disproportionate burden on the least well-off in society. This is
     the *equity* principle.
(d) the El should have both low bureaucratic and compliance cost (i.e., the
     practical difficulties of calibration, collection, monitoring and control should
     be minimised). This is the *cost-effectiveness* principle.
(e) simple and transparent Els are more easily internalised by the existing market
     and institutional system. This is the *acceptability* principle.

Two further criteria can be added:

(f) the chosen El should be compatible with national, or in Europe, EC regu-
     latory objectives and existing legislation. In the EC, the El would need to
     represent minimum requirements for countries newly embarked on a policy
     course and not in breach of the Treaty of Rome and the Internal Market
     provisions. Additionally, the El would have to be recognised as a credible
     substitute for or supplement to regulatory legislation. This is the principle
     of *institutional concordance*.
(g) given that household source separation recycling schemes carry a heavy
     collection cost burden, the revenue raising properties of a given El should
     be considered.

6. Types of Economic Instruments

A **materials levy** is an example of an input tax and would be imposed on the raw
materials used to manufacture packaging, with due account being taken of existing
rates of recycling and reuse. To meet the criterion of economic efficiency and to
conform to the strict Polluter Pays Principle (PPP), the size of the levy needs to
be related directly to the environmental damage done by the production and
consumption of the packaging, plus any scarcity premium if relevant. However,
where existing legislation covers environmental impacts from earlier stages of the
life cycle, a levy may need to reflect only the MSW environment costs.

A **product charge** is by contrast an *output* tax, a charge on the packaging end-product itself. The tax would be related to the potential waste disposal and pollution impact. Products made from wholly recycled materials could be exempted and products made partly from recycled materials could carry a reduced charge.

Both the material levy and product charge can in principle induce a change in the amount of packaging per product, i.e., a source reduction impact; and a change in the level of recycling that takes place at the point of consumption. The levy stimulates recycling because it raises the price of virgin materials relative to recycled (secondary) materials. It may also stimulate some source reduction if overall net production costs rise and this reduces the demand for packaging. The charge would again penalise products according to their 'embodied' waste and would stimulate a switch in the packaging mix towards lighter packaging. Differential charge rates could be set to allow for recycling performances.

In the UK a system of 'recycling credits' has been introduced in 1992. The credits are financial payments to waste collection authorities and in some circumstances private reclamation agencies, based on waste disposal cost savings which accrue wherever recycling takes place. The disposal cost saving credit is based on a calculation of half of the relevant long run marginal costs of the highest cost disposal option. In cases where waste disposal authorities are unable to calculate their own long run marginal cost savings an official schedule of representative savings can be utilised:

Inner London WDAs	£16.50
Outer London WDAs	£14.00
Metropolitan WDAs	
Shire counties:	£11.00
Transport cost paid	£8.00
No transport costs	£4.50

Cooper (1992) has noted that the establishment of a nationwide system of recycling credits has been viewed by several reclamation industries as an opportunity for making adjustments to their prices or provision of services. The exact status of credit payments to private recyclers is also somewhat unclear.

Waste disposal charges (user charges) should also induce more recycling as disposal becomes more expensive. A system that perfectly charged each consumer all of the social costs of disposal of each item of refuse would require comprehensive monitoring and enforcement and would therefore carry prohibitively high transactions costs. Real world systems (e.g., simple curbside charges based on volume or weight of mixed refuse) represent pragmatic balancing of the efficiency gains of a perfect pricing system and the transactions costs of such a system in practice (Menell, 1990).

Two communities in the USA have implemented (minimum transactions cost) curbside charging schemes, Seattle and Perkasie, Pennsylvania. In Seattle house-holds are given trash cans with differentiated charges according the size and number of cans provided. Residents are not charged for the removal of various types of separated wastes. In Perkasie, bags are provided for unseparated waste and aluminium cans, glass, cardboard and newspapers are collected separately. Residents are charged per bag which seems more effective than the can system in which residents are charged on a monthly basis for the use of a specific number of cans per week. Bag users can save money by putting out fewer bags in a given week.

Menell (1990) has further speculated that recent technological advances in scanning technology and the widespread adoption of the product bar code system could lead to the implementation of a fairly low cost yet flexible system of *adjusting relative retail prices* to reflect social costs of disposal.

7. Some Simple Analytics

Packaging tax (product charge): the nature of the external costs from packaging need to be determined. Using the cost-benefit 'with/without' principle we have the following:

(a) without packaging, we would not have *disposal costs* which are borne by society, not producers or users.
(b) without packaging we would not have *packaging litter*.
(c) without packaging we would save
    (i)   the energy/materials costs of packaging;
    (ii) the externalities associated with the energy/materials content of pack-aging with the production of packaging.
(d) without packaging we would reduce resource scarcity – e.g., the scarcity value of energy.

Items (a) and (b) are relevant to the design of a packaging tax. But, we argue, c(i) and c(ii) and (d) are unlikely to be as relevant as is widely thought (Pearce and Turner, 1992a). Since there is a fashion for 'cradle-to-grave' energy and materials analysis of producer and consumer products, we need to discuss the rationale for these conclusions.

Consider the costs of energy used up to produce packaging. These are *private* costs – i.e., they are part of the costs of production of packaged goods. As such, they are already 'internal' to the decision to produce and consume packaging. We are interested *only* in 'external' costs since these characterise market failure. Hence c(i) is not relevant to a packaging tax.

The *external* costs of energy use (e.g., CO_2, SO_x emisssions) *would* be relevant if these were not tackled anywhere else in the policy system. In such circumstances, the packaging tax should reflect the environmental damage done by energy used in the manufacture and transport of packaging. However, such external costs are typically *not* neglected in environmental policy. For example, in Europe sulphur oxide and nitrogen oxide emissions are the subject of agreements under the auspices of the Economic Commission for Europe (ECE) and the Large Combustion Plants Directives of the EC. Carbon dioxide taxes are also under consideration in a number of countries and exist in a modest way in several countries (Netherlands, Sweden, Norway).

If these externalities are regulated to an 'acceptable' level then it would be wrong to argue that the *same* externality should be regulated again through a packaging tax. This would amount to double taxation. Hence we reject the *general* relevance of item c(ii) for additional regulation. Even if current environmental protection policy is judged to be sub-optimal it can itself be made more stringent in the future thus avoiding the danger of double taxation and saving on implementation and monitoring costs.

There are two caveats to the view that life cycle impacts are not wholly relevant to packaging waste tax policy;

(a) if pollution taxes are meant to include taxes on *optimal* externality, then it *may* still be arguable that a packaging tax should be imposed on *all* life cycle emissions. However, even if this principle is accepted, it is widely argued that a tax which is targeted on the actual emission is more efficient than a tax on a product, the production of which has caused the emission. That is, a packaging tax to capture all 'embodied' life cycle impacts would still be inefficient relative to a direct emission tax;

(b) a life cycle analysis is needed to establish that life cycle impacts have been accounted for.

Thus, while life cycle *analysis* is relevant to the determination of tax policy, measurement of life cycle *impacts* is not relevant to the determination of a packaging tax.

The appraisal of natural resource availability and scarcity (item d) involves a combination of physical science, materials science and economic considerations. It is a complex process because scarcity is not the only influence in resource prices and prices often do not fully reflect scarcity, especially if the term 'resource use' encompasses the full range of environmental functions (amenity provision, waste assimilation and life-support) as well as raw materials supply.

Absolute physical scarcity is unlikely to be a significant problem for the exhaustible resource-based materials currently in use in packaging, i.e., aluminium, oil (plastics), paper, glass. The *user cost* of current resource extraction (i.e., the losses incurred in the future due to current extraction of exhaustible resource stocks) is therefore likely to be very small.

The exception to this rule would be the scarcity of final disposal sites themselves. If 'holes in the ground' become scarce either through physical non-availability (as in some cases in the USA and more generally in the Netherlands and Germany) or through social non-acceptability, then a 'landfill user cost' (LUC) might legitimately be added to the marginal external cost (MEC) tax. Ignoring LUC for simplicity, the general pricing rule for packaging becomes:

$$P = MPC + MEC \qquad (1)$$

where P is the price of packaging, MPC is the marginal private cost of production of packaging, MEC is the marginal external cost (disposal costs plus litter)

$$P = MPC + MDC + MLC \qquad (2)$$

where MDC = Marginal disposal cost
       MLC = marginal litter cost

if MDC and MLC are not already incorporated into the price of packaging through regulation, the tax t that is needed is:

$$t = MDC + MLC$$

Pearce and Turner (1992a) show how such a tax can be computed in practice, in the case of a tax on beverage containers in the UK

The beverage container tax can be calculated as follows:

$$t_i = \frac{W_i}{L_i} \cdot [1 - r_i] \cdot [MDC + MLC] \qquad (4)$$

where t_i = tax on the ith container in cents or pence per 100 litres
       W = weight of container – i.e., we assume external costs are related to weight, not volume, in kg/100 litres
       L = litres per container, so that W/L is weight per litre of beverage
       r = recycling rate as a fraction (e.g., 20% of 0.2)

Table 4 shows that a UK beverage container tax can be estimated simply on the basis of disposal costs, trippage rates, and container weight. On this analysis the ranking in terms of the lowest-to-highest product tax rates is:

1. cartons
2. PET
3. returnable bottles with T = 14
4. aluminium cans

The high ranking of cartons and plastics is perhaps counter-intuitive from an environmentalist viewpoint. However, inspection of the low weight-to-product ratio explains the ranking. If the basis was switched to packaging *volume*, it is possible

Table 4. Some preliminary estimates of a UK tax on liquids containers

	Type of container							
	Pet plastic	Aluminium can		Glass bottle				Carton
				One way		Returnable		
[1] Weight kg/100 litre	3.0		5.1	36		45		2.8
[2] Trips	1.05	1.05	1.11	1	7	10	14	
[3] = [1/2] Weight/trips	2.9	4.9	4.6	36	6.4	4.5	3.2	2.8
[4] Disposal Cost p/kg			◄------------ 2.0 ------------►					
[5] = [4 × 3] Tax in pence per 100 litres	5.8	9.8	9.2	72	12.8	9.0	6.4	5.6
[6] = [5/1] Virgin materials tax £/tonne	19.3	19.2	18.0	20.0	2.8	2.0	1.4	20.0

that ranking would change. The returnable bottle's rank order is determined largely by the trippage rate that is achievable. In terms of raw materials the tax ranking (lowest first) is:

1. glass (k > 1)
2. aluminium
3. plastics
4. paper

A **deposit-refund** system is essentially a combination of a tax and a subsidy. The consumer of packaging/container materials is given the right to a refund if he/she returns the waste product to the seller, i.e., to an authorised recycling/reuse point. For this right the consumer may have had to pay a formal deposit at the time of the purchase or have paid a higher product price. The superficial evidence drawn from schemes that have actually been implemented (most for beverage containers) suggests that DRSs may impose net costs on society. Actual schemes have led to only relatively small reductions in the volume and cost of waste disposal and litter reduction cost savings have usually been experienced but their magnitude has varied quite widely and such schemes have also been expensive to operate and have pushed up product prices.

   DRS may be **market-generated systems** or schemes imposed by law. This latter category of *government-initiated systems* can operate with or without the government being financially involved, i.e., owning the deposit. It is also the case the governments may intervene in existing market-generated systems. Systems (return offers made by firms) that have been generated by market forces have come into existence because the expected costs of handling and reusing the returnable items are lower than the expected overall revenues to the producer. This is usually because V (the net reuse value of the scrap item) is positive, or because the refund, R, stimulates a significant increase in demand, sufficient to offset a negative value of V.

For government initiated DRSs, *deposits* (D) must be related to the environmental damage caused by the disposal of the product (negative externality costs = E_x). Consumers who return the product in the prescribed manner get paid a *refund* (R), such that $R = D = E_x$, plus V the *net reuse value* of the scrapped product.

Figure 2 illustrates the case of a DRS introduced by the government to reduce litter and disposal costs. The consumer is paid R + V for a product return. If the PR curve is the *social marginal costs* to consumers who return the used product and the *social marginal benefit* is the disposal/litter costs savings (E_x) + V (reuse value), then the optimal deposit rate is $\overline{D} = E_x$ and the optimal return quantity is X_R. The amount of product waste $X_o - X_R$ is the optimal quantity of waste still requiring disposal.

In situations where the net reuse value of the scrap product is low or negative (usually because of high system set-up costs and storage and handling costs) there is a built-in, short run, incentive to firms to obstruct the system and make returning

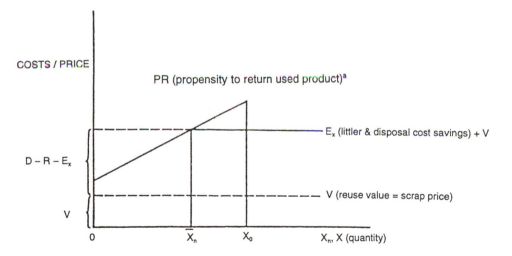

Note: (a) PR assumed to increase as R (R = D) increases.
Source: Adapted from Bohm (1981).

Fig. 2. Deposit-Refund System: Government-initiated.

by consumers more inconvenient, while retaining the unredeemed deposit income. Such a situation would require more extensive government intervention in the operation of the scheme.

Overall, on the basis of the cost-benefit principle the *net social benefits* of a DRS should be estimated by quantifying the following costs and benefits:

(i)   benefits from reduced waste collection and disposal induced by the oper-
        ation of the DRS (+)
(ii)   benefits from reduced litter caused by the DRS (+)
(iii)   benefits from reduced inputs to container production (+)
(iv)   costs due to increased storage and handling (–)
(v)   costs to householders in terms of inconvenience (carrying returnables, etc.)
        (–).

Government initiated DRSs should therefore not be viewed as a simple extension of the systems that would be generated by the market process. The market gener- ated systems will not operate efficiently if refund levels (R) are greater than (V), net reuse value, for a given product. The government has to intervene, and deposits related to the environmental damage caused by the disposal of the product would have to be paid to the government. Refunds equivalent to the damage costs plus the reuse value of the scrap product would also be paid by the government to avoid having the system obstructed by the market. A number of the mandatory beverage container deposit schemes that have been introduced in the real world have, however, been closer in design to the simple market systems than to the govern- ment-initiated and economically efficient system proposed by some economists (Bohm, 1981) An exception is a scheme introduced under Florida's solid waste law of 1988. A deposit of 1 cent per container will be charged from October 1992 on all containers made of materials that are not recycled at a rate of at least 50%. This deposit plus the market value of the recycled container will be redeemable at recycling centres.

A number of actual beverage container deposit schemes have had to operate, in the short run, with negative net reuse value (V) because of initial handling, storage and return/reuse/recycling system costs. Consumers have also had significant costs imposed on them in the form of lost consumer surplus as product prices have risen above the level of the deposit set. From the economic perspective, one important issue here is whether these price increases have been wholly or substantially due to real resource costs imposed on firms (and passed on to consumers), or whether they are more a reflection of pricing imperfections in the beverages market(s). It is also important to determine whether or not the resource costs imposed on firms are significant long run cost penalties of the return system.

If such DRSs are to represent increases in economic efficiency then the deposit set D must be equal to waste disposal and litter cost savings, which in turn equals

R (refund). V (net reuse value) will be greater, over the longer run, the greater is the switch to refillable beverage containers, and the higher the trippage rate (reuse rate) such containers achieve. An 'all refillables' system offers the best prospect for a positive V value which is also greater than R, and therefore a smoothly running and efficient system, provided that handling, storage and transport costs for the returnable system are not prohibitively high.

In order to facilitate the optimum DRSs, the government could pay lump-sum compensation to firms faced with genuine (short run) 'set-up' resource costs connected to handling, storage etc facilities. The government could, in the short term, also subsidise collection costs for those groups of consumers likely to be non-returners. Monopoly pricing practices should be covered by prevailing anti-trust legislation and regulation. In the UK, for example, three conglomerates control 40% to 50% of the soft drinks market and over 50% of the carbonated drinks market. The other 50% of both markets is taken up by around 200 smaller manufacturers which supply own label products.

Actual DRSs have generated both litter and disposal cost savings, although the exact magnitude of these social gains have varied from scheme to scheme and have proved difficult to value to everyone's satisfaction. Handling, storage and transport costs also seem to have been significant.

Evidence from a number of DRSs has also indicated that return rates are not very sensitive to the size of the deposit. A much more important factor in this context has been the number, knowledge and convenience of return points. Inconvenience costs to consumers may well fall over time as individuals adjust to the returnable system. Government regulation/legislation could mandate the required number and type of returning points, which in turn would boost trippage (i.e., return) rates. The downside of this suggestion is that the greater the number of returning points the higher will be the overall system costs for handling, storage and transport of returns.

A more detailed anslysis of the social costs and benefits associated with beverage container DRSs, with special reference to US and Australian experience can be found in Pearce and Turner (1992a).

Marketable permits have been proposed as a means of increasing the recycling of old newspapers, used oil and scrap tyres, in the USA (Dinan, 1990). EPA has been evaluating a scheme which seeks to establish a minimum recycled content for newsprint. this requirement would not, however, be imposed on a uniform basis, rather a permit market would be set up. The permit market would be designed to achieve an industry-wide recycled content standard, yet still provide flexibility to individual firms responding to the policy. By allowing firms flexibility, those with the lowest cost of increasing their recycling activities are encouraged to do so, whereas firms with high costs are able to purchase virgin material rights.

The full measure of potential cost savings associated with the permit system can be realised only when a market for permits develops and results in an efficient allocation of permits. four conditions are necessary for this result:

(a) firms comply with the policy;
(b) transactions costs are sufficiently low that they do not prevent efficient permit exchanges from taking place;
(c) there is enough certainty regarding the permit policy that firms are willing to engage in permit transactions;
(d) the market for permits is competitive.

In the case of newsprint, newsprint producers/importers would need to determine their individual 'new permit requirement' (NPR) by comparing the recycled content of the newsprint that it produced/imported with the recycled content standard (as laid down by the authorities). If the recycled content standard was less than a firm's product content then it would have a negative NPR would be able to sell surplus permits. If the recycled content standard exceeded the firm's product content then it would have a positive NPR and would be required to purchase permits from another producer/importer.

In principle, permit system induced efficiency gains are possible in the USA because the relative costs of producing recycled newsprint vary among firms (largely due to regionalised markets and the fact the pulping technologies in place vary in size and vintage). If all potential gains from trade are captured, permits will be traded up to the point where the marginal cost of expanding recycled newsprint capacity is equated across all firms. Thus the total cost to society of increasing the recycled content of newsprint is minimised. In contrast, a uniformly applied regulatory standard on recycled content would require that all firms produced a minimum percentage of recycled newsprint regardless of their relative costs of recycled-based and virgin-based inputs and production.

If the permit market is not competitive, or there are barriers to permit trading, the marginal cost of increasing recycled newsprint production will not be equal across firms and some efficiency gains would be lost.

Firm compliance with the permit policy is more certain the smaller the number of producers/importers that are covered by the policy. As the number of firms increases so does the cost and difficulty of monitoring and enforcement of the policy. The number of firms involved will also influence transaction costs. Firms must be able to easily identify potential permit buyers and sellers if transactions costs are to be kept low. In the newsprint case, regulatory constraints on trades are not required (as they are in water/air pollution situations when potential localised pollution 'hot spots' can become a problem) and this serves to keep down transaction costs.

The emerging permit market must be competitive in the sense that each firm acts as a 'price taker', i.e., it takes the market price for permits as given and makes it profit maximising decision accordingly. If on the other hand, 'price setting' behaviour evolves then the market price of permits will not reflect the minimum cost to society of incremental increases in the use of recycled newsprint. The target level of newsprint recycling would not be achieved at minimum social cost.

In uncompetitive markets the dominant firm(s) may attempt permit market optimising behaviour or exclusionary pricing in the final product market. In the former market, a dominant firm will try to increase permit prices if it has a negative NPR (seller of permits) or decrease the permit price if it has a positive NPR (permit buyer).

Dominant firms with market power in both the permit and the final product market can engage in exclusionary pricing in the final product market. The price-setting firm will use the permit market to increase the production costs of its competitors, in the expectation of gaining a larger share of the final product market. The dominant firm's aim is to increase the price of permits, thereby forcing up firm costs and reducing rival firm supply. However, the price-setter has to balance the loss of profits in the permit market (loss of permit sales if it has a negative NPR or increased cost of permit purchase if it has a positive NPR) against the gain in profits in the final product market.

Firms are unlikely to be able to engage in price setting behaviour if they control less than 10% of the market. The threat of new rivals entering the permit market may constrain such price setting behaviour and lead to the establishment of some 'limit' price for permits. It seems possible in the US newsprint situation that the demand for permits will be relatively inelastic and potential entrants will have to be large in order to command the necessary production economies of scale. Thus existing producers of recycled newsprint will be able to hold permit prices above a competitive market price (i.e., by selling permits at high prices, given their negative NPRs) and engaged in exclusionary price setting.

One further problem has been identified which will affect the firms 'commitment' for the permit policy. The duration of each permit is only one year, while the installation of the necessary de-inking equipment will take up to 3 years. Long-term contracts will have to evolve in order to resolve the uncertainty that permit purchasers will face.

8. Comparative Evaluation of Taxes, Deposit-Refunds and Permits

On the basis of the evaluation criteria set out earlier in this paper (i.e., environmental effectiveness; economic efficiency; equity; administrative cost-effectiveness; institutional acceptability; institutional concordance and revenue raising properties) a brief comparative assessment of the different EIs in the context of the packaging waste problem is set out in this sub-section.

The **packaging tax** instrument, in principle, scores well on both the environmental effectiveness and economic efficiency criteria. It does not itself need to involve the calibration of the entire life cycle (LCA) impacts of a given packaging product, though LCA may be needed anyway in order to determine that such impacts exist. Administration of the tax should be highly cost-effective, especially since it has been demonstrated that in practice it can be computed easily and quickly. The tax fulfils the Polluter Pays Principle and scores well in terms of the principle of institutional concordance. If market/institutional acceptability constraints emerge then the instrument is flexible enough to stand conversion into a materials levy, which might be more attractive to some industrial interests. Finally, the nature of this instrument ensures that a revenue raising capacity is in-built.

Disposal Charges (Curbside) based on volume or weight of mixed waste score reasonably well on the environmental effectiveness and economic efficiency criteria. Some US communities seem to be able to operate such simple systems without prohibitive transactions cost penalties (moderate administrative cost-effectiveness).

Deposit-refunds, in principle, score well on environmental effectiveness and equity grounds. DRSs can be aimed at recycling, but also at safe-disposal – i.e., an assurance can be given that more material will be disposed of through an authorised outlet, which is important for hazardous material. US beverage container DRs have been effective in terms of their return rates, which ranged from 72% to 98 in some seven states for which data was available. These container returns account for some 80% and 98% of the total national recycling of glass and PET plastic respectively (and some 64% of aluminium can recycling in the USA). Because DRs can target specific types of containers, without collecting other materials that might be contaminants, they have an advantage over other recycling collection systems. They may also discourage anti-social littering behaviour. Conversely, targeting means that DRs do not reduce the overall volume of MSW significantly.

In terms of equity, DRSs may be relatively less regressive depending on whether packaging product prices increase significantly because of extra system costs and on whether less well off individuals are the main returners. Price increases born by consumers through the deposit scheme are to some extent offset by securing the refund.

Actual DRSs do not appear to be economically efficient in terms of generating net social benefits. Much depends on the prevailing market conditions related to a given packaging product(s), but to date, cost-benefit studies have not indicated that DRS generate significant net social gains. The administrative cost-effectiveness of these schemes has been open to doubt, at least in the short to medium run, when 'transitional' costs are high.

With the exception of hazardous materials (e.g batteries, used oil, etc.) the general acceptability of DRSs in industrial and some institutional circles is quite low. There is a risk of competitive distortion particularly within the containers market. Carton and plastics containers manufacturers could impose a deposit for return of materials to an authorised site, but such materials could impose a deposit for return of materials to an authorised site, but such materials would not be re-used because of health regulations covering the use of recycled fibres in liquids containers and sterilisation of plastic containers. The carbon and plastics container manufacturers would have therefore to bear the cost of the DRS. Other container manufacturers would bear the DRS costs but would gain a supply of directly recyclable secondary material. Some recycled plastics may find a limited end-use in alternative products (indirect recycling).

No significant revenues are generated (unless return rates are low) by a DRS and hence recycling cannot be stimulated by a transfer of funds.

Finally, although the acceptability of DRs amongst industrial groups has been low, the general public in the US states that have such schemes seem very supportive of these ventures.

A Combined Deposit-Refund and Curbside Collection System has been in operation in California since 1987. Manufacturers of most beverage containers pay a fee of $0.02 per container to a State recycling fund. Returned containers are channelled through recycling centres or curbside collection programmes. The recycling fund pays $0.025 to the recycling centre or programme which presents documentation of having handled the container. Small retailers are exempt for handling returned containers, and large retailers may also gain exemption if they can demonstrate that there is a recycling centre located within a one mile radius of their store ('convenience zone').

The scheme also requires the State to calculate a 'processing fee' for each type of container. The fee is the difference between the average cost to recyclers of handling returned containers and their scrap value. The container manufacturer must either guarantee a scrap price equal to the cost of processing, or pay the State fund a processing fee equal to the difference between the two. It is also possible for the State to provide subsidies ('convenience incentive payments') to low-volume recyclers to help keep them in business.

The main drawback of this combined system seems to be the high administrative costs that are involved.

Marketable permits depend heavily on the market conditions in a particular industry if they are to generate efficiency gains. The competitive nature and size of the market are critical factors. The market needs to be big enough to allow competition but not so big as to cause significant transactions costs (i.e., low administrative cost-effectiveness). Environmental effectiveness may be a problem if regulatory constraints on permit trading are required in order to control potential localised pollution 'hot spots'. Acceptability, amongst industrial interests, will be low unless long-term contractual arrangements or brokering facilities can be established.

9. Conclusions

Cost-benefit analysis can be used to rigorously determine the optimal amount of waste that is directed to final disposal environments. The implication of this economic analysis is that 'waste minimisation' and 'maximisation recycling' are not necessarily socially worthwhile things in themselves. Each waste management option must be evaluated both in terms of its social costs and social benefits, indeed not doing so may actually induce more resource use than at the economic optimum.

The least cost principle determines the optimal combination of waste reduction and recycling, as well as the optimal combination of re-use (closed-loop recycling) and indirect (open-loop) recycling.

It is possible to use either command-and-control regulations or economic instruments to achieve some optimum, or target, level of waste minimisation and/or recycling. The primary virtue of economic instruments is that they provide for the economically efficient achievement of the optimum standard or target.

Choosing between individual economic instruments involves a complex mixture of issues and some situations will require either a combination of economic instruments, or a combination of regulatory and economic instruments. A range of general criteria can be listed against which individual instruments or combinations of instruments can be evaluated:

- environmental effectiveness;
- economic efficiency;
- equity;
- administrative cost-effectiveness;
- acceptability;
- institutional concordance;
- revenue raising properties.

On this basis, a packaging tax is conceptually simple, need not involve life cycle impacts and has the virtue of being computable in practice. The tax is also flexible enough to be convertible into a materials levy.

It seems possible to design simple curbside disposal charges (e.g., Seattle and Perkasie in the USA) which produce more efficient consumer decisions about product and disposal choices while at the same time not requiring prohibitively high administration costs. Future technological innovation might make a perfectly calibrated (in terms of full social costs of disposal) retail pricing system for individual products a feasible proposition.

Deposit-refund systems are best directed at waste management contexts which involve hazardous substances, in which 'safe disposal' is a priority requirement. Market imperfections cause significant complications for the efficient operation of DRSs, and cost-benefit studies of actual beverage container-related schemes have failed to demonstrate that such schemes generate net benefits. Part, but not all, of the reason for this scheme efficiently failure may lie with the original design of some of these returnable container systems.

Permits have not yet been actually applied in waste management. Their efficiency advantages rely on the right balance between market size and market competitiveness conditions. This will probably restrict an extensive application of this particular policy instrument. Permit trading will require long-term contracts and/or brokering facilities. Candidate materials suggested so far for this instrument are, newsprint, waste oil and used tyres, so applications in the packaging sector seem quite limited.

Acknowledgments

We are grateful to J. B. Opschoor and the other members of the European Science Foundation Task Force II; Environment Policy Instruments for comments on an earlier draft of this chapter.

References

Alter, H. (1991) The future course of solid waste management in the US, *Waste Mgm. & Research* **9**, 3–20.

Bohm, P. (1981) *Deposit-Refund Systems*, Johns Hopkins University Press, Baltimore.

Cooper, J. (1992) Recycling credits, *Materials Reclamation*, Feb. 15, 8–11.

Dinan, T. M. (1990) Increasing the demand for old newspapers through marketable permits: will it work? Paper presented at the AERE Workshop, Natural Resource and Market Mechanisms, Waunakee, Wisconsin, 7–8 June.

Evans, J. W. and Szekely, J. (1985), Newer versus traditional industries: a materials perspective, *J. of Metals* **37**, 12–20.

Menell, P. S. (1990) Beyond the throwaway society: An incentive approach to regulating MSW, *Ecology Law Quarterly* **17**, 655–739.

Opschoor, J. B. and Vos, H. B. (1989) *Application of Economic Instruments for Environmental Protection in OECD Countries*, OECD, Paris.

Pearce, D. W. and Turner, R. K. (1993) Market-based approaches to solid waste management, *Resources, Conversation and Recycling* **8**, 63–90.

Pearce, D. W. and Turner, R. K. (1992a) Packaging waste and the polluter pays principle – A taxation solution, *J. Environment Management and Planning* **35**, 5–15.

Pearce, D. W. and Turner, R. K. (1992b) The economics of packaging waste management: conceptual overview, Centre for Social and Economic Research on the Global Environment (CSERGE), Discussion Paper, WM 92-03, University of East Anglia, Norwich and University College London.

Turner, R. K. (1991) Municipal solid waste management: An economic perspective, in A. D. Bradshaw, R. Southwood and F. Warner (eds), *The Treatment and Handling of Wastes*, Chapman and Hall, London, pp. 85–104.

Turner, R. K. and Powell, J. C. (1991) Towards and integrated waste management strategy, *Environm. Mgm. and Health* **2**, 6–12.

13. Policy Instruments to Stimulate Cleaner Technologies

RENÉ KEMP,[1] XANDER OLSTHOORN,[2] FRANS OOSTERHUIS[2] and
HARMEN VERBRUGGEN[2]
[1] *University of Limburg, Maastricht, The Netherlands*
[2] *Free University, Amsterdam, The Netherlands*

1. Introduction

We know a great deal about innovations that help save costs or that render superior
services. The economics of the innovation and diffusion processes of such
innovations have been studied quite extensively. Our knowledge, however, of the
economic stimuli for innovations that help save the natural environment is rather
limited. We know that such innovations depend to a large extent on government
interventions. But how and to what extent government policy and different policy
instruments affect firms' and consumers' willingness to develop and use cleaner
innovations is quite unclear.

Up to now, the relation between policy instruments and innovation in pollution
control has primarily been analysed in theoretical models, as for instance in Wenders
(1975), Magat (1978), Downing and White (1986), and Milliman and Prince (1989).[1]
Although these models are useful attempts to provide clarity in the above-mentioned
relation, their conclusions are only valid in the narrow theoretical framework. To
differing extents, these analyses fail to take account of the available technological
opportunities and costs for developing new technologies, the supply of innovations by special suppliers, the time element in the adoption of the innovation, the
dissemination of knowledge and learning processes that are necessary for the
technology to be adopted, the appropriability conditions that determine the ability
of the innovator to capture the benefits from the innovation, the uncertainty involved
in developing and using a new technology, and the presence of multiple technological solutions.[2] As a result, these models are of little practical use for policy
purposes. In this chapter we will not pay further attention to such models.

This chapter tries to contribute to the understanding of the factors that determine the decision of possible suppliers to develop cleaner technologies and the
willingness of potential users to adopt such innovations. Government policy is
considered as an important stimulus amongst others. The effects of various policy
instruments (taxes, tradable pollution permits, subsidies and information) on the
supply and demand for cleaner technologies are analysed and compared. Besides

Hans Opschoor and Kerry Turner (eds), Economic Incentives and Environmental Policies, 275–300.
© 1994 *Kluwer Academic Publishers. Printed in the Netherlands.*

a theoretical part, in which determinants of the decisions to develop and use cleaner technologies are identified, and the effects of policy instruments on these decisions are explored, the chapter contains the results of three case studies on cleaner technologies: CFC substitutes, low-solvent paints and coatings, and membrane technology (in the metal-plating industry). The case studies examine the importance of the earlier identified factors, especially the role of government policy. This chapter also deals with the question of how policy may be better used to stimulate innovation in and diffusion of cleaner technologies. Although economic instruments are believed to have certain advantages, it is argued that there is also room for other policy instruments.

The chapter is divided in five sections. In Section 2 we identify and analyse determinants of supply and demand of cleaner technologies. In Section 3 the effects of various policy instruments for environmental protection on the development and use of four types of cleaner technologies (input substitution and savings, pollution control technologies, recycling, and environmentally-friendlier consumer products) are explored. Section 4 contains the results of the three case studies on cleaner technologies. Section 5 gives some conclusions and policy implications.

2. Determinants of the Decision to Develop and Adopt a Cleaner Technology

Introduction

In this section we identify and analyse the factors that influence the decision to develop and adopt an innovation in cleaner technology. To this end, we make use of the economic literature on technological change and the available literature on cleaner technologies. The term cleaner technology is used here as a general term for all techniques, processes and products that avoid or diminish environmental damage and/or the usage of natural resources and energy.

Before we go into the determinants of technical change which preserves and protects the natural environment, a few distinctions common within the field of the economics of technological change need to be made. First, technical change consists of three phases. The basis of technical change is scientific and technical research. This may result in a new finding or *invention*, such as new device, product, substance or material. The second phase of technical change is the 'development phase', in which 'upscaling' of research takes place, from pilot configuration to pilot plant. The third phase is the phase of 'market introduction'. When the invention is available to the market, or when it is used by the innovating firms themselves, we speak of an *innovation*. Usually feasibility studies precede market introduction. The last phase is the phase of *diffusion*, the rate at which the new technology is adopted by firms and sectors. Second, innovations can be divided into process and product innovations. A *process* innovation is a new or improved production technique, for example a computer-numerically controlled (CNC) machine or a cleaning device. A *product* innovation, here, is a new or improved consumer product. Third, innovations can be subdivided into radical innovations (a new technique or product or important, new applications) and incremental innovations (minor improvements of existing techniques and products). Below we will focus upon the factors which influence the development and diffusion of important new products, techniques or substances rather than that of incremental innovations.

Determinants of the Decision to Develop an Innovation in Cleaner Technology

Within the field of the economics of technical change there has been a fierce debate amongst economists on the question of whether innovations were determined by new knowledge and technological opportunities (the 'technology push' or 'supply push' view, inspired by Schumpeter), or whether the supply of innovations was predominantly determined by economic stimuli, in particular market demand (referred to as the 'demand pull' or 'market pull' view, with Schmookler as one of its important representatives). Since both factors are complementary and necessary, this seems to be a 'chicken or egg' problem. For our purposes this debate is less relevant; we simply consider both factors without elaborating on the relative importance of them.[3]

Apart from the technical opportunities and necessary market demand, more recently, another factor is found to be relevant to the realisation of an innovation in a market economy: the so-called 'appropriability conditions' that constitute the protection of an innovation against imitations by competitors. Together with the market demand, appropriability conditions determine the extent of the innovating company's ability to appropriate the benefits of the innovation. Protection against imitation may take place in various ways, varying from legal protection in the form of patents to secrecy or a technical lead, as described in Levin (1986). Just as the direction and rate of technical change may be understood *conceptually* in terms of the three following factors: (i) technology opportunities; (ii) market demand, and (iii) the appropriability conditions (see Dosi, 1988a), so may the decision to develop an innovation. Of course, the actual decision to innovate may be obstructed by specific problems such as management and engineering resistance, lack of technical expertise and skills, and insufficient financial resources. Also uncertainty about the technical success of the R&D project, of R&D cost and the costs of producing the innovation, and uncertainty about consumer needs and future government regulation may hinder or obstruct the innovation process.

(i) *Technological Opportunities.* To develop a solution for a specific environmental problem, certain technological opportunities have to be available. These technological opportunities are closely related to the existing scientific knowledge and technology, i.e., the 'pool of knowledge' or the whole of fundamental scientific knowledge and the knowledge that is embodied in machines, human beings and organizations. Such knowledge is not immediately available or free of charge. To develop such opportunities requires research effort and money. The development of innovation also involves risk. Many research projects and innovations fail, either technically or commercially.

The technological opportunities are related to the size and nature of the knowledge base existing within organizations. This knowledge base often is rather restricted and very much shaped by past activities. Thus, technological capabilities differ between firms. This explains why the innovation record is so different between sectors and firms. Pollution control technologies are usually provided by specialist firms in machine building and equipment industries. Only knowledge-intensive polluting sectors, such as the chemical and the (advanced) electro-technical industries, have the possibilities to develop cleaner production processes, usually with the help of suppliers of capital goods. Product innovations on the other hand are usually developed by the regular manufacturers of the products, either independently or with the help of special suppliers of equipment and materials.

(ii) *Market Demand.* The willingness to innovate also depends on the sales potential of an innovation. As a rule, the development of a new, cleaner technology for a firm's own use only is not profitable. Here too, a distinction must be made between product innovations and process innovations. Demand for cleaner consumer products manifests itself more easily through the market without government interference (despite the free-rider problem), and is a stimulus for firms to develop cleaner products. In contrast, the demand for cleaner production methods is stimulated mainly through environmental regulation, since cleaner production generally leads to higher costs.[4] Below we will go deeper into the determinants of market demand when we discuss the factors that affect the willingness of potential users to adopt a cleaner innovation.

(iii) *Appropriability Conditions.* For a firm to engage in R&D and to develop an innovation, it must be able to appropriate the benefits from the innovation. Imitations of an innovation by competitors undermine this. The danger of imitation is high in general because the knowledge which is embodied in a new technology becomes available to others when this technology is introduced into the market; knowledge which usually can be reproduced or used at much lower development costs.[5] Thus, the willingness of potential innovators to develop an innovation depends on the appropriability conditions. These appropriability conditions may be defined as the means of capturing and protecting the competitive advantages of new and improved products or processes (Levin, 1986).

Levin (1986) distinguishes the following appropriability conditions: (i) patents (as a means to protect from imitation and to receive royalties), (ii) secrecy, (iii) the technical lead of competitors, (iv) learning curve effects, and (v) the extent to which a strong market position can be built up (through reputation or the set-up of distribution channels). Dosi (1988a) adds scale economies to these factors. Appropriability conditions differ for each type of innovation. Technical lead and learning effects, together with additional marketing efforts, are the most important appropriability mechanisms for product innovations, whereas learning curve effects, secrecy and technical lead are relatively important in the case of process innovations (see Levin, 1986). In most cases, patents are additional appropriability conditions: they are important in some industries (such as the chemical industry and mechanical equipment industry) as well as for smaller companies. The benefits from the innovation may be reaped by firms with complementary assets as well as by imitators (Teece, 1986). There is also a relation between market power and approachability conditions. Monopolistic firms may be in a better position to reap the benefits of an innovation. On the other hand, if the invention is a substitute for their own products, such firms may successfully withhold it.

As far as we know, no specific research has been carried out into the appropriability conditions of cleaner technologies. When the appropriability conditions for certain types of cleaner technologies are inadequate, this may be reason for the government to conduct or finance research itself, or to stimulate cooperation between companies. It can also try to change the appropriability conditions although this is rather difficult.

Determinants of the Decision to Adopt an Innovation in Cleaner Technology

In economic models, economic actors are believed to buy a certain good or service if the benefits outweigh the costs. It is often forgotten that the realization of a transaction requires dissemination of knowledge and information about the technology and the economic consequences of adoption. Transfer of knowledge and information is especially important for new technologies to be adopted. This explains why the diffusion of an innovation, analogous to epidemics, in many cases follows a sigmoid or S-shaped curve. The diffusion of new technologies, however, does not depend on information transfer and learning only, but also on price and quality changes of the innovation, changes in market conditions (price changes, the obsolescence of capital goods), and, finally, changes in consumer preferences and government intervention. As noted before, government intervention is particularly important for cleaner technologies to be adopted. Such intervention may be in the form of economic instruments that affect the costs and benefits of pollution control and of R&D; in the form of emission standards that require the adoption of pollution control technologies (sometimes these technologies are prescribed); or in the form of communicative instruments aimed at a better understanding and environmental awareness of firms and consumers. In section 3 we analyse the effects of policy instruments for environmental protection on innovation and diffusion of cleaner technologies, and how policy instruments may be better used in this respect. Here we examine the influence of the following factors that affect the adoption and diffusion process of cleaner technologies: (i) the price and quality of the innovation (quality in terms of service characteristics) as an important determinant of the costs and benefits related to the adoption of the technology, (ii) the transfer of knowledge and information about the innovation which is required to realise a transaction, and (iii) risk and uncertainty about the economic consequences of the adoption of a new technique.

(i) *Price and Quality of the Innovation.*   The price and service characteristics of the innovation determine to a large extent the costs and benefits of the innovation for the individual adopters, and accordingly, its attractiveness to the potential adopter. These costs involve the costs of purchasing the technology, of implementing the technology, financial costs, operating costs. The benefits of adoption are possible savings on waste disposal costs, on inputs, a better image, and, in the case of consumers, higher satisfaction. With respect to these costs and benefits, we must distinguish between firms and consumers.

For firms, the cost consequences of adopting cleaner technologies differ strongly, depending on the size of the firm and the nature and age of production process. Smaller firms often experience relatively higher compliance costs as a result of scale disadvantages. Also, costs are high for firms that have to change or replace production modes. Despite of the importance of cost factors, the environmental aspects of production and products are becoming more and more important. A bad environmental reputation may have a negative effect upon the sales of products and may lead to personnel problems (such as problems of motivation or difficulties in hiring people). However, such stimuli are still rather weak.

For consumers, a high price and unfavourable quality characteristics of the innovation may inhibit the purchase of a more environmentally friendly consumer product. A hazardous consumer product may be superior to its cleaner alternative in some respects. There is also an opportunity for free-rider behaviour of individual consumers who may decide to benefit from changes in purchases and behaviour of others. On the other hand, as noted before, consumers' willingness to buy cleaner products is growing.

Again, we like to emphasize that the costs and benefits related to the adoption of the technology are not constant but change over time. They vary with the ageing of the capital goods and with price changes and post-innovation improvements of the technology as a result of dynamic scale and learning effects.[6]

(ii) *Knowledge and Information Problems.* The realisation of a transaction requires the transfer of knowledge and information. In actual practice, there exist numerous problems relating to knowledge and information which hinder the purchase of a cleaner product or technique. Apart from being unaware of the ecological damage they cause, firms often do not know which cleaner technologies are available, where to go to get information about the technologies or to find out which forms of technical and financial support may be obtained. Small firms in particular face knowledge and information gathering problems. In addition, firms often feel the need for independent advice. These problems of knowledge and information are particularly important with respect to cleaner technologies, since the knowledge of environmental aspects of products and production has barely been organized in firms.

Transfer of knowledge and information may be realised in several ways: besides through contacts with suppliers, it may take place through information (data) banks, congresses and trade fairs, demonstration projects, professional journals, informal contacts, or through special intermediaries such as advice and consultancy agencies.

Apart from firms, also consumers – being buyers of products – face problems relating to knowledge and information. Consumers are often unaware of the environmental damage of products they use and of the existence of environment-friendlier alternatives. Furthermore, it is very difficult for consumers to compare the environmental aspects of products on the basis of product information.

(iii) *Risk and Uncertainty.* Also risk and uncertainty about the economic consequences of adopting the technology affects the willingness of firms to employ such a technology. A lot of firms do not apply cleaner techniques because of the associated technical and economic risks. It may be necessary to change production routines and the work organization (new tasks, jobs, rewards, etc.). Moreover, personnel must gain knowledge of and experience with new machines. Process-integrated facilities that lead to radical changes in the production process, particularly involve much risk and uncertainty (see Hartje and Lurie, 1984). Such uncertainty may be reduced by a better transfer of users' experiences and guarantees from suppliers.

3. The Impact of Policy Instruments on Cleaner Technology

Introduction

In the previous section we pointed out that government policy, particularly the environmental policy, exercises an important influence on the supply of and demand for cleaner technologies. A wide array of policy instruments are available to the regulator: product and emission standards, pollution charges on inputs and waste material, R&D subsidies, special tax facilities for investments in cleaner technologies, compulsory environmental audits, information campaigns, 'green' product labels et. Further, cleaner technologies may also be stimulated by the government through its science and education policy, its procurement policy and by the integration of environmental aspects in other policy areas.

Since the available policy instruments do not only differ in a technical sense but also affect the process of technological change which helps to save the natural environment differently, it becomes important to investigate and assess the impact of the different policy instruments on innovation in and diffusion of cleaner technologies, especially to understand which instrument can be used best to stimulate which technology, and under which circumstances.

As one might suspect, the impact of policy instruments on technological change is difficult to assess. Policy instruments are but one of the many stimuli. Their effects differ between sectors and firms. Little information is available about what would have happened in the absence of a certain policy. Additionally, little experience has been gathered regarding some instruments, such as technology-forcing emission standards, effluent charges and tradable pollution permits. And finally, the effects of different instruments on environment-saving technological change depend on their implementation: their tightness, time path, differentiation and flexibility. All this seriously complicates a comparison of the instruments with respect to their impact on innovation in and diffusion of cleaner technologies. Our conclusions on the impact of different policy instruments on environment-saving technological change should be read with this in mind. They are rather tentative and rest on certain theoretical a priori's and notions of the economic reality.

The Factors Hindering Supply and Demand of Different Categories of Cleaner Technologies

As stated above, in analysing the impact of policy instruments on environment-saving technological change one should aim to take account of the supply and demand relations of cleaner technologies. Suppliers and users of particular cleaner technologies operate in strongly differing markets with the associated stimuli. In order to generalize about the specific factors that hinder or facilitate innovation in and diffusion of cleaner technology, a distinction is made between four categories of cleaner technologies: (i) input substitution and savings, (ii) pollution control and prevention, (iii) waste recycling, (iv) cleaner consumer products.[7]

Examples of input substitution are the replacement of CFCs by other substances and the switch to coal with a lower sulphur content. Pollution control and prevention technologies are technologies that avoid or treat hazardous emissions such as desulphurization techniques and anaerobic water cleaning. They can be divided into end-of-pipe and process-integrated technologies. Recycling consists of in-process recycling and the use of waste materials by other firms. Examples of cleaner consumer products are cleaner automobiles (for instance automobiles with catalytic converters) and low-solvent paints.

The demand and supply relations for these four categories differ. In relation to this, innovation in and diffusion of technologies in these categories is hindered by particular problems. In Table 1 a (general) overflow is given of the problems related to innovation in and diffusion of the cleaner technologies belonging to the four categories. In the case studies in the next section more explicit attention is given to the particular obstacles.

With respect to input substitution, technological opportunities are usually available. Suppliers of substances and materials are mostly large-scale and/or knowledge-intensive, industries such as the chemical, building materials and compound animal stock feeds industries. Such industries have a substantial knowledge potential which can be used for the development of substitute, less harmful substances and materials and for associated knowledge transfer. A problem which poses itself here is that demand for these substitutes has to be rather strong if these substances are

Table 1. Factors hindering innovation in and diffusion of cleaner technologies

	Input substitution and savings	Pollution control	Recycling	Cleaner consumer products
Innovation				
Technological opportunities	+	+	+	+/0
Market demand	++	++	+	+/0
Appropriability conditions	0	+/0	+/0	++/0
Diffusion				
Price and quality characteristics	++	++/+	+/0	+
Knowledge and information	+/0	+	+	++
Risk and uncertainty	+	++/+	+	+/0

++   serious problem
+   problem
(+)+/0 in some cases a (serious) problem.

developed and produced, since the production of new substances usually calls for rather large investments. Also, scale economies that result in lower production costs and prices are important. This hinders a substitution of inputs that have not benefited from dynamic scale and learning effects.

Also technologies which help reduce pollutant emissions and harmful waste material are usually provided by special firms outside the using industry. Pollution control technologies, especially end-of-pipe technologies, are generally provided by (rather small) specialised suppliers in the machine building and equipment industries. Process-integrated facilities are often developed by regular suppliers of capital goods in cooperation with their users. Also here, market demand seems to be the problem. Since these technologies usually lead to higher costs, demand for pollution control techniques depends strongly on government regulation. Policy that is based on available 'best practicable means' or 'best available control technology' (usually end-of-pipe technologies) however hardly gives an impulse to the development of new and more effective technologies. In addition, government policy is rather unpredictable which makes the business of innovating in pollution control uncertain and risky.[8]

With respect to the third category, recycling and reuse systems, technical recycling opportunities within and outside the firm are usually present, but in many cases waste material is not recycled as a result of economic and organizational obstacles. It is often cheaper to buy virgin materials. The recycling of waste does not only require some organizational changes within the firm but also new relations between firms, special intermediaries and a new infrastructure (for instance waste storage stations).

In the case of cleaner consumer products, insufficient appropriability conditions (that determine the benefits the innovator can reap from the innovation) might be a barrier to the development of cleaner innovations. Patents are relatively important for product innovations but may not provide enough protection. Also, the new product may be a substitute for one's own products, which reduces the willingness of firms to supply a cleaner innovation. On the other hand, the increasing environmental awareness of the public and the corresponding demand for cleaner products constitutes a strong market impulse for firms to develop cleaner consumer products. The actual adoption of cleaner technologies, however, is often hindered by specific problems. Cleaner consumer products are often more expensive and inferior in some aspects (e.g., recycled paper, which is less white and has a shorter lifetime) and there are serious information problems. Consumers are often not aware of the environmental aspects of the products they use and unaware of the existence of available cleaner alternatives. Also, the use of new technologies may involve differences in life style and behaviour and depend on social and cultural changes which are known to come about slowly.

The Effects of Policy Instruments on the Development and Use of Cleaner Technologies

The usefulness of the specific policy instruments to stimulate cleaner technologies depends on the way in which these instruments deal with the above problems, either directly or indirectly. As will be argued, no single instrument is considered to be optimal in all cases, although economic instruments have a number of advantages. When comparing different policy instruments, we focus on the effects of the instruments on the development of cleaner technologies and the use of these technologies. Other aspects such as their acceptability to society and their distributional effects are – despite their importance – not considered here.

In the economic literature, the whole debate on the choice of policy instruments in environmental policy is primarily on the question of whether economic instruments such as effluent charges (emission taxes) and tradable pollution permits should be used instead of emission standards. The benefits of economic instruments or price incentives to reduce pollutant emissions are many. First, effluent charges and tradable pollution permits are more efficient because every polluter is given the choice between compliance and paying the polluter's bill. The polluting firm cannot be forced to undertake emission control the marginal costs of which are higher than the effluent charge. Second, there is a financial incentive to diminish all pollution – not merely up to the level of emission standards. Third, such a system depends less on the availability of pollution control technology, therefore it can be introduced more quickly and adjusted, and once such a system is implemented it generally provides stronger incentives for the development of cleaner technologies than the present policies. And fourth, economic instruments stimulate much more process-integrated technology (including recycling technology) instead of end-of-pipe technology that is often chosen to comply with standards. A disadvantage of effluent charges is the uncertainty about their effectiveness since the abatement cost curves and the responses of the polluters are not known to the regulator. Tradable pollution permits do not suffer from this property, since a maximum level of emissions is set. Effluent charges can also be used to stimulate input substitution and savings, waste recycling and cleaner consumer products. The advantages are similar to the ones above. Whether such a system can be implemented, at low enough administrative costs, has to be studied on a case-by-case basis.

As mentioned before, an extremely unfavourable property of standards, at least in the way they have been used in the past, is that they barely provide an impulse to develop new, more effective abatement technologies. To deal with this unfavorable property technology forcing standards and innovation waivers may be considered. However, the chance that these instruments lead to high costs is large, unless the regulator is willing to soften and delay standards. But this would have a negative effect on the willingness to develop these innovations. They should only be used in case of good prospect of technological opportunities that can be developed at a low enough cost. Moreover, the chance that these opportunities are developed is greater when potential suppliers are located outside the regulated industry.

Economists have traditionally argued for the use of economic instruments in environmental policy. The social costs of production and consumption may be internalized and economic instruments are more efficient, so environmental improvements can be achieved at lower costs. Although there are good arguments for the use of economic instruments in environmental policy, the above anlaysis suggests that there might also be room for other instruments.

Uncertainty about the demand for cleaner technologies, partly related to unpredictable government policy, may call for the use of R&D subsidies or special loans. Communicative instruments can be useful in dealing with information problems related to the environmental aspects of products and processes. Environmental care systems (that are required in the Netherlands), demonstration projects and information campaigns can be useful in ensuring that firms make full use of the possibilities available for emission reduction. Firms are often not familiar with available cost-reducing environmental measures. These profitable environmental measures are especially connected with good housekeeping and waste prevention.[9] Information disclosure requirements, such as in the U.S., that force the firm to communicate, may also be useful. And finally, instruments of information, such as 'green' labels and product information, are in our view not only useful but also necessary to stimulate environment-friendlier products in view of the extensive information problems about the environmental aspects of products.[10]

Subsidies for investments in pollution control technology are in our view less useful. They are expensive and evaluation research in the Netherlands have proved them to be of little effect. Therefore there exists a big risk that these are 'windfall gains' for the receiving firm. They should only be used in case of high costs for a polluting industry and competitive disadvantages due to less strict regulation in other countries or regions.

Although it is dangerous to compare instruments on their intrinsic characteristics only for such broad categories of technologies, some qualitative conclusions are drawn. A survey of the usefulness of four types of instruments to stimulate the four types of cleaner technologies is given in Table 2. It should be noted that these results are rather tentative and need to be validated.

Charges are considered to be especially useful to induce changes in the mix of inputs, emission reductions and the recycling of waste material in view of the cost-inefficiences of standards, whereas standards and information transfer are believed to be more useful to stimulate the development and use of cleaner consumer products in view of the information problems and low responsiveness of consumers to price changes (especially with respect to the use of automobiles). With respect to subsidies,

Table 2. The usefulness of policy instruments to stimulate cleaner technologies

	Standards	Charges	Subsidies[12]	Information
Input-savings	+	++	+	+/0
Pollution control	+	++	+/0	+/0
Waste recycling	–	+	+/0	+/0
Cleaner consumer products	++	+	+/0	+

++	very useful
+	useful
+/0	in some cases useful
–	not useful

R&D subsidies are believed to be more useful than subsidies for investments in cleaner technologies but the latter may be necessary to compensate for competitive disadvantages due to less strict regulation elsewhere.

4. Three Case Studies of Cleaner Technologies

Introduction

In the previous sections we discussed the factors, besides environmental regulation, which (may) influence the innovation and diffusion of cleaner technology. Little empirical evidence is available on the supply and demand factors of cleaner technologies, and especially the role and importance of government regulation. In an earlier research project of the Maastricht Economic Research Institute on Innovation and Technology (MERIT) and the Institute for Environmental Studies (IVM), the factors identified as influencing the innovation and adoption process of three kinds of cleaner technologies, were investigated.[12] The three case studies are: (i) CFC substitutes, (ii) low-solvent paints and coatings, and (iii) membrane technology in the metal-plating industry. These technologies constitute different types of cleaner technologies: CFC substitutes belong to environment-friendlier substances (which result in cleaner processes and products), low-solvent paints and coatings are examples of cleaner (intermediate) products, and membrane technology is an example of a pollution control technology which allows for the recycling of waste material.

Although the focus was on the innovation and adoption process of these technologies in the Netherlands, the results are believed to apply to other Western countries as well. The research project involved an extensive literature survey of the technologies plus interviews with suppliers and (potential) adopters of the innovation.[13] It should be noted that although the approach followed provided us with a lot of qualitative information about the factors influencing the innovation and adoption process of these technologies, it was not possible to assess the importance of the individual factors in a more quantitative way. Despite this, the adopted perspective proved to be useful for this kind of research. Some conclusions and policy implications could be drawn from the case studies. These are discussed in the next section.

CFC Substitutes

Chlorofluorocarbons, abbreviated to CFCs, have been applied in a broad range of products ever since their 'invention' in the 1930s. Originally developed as coolants, they have also been used on a large scale as aerosol propellants, foam blowers (sometimes they also serve as an insulator), and as solvents in a range of cleaning application in the metal and electrotechnical industries. Important properties of CFCs are their low toxicity and high level of stability (they are, for instance, non-flammable). However, as a result of this stability, CFCs can reach the ozone layer once they have entered the atmosphere. There they destroy the ozone which protects the earth from ultraviolet rays. In addition, they contribute to global warming (assuming it does exist). Their chemical stability eventually appeared to be a crucial unfavourable property. In the Montreal Protocol (further adjusted in June 1990 in London) it was agreed that their production would be ended before the year 2000.

It is expected that about a third of the current CFC market will disappear as a result of the transition to non-CFC technologies, for example the wider application of ammonia as coolant, or more CO_2 instead of halons in fire extinguishers (UNEP, 1989). For other CFC applications a shift to 'CFC-likes' will take place. CFC-likes consist of HCFCs, so-called 'soft' CFCs, having a low ozone-depletion potential, and HFCs, which do not contain chlorine or bromine and therefore do not affect the ozone layer. The use of CFC-likes is expected to count for about one-third of CFC-use. Another reduction of one-third will be achieved through a more careful use of these substances, so that unnecessary loss is avoided.

We now come to the factors influencing the development of CFC substitutes. Worldwide there are some 20 CFC manufacturers, six of which account for the bulk of the CFC production. These are large chemical firms, in other words a 'science-based' sector, which has ample opportunities to develop new substances and products. These firms mainly focus their attention on 'soft' CFCs, a continuation of the CFC trajectory, so that they can benefit from the scale and learning effects achieved in that trajectory.

Market demand for CFC substitutes is guaranteed by the future ban of CFCs. Except for aerosol propellants that have become a 'contaminated' product, autonomous demand is not strong enough to establish a serious substitution of CFCs. In most applications, CFCs are 'ideal' substances to use. Substances that perform as well as CFCs against a lower price, are mostly inflammable, toxic and/or strongly reactive.

Appropriability conditions do not constitute a barrier to the development of (H)CFCs. All CFC manufacturers are presently developing substitutes for CFCs.

Next, we will discuss factors influencing the demand for CFC substitutes. The price and quality do not greatly influence the question of whether or not substitution of CFCs takes place (for this is inevitable). They do play a role in the direction towards which firms look for substitutes. Due to their complex production process, it is estimated the H(C)FCs will become two to five times as expensive as CFCs. The costs of a substitute technology are not, however, exclusively determined by the price of the substance concerned, but also by the amount needed and the cost of the equipment in which it is used. In the cooling sector, the price/quality ratio is likely to be to the advantage of H(C)FCs, whereas in the remaining areas of application, serious competitors will also be found outside the CFC trajectory.

With respect to the needed information transfer, big CFC users have sufficient knowledge of the available alternatives. They are also involved in the development and testing of CFC-replacing technology. Furthermore, in the Netherlands, sector-specific organizations play a significant role in the transfer of knowledge and information regarding alternative technologies, through the set-up of demonstration projects, admission rules, etc. Lack of information usually occurs in smaller firms. Also consumers suffer from inadequate knowledge.

Although there do exist some technical-economic risks inherent in the shift to CFC substitutes in the various application areas of CFCs, these are 'normal' business risks which result from the shift to a new technology. Users tend to reduce the technical risk by making use of 'drop-ins' as much as possible: substances which can be used in existing installations with little adaptions. This is favourable for H(C)FCs. Competitive disadvantages are averted since all industries are faced with the need to substitute CFCs.

The dominant policy instrument relating to the CFC problems is direct regulation in its most extensive form: a future, general ban on its production and use.[14] This general ban can be considered as a form of a technology-forcing standard. It may be assumed that this will be a strong enough incentive for CFC-substituting innovations and their diffusion.

The role of economic instruments and information and communication is complementary in nature. They can be used to accelerate and/or facilitate the transition to CFC substitutes. In the United States, for example, rights are allocated for CFC production and use. These rights are gradually reduced and are tradable. The aim of the CFC charge that is also used in the US, is mainly to skim off 'windfall profits' which may arise from the artificial scarcity of CFCs.

Low-solvent Paints and Coatings

In the 1950s, the traditional (linseed) oil paints were replaced by paints based on synthetic binding agents. A basic component of most of these paints were organic solvents (the percentage of which is usually between 30 and 65%, but can be as high as 90%). It was not discovered until much later that the solvents which were released at application had negative consequences for public health and the environment (for instance through the formation of smog).

There exist various kinds of low-solvent paints: water-based (or water-borne) paints (5–10% solvents), 'high solids' (20–30 solvents), powder coatings, and UV- and EB-curing coatings. The first three types are candidates for widespread application, both within the architectural and industrial market (although to different degrees).

We turn to factors influencing the development of paints and coatings. Research into low-solvent paints and coatings started already in the 1960s, particularly in the laboratories of the bigger paint manufacturers. Currently, practically all paint makers are developing water-based paints, both for the industrial and architectural market. Small firms are strongly dependent upon their suppliers (subsidiaries of the large chemical concerns) of raw materials, which provide directive recipes for paints. Other low-solvent paint products such as powder coatings, high solids and UV- and EB-curing coatings are developed by large paints manufacturers and some specialized suppliers. It can be concluded that there are vast technological opportunities for low-solvent paints available. However, paint makers are sometimes criticised for conservatism and the under capitalization of research efforts. Although many different formulations for new products are constantly being developed, only a small number of these formulations reach the production stage. This is related to market demand and appropriability conditions as will be explained below.

The history of paints is strongly associated with changes in demand. For example, the development of high-solvent paints was stimulated by the demand for paints with a shorter drying time (especially by the car industry). The demand for low-solvent paints has mainly been a derived demand, depending on government policy. Important in this respect were emission requirements in the United Sates and West Germany and the legislation relating to working conditions in Scandinavian countries. Recently, industrial demand for new paints and coatings and consumer preferences play a role. Industrial demand for these new paint products is often for normal business reasons (for instance because of less losses of paint material during application). In 1983 the market share of low-solvent paints for industrial application was 32% in the US and 25% in Europe. In the Netherlands, the sales of powder coatings and water-borne paints for industrial application are presently increasing 15–20% annually. The share of low-solvent paints for other purposes (except for wall painting) is much lower and increasing less rapidly.

The paint industry takes up a special position as far as appropriability conditions are concerned. Imitation of paint products is relatively simple. By means of chemical analysis, the global composition of paints can be relatively easily discovered (even though its production calls for some additional research work). Protection of paint through patents is practically impossible, since the preparation of paint comes down to 'mixing and stirring'. In order to be able to patent something new technical principles have to be developed. Suppliers of raw materials do patent new procedures more frequently. The most important protection of paint products in the Netherlands lies in their distribution. The large paint manufacturers have their own distribution networks (service stations for the professional user and paint shops for consumers), where users can turn to and receive advice about the paint product to be used. This is quite different from the situation in Germany, where advice is much less important and paint is usually diffused via the wholesale trade. The fact that paint companies sell their products through their own channels, however, is an obstacle to developing innovations rather than a stimulus. The innovating firm mainly reaches its own clients. Thus, new products of a paint company are competitors of a firm's existing own products in the first instance. This has a negative effect on the willingness of firms to perform R&D activities with respect to low-solvent paints.

Next, we shall discuss factors influencing the demand for low-solvent paints and coatings. Although the quality of the paint products differs considerably, it may be said that water-based paints are market-ripe products. However, professional painters and private clients still have a strong preference for the high-solvent paints. Apart from being unfamiliar with low-solvent paints, and the necessary extra cleaning of older layers of paint, (partly unfounded) prejudices against the quality of water-based paints play a role here. The price of water-based paints is about 10% higher than that of high-solvent paints. According to paint manufacturers, no major price falls are expected. However, the costs of application and maintenance often turn out in favour of low-solvent paints. Over the last years, the assortment of low-solvent paint products has steadily increased. Nowadays also some high-gloss water-based paints are available. Further improvement of the paint products are to be expected.

There exists a serious lack of knowledge and information regarding both the environmental damage of high-solvent paints and the availability of alternatives, as well as the quality and processing of low-solvent paints. These information problems are particularly important to painters and private users. Another obstacle is that in the past water-based paints were presented as being overly promising. This publicity has been counterproductive.

Although there exists some uncertainty regarding the quality of paints (its gloss, durability, etc.) and there are some risks to the professional applicator (unsatisfactory results may lead to financial claims), this uncertainty and these risks are relatively small, especially for the non-industurial user. In the case of an industrial user, it is often necessary to change the production routines and the work division, since the new paints and coatings require different machines and tools.

Until recently most countries have barely pursued an environmental policy regarding high-solvent paints. Policy has been directed towards emissions (during production and application) rather than towards products. At present, in the Netherlands, Germany and Switzerland convenants between governments and business community are used or considered. Also, the use of charges on high-solvent paints is considered by some countries (for example the Netherlands, Switzerland and the United States). Standards based on environmental considerations for the maximum level of solvents in paints are not used anywhere as far as we know. Currently, the need for specific stimuli to encourage innovations in low-solvent paints is probably smaller than that for promoting their diffusion, particularly among professional painters and private consumers. A charge imposed on solvents may contribute to the diffusion and further development of low-solvent paints, but such a charge must be considerable in order to be effective. Information and communication are particularly important to increase the acceptance of the new paint types and to take away negative prejudices. The government's own purchase policy may also contribute to this end.

Membrane Technology in the Metal-plating Industry

In the metal-plating industry, large amounts of heavy metals are released into the waste water. In the 1970s a policy was followed in the Netherlands which was aimed at combating the discharge of these emissions into the surface water. At that time, many firms in the metal-plating industry purchased a so-called 'ONO installation', a typical end-of-type solution (ONO in Dutch stands for: Detoxication, Neutralisation, Dehydration). It is a technique whereby substances are extracted from the industrial water. Although the resulting waste water is cleaner, the ONO techniques produces chemical waste which in turn must be taken care of. In contrast, membrane technology can be considered a typical process-integrated technique. Using this technique, metals can be removed from industry water, and be reused. Up until now the metal-plating industry has made little use of the various membrane techniques for the purification of industrial water.

On factors influencing the development of membrane technology for the metal-plating industry, we would like to mention the following. Membrane separation or purification techniques were developed in the 1950s, as a result of the technological development in the plastic producing and processing industry. The problems surrounding waste water in the metal-plating industry have played little or no role in this development. On a world scale, the market for membranes is controlled by firms in the united States and Japan, where the governments put large amounts of money into research and development in this area in the 1960s.

For firms in the metal-plating industry, membrane technology is not directly relevant to their product but only to the process. The application of a membrane technology does not provide a firm with extra opportunities to increase its sales by creating or conquering new markets. It is to be expected that the demand for membrane technology in the metal-plating industry will increase, because of higher costs for waste. The cost of treatment and disposal of chemical waste in the Netherlands will probably double or triple within the next few years.

The knowledge needed for the production of membranes and membrane installations is generally in the hands of the manufacturers. Protection of this knowledge is usually fixed in the form of patents, being the most important appropriability condition. However, in the specific case of membrane techniques for the metal plating industry, appropriability conditions are found to be of little importance due to the small and difficult market for this technology.

Next, we shall discuss factors influencing the demand for membrane technology in the metal-plating industry. The (limited) experience gained by firms in the metal-plating industry with membrane techniques is largely negative. There have been a great deal of problems with the installations (such as the pollution of the membranes). In addition, the follow-up care of suppliers often left much to be desired. These negative experiences have led to a bad reputation of the membrane technology within the sector concerned. In general, the price of membrane equipment plays a lesser role. A well-functioning installation might lead to cost savings for some firms. This number may rise substantially as the costs of the transport and disposal of sludge increase.

The knowledge users have of membrane technology is minimal and what firms do know about membrane technology is limited to a number of bad experiences, which has a negative effect on demand. Furthermore, smaller firms especially lack the expertise to apply membrane technology. The lack of knowledge of membrane technology is partly related to insufficient transfer of knowledge by the suppliers of membrane technology. Suppliers experience the metal-plating industry as a 'difficult' market and orientate themselves preferably towards other markets.

Firms in the metal-plating industry are often insecure about the well-functioning of the membrane installations. They are afraid of breakdowns, involving financial risks and time losses. Particularly small firms cannot afford the risk of spending much time on matters which do not directly benefit production.

Finally some words on the environmental policy with respect to membrane technology in the metal-plating industry. In the Netherlands a standard-based policy has been implemented with respect to heavy metals in the waste water of the metal-plating industry. The standards were based on the 'best-practicable-means'. Membrane technologies have not been part of this category up until now. Since the standards exclusively pertained to emissions into water, the environmental problems have shifted: the heavy metals are now released in the sludge. The charges imposed upon heavy metals in waste water have also contributed to this, as well as the allocated investment subsidies (which have been used especially for ONO installations).

In order to make recycling of metals in the metal-plating process attractive, policy must focus on the integral environmental damage of business activities, e.g., also on the environmental damage of the sludge which is polluted with heavy metals. In view of the heterogeneous character of the sector in question (strongly varying production processes and, consequently, substantial differences in abatement costs) economic instruments are to be preferred to direct regulation. For that matter, the sharply rising costs for the discharge of chemical waste may have the same effect as a charge imposed on metals in sludge. In order to prevent illegal dumping, a deposit premium for chemical waste may also be considered. Investment subsidies may be necessary to prevent the closing down of some firms in the metal-plating industry.

Additional outlets of information and communication can be of great importance. Information should not only be concerned with reinforcing environmental awareness and the knowledge of the various techniques to reduce heavy metal emissions, but also with removing (whether or not unfounded) prejudices against process-integrated facilities such as membrane installations. Demonstration projects may make a significant contribution to this.

5. Conclusions and Policy Implications

In the earlier sections we investigated the factors that affect the decision to develop and to adopt cleaner technologies, both theoretically and empirically. Here we try to derive some general conclusions on these factors and the way in which policy instruments can be used to stimulate supply and demand of cleaner technologies.

In the case studies, the technological opportunities and appropriability conditions do not appear to be distinct obstacles to the realisation of cleaner innovations. One might reply that this is hardly surprising, since if technological opportunities are absent and appropriability conditions insufficient, there would not have been a case to study. A more general conclusion, however, is that for almost all environmental problems, many technological opportunities for cleaner technologies are available and that firms in one way or another can protect an innovation against imitation for a long enough period.

The multiple technological opportunities may pose policy makers with a problem. Since the success of a certain technology depends strongly on the government policy, policy makers should be careful not to induce the selection of the 'wrong' technology, and, as a result, be 'locked-in' to a sub-optimal technological trajectory. This point is less academic than it might seem. In the case of the metal-plating industry, the market for membrane technologies has been blocked for years because of the widespread adoption of ONO-installations, a typical end-of-pipe device which led to a transfer of environmental problems. Another example is the legislation on emission of SO_2 and NO_x in Europe and North America which led to a fast development of the catalytic converter and at the same time caused a considerable delay in the development of the lean burn engine. The same emission standards led to the development of flue gas desulphurization at the cost of e.g., the combined cycle coal gasification.[15] In the case of the substitution of CFCs, policy makers are currently facing such a dilemma: i.e., should HCFCs (so-called 'soft' CFCs), which also affect the ozone layer, be allowed for a certain period, or should other solutions which are currently less suitable and more expensive be stimulated? The choice between technological solutions is very difficult, since the future costs and benefits of possible technological solutions to the environmental problems are usually not well known, neither to policy makers nor to possible suppliers of these technologies. These costs and benefits depend on post-innovation improvements in the technology, price reductions due to cost-reductions in manufacturing and competitive pressure, new technological options that become available and the obsolescence capital goods.

If the appropriability conditions are insufficient, policy makers can do little to overcome this, but as stated above, few technological opportunities are not exploited because of inadequate appropriability conditions (although they can be unfavourable, as in the case of paints and coatings, and, as a result, delay the development of new products).

Market demand seems to be the crucial factor for the successful exploitation of technological opportunities. As indicated above, market demand for cleaner technologies often depends strongly on government policy. Also the perspective of a certain policy can exercise an important stimulus. A clear policy objective for the medium term gave a strong impulse to the developments of CFC substitutes and low-solvent paints and coatings. However, government policy is not the only stimulus. There are other pressures form the firm's environment which may induce polluters to take environmental measures. Local communities, insurance companies, investors, special environmental interest groups and the wider public are increasingly putting pressure on firms to improve their environmental record. Although these stimuli are quite diffuse and still less important than environmental legislation, they are gaining importance (for an assessment of the relative importance of these factors, see Williams *et al.*, 1991). The increasing environmental awareness of the public and the corresponding demand for environmentally sound products already constitutes a strong market impulse for firms to develop cleaner consumer products.

The case studies also provide us with information about the factors that affect the diffusion of cleaner technologies. These factors appear to be closely related. The risk and uncertainty regarding the adoption of the technology depend on the price and technical properties of the innovation and the perceived adaptation problems. It is essential therefore to take away possible obstacles here. This not only involves actual risks and lack of information, but also correcting distorted images or false information. Even more importantly, it is found that the purchase price of a cleaner technology is often not the most important factor. Whether or not a firm switches to another technology implies a simultaneous change in a large number of financial and non-financial components regarding costs and benefits. As a result, a complex decision-making situation often arises. However, this does not exclude that price ratios may play a crucial role eventually.

With respect to the choice of policy instruments, the above suggests that no single instrument is optimal, but that instead the stimulation of innovation in and diffusion of cleaner technologies call for a mixture of instruments, depending on the specific factors and circumstances. Suppliers and users of particular cleaner technologies (pollution abatement technologies, reuse systems, environmentally-friendlier consumer products and materials) operate in strongly differing markets with the associated stimuli and obstacles. The policy choice for instruments to stimulate cleaner technologies should be based on the different characteristics of these firms and the markets they operate in, the available technological opportunities, and the seriousness of the environmental problems. However, economic instruments have a number of advantages. Economic instruments such as effluent charges (but also charges on inputs and waste) and tradable pollution are more efficient, since, in principle, the private marginal cost of abatement for all pollution sources are equalized. Thus, in the case of heterogeneous polluters with large differences in compliance costs, economic instruments are generally preferred to standards. In addition this, a system of effluent charges of tradable pollution permits depends less on the availability of pollution control technology, therefore it can be introduced more quickly and more easily adjusted, and, once such a system is implemented, it generally provides stronger incentives for the development of more effective technologies than the present policies. Also, such systems are likely to stimulate preventive technologies instead of end-of-pipe technologies which have been adopted overwhelmingly in the past. And, in the case of economic instruments, there is an incentive to reduce *all* emissions, especially in the case of effluent charges.

To stimulate innovation in pollution control also technology-forcing standards and innovation waivers may be considered. They may create a more certain and predictable market for new technologies, maybe even more than effluent charges can. However, these instruments are likely to lead to high costs and the risk of being locked into a certain technology or trajectory, which may be sub-optimal in the long run, is relatively high. Further, uncertainty about the demand for cleaner technologies, partly related to unpredictable government policy, may call for the use of R&D subsidies or loans. Thus, in the case of cleaner technologies there may be an extra argument for the use of R&D-subsidies, besides the traditional 'public good' argument. And finally, communicative instruments such as compulsory environmental care systems, information disclosure requirements and 'green' product labels can be useful to deal with information problems related to the environmental aspects of products and processes. The environmental awareness and knowledge of firms and consumers, which is a prerequisite for environment-friendlier actions, will increase as a result of the use of such instruments.

Technological change which helps save the natural environment may be stimulated by the government in other ways: through its science and technology policy, education, and the integration of ecological aspects in other areas of policy (especially the agricultural and transport policy). Also, public procurement may be much better used for environmental purposes. Especially in the beginning of the product life cycle, when technologies have benefited little from dynamic scale and learning effects and the adaptation of the selection environment, a market niche may be created by procurement policy which enables a technology to survive the hard market selection for a certain period. Such a policy may give an important and decisive impulse to the further development and success of the technology.

Finally, the case studies show that a short-term transition towards cleaner technologies can lead to a high costs and serious adjustment problems for the adopters. New and cleaner technologies will always be less suited for some adopters, because of specific technical requirements or high costs (for instance when production techniques have to replaced early). Especially in the case of standards, the costs related to such a short-term transition can be high. This means that the combination of patience and persistence in environmental policy making may prove to be the optimal strategy.

Acknowledgements

This paper is based on a research project for the Ministries of Economic Affairs and the Environment in the Netherlands, and is a revision of an earlier paper 'Policy Instruments to Stimulate Cleaner Technologies', which was prepared for the EAERE conference in Stockholm, 11–14 June, 1991. The authors thank Hans Opschoor and two referees for helpful comments.

Notes

[1] A survey of the theoretical literature about the relation between environmental policy and technical change in pollution control is in Kemp (1992).

[2] It should be noted that the model of Milliman and Prince (1989) differs from the other theoretical models in that it considers the provision of innovations in pollution control by special suppliers outside the polluting industry, the possibility of innovator gains related to the adoption of the technology by other firms, and protection of the innovation against imitation through patents.

[3] For a critical discussion of research which attempts to answer such questions, particularly the empirical research of the 'demand pull' advocates, we refer to Mowery and Rosenberg (1979).

[4] The relation between environmental regulation and innovations that help save the natural environment is a complex one. Such innovations may require stricter regulation which is known to come about slowly, due to bureaucratic inertia and polluters' opposition, despite of attempts of firms in the pollution control industry to influence environmental policy. This creates some extra uncertainty to the supplying firm.

[5] Imitation of innovations is analyzed by Mansfield *et al.* (1981), who find that within four years of the introduction, 60% of the patented successful innovations, studied in the chemical, drug, electronics and machinery industries, were imitated. On the whole, for patented and non-patented innovations, they find that the ratio of the imitation costs to the innovation cost is about 0.65, and the ratio of the imitation time to the innovation time is about 0.70.

[6] In Kemp and Soete (1992) it is argued that the older technologies and technological trajectories are dominant and not abandoned quickly, precisely because these technologies have benefited from dynamic scale and learning effects (resulting in lower costs in the manufacturing, lower prices, evolutionary improvement of the technologies) and the adaption of the selection environment to these technologies (production and organization at the user's side, training, regulation, social values, life styles etc.).

[7] Of course, the distinction between these categories of cleaner technologies is often not so clear. For instance, recycling system lead to input savings and can prevent hazardous emissions. Input substitution can occur in product, etcetera.

[8] Research among suppliers of pollution control technologies in the Netherlands by IJ1st *et al.* (1988) refers to the following factors as being the most important obstacles to offering these techniques: unpredictable government policy (51%), low profits (42%), and insecure market development (38%).

[9] For a large number of examples, see Huisingh *et al.* (1986).

[10] Of course, information transfer can also be left to the market. But as noted by Arrow (1962, p. 615) there is a fundamental paradox in the determination of demand for information; its value for the purchaser is not known until he has the information, but then he has in effect acquired it without cost. In addition, it may be more efficient for some collective body to provide knowledge and information in view of the indivisibilities involved.

[11] Subsidies for R&D and/or for investments in cleaner technology (not emission subsidies, i.e., subsidies per unit of emission reduction).

[12] The focus is on the innovation process and diffusion of cleaner technologies and the way it is affected by environmental regulation and *not* on the achieved emission reductions and the costs involved. This would require a study of its own.

[13] For references to the literature used in the case studies and for more details we refer to the original research report (only available in Dutch).

[14] 'Use' is defined in the Montreal protocol as production minus export plus import. Substances with a limited ability to affect the ozone layer (the so-called 'soft' CFCs or H(C)FCs) will be allowed until far into the next century according to the Montreal protocol.

[15] These examples were brought to our attention by one of the referees.

References

Arrow, K. J. (1962) Economic welfare and the allocation of resources for invention, in R. R. Nelson (ed), *The Rate and Direction of Inventive Activity: Economic and Social Factors*, NBER, Princeton University Press, Princeton, pp. 609–625.

Baumol, W. J. and Oates, W. E. (1988) *The Theory of Environmental Policy*, 2nd edition, Cambridge.

Brumm Jr., H. J. and Dick, D. T. (1976) Federal environmental policy and R&D on water pollution abatement, *American Economic Review*, papers and proceedings 66(2), 448–453.

Cramer, J. and Schot, J. (1990) Innovation and diffusion of environmental technology: Opportunities for research from a technology-dynamics perspective, RMNO publication, nr. 44A, the Netherlands.

Dosi, G. (1988a) The nature of the innovative process, in C. Freeman, R. Nelson, G. Silverberg and L. Soete (eds), *Technical Change and Economic Theory*, pp. 221–238, Pinter Publishers, London, New York.

Dosi, G. (1988b) Sources, procedures and microeconomic effects of innovation, *J. Economic Literature* 1120–1171.

Downing, P. B. and White, L. J. (1986) Innovation in pollution control, *J. Environmental Economics of Management* 13, 18–29.

Hartje, V. J. and Lurie, R. L. (1984) Adopting rules for pollution control innovations: End-of-pipe versus integrated process technology, International Institute for Environment and Society (IIUG), Wissenschaftszentrum Berlin.

Huisingh, D., Martin, L., Hilger, H. and Seldman, N. (1986) Proven profits from pollution prevention, Institute for Local Selfreliance, Washington D. C.

IJ1st, P., Stokman, C. T. M. and Visser, E. T. (1988) Informatieoverdracht en informatiebehoefte in de milieuproduktiesector in Nederland (Information Transfers and Information Needs in the Environmental Industry in the Netherlands), EIM, Zoetermeer.

Kemp, R. P. M. and Soete, L. L. G. (1992) The greening of technological progress: An evolutionary perspective, *Futures* 24(5), 437–457.

Kemp, R. P. M. (1992) Environmental policy and technical change in pollution control: A critical assessment of the existing theory, mimeo, MERIT, Masstricht, The Netherlands.

Levin, R. C. (1986) A new look at the patent system, *American Economic Review*, papers and proceedings, May, pp. 199–202.

Magat, W. A. (1978) Pollution control and technological advance: A dynamic model of the firm, *J. Environmental Economics and Management* 5, 1–25.

Mansfield, Schwartz, E. M. and Wagner S. (1981) Imitation costs and patents: An empirical study, *Economic Journal* 907–918.

Milliman S. R. and Prince, R. (1989) Firm incentives to promote technological change in pollution control, *J. Environmental Economics and Management* 17(3), 247–265.

Mowery, D. C. and Rosenberg, N. (1979) The influence of market demand upon innovation: A critical review of some recent empirical studies, *Research Policy* 8, 102–153.

Nelson, R. R. and Winter, S. G. (1977) In search of useful theory of innovation, *Research Policy* 6, 36–76.

OECD (1985) *Environmental Policy and Technical Change*, Paris

Pearce D. W. and Turner, R. K. (1984) The economic evaluation of low and non-waste technologies, *Resources and Conservation* **11**, 27–43.

Schmookler, J. (1966) *Invention and Economic Growth*, MIT Press, Cambridge.

Schot, J. W. (1991) Constructive technology assessment and technology dynamics: Opportunities for the control of technology – the case of clean technologies, *Science, Technology and Human Values* **17**, 36–57.

Teece, D. J. (1986) Profiting from technological innovation: Implications for integration, collaboration, licencing and public policy, *Research Policy* **15**, 285–305.

UNEP (1989) Technical progress on protecting the ozone layer.

Vollebergh, H. (ed) (1989) *Milieu en innovatie* (Innovation and the Environment), Wolters-Noordhof, Groningen, the Netherlands.

Wenders, J. T. (1975) Methods of pollution control and the rate of change in pollution abatement technology *Water Resources Research*.

Williams, H. E., Medhust, J. and Drew K. (1991) Corporate strategies for a sustainable future, paper prepared for the Greening of Industry Conference, November 17–19th, 1991, Noordwijk, The Netherlands.

List of Contributors

Authors*

*Dr. G. (Gerard) Bertolini**
   Director of Research, Centre National de la Recherche Scientifique, Université
   de Lyon 1, Batiment 101, 43 Bld. du 11 Novembre 1918, F-69622 Villeurbanne
   Cedex, France.

Prof. A. (Alberto) Cassone
   Professor of Economic Policy, Department of Economics, Univ of Torino, Via
   S. Ottavio, 20, 10124 Torino, Italy.

*Prof. Dr. K. (Klaus) Conrad**
   Professor of Microeconomics, University of Mannheim, Seminargebaude A5,
   D-6800 Mannheim, Germany.

*Prof. A. (Angela) Fraschini**
   Member, Steering Committee ESF-Programme: Environment, Science and
   Society.

   Associate Professor of Local Government Finance, Institute of Economics and
   Finance, Corso Ercole 1 d'Este, 44, University of Ferrara, 44100 Ferrara, Italy.

*Dr. I-M. (Ing-Marie) Gren**
   Researcher, Beijer International Institute of Ecological Economics, Royal Swedish
   Academy of Sciences, Box 50005, 10405 Stockholm, Sweden.

* The authors indicated with * were members of the ESS-Task Force on Economic Analysis of
Environmental Policy Instruments.

Mr. R. Kemp
Researcher, Maastricht Economic Research Institute on Innovation and Technology, University of Limburg, P.O. Box 616, Maastricht, The Netherlands.

Prof. Dr. H. G. (Hans) Nutzinger*
Professor of Economics, University of Kassel and Institute for Advanced Studies, Berlin, Fachbereich Wirtschaftswissenschaften, Postfach 101380, D-3500 Kassel, Germany.

Dr. A. A. (Xander) Olsthoorn
Researcher, Economics and Technology Division, Institute for Environmental Studies, Free University, De Boelelaan 1115, 1081 HV Amsterdam, The Netherlands.

Mr. F. (Frans) Oosterhuis
Researcher, Economics and Technology Division, Institute for Environmental Studies, Free University, De Boelelaan 1115, 1081 HV Amsterdam, The Netherlands.

Prof. Dr. J. B. (Hans) Opschoor*
Member Steering Committee ESF-Programme: Environment, Science and Society (ESS); Chairman of the ESS-Task Force on Economic Analysis of Environmental Policy Instruments.

Professor of Environmental Economics, Department of Spatial and Environmental Economics, Free University, De Boelelaan 1105, 1081 HV Amsterdam, The Netherlands.

Chairman Advisory Council Environment and Nature Research, P.O. Box 5306, 2280 HH Rijswijk, The Netherlands.

Prof. D. W. (David) Pearce
Director, CSERGE (Centre for Social and Economic Research on the Global Environment), University College London, and University of East Anglia, Norwich, UK

Professor of Economics, University College London.

Dr. D (Diego) Piacention*
Associate Professor of Public Finance, Faculty of Law, Universita di Urbino Via Matteotti 1, 61029 Urbino, Italy.

Mr. A. F. de Savornin Lohman*
Environment Economist, Institute for Environmental Studies, Free University, De Boelelaan 1115, 1081 HV Amsterdam, The Netherlands.

Dr. M. (Michael) Schröder
Researcher, University of Mannheim, D-6800 Mannheim, Germany

Prof. R. K. (Kerry) Turner*
Professor of Environmental Sciences, University of East Anglia, Norwich, and University College London.

Executive Director CSERGE (Centre for Social and Economic Research on the Global Environment), Univ. of East Anglia (see above).

Dr. H. (Harmen) Verbruggen*
Head, Economics Division (and Deputy Director of) Institute for Environmental Studies, Free University, De Boelelaan 1115, 1081 HV Amsterdam, The Netherlands.

Dr. J. (Jianmin) Wang
Researcher, University of Mannheim, Seminargebaude A5, D-6800 Mannheim, Germany.

Reviewers

Mr. J.-Ph. Barde
Environment Directorate, OECD, Paris, France.

Dr. F. Brouwer
Institute for Agricultural Economics (Landbouw Economish Instituut), The Hague, The Netherlands.

Prof. Dr. L. Hordijk
Director, Centre for Environmental Studies, Agricultural University, Wageningen, The Netherlands.

Prof. Dr. D. Wolfson
Member, Scientific Council of Government Policy, The Hague, The Netherlands.

Chairman, Steering Committee Regulatory Energy Charges, Min. of Economic Affairs, The Hague, The Netherlands.

Subject Index